Within the literature on industrial economics and innovation there have been surprisingly few attempts to build analytical frameworks that are based on the distinctive features and institutional characteristics of Europe, and especially of the European Union.

This collection explains the organization and dynamics of innovative activities in Europe. It is the first time that theoretical advances in the economics of technological innovation have been placed alongside empirical research relating to the interaction between the industrial structure of individual member nations and the policies and regulations of the European Union. The team of distinguished international contributors includes Paul David and Nick von Tunzelmann.

ALFONSO GAMBARDELLA is Associate Professor of Economics and Management at the Faculty of Economics, University of Urbino, Italy. He is the Director of the Inter-University center CUSTOM (Cheiti, Urbino, Siena, Technology, Organization, and Management). His books include *Science and Innovation* (Cambridge University Press, 1995).

FRANCO MALERBA is Professor of Industrial Economics at the Università "Luigi Bocconi", Milan, and Director of CESPRI, a leading research centre on industrial and international economics at Bocconi University. He is editor of *Industrial and Corporate Change*. His books include *The Semiconductor Business* (University of Wisconsin Press, 1985) and *Organization and Strategy in Evolution of the Enterprise* (Macmillan, 1996).

The Organization
of Economic Innovation
in Europe

Edited by
Alfonso Gambardella and Franco Malerba

CAMBRIDGE
UNIVERSITY PRESS

CAMBRIDGE UNIVERSITY PRESS
Cambridge, New York, Melbourne, Madrid, Cape Town, Singapore, São Paulo

Cambridge University Press
The Edinburgh Building, Cambridge CB2 8RU, UK

Published in the United States of America by Cambridge University Press, New York

www.cambridge.org
Information on this title: www.cambridge.org/9780521643030

First published 1999
This digitally printed version 2008

A catalogue record for this publication is available from the British Library

Library of Congress Cataloguing in Publication data

The organisation of economic innovation in Europe / edited by Alfonso
    Gambardella and Franco Malerba
        p. cm.
    ISBN 0 521 64303 1
    1. Research, Industrial – Europe.   I. Gambardella, Alfonso.
    II. Malerba, Franco, 1950– .
    T177.E80724   1999   338.9407–dc21   98-39111   CIP

ISBN 978-0-521-64303-0 hardback
ISBN 978-0-521-06571-9 paperback

Contents

Figures

Tables

1 The organization of innovative activity in Europe: towards a conceptual framework

Alfonso Gambardella and Franco Malerba

Aims of the book

Why a book on the organization of innovative activity in Europe? While one can think of several obvious reasons (the topic is important, interesting ...) there are more subtle reasons as well. Europe is a large economic area similar to the United States, but unlike the United States it is an amazingly heterogeneous continental economic system, with considerable diversity among countries and regions in terms of income *per capita*, industrial structure, specialization, institutional setting, culture, and history. This diverse set of countries and regions is linked together by a supra-national institution, the European Union, which governs the unified market and monetary union, and aims at economic efficiency, social objectives, and dynamic progress in the continent as a whole. In science, technology, and innovation, the European Union also acts as an organism for fostering European cooperation, standard-setting, and advancement of key scientific disciplines and technologies. In all these dimensions one finds the advantages of scientific, technological, and productive specialization among countries and regions, and the disadvantages of increasing economic gaps between strong and weak areas, as well as duplication of resources and activities at the national level. These (and other) conditions imply rather marked differences with other countries, and particularly with the more homogeneous areas of the United States and Japan. This also implies that in analyzing the organization of innovative activity in Europe one cannot neglect this interplay between diversity of contexts and socio-economic environments that are nonetheless linked together by a unified market and a common supra-national political institution.

In this respect, it is surprising that in the field of industrial economics

This book is the result of a research project funded by the European Union under the Human Capital and Mobility Program (Contract no. ERBCHRXCT920002), which we gratefully acknowledge.

1

there have been so few attempts to build analytical frameworks that are based on the distinctive features and institutional characteristics of Europe, including the peculiar role of the European Union. The neoclassical approach in industrial economics has developed several sophisticated tools to analyze microeconomic behavior at the level of firms and industries (agency theory, contract theory, game theoretic models of strategic interactions, etc.). But the theory was built with a special institutional framework in mind – the United States or, more generally, the Anglo-Saxon system. Similarly, the evolutionary approach has gone a long way in trying to understand learning processes, firms' competencies and routines, industry dynamics, and the role of institutions in economic evolution. But there has been no systematic attempt to cast this approach in the special conditions of the European environment. The evolutionary approach and developments in system theory have developed the concept of "national and local systems of innovations," which has led to numerous studies of individual European countries and regions. There have also been studies that have provided a comprehensive framework of the characteristics of European industries in different countries, and have compared the differences among them. However, there is still a long way to go in order to assess the specificities of the European system as a whole, and particularly of the special role of the European Union with respect to the American and the Japanese cases, or to the emerging economies.

In looking at the organization of innovative activities in Europe, there are some questions that one may still need to address. How does the considerable heterogeneity of firm sizes, competencies, industry structures, and national environments affect the specialization of firms, their growth, degree of vertical integration and diversification, innovative performance, and innovation strategies? How does the fragmentation of the continental market affect the organization of innovative activities and the dynamics of industries – compared with the more homogeneous continental American market or the large Japanese market? How different is the pattern of entry of new innovators across European countries? How important is innovation-clustering in key European regions? How are networks of innovators organized and how industry-specific are they? What are the implications for innovation of the Union's role as a source of allocation of resources for invention?

This book will not give comprehensive answers to all these questions. Nor does it offer a comprehensive description of the organization of innovative activities at the firm or industry level through a complete set of industry or firm case studies. The book does not look at the international performance of European industry (although some lessons can be drawn from this collection of studies); it is simply an attempt to look in a new way at the organization and dynamics of innovative activities in Europe, by drawing from recent theoretical and empirical literature in the economics of technological innovation.

In recent years there have been several developments in the economics of technological innovation that have examined many aspects of the innovation process, firms' strategies and organization, technological environment, relationship between innovation and industrial dynamics, institutions, and science. First, many studies have emphasized the importance of firms' *learning, routines, and competencies.* Learning is one of the key dynamic mechanisms of firms' knowledge-accumulation, innovation, and growth. Routines have recurrent and automatic action patterns of firms and have an organizational dimension. Competencies underpin persistent differential performance among firms. Competencies are, moreover, often of a tacit nature, they cumulate over time and create persistent heterogeneity and distinctive competitive advantages among firms. Competencies affect the ability of firms to innovate in certain directions rather than others, and shape their technology strategies.

Second, the link between *innovation and industrial dynamics* has been increasingly at the center of analyses. Innovation has been interpreted as the driving force of industrial dynamics, affecting entry, firms' growth and diversification, and changes in market structure. At the same time, technological change has been closely connected with the evolution of firms' learning and competencies and with their innovative behavior.

Third, other studies have highlighted the *sectoral-specificity of industrial and technological change.* The idiosyncratic features of technologies and the technological environment (so-called "technological regimes," defined in terms of the knowledge base and of opportunity, appropriability, and cumulativeness conditions) are major determinants of differences in the patterns of innovation across industries.

Fourth, a great deal of effort has been spent in trying to understand aspects of innovation such as *interactive learning, local externalities, and networks* among firms and other organizations. These aspects emphasize the "system view" of the innovation process, which has implications for the accumulation of technological capabilities, the organization of innovative activities, and the geographical agglomeration of firms.

Finally, recent work in the *economics of science* have discussed the economic implications of the distinctive features of organizations such as universities and other non-profit research centers for the generation and diffusion of innovation, and more generally for the growth of scientific and technological knowledge.

These are heterogeneous approaches. However, they share a common evolutionary framework. Change is at the center of the analysis and uncertainty surrounds the outcomes of firms' actions. Industrial dynamics is characterized by the generation of innovations and the entry of new firms which increase variety in the system, and by selection mechanisms that in turn reduce the variety of products, processes, and firms' heterogeneity. More broadly the evolution of industries is characterized by path-dependent processes and the coevolution of technology, firms' behavior, competencies and organization, market structure, and institutions. This book shares this framework and presents a collection of theoretical and empirical studies in these areas applied to the European scene. It thus builds on concepts such as learning, competencies, technological regimes, interaction, and networks, and addresses broader issues such as increasing returns, variety, and selection.

We initially thought to make all the contributions in this volume more homogeneous in terms of their approach to the problem, and in their methodological background. We then realized that this would not do justice to the fact that a field such as the economics of innovation has prospered *because* of its variety of viewpoints and contributions. Therefore, although the chapters have been revised several times to find common themes and a consistent overall structure among the various contributions, we deliberately chose to maintain a variety of perspectives in order to take advantage of the richness of ideas, topics, and insights that can be created by an underlying diversity of approaches and methods.

We are not disappointed with the outcome, and we think that one important aspect of the volume is that it looks at the organization of innovative activity in Europe from several viewpoints and tackles different analytical and empirical dimensions. Indeed, the book touches upon issues such as the sectoral and geographical patterns of innovative activities in Europe; the role of large innovative firms, the way they accumulate and use their internal competencies, and the factors that influence their ability to create competitive advantages; the rise of and the opportunities of growth for new innovators, and more generally the extent to which Europe benefits from the creation of new firms that threaten the position of established producers in given markets and industries; technical progress, localized learning, and corporate change in electronics and mechanical engineering; the formation of geographic clusters in Europe, and the role of inter-firm linkages; the structure and dynamics of innovative networks in some key sectors such as software and biotechnology; science–technology interfaces and the evolution of research networks, including universities; and finally the role of the European Union in encouraging the formation of these networks at the European level. Whenever possible, the chapters also present comparative analyses with respect to the United States and Japan.

The structure of the book

The book is divided into two parts. Each part corresponds to a general topic and deals with some special features of the organization of innovative activities in Europe.

Part I focuses on the *patterns of innovative activity in Europe*. This introduces the reader to some of the main features of the European system of innovation, such as the role and characteristics of large firms and the formation of their technological competencies; the vitality of the European innovation process through an analysis of the entry and exit of new and old innovators; the patterns of geographical agglomeration of innovation activities, and the importance of localized vs. generalized technological change.

Part II focuses on *inter-firm collaborations and research networks*. This is a key topic in Europe. While in the United States collaborations among firms have always been treated with suspicion because of their inherent relationship with collusion, Europe has more often regarded collaboration as a means for encouraging effective sharing of complementary resources. Moreover, as noted earlier, unlike the American antitrust authorities, the European Union is especially keen on encouraging collaborations among firms and other organizations of different member countries. This part of the book then examines in some detail the relevance of networks of collaborations among firms and other organizations in the innovation process and the dynamics of research networks in Europe.

Part I begins with an introductory chapter by Giovanni Dosi and Luigi Marengo. *Dosi and Marengo* emphasize in chapter 2 the key role of knowledge in the competitive outcome of individual companies, sectors, regions, and countries. They claim that the specificity of learning, knowledge-accumulation, and competencies is a primary determinant of the observed patterns of innovative activities of firms and industries, organizational forms, dynamics and revealed competitive performances. Learning tends to be technology- and firm-specific, and is also affected by the market and institutional environment. Among the characteristics of the learning processes, three are particularly relevant: path-dependency, locality, and tacitness. Chapters 3 and 4, by Keith Pavitt and Pari Patel, and by Franco Malerba and Luigi Orsenigo, look at two different aspects of the patterns of innovative activities in Europe. *Pavitt and Patel* focus on large firms. They use comprehensive data on patents to discuss how large European firms learn about technologies, how they form their competencies, and their patterns of technological diversification. One of their main conclusions is that in-house learning is an important determinant of the accumulation of such competencies. *Malerba and Orsenigo* examine the entry and exit of firms in different patent classes in Europe. They look at whether new innovators in a certain class are newly established firms or constitute lateral entries from firms that already innovate in other fields. They also look at the patterns of exit from given patent classes, and examine the characteristics of what they call "ex-innovators." This chapter provides new evidence on the extent to which the European system encourages the rise of new innovators, and the extent to which innovation in Europe is still the domain of established firms that diversify onto related technologies.

Chapters 5 and 6, by Stefano Breschi and Peter Swann, look at the relationships between innovative activity, geographical concentration and regional agglomeration. *Breschi* uses European patent data, along with information about the geographical localization of patent holders, and finds that in Europe spatial agglomeration is an important determinant of innovation because of the knowledge spillovers generated by geographical proximity. He also finds that the importance of spatial agglomeration differs across sectors and technological regimes. He ascribes these differences to differences in the nature of the underlying knowledge bases, in the related opportunity and appropriability conditions, and in the extent to which the benefits of technological knowledge depend on the cumulativeness of the learning processes. *Swann* asks what is the size of industrial clusters after which one observes an acceleration in their growth rates (take-off), and what is the size after which growth vanishes (peak level). Among other things he suggests that in large European countries (Germany, France, Britain, and Italy) many industrial clusters have already reached the peak-entry level, while the clusters in smaller countries (the Netherlands, Denmark, Belgium, Spain, Greece, Ireland, and Portugal) are probably too small to "take off." These are important conclusions which have significant implications for a European policy of industrial growth based on the potential that can be created from regional agglomerations.

The final two chapters in part II – chapters 7 and 8, by Nick von Tunzelmann, and Cristiano Antonelli and Marco Calderini – are related to some of the aspects dealt with in chapters 3–6, by focusing on two different industries: electronics and mechanical engineering. *Von Tunzelmann* looks again at the accumulation of firm competencies by analyzing the behavior of large European electronics companies. He discusses in detail the characteristics of the competence-accumulation process of these firms, their patterns of specialization and diversification, and the ensuing trends towards technological convergence among the different sub-fields of this industry. The analysis provides a comprehensive view of these firms, and discusses the related implications for competitive advantages. *Antonelli and Calderini* analyze the importance of localized technological change in skill-intensive industries such as mechanical engineering. Localized technological change is due to "bottom-up" processes based on generic as well as on tacit knowledge, and on the improvements in design and production processes. The generation of innovation is thus mainly the outcome of the efforts of innovators that draw on learning processes highly specific to the history, context, and experience of innovators. Among other things, they use data on 136 Italian firms in the mechanical sector during 1988–93, and measure their "efficiency" by the error of a production function which relates the value-added of these firms to some of their tangible inputs. Using non-parametric estimation techniques, they show that the efficiency of these firms is highly correlated with demand shocks.

Part II is about inter-firm collaborations and research networks. It opens with chapter 9, by Patrick Llerena and Mireille Matt, which discusses policy aspects of inter-firm collaborations. *Llerena and Matt* contrast a "static" approach to the problem of inter-firm collaborations with a "dynamic" one. In a static approach, inter-firm collaborations tend to be viewed as a vehicle for collusion. As a result, the emphasis is on policies that restrict collaborative agreements because of the implied restraints on competition. But, as Llerena and Matt argue, collaborations should be examined primarily from a dynamic, evolutionary perspective. The emphasis should be on the implications for inter-firm learning and the exchange of complementary assets and capabilities. In short, a dynamic perspective underscores the beneficial effects of collaborations, and therefore calls for policy interventions that encourage agreements among firms endowed with complementary assets and capabilities.

While Llerena and Matt set the framework for analyzing inter-firm collaborations and research networks, chapters 10–12 look specifically at collaborative relationships among firms, with special emphasis on European collaborations in three main industries. *Antoine Bureth, Sandrine Wolff, and Antonello Zanfei* in chapter 10 examine an important feature of the dynamics of collaborations, and apply their framework to the case of the European electronics industry. They analyze whether, and to what extent, the stability of collaborations is influenced by the underlying characteristics and objectives of the partners. They discuss the tensions that arise in these collaborations, and the ensuing stabilizing and destabilizing forces. *Salvatore Torrisi* in chapter 11 looks at the software industry. He uses data on the growth and restructuring processes of 38 large US and European software firms during 1984–92. His main research hypothesis is that both internal and external growth operations (e.g. formation of new subsidiaries, or inter-firm agreements) reinforce firms' specialization rather than business diversification, and his empirical results find evidence that is consistent with this hypothesis. *Margaret Sharp and Jacqueline Senker* look at inter-firm collaborations in European biotechnology. They discuss in detail case studies of inter-firm agreements in this industry which offer a comprehensive view of these relationships. Some of the agreements in their case studies are between large established pharmaceutical multinationals and newly formed biotechnology firms, while others are between more established biotech companies and large firms. Moreover, while some of the case studies are of US and European firms, others are intra-European collaborations. The case studies also highlight the factors that encourage and lead to successful relationships.

Chapters 13–15 deal specifically with research networks. These build on the theoretical framework of the so-called "new economics of science," advanced in particular by the work of Paul David. As we shall see below, this framework proves to be useful in analyzing an important dimension of research networks in Europe – the research networks created through research funding by the European Union and, more generally, the effects on the formation of these networks produced by the deliberate and systematic attempt by the European Union to enhance continent-wide R&D collaborations among firms and non-profit institutions (government research labs and universities).

Chapter 13, by *Paul David, Dominique Foray, and Edward Steinmueller*, offers a comprehensive survey of the approach underlying the new economics of science, its application to the formation and development of research networks, and related public policy implications. The chapter also opens some new issues in the agenda of the new economics of science, perfects others that were dealt with in other contributions, and suggests how this framework can be applied to understanding research networks and collaborations in Europe. Among other things, a relevant contribution of this chapter to the purpose of this volume is that it shows how the framework can be used to deal with the phenomenon of research networks among public and private institutions (and particularly of networks promoted by the European Union in the field of research and development of new technologies).

Following this line of analysis, chapter 14, by *Walter Garcia-Fontes and Aldo Geuna*, uses data on the BRITE-EURAM contracts from 1989 to 1993. Interestingly enough, this is one of the first times that a comprehensive data set of European research programs has been used to analyze a number of issues about the formation of research networks funded by the European Union. The interesting finding of the chapter is that it confirms the existence of a core set of institutions that participate repeatedly in many European-funded networks. However, the authors also find that these institutions have produced significant knowledge spillovers. The "hub" institutions typically link, in different networks, with different institutions (or firms) that do not participate repeatedly in them. The hub group then appears to be a vehicle for enhancing the participation of new partners in the European-funded networks.

Chapter 15, by *Aldo Geuna*, looks at the determinants of university participation in the R&D programs of the European Union. The chapter uses data on the number of participations of a fairly comprehensive sample of "higher-education" institutions. The sample was chosen independently of the participation in European programs, and includes institutions that did not participate in any of them. The interesting result of this analysis is that, after controlling for a number of factors (e.g. scale or the composition of scientific fields in the institution), scientific quality influences both whether a given institution participates or not in any program, and how many times it participates (i.e. the number of participations). As discussed in the chapter, this is suggestive of some sort of increasing returns in the participation in European R&D projects.

Some general conclusions

There are a few analytical conclusions that can be drawn from this collection of studies.

First, these studies confirm an important insight of recent work in the economics of innovation and related fields, such as organization theory and strategic management – that firms' competencies are characterized by *stability and inertia*. Competencies are hard to change, and companies tend to exploit systematically the special set of competencies that they have accumulated over time. Lock-ins and competence traps may thus take place, in that successful firms may be driven by their success in existing technologies to disregard new alternatives. Learning may then also contain the seeds for future failure.

Second, there is a considerable degree of *sectoral specificity* in the organization of innovative activities. This means, for instance, that one observes greater differences in learning patterns, entry rates, sources of innovation, and concentration of innovators across sectors in the same country than across countries for the same sectors. These invariances are the consequence of the type of knowledge base of innovative activities and the working of technological regimes which differ across sectors more than they differ across countries.

However, as some of these studies show, there are also important differences across countries and regions which can be ascribed to factors related to the specific characteristics of the *national and local systems of innovation*. Thus the role of institutions in various European countries seems to modify in different degrees the sectoral specificities of the organization of innovative activities. At the European level, this means that the forces promoting the convergence of the organization of innovative activities across countries due to technological regimes may be attenuated by the tendency towards diversity caused by historical or socio-cultural differences, processes of division of labor or persistent differences in performance. As a consequence, tensions between sector specificity and national systems seem to play a relevant role in shaping the organization of innovative activity. The prevalence of one effect over another depends on the intensity of technological invariances, differences in the institutional settings and national systems of innovation, history and competitiveness of national companies, and degree of internationalization of R&D and production by companies.

One final set of insights produced by this collection is that the phenomena of *increasing returns* and *path-dependence* affect the nature of the innovation process and the dynamics of industries in Europe. There is a strong concentration of innovative activities in Europe; this emerges, for instance, from the analysis of the sectoral patterns of innovation and the geographical agglomeration processes in the continent. At the same time, the analyses of the European research networks in BRITE-EURAM and other programs, as well as the analysis of university participation in European R&D programs, provide empirical support to the idea that not only are these capabilities highly concentrated, but that this concentration may be reinforced by these programs. However, as discussed in the volume, there are offsetting factors as well, such as the fact that the hub institutions produce knowledge spillovers to other institutions.

Policy implications

What all these contributions suggest is that the balance between economic growth and European "cohesion" and integration is not an easy one to attain, and that considerable attention should be paid to finding policies that can effectively address the underlying trade-off. Although the book is not meant to provide policy prescriptions, some possible directions for further discussion of policy implications can be drawn from these studies.

Many of the studies suggest that innovation policy – or, more generally, industrial policy in Europe – has to take very seriously into account that the nature of technical change, and the related economic characteristics of the innovation process, display differences across industries that reflect differences in technological regimes. As a result, technology policy prescriptions cannot be formulated only general basis, but must also be made selective and sector-specific. They have to be based on the peculiar features of the different industries, with implied specificity in the instruments used and in prescriptions being made.

At the same time, the stability and inertia of firms' competencies create problems in the face of radical changes in technologies. Policy should in the first place try to reinforce existing competencies and specializations, and rely on international trade and the international diffusion of knowledge for products, information, or knowledge where other continents or areas show greater comparative advantages. This is not to say that Europe should not stimulate dynamic competencies in order to change and move to new technologies: quite the opposite. Together with policies aiming at strengthening existing competencies, Europe should develop policies aiming at shifting from one key technology to another, in order to avoid being trapped in competence-destroying technical change. However this implies that Europe should also rely to a large extent on international trade, and particularly on the international flow of technologies and ideas. This in turn calls for a policy aimed at basic research and human-capital formation.

One should also keep in mind that drastic "jumps" in technological competencies can rarely produce immediate results. By reinforcing existing competencies and specializations one can gain complementary expertise at the international (both inter-continental, and intra-European) level, while encouraging at the same time some diversification of capabilities through gradual shifts into related knowledge fields. In this respect, a key issue for Europe is to encourage *innovative entry* by new firms in new technologies and sectors. New firms are important means for creating new capabilities at the industry level, as these firms do not bear the "sunk" costs related to existing technologies and products associated with large established companies.

Another set of policy implications concerns the role of *collaborations* and the formation of *research networks*. On these matters, one can only endorse the present policy of the European Union. By encouraging these alliances – or at least by pursuing policies that are not as stringent as the US anti-trust policy – Europe has given rise to a host of interactions and exchanges of complementary knowledge and assets among many firms, organizations and institutions. One can fairly say that this has been one of the most important achievements of the industrial (and social) policies of the European Union. Over the past 10–15 years, these policies have encouraged much more profound and systematic linkages among European economic agents in different countries than in the past, thereby enhancing tighter relationships among the diverse cultures and institutions of the various European nations and regions. This emphasis on European collaboration has created the conditions for cross-country interaction of many local European organizations that had previously rarely moved outside their boundaries, as well as the conditions for interactions of partners that were already "internationalized," but that (especially in science and technology) typically looked for partners outside Europe (particularly in the United States), in spite of the fact that some of the competencies or resources that were sought could be found in the continent as well. Clearly, this cannot be the end of the story, and one still needs some considerable effort to enhance the participation of some European regions, especially in less advanced areas, in the continental networks.

Europe must be encouraged to insist on its underlying assumption that one must take a *dynamic* rather than a static perspective when assessing the social advantages of collaboration. Here the role of *diversity* among different European local or national systems of innovation may prove quite fruitful for effective collaboration, particularly if this diversity has generated complementarities in knowledge and competencies. The book also suggests that an important area where one needs deeper understanding of the policy implications of specific actions is the criteria on which to allocate resources for research. As noted in this book, the policy undertaken so far has maintained a sufficient degree of efficiency in the allocation process, while encouraging some diffusion of knowledge and technological information. Yet, one needs to dig more deeply into the specific mechanisms of these policies, and the underlying criteria for resource allocations, to examine their dynamic and long-run effects. One would like to know for instance whether concentration of research capabilities is actually being reinforced by these programs or not, in addition to what the studies in this volume have disclosed. The point is not that less concentration is socially desirable, but the implications of higher or lower concentration should be assessed more carefully. One should then evaluate more profoundly how one could resolve the trade-offs between short-run research efficiency, long-run innovation and growth, and long-run objectives of social cohesion.

Part I
Patterns of innovative activity

2 The co-evolution of technological knowledge and corporate organizations

Giovanni Dosi and Luigi Marengo

In spite of their richness and diversity, several major themes cut across most of the chapters contained in part I of the book. In this introductory chapter we discuss some of these themes, along with a brief outline of the theoretical background into which they could fit (wearing our, admittedly, biased interpretative spectacles), and some policy implications.[1]

Knowledge diffusion and learning

All the chapters in this section appear to share some common ground. First, patterns of creation and diffusion of technological innovations have a fundamental influence on patterns of industrial dynamics. Second, understanding the nature and dynamics of technology- and sector-specific knowledge bases is a major ingredient of the interpretation of competitive outcomes at the level of individual companies, sectors, regions, and countries.

Conversely, in modern economies, firms are major – albeit by no means unique – repositories of knowledge. Individual organizations embody specific "ways of solving problems" that are often very difficult to replicate in other organizations or even within the organization itself. In turn, organizational knowledge is stored to a great extent into the operating procedures (the "routines"[2]) and the higher-level rules (concerning, for example, "what to do when something goes wrong," or "how to change lower-level routines") that firms enact while handling their problem-solving tasks in the domains of production, research, and marketing. Such organizational knowledge usually comes under the heading of "organizational competencies" (cf. Chandler, 1992; Prahalad and Hamel, 1990; Teece and Pisano, 1994; Dosi and Marengo, 1994) – that is, those problem-

---

[1] Broader discussions along similar lines are found in Dosi (1997); Dosi and Marengo (1994); Dosi *et al.* (1997), from which the following discussion is partly drawn.
[2] Cf. Nelson and Winter (1982), Cohen *et al.* (1996).

solving capabilities which emerge out of the interaction among distributed pieces of knowledge within the organization. Such competencies have often (though not exclusively) a technological nature, but since they emerge out of distributed interactions, the technological and organizational dimensions can hardly be separated.

Corporate organizations "learn" in ways that – as we shall briefly discuss below – are shaped by what the organizations already "know," and by the collective interactions within the environment where the organization happens to be nested. In turn, these collective interactions partly have to do with *lato sensu* cooperative and symbiotic phenomena, such as mutual imitation, externalities of some sort, explicit collaborative links, etc. However, to a large extent, interactions straightforwardly depend on market-selection mechanisms. Hence, in the view suggested here, the analysis of technological and industrial dynamics basically nests in the understanding of the interplay between the accumulation of techno-organizational competencies (within and across firms) on the one hand, and by market-selection processes on the other.

Learning tends to be highly technology- and firm-specific. However, common knowledge bases shared by a multitude of firms within the same production activities, often cutting across regional and national boundaries, are likely to limit and order such corporate specificities. Moreover, market selection – operating through differential economic performances – is another powerful force reducing and, so to speak, "patterning", the variety of both technological and organizational innovations which are observed over time.

Given all that, a puzzling issue addressed from different perspectives in all the chapters which follow concerns the explanation of long-lasting inter-firm asymmetries in performances and equally long-lasting sectoral and regional specificities in the patterns of innovation. Part of the causes probably rest upon the "locality" of learning, the "opaqueness" of the environment, and the positive feedbacks linking particular directions of technological learning with particular organizational set-ups, all implying the persistence of different forms of corporate and industrial organization, even when *ex post* they yield different competitive performances. As one can easily generate multiple equilibria stemming from non-convexities and increasing returns in the space of technologies, so one can easily conjecture multiple "organizational trajectories" stemming from organizational learning about norms, competencies, and corporate structures.

As already mentioned, the variations observed in organizational and behavioral traits are not unbounded: the institutional and market environments in which each firm operates are also likely to set some viability constraints on such variety.

Dynamically, technological knowledge is modified and augmented partly within individual firms and partly through interaction with other firms (competitors, users, suppliers, etc.) and other institutions (universities, technical societies, etc.). In sketchy evolutionary terms, we can characterize each competing firm by a set of largely complementary, interrelated, and rather inertial traits which map into organizational actions and determine, in a given competitive environment, the relative performance of the organization. (In Nelson and Winter, 1982, and Cohen *et al.*, 1996, some of these inertial organizational characteristics are defined as "quasi-genetic", and, loosely borrowing from biology, one may say that many organizational traits are *epistatically correlated* in the sense that "competitiveness" is the point outcome of the interrelation of bundles of them.)

Research agenda

Such a view implies a research agenda which is focused on the following three interlinked issues:

- understanding the nature and the dynamics of such "quasi-genetic" traits, which are the carriers of the firm's organizational capabilities (cf. Nelson and Winter, 1982, Cohen *et al.* 1996) and constitute what are usually called organizational competencies;
- understanding the technological and organizational constraints which limit the possible directions of evolutionary change and constitute a sort of "grammar" of the possible organizational and technological configurations;
- understanding the interactions between market-selection processes and internal constraints which limit the patterns which can emerge out of selection.

Patterns of innovative activities are the result of complex interaction between micro-processes of learning and adaptation and competitive selection forces. In particular, it must be stressed that if selection forces tend to pull organizational adaptation in some particular directions, how organizations *actually move* in such a selection environment depends also on their pre-existing features, on the distribution of these across firms, and the dynamics of technological and organizational knowledge. The same issue can be framed in terms of the so-called "fitness landscape" (cf. Kaufman, 1993), representing in some reduced form the interactions between firm-specific traits and collective competitive advantages/disadvantages.[3]

---

[3] In terms of organizational features, the shape of the "fitness landscape" in which an organization learns and adapts (number of local optima, size of their basins of attraction) depends on the features and dynamics of the underlying technological and organizational

Crucial questions and dimensions

In brief, crucial underlying questions concern, for example:

- What are the main technological and organizational traits and how are they interrelated?
- What are the collective properties of technological and organizational learning?
- How do such properties interact with specific features of market selection?

Among the characteristics of learning processes there are some dimensions which are particularly important for these purposes, grounded in some rather general features of the underlying knowledge bases. Such dimensions are path-dependency, locality, and tacitness.

Path-dependency arises from complementarities within the technological and organizational system: such complementarities increase the ruggedness of the "fitness landscape" (cf. Kaufman, 1993) in which organizational adaptation takes place and therefore increase the chance that organizations are trapped on different local optima. Path-dependency thus generally implies history-bound diversity among organizations, diversity which can persist in spite of selective pressure. It must be pointed out that such complementarities are not necessarily located within the borders of a single organization, but can spread across organizations, forming a *co-evolving system* of interrelated organizations. Such co-evolving complementarities can be spatially determined, either in the physical geographical space – as pointed out in chapter 3 by Pavitt and Patel (on national systems of innovation), by Swann (on geographically limited knowledge spillovers), and 5 by Breschi (on clustering in industrial districts) – or in some technological space (see the concepts of technological proximity explicitly or implicitly employed in all the chapters in part I, and in particular chapter 7, by Von Tunzelmann).

Relatedly, locality means that learning and adaptation proceed, in probability, by "small" steps in the neighborhood of the current state. This implies that long jumps in the fitness landscape are quite unlikely and

---

knowledge. The fundamental questions to be answered can then be phrased in the following terms:
- what are the main technological and organizational characteristics, and how are they inter-related?
- What are the dynamic systemic properties of technological and organizational learning?
- How do such characteristics and dynamics interact with the competitive selection process, and which sets of inter-related characteristics are likely to be selected, for or against?

learning and adaptation is likely to happen by small increments.[4] Different aspects of "locality" are addressed by Breschi in chapter 5, whose evidence suggests the widespread existence of dynamic increasing returns which are "local" in terms of both knowledge and of geographical space; conversely, Antonelli and Calderini in chapter 8 study the impact of "local" market-specific influences upon some proxies of productivity growth.

Tacitness, as opposed to codification, is a feature of the organizational knowledge basis which make its transfer more difficult. Tacit knowledge components cannot be transferred through a set of instructions in some formal language, but only through direct imitation and practice. Tacitness has a much deeper dimension than the one usually considered in the literature on technological change, where it is usually seen in connection with skills acquired through repeated practice when all the components required for a good performance are never entirely transparent, even to the executor. The examples which are usually referred to are those of skillful physical activities, such as riding a bicycle or playing soccer: it is clear that nobody will ever learn to ride a bicycle or become a good soccer player just by studying a handbook, however detailed and complete it may be.

But there is a more fundamental sense in which knowledge has a tacit component well beyond skillful physical activities: this has to do with the tacit component in every act of interpretation and meaning attribution, whereby *even codified knowledge is deeply rooted in tacit knowledge*. In particular, categories through which individuals interpret and process signals have a tacit and idiosyncratic dimension which prevents groups from ever exactly sharing meaning. Economic organizations are therefore systems of interpretation and meaning (cf. March, 1988), where interpretation of past experience

is captured by routines in a way that makes the lessons [of history], but not the history, accessible to organizations and organizational members who have not themselves experienced the history (Levitt and March, 1988, 320).

Organizational routines, practices and procedures (cf. Nelson and Winter, 1982; Cohen *et al.*, 1996) are systems of interpretation and meaning which encode past experience, store interpreted experience in the

---

[4] Note that even when adaptation proceeds by small increments at the level of "quasi-genetic" traits, this does not necessarily imply that the same gradual pattern of change is observed at the corresponding organizational (phenotipic) level of revealed "fitness": on a rugged landscape, such small steps can trigger dramatic change when a new basin of attraction is reached.

organizational memory and direct organizational decision-making through a *logic of appropriateness.*[5]

"Locality" broadly means that new knowledge is built upon – what is already known: learning is typically a local search process in some knowledge space. This implies that knowledge is often built in a *cumulative fashion*, and that patterns of knowledge-accumulation and exploration tend to remain relatively coherent within individuals, organizations, and possibly also countries (an obvious underlying assumption is that competencies developed in a given domain do not make it easier to acquire other competencies in different ones).

Locality is likely at work in various different spaces, defined by the dimensions of technological knowledge, organizational traits, geography *stricto sensu*, market characteristics, etc. While geographical proximity relates more closely to notions such as industrial districts, market proximity relates primarily to user–producer interaction, organizational proximity to the existence and intensity of communication and interaction links within an organization, etc. Admittedly, the definition of a clear-cut concept of proximity in knowledge and technological spaces is not an easy task – if anything, because such spaces and their topologies are not given independently from the very process of learning.

In order to characterize such spaces and the systems of knowledge accumulation at work in them, taxonomic exercises (Keith Pavitt's taxonomy is probably the most famous one, cf. Pavitt, 1984), try to map "families" of technologies and sectors according to their sources of innovative knowledge and their typical innovative procedures.

A property – broadly acknowledged by most studies on the economics of innovation – is the diversity of learning modes and sources of knowledge across technologies and across sectors. For example, in some activities, knowledge is accumulated primarily via informal mechanisms of learning-by-doing, learning by interacting with customers and suppliers, etc. In others, it involves much more formalized activities of search (such as those undertaken in R&D labs). In some fields, knowledge is mostly generated internally and is specific to particular applications. In others, it draws much more directly upon university research and scientific advances.

At the same time, one has tried to identify possible invariances, which hold across technologies, in the patterns of learning (notions such as "technological paradigms," "regimes," and "technological trajectories"

---

[5] Appropriateness, as a logic for action, means that action is not so much driven by rational calculation of the value of the consequences to alternative courses of action, but rather by recognition of familiar patterns in the present state of the world and application of known procedures "appropriate" to such patterns (cf. Cyert and March, 1963; Nelson and Winter, 1982; Levitt and March, 1988).

belong to this domain of analysis), and descriptive indicators for these same patterns. So, for example, variables such as the levels of "innovative opportunity" associated with each technological paradigm, the degrees of "cumulativeness" displayed by technical advances, etc. have turned out to be quite useful in interpreting the determinants of the particular "trajectories" of innovation that one observes.

In brief, the general message of an increasing number of studies – including those which follow – is that the specificities of knowledge-accumulation might well be primary determinants of the observed dynamics in both organizational forms and revealed competitive performances.

As already mentioned, the following chapters also bring quite a few insights with respect to (1) the processes through which knowledge-accumulation occurs; (2) their embodiment within largely path-dependent organizational set-ups; and (3) the patterns – within and across technologies, industrial sectors, and regions – which emerge as a result. By reflecting on these contributions, if we had to choose some concluding hints on some topical research tasks ahead, they would include the following.

Policy and research implications

First, the time might be ripe to engage in a thorough discussion of the comparative merits of interpretations of industrial performances and dynamics based, *in primis*, on largely discretional strategic deliberation (in the spirit of a lot of contemporary IO theory) as distinguished from the stream of much more "destrategized" and knowledge-based interpretations which appear prominently below.

Second, there are encouraging signs of emergence of different but complementary topologies of innovative patterns. Some have to do with proxies of technological distances (here, an urgent challenge is the reduction of their metaphorical fuzziness and the identification of more precise indicators of learning activities and their outcomes). Other topologies have sectors, lines of production, and markets as the primary units of analysis (in this vein, rediscovering and refining earlier intuitions on the importance of such things as "development blocks," Dahmen, 1988, *"filières"* Jacquemin and Rainelli, 1984, etc.) And, finally, it is clear that down-to-earth "geography" – i.e. the space of regions, nations, language barriers, institutional differences, etc. – implies much more than sheer transport costs and local demand externalities. Indeed, specific interactions across "cognitive", organizational and institutional spaces are more likely to explain the diverse patterns of innovation and competitiveness that we actually observe.

Third, and relatedly, it seems to us that precisely the richness of all empirical insights into these different processes of learning, adaptation, and selection also favors and urges further advances on the side of more formal (and, inevitably, more "reduced-form") theories, whereby one will also be able to explore some general properties of different forms of interaction mechanisms (e.g. across knowledge bases, organizations, institutional arrangements, etc.).

Fourth, the wealth of policy implications which can be derived from the knowledge- and organization-focused views presented below appears to be still strikingly under-explored. The contributions which follow also help set more solid foundations for policy perspectives whereby central tasks are nurturing organizational learning, stifling likely organizational inertia through novel competitive challenges and institutional designs which help in ameliorating the persistent dilemmas between "exploitation" of what is already known and "exploration" of much more uncertain notional opportunities.

References

Chandler, A.D. (1992). "Organizational Capabilities and the Economic History of the Industrial Enterprise," *Journal of Economic-Perspectives*, 6, 79–100

Cohen M., R. Burkhart, G. Dosi, M. Egidi, L. Marengo, M. Warglien, S. Winter, and B. Coriat (1996). "Routines and Other Recurring Action Patterns of Organizations: Contemporary Research Issues," *Industrial and Corporate Change*, 5, 653–721

Cyert, R.M. and J.G. March (1963). *A Behavioral Theory of the Firm*, Englewood Cliffs, NJ: Prentice-Hall

Dahmen, E. (1988). "'Development Blocks' in Industrial Economics," *Scandinavian Economic History Review*, 36, 3–14

Dosi, G. (1997). "Opportunities, Incentives and the Collective Patterns of Technological Change," *Economic Journal*, 107, 1530–47

Dosi G., F. Malerba, O. Marsili, and L. Orsenigo (1997). "Industrial Structures and Dynamics: Evidence, Interpretations and Puzzles," *Industrial and Corporate Change*, 6, 3–25

Dosi, G. and L. Marengo (1994). "Toward a Theory of Organizational Competencies," in R.W. England (ed.), *Evolutionary Concepts in Contemporary Economics*, Ann Arbor: Michigan University Press, 157–78

Jacquemin, A. and M. Rainelli (1984). "Filières de la nation et filières de l'entreprise," *Revue Economique*, 35, 379–92

Kauffman, S.A. (1993). *The Origins of Order*, Oxford: Oxford University Press

Levitt, B. and J.G. March (1988). "Organizational Learning," *Annual Review of Sociology*, 14, 319–340

March, J.G. (1988). *Decisions and Organisations*, Oxford: Basil Blackwell

Nelson, R. and S.G. Winter (1982). *An Evolutionary Theory of Economic Change*, Cambridge, Mass., The Belknap Press of Harvard University Press

Pavitt, K. (1984). "Sectoral Patterns of Technical Change: Towards a Taxonomy and a Theory," *Research Policy*, 13, 343–74

Prahalad, C.K. and G. Hamel (1990). "The Core Competence of the Corporation," *Harvard Business Review*, 68, 79–91

Teece, D. and G. Pisano (1994). "The Dynamic Capabilities of Firms: An Introduction," *Industrial and Corporate Change*, 3, 537–56

3   Large firms in Europe's innovative activity

Keith Pavitt and Pari Patel

Introduction

This chapter summarizes the results of our research on the role of large firms in the innovative activities of Europe. Our data is based on information on the large firms listed in *Fortune*, in particular on their R&D expenditures (when available), and on the patents granted to them in the United States. We shall address the following questions:

- How important are large firms in the technological activities of European countries, and how closely linked are they to their home countries?
- How important are large firms in various fields of technology?
- How do European large firms relate to those in other parts of the world?

We begin with a brief description of our data.

Data sources and limitations

Our population is made up of the world's largest firms that were technologically active in patenting in the United States in the 1980s. It consists of 587 firms, of which 249 were US-owned, 17 from Canada, 143 from Japan, and 178 from Europe (Patel and Pavitt, 1991). In some analyses, we have excluded firms (usually towards the smaller end of the population) whose volume of patenting was inadequate for the type of statistical analysis that we intended to undertake (Patel and Pavitt, 1994c).

The essential data that we have for each firm are its sales, principal sector of activity, country of origin, and the US patents granted to it since 1969, including those granted to divisions and subsidiaries with names different from the parent company. For each patent, we have the following information:

This chapter is based on research at the Centre for Science, Technology and Energy and Environment Policy (STEEP), funded by the Economic and Social Research Council (ESRC) within the Science Policy Research Unit.

- *The technical field:* We have developed and used different levels of dis-aggregation – 34 fields, and 5 or 11 broad fields, depending on the purpose of our analysis. All are based on the US patent classification.
- *The country of residence of the inventor:* This is *not* necessarily the country from which their patent application was filed, and is a more accurate reflection of the country in which the technological activity was performed.

The advantages and drawbacks of patenting statistics as indicators of technological activities have been discussed extensively elsewhere.[1] For the purposes of our analysis, the main drawbacks are that US patenting does not fully reflect improvements in software technology, since the practice in the United States of protecting software technology through patents is of recent origin. On the other hand, our patenting database offers greater coverage, comparability, and detail than any other available measure of technological activities. It also yields results that are consistent with those derived from other measures (such as R&D activities), when the two can be compared.

How important are large firms in Europe's innovative activities?

Major differences among countries in shares of national totals

In the late 1980s (1985–90) our large firms' share of total US patenting was about 45 percent. Although difficult to compare directly, this is probably much smaller than their share of R&D activities, which in most countries is heavily concentrated in firms with more than 10,000 employees. This is because US patenting also reflects technological activities performed outside R&D departments – in particular, the largely machinery-related technological activities of small firms.

Table 3.1 shows that, in Europe, the overall share of large firms in total innovative activities is higher than in the United States, but well below that in Japan. Within Europe, the shares of large firms vary considerably amongst countries, from above 60 percent in the Netherlands to below 30 percent in Italy, Norway and Finland. These international differences in the relative importance of large firms are *not* reflected in international differences in technological performance, as measured by the share of business-funded R&D activities in GDP (Patel and Pavitt, 1991). Rather, they reflect differing sectoral patterns of national technological advantage, with high shares of large firms reflecting national advantage in industries where technological activities are concentrated in large firms – chemicals, vehicles,

[1] See, for example, Basberg (1987); Griliches (1990), Pavitt (1988).

Table 3.1. *Large firms in national technological activities, 1985–1990*

| | Large firms | | Other firms and | |
Country	National (%)	Foreign (%)	institutions (%)	Total (%)
Japan (143)	64.9	0.7	34.4	100.0
Europe[a] (178)	41.2	10.9	47.9	100.0
United States (249)	37.0	2.6	60.5	100.0
Canada (17)	7.6	13.5	78.9	100.0
Netherlands (9)	53.5	8.1	38.4	100.0
Germany (43)	43.0	9.9	47.1	100.0
Switzerland (10)	37.6	5.8	56.6	100.0
France (26)	31.5	9.3	59.2	100.0
United Kingdom (56)	28.8	17.7	53.5	100.0
Finland (7)	20.7	0.2	79.1	100.0
Sweden (13)	20.5	11.5	68.0	100.0
Italy (7)	19.0	9.0	71.9	100.0
Norway (3)	13.9	9.2	76.9	100.0
Belgium (4)	7.1	35.8	57.1	100.0

Notes:
[a] "Europe" is the aggregate of all the European countries in this table. "Foreign" here refers to the share of all non-European firms.
( ) = number of firms based in the country.

electronics – and low shares of large firms reflecting national advantage in sectors where they are not – non-electrical machinery (See table 3.1 above).

Table 3.1 also shows that foreign large firms are relatively much more important sources of innovative activities in Europe than in either Japan or the United States. Within Europe, foreign large firms vary from less than 1 percent of the total in Finland to more than 10 percent in Sweden and the United Kingdom, and more than 30 percent in Belgium. Cross-country comparisons show no statistically significant relationship between strong national technological performance (as measured by industry-funded R&D as a percentage of GDP), and the share of either national or foreign large firms in national technological activities (Patel and Pavitt, 1991).

Strong links between large firms and their home countries

Our analysis confirms the conclusions of Porter (1990) that the rate and direction of technological activities in large firms are strongly conditioned

Table 3.2. *Large firms' patenting in the United States, by home country, 1985–1990*

Firm nationality	% share		% abroad, of which			
	Home	Abroad	United States	Europe	Japan	Other
Japan	98.9	1.1	0.8	0.3	—	0.0
United States	92.2	7.8	—	6.0	0.5	1.3
Europe[a]	82.0	18.0	16.7	—	0.4	1.0
Canada	66.8	33.2	25.2	7.3	0.3	0.5
Italy	88.1	11.9	5.4	6.2	0.0	0.3
France	86.6	13.4	5.1	7.5	0.3	0.5
Germany	84.7	15.3	10.3	3.8	0.4	0.7
Finland	81.7	18.3	1.9	11.4	0.0	4.9
Norway	68.1	31.9	12.6	19.3	0.0	0.0
Sweden	60.7	39.3	12.5	25.8	0.2	0.8
United Kingdom	54.9	45.1	35.4	6.7	0.2	2.7
Switzerland	53.0	47.0	19.7	26.1	0.6	0.5
Netherlands	42.1	57.9	26.2	30.5	0.5	0.6
Belgium	36.4	63.6	23.8	39.3	0.0	0.6
All firms (587)	89.0	11.0	4.1	5.6	0.3	0.9

Note:
[a] For European firms as a whole, "share abroad" refers to their activities outside Europe.

by their home country. Table 3.2 shows that our large firms continue to perform a high proportion of their innovative activities in their home countries. According to Cantwell (1992), the share of large firms' innovative activities performed outside their home country is significantly related to the share of foreign production. About 25 percent of the firms' production is performed abroad, compared to only 11 percent of their innovative activities, which shows that foreign production is in general much less innovation-intensive than domestic production. Surveys show that the purpose of most foreign innovative activities is to adapt products and processes to local factor endowments and consumer tastes (Casson, 1991). Table 3.2 also shows that the main differences among countries and regions are that:
• Japanese firms have the least "globalized" structure of innovative activities, and European firms the most, with one-sixth of their innovative activities located in the United States.
• Within Europe, the degree of "globalization" of firms' innovative activities varies considerably, largely as a function of the size of the home

country. However, only Belgium and Dutch large firms perform more than half their innovative activities outside their home country, while German, French, and Italian firms perform more than 80 percent domestically.[2]

- Europe is the preferred location of foreign innovative activities for most large European firms. Within Europe, Germany is the first choice, probably reflecting its position as both the largest market and the largest European location of innovative activities.
- United Kingdom large firms do not fit this pattern. Although from a large country, they perform 45.1 percent of their innovative activities abroad. Although from a European country, they perform more than a third in the United States, partly reflecting past mergers and acquisitions.[3]

Further analyses show that the proportion of innovative firms' activities performed abroad *decreases* with the technology intensity of the industry and the firm (Patel, 1994b, 1995). This probably reflects the influence of the following factors:

1. At the industry level, the need to adapt "traditional" products to local tastes (e.g. food and drink, building materials), and to locate innovative activities close to available raw materials (e.g. petroleum, food and drink, building materials).
2. At the industry level, the smaller need to adapt high-technology products (e.g. civil aircraft, automobiles) to local requirements.
3. At the industry and the firm level, the concentration of innovative activities in the home country, probably reflecting (a) the positive external economies of links with the local science base and supply of skills, sources of finance, and local suppliers and customers; (b) the efficiency gains within firms from the close coordination of functional activities, and integration of tacit knowledge, necessary for the launching of major innovations (Patel and Pavitt, 1991).

In addition, we have found that country effects dominate over company effects in explaining large firms' technological performance. Cross-country comparisons show that domestically controlled large firms' technology intensities – and their rates of growth of technological activities – correlated significantly with those of other national firms, but not with their own foreign technological activities[4] (Patel and Pavitt, 1991).

---

[2] High R&D-spending firms with more than 50 percent of their technological activities performed outside their home countries include AKZO, Nestlé, Philips, Racal, ITT, Electrolux, SKF, Solvay, GKN, Wellcome, Roche, and Sandoz.

[3] See p. 000 for further elaboration.

[4] An important exception to this general rule was the pharmaceutical industry.

Large foreign firms in host countries' innovative activities.

On the whole, foreign large firms establish technological activity in host countries in fields reflecting the parent firm's (and often the home country's) strengths, rather than the particular technological strengths of the host country. This is the case for firms from Japan, (FR) Germany, the Netherlands, Switzerland, and Sweden, although the pattern is inconclusive for firms from France and the United States (Patel and Pavitt, 1991).

From the side of the host country, the technological activities of foreign large firms are most strongly established in fields of relative national weakness in Canada, France, (FR) Germany, and the United States. Only in Belgium are the fields of overall national, and of foreign firms', technological strength closely correlated, reflecting the unusually strong position of foreign firms there (Patel, 1994b).

Large firms and technological fields

Varying Contributions amongst Fields

Table 3.3 shows that the relative importance of our large firms in total technological activity varies considerably among 11 core technological fields, being highest in electronics, chemicals, and automobiles, and lowest in non-electrical machinery. There is no discernible difference in this pattern among countries or regions.

Table 3.3. *Share of large firms in different technological fields, 1985–1990*

Percentage of total patenting in 11 broad fields, covering all US patenting

Technological field	Top 20 firms	All firms (587)
Electronic consumer goods and photography	50.8	69.9
Electronic capital goods and components	45.2	69.2
Motor vehicles and parts	50.1	65.0
Other chemicals	25.8	61.3
Materials	23.2	57.0
Telecommunications	34.3	56.5
Fine chemicals	29.4	50.3
Electrical machinery	26.1	47.7
Raw materials-related technologies	25.3	43.2
Non-electrical machinery	10.9	34.4
Defense-related technologies	22.9	33.1

Multi-technology large firms

Table 3.4 shows that the correspondence between large firms' principal products, and their technological competencies is not simple and straightforward:
- Large firms are technologically active in a wide range of technologies outside what might be considered as their "core fields." In particular, firms in all sectors are active in machinery technologies, where they often do not have a distinctive technological advantage, where smaller firms are particularly active, and where the processes of "technological convergence" and "vertical disintegration" described by Rosenberg (1976) remain of central importance (Patel and Pavitt, 1994a).[5]
- Specific firms' technological mixes (or profiles) are closely related to the products that they make. They are typically spread over a wide range of

Table 3.4. *Shares of large firms' technological activities, five broad technological fields, by principal product group*

Principal product group (PPG)	Chemical	Non-electrical machinery	Electrical	Transport	Other	Total
Chemicals (66)	71.0	16.9	8.9	0.6	2.6	100.0
Pharmaceuticals (25)	80.2	8.0	2.1	0.0	9.7	100.0
Mining and petroleum (31)	57.1	34.2	6.7	0.9	1.1	100.0
Textiles, etc. (10)	52.9	31.7	9.5	0.6	5.3	100.0
Rubber and plastics (9)	43.2	29.3	4.7	20.1	2.7	100.0
Paper and wood (18)	25.4	47.1	12.4	0.4	14.6	100.0
Food (14)	70.6	21.9	3.0	0.1	4.3	100.0
Drink and tobacco (8)	40.8	50.3	4.6	0.3	3.9	100.0
Building materials (16)	30.5	51.3	10.0	0.9	7.3	100.0
Metals (38)	26.8	54.9	13.9	2.1	2.2	100.0
Machinery (58)	7.6	64.9	13.9	10.2	3.3	100.0
Electrical (56)	7.6	21.2	67.0	1.3	2.8	100.0
Computers (17)	5.2	16.3	77.3	0.2	1.0	100.0
Instruments (21)	14.3	18.3	64.2	0.1	3.0	100.0
Motor vehicles (35)	3.8	44.8	20.7	28.8	1.9	100.0
Aircraft (35)	8.1	48.5	31.2	8.3	3.9	100.0
All large firms (440)	28.8	27.9	35.7	4.4	3.1	100.0

Note:
( ) = number of firms.

[5] As a consequence, the large firms making electrical and electronic products develop more mechanical technologies than the large firms producing non-electrical machinery.

sectors: more than 95 percent of the firms were active in the 1980s in more than 10 of our 34 technical fields, and more than 40 percent in more than 20 (Patel and Pavitt, 1994c).

• Firms' technological profiles change only very slowly over time, reflecting the localized and cumulative nature of technological learning. Fewer than 10 percent of our firms have no significant correlation between their patent shares in 1969–74 and in 1985–90, and their revealed technology advantage (RTA, see table 3.5 for definitions) over the same period.

Table 3.5. *Stability of firms' technological profiles, including acquisitions and divestments*

	Correlation Coefficients[a]				
Firm	RTA[b]	Shares[c]	Firm	RTA[b]	Shares[c]
Rolls Royce	1.00	0.97	Canon	0.92	0.81
Bosch	0.99	0.95	MAN	0.92	0.97
Kodak	0.99	0.91	Thomson	0.92	0.94
Merck	0.99	0.99	Zeiss	0.92	0.97
NEC	0.99	0.97	Texas Instruments	0.91	0.87
Sony	0.99	1.00	Takeda Chemical	0.90	0.96
Xerox	0.99	0.99	Dow Chemical	0.89	0.99
Ciba–Geigy	0.98	0.99	United Technologies	0.89	0.93
Fujitsu	0.98	0.97	Caterpillar	0.88	0.86
Hitachi	0.98	0.91	Komatsu	0.87	0.82
IBM	0.98	0.98	Gould	0.86	0.91
Nissan	0.98	0.94	Alcatel	0.84	0.85
Philips	0.98	0.99	Bayer	0.84	0.99
ABB	0.97	0.84	ICI	0.82	0.96
Du Pont	0.97	0.98	Mitsubishi Denki	0.77	0.66
Olivetti	0.97	0.94	NTT	0.76	0.81
Sumitomo Chemical	0.97	1.00	General Motors	0.71	0.74
Nippondenso	0.96	0.92	General Electric	0.70	0.81
ATT	0.95	0.94	Black & Decker	0.51	0.61
Fanuc	0.94	0.95	Nokia	0.00	0.07
Siemens	0.94	0.96			

Notes:

[a] Correlations between (i) patents in 1979–84 to company as it existed in 1984, and (ii) patents granted in 1987–92 to company as it existed in 1992.

[b] RTA = company patent share in each of the 34 technological fields, divided by the share of total patenting in the same field.

[c] Patent shares = share of total company patenting in each of the 34 technological fields specified in table 3.6.

- Even when acquisitions and divestments are taken into account, firms' technological profiles remain remarkably stable. A detailed examination of their effects on the 41 firms listed in table 3.5 shows that profiles were significantly similar (at the 1 percent level) over the period 1979–92 in nearly two-thirds of the firms. Only in one case was the correlation not significant at the 5 percent level (Patel, 1994a).
- Furthermore, in only very few of the cases involving substantial technological activities were the technological profiles of the acquired firm different from the acquiring firm. All these cases involved US-owned firms (Black and Decker's purchase of Emhart, General Motors of Hughes; General Electric of RCA, and Kodak of Sterling Drug). In contrast, ATT and the European firms (ABB, Alcatel, Philips, Thomson, and Olivetti) reinforced their existing profiles through their acquisitions, as did Hitachi and Fujitsu. This suggests that, in their corporate acquisitions, European and Japanese firms are more heavily driven than their US rivals by strategies of cumulative competence-building.

Increasing technological diversity of large firms

Columns (4)–(7) in table 3.6 show marked differences amongst European, Japanese and US firms in the *trends* in their technological diversity between the early 1970s and the late 1980s, with Japanese firms increasing, and US firms decreasing. However, this may be an illusion created by the method of measurement, since we are comparing trends in *domestic* patenting by US firms with *international* patenting by Japanese firms at precisely the time that they were reaching the world technological frontier, and increasing their international sales. At the end of the period, the degree of diversity of Japanese firms was not significantly different from that of US and European firms.

Within Europe, the picture is more mixed. More firms based in Germany, Switzerland, and France increased than decreased their diversity, while the two trends were more or less equal in Belgium, Italy, Netherlands, Sweden, and the United Kingdom. Amongst the firms increasing their technological diversity most extensively were BMW, Degussa, ELF, and Metal Box. Amongst those decreasing it were Linde, Grundig, Michelin, BOC, and BTR. Often (but not always) increasing technological diversity appears to be associated with expanding technological activities, and vice versa.

Stronger conclusions can be reached about the technical fields into (and out of) which firms are moving over time. Columns (1)–(3) of table 3.6 show the total number of large firms that have been active (i.e. have patented) in each of our 34 technical fields in 1969–74 and 1985–90. It thereby compares

Table 3.6. *Number of firms out of 440 that are active in each of 34 technical fields*

Sorted by total change (1)	1969–74 (2)	1985–90 (3)	Change, of which			
			Change (4)	European (5)	Japanese (6)	American (7)
Calculators and computers, etc.	215	285	70	14	34	22
Drugs and bioengineering	159	204	45	18	27	0
Materials (inc. glass and ceramics)	321	362	41	7	28	6
Plastic and rubber products	251	287	36	10	37	−11
General electrical industrial apparatus	331	367	36	6	38	−8
Instruments and controls	373	407	34	8	31	−5
Metallurgical and metal treatment processes	238	270	32	0	29	3
Dentistry and surgery	143	173	30	17	34	−21
Miscellaneous metal products	351	380	29	5	26	−2
Other (ammunitions and weapons, etc.)	314	337	23	4	26	−7
Image and sound equipment	209	231	22	6	33	−17
Chemical processes	392	413	21	4	18	−1
Mining and wells: machinery and processing.	117	137	20	12	15	−7
Hydrocarbons, mineral oils, fuels, etc.	135	152	17	14	5	−2
General non-electrical industrial equipment	363	377	14	2	18	−6
Agricultural chemicals	96	108	12	7	17	−10
Semiconductors	154	166	12	3	23	−14
Photography and photocopy	137	147	10	−1	38	−28
Appliances for chemicals, food, glass, etc.	384	393	9	−4	23	−10
Assembling and material handling appliances	310	319	9	−2	21	−10
Road vehicles and engines	134	142	8	6	11	−9
Electrical devices and systems	259	267	8	5	22	−19

Table 3.6. (*cont.*)

Sorted by total change (1)	1969–74 (2)	1985–90 (3)	Change (4)	Change, of which		
				European (5)	Japanese (6)	American (7)
Organic chemicals	281	284	3	8	14	−19
Non-electrical specialized ind. equipment	391	394	3	−2	17	−12
Power plants	135	138	3	−2	19	−14
Inorganic chemicals	181	183	2	−2	14	−10
Aircraft	71	73	2	5	3	−6
Metallurgical and metal working equipment	366	366	0	−1	21	−20
Telecommunications	253	252	−1	−2	15	−14
Bleaching, dyeing and disinfecting	113	110	−3	2	13	−18
Other transport equipment (exc. aircraft)	211	206	−5	−4	15	−16
Food and tobacco (processes and products)	127	119	−8	4	9	−21
Induced nuclear reactions	48	30	−18	−7	3	−14
Textile, clothing, leather, wood products	119	94	−25	−2	11	−34

the degree of pervasiveness of technological competencies in different fields; the most pervasive competencies are highlighted – instruments and controls, chemical processes, chemical and other apparatus, and specialized machinery. Column (4) shows the changes over time in the number of firms that have patented in each of the 34 technological fields, which are sorted according to the increase in the number of active firms between the two periods. It emerges that:

- *New technological opportunities have been emerging in the past 20 years.* The highlighted fields in which the number of active firms increased most rapidly were computing, drugs and bioengineering, and materials – precisely the fields that have seen the most rapid growth of strategic alliance among firms (Hagedoorn and Schakenrad, 1992).
- *New technologies build on the old.* For firms from Japan, Europe, and the United States, the most pervasive fields remained the same over the period. In other words, the emergence of new fields of technological

opportunity has not destroyed the relevance of established fields of competence.

- *New technologies can fail.* The rapidly declining number of firms with competencies in textiles is to be expected. The rapid decline in nuclear energy shows that the optimistic expectations in the 1950s and 1960s of many firms in the electrical and machinery industries have turned out to be fallacious.

European firms in global competition

European firms in major technological fields

Table 3.7 shows that, in general, the global technological competitiveness of large firms in major technological fields is the same as that of their home country.[6] US firms are relatively strong in defense and raw materials technologies, Japanese firms in consumer electronics and motor vehicles, and European firms in chemicals and defense-related technologies. However, the relative European strength in non-electrical machinery is not apparent, given the predominance of small firms. Column (5) shows that European firms have been relatively more successful in technological fields where the positions of the leading firms have not changed radically over the past 20 years.[7]

Within Europe, the leading firms again reflect the strengths of their home country: Germany in chemicals, motor vehicles, and defense-related technologies; France in defense-related technologies and telecommunications; the United Kingdom in defense-related technologies and chemicals, and the Netherlands in electronics.

Rivalry versus concentration

Among our large firms we have found no sign of either increasing or decreasing returns to scale in R&D or patenting activities: in other words, firms' R&D or patenting increases more or less linearly with their sales or employment. There is, therefore, no justification for either mergers or deconcentration in order to increase the volume of innovative activities (Patel and Pavitt, 1992). Fields of relative technological strength in each of the three regions (Japan, the United States, and Europe) are associated with a relatively large *number* of firms, thereby confirming another of Porter's (1990) conclusions regarding the importance of rivalry in domestic

---

[6] In fact, we have shown elsewhere (p. 28) that the causality probably runs from country performance to company performance.

[7] Or, put another way, European firms have not been challenged by Japanese firms in chemicals with the same vigor and success as in electronics.

Table 3.7. *Nationalities of the top 20 firms in US patenting, 1985–1990*

Broad technological field	Japan	United States	Europe	Correlation[a]
Industrial chemicals	1	11	8	0.66[b]
Fine chemicals	1	12	7	0.54
Defense-related technologies	0	14	6	0.37
Electrical machinery	6	10	4	0.68[b]
Telecommunications	6	10	4	0.70[b]
Motor vehicles	11	5	4	0.15
Raw materials-based technologies	1	16	3	0.45
Materials	4	13	3	0.41
Electronic capital goods	8	9	3	0.51
Non-electrical machinery	9	8	3	0.41
Electronic consumer goods	14	4	2	0.27

Notes:
[a] Correlation of shares of the top 20 in 1985–90 with their shares in 1969–74.
[b] Denotes coefficient significantly different from zero at the 5 percent level.

markets. Only for Europe is the above-average size of firm associated with technological fields of international competitive advantage. But even this is not a sufficient justification for public policies to increase company size, which (like a relatively large number of firms) may be as much the *result* of innovative dynamism as its cause.

Increased globalization in the 1980s?

In spite of the increasing talk of "techno-globalism," there is no strong evidence that most of our firms are consciously restructuring and internationalizing their innovative activities. Table 3.8 shows that, between the early and the late 1980s, large firms did on the whole increase the proportion of their innovative activities performed outside their home country. The increase was biggest for European firms, was concentrated mainly in the United States, and more than half came from mergers and acquisitions. The foreign shares of Japanese and US firms increased much less, and mainly as a result of internal redeployment, rather than mergers and acquisitions. Within Europe, the trends varied greatly among countries. The increases were highest for the United Kingdom and Swedish[8] firms, where most of

[8] According to Hakanson (1992), some Swedish firms' R&D was located elsewhere in Europe as part of a political campaign to join the European Union.

Table 3.8. *Trends in the internationalization of large firms' technological activities, 1979–1984 to 1985–1990, as percentage of firms' total patenting*

| | Increase abroad | | Of which | | | |
| | | | United States | Europe | Japan | Other |
Home country	Firms' total (%)					
Europe	4.2	[57][a]	3.8	–	0.2	0.2
United States	1.5	[−12]	–	1.3	0.0	0.2
Japan	0.3	[34]	0.1	0.1	–	0.0
United Kingdom	12.1	[59]	13.9	−2.4	0.1	0.4
Sweden	9.3	[95]	7.1	1.7	−0.0	0.5
Belgium	7.4	[53]	1.5	6.0	−0.3	0.3
Norway	6.9	[65]	−9.1	16.0	0.0	0.0
Switzerland	5.9	[127]	0.3	6.1	0.0	−0.5
Finland	5.4	[88]	−0.3	3.1	0.0	2.7
Netherlands	5.1	[5]	2.2	2.2	0.3	0.4
France	5.0	[44]	0.9	3.7	0.2	0.2
Germany	2.1	[88]	1.7	0.0	0.3	0.0
Italy	1.4	[234]	−1.9	3.2	0.0	0.1
All firms (587)	1.4	[37]	0.9	0.5	0.2	0.5

Note:
[a] Numbers in square brackets are the percentage shares of total increase of international patenting due to mergers and acquisitions, as distinct from redeployment of internal resources. Numbers >100 show that increasing internationalization through mergers and acquisitions was counterbalanced by decreasing internationalization of internal technological resources. Numbers <0 indicate the contrary: mergers and acquisition decreasing internationalization, and internal redeployment increasing it.

the expansion of activity was in the United States, as a consequence of mergers and acquisitions. Firms from all other European countries except Germany and the Netherlands increased their international technological activities more in Europe than the United States. The increases in foreign shares in German, French, and Italian firms were relatively small (Patel, 1995).

Despite these increases, about 60 percent of our large firms still had no foreign technological activity at the end of the 1980s, about a quarter were active in one or two foreign countries, and only about 15 percent in more than two (Patel, 1994b) clearly not a process that can reasonably be described as "globalization". However, since the late 1980s, the shares of

European firms' US patenting in medical (and to a lesser extent electronics) technology has increased considerably, mainly through local acquisitions. Companies with major increases in their US technological activities include Ciba-Geigy, Siemens, and Thomson, whilst Nokia and ICI have seen a decrease. Firms with substantial increases in the share of their technological activities in other European countries include Alcatel, Thomson, and Olivetti (Patel, 1994a).

Conclusions

Our analysis casts doubt on three of the most cherished beliefs and assumptions about trends in technological developments in the 1980s and 1990s: the increasing focus on firms' core technological competencies, increasing techno-globalism, and the emergence of a European system of innovation. The implications for European policy are both important and uncomfortable.

More focus on firms' core competencies?

According to Prahalad and Hamel (1990),

Few companies are likely to build world leadership in more than five or six fundamental competencies. A company that compiles a list of 20 to 30 capabilities has probably not produced a list of core competencies.

Our analysis shows that large firms do *not* concentrate on a few, fundamental core competencies, but instead are technologically active in a *range of technologies* where they have no distinctive advantage compared to their competitors. In industries such as automobiles, aerospace, and even electronics, high shares of firms' technological resources are devoted to maintaining an active technological interface with suppliers of components, sub-systems, machines, and materials, from whom they require a continuous path of technological change that is compatible with the changes in their own complex products and processes. For this reason, firms' core competencies are often distributed over a wide range of fields and in different parts of the organization.

In addition, our firms have increased their technological activities in precisely the same fields that have witnessed the most rapid growth of inter-firm technological alliances: IT, biotechnology, and materials. Here, our results are consistent with those of Granstrand and his colleagues at Chalmers in Sweden,[9] who conclude that the number of technological fields that large firms must master is increasing with the widening range of

[9] See, in particular, Granstrand and Sjolander (1990).

technological opportunities emerging from improvements in computing and other technologies. The observed increases in the external acquisition of technology are not therefore a *substitute* for in-house technological activities resulting from lower transaction costs, and thereby enabling reductions in R&D expenditures. On the contrary, internal technological activities and external linkages are *complementary* activities in the dynamic process of learning to cope with ever-more complex products, and requiring increases in R&D expenditures.

Given these findings:

- we should be skeptical about the applicability of static concepts taken from marketing (e.g. "focus") and from production (e.g. "make or buy") to the dynamic processes of technological learning
- we should not expect the growth of "strategic alliances" in technology to enable Europe to obtain technological competencies on the cheap; there is no substitute for in-house technological investment and learning
- we should distinguish carefully, at both the national and European levels, between policies to promote technological competencies that are increasingly useful over a wide number of firms and sectors (i.e. computing), and policies to promote specific firms and sectors (e.g. those developing and making computers and semiconductors).

Techno-globalism?

Certainly, national innovative activities, and those of national firms, are not the same thing. Foreign firms' innovative activities can help alleviate domestic technological weaknesses, and domestic firms can compensate for domestic technological weaknesses by establishing or acquiring foreign competencies.[10] Nevertheless, national systems of innovation will continue to be important for the foreseeable future. Our analysis shows that the technological activities of large firms remain firmly embedded in their home countries, and there are strong managerial reasons for concluding that they will continue to do so in the future.

A European system of innovation?

Our data also show that technological activities in the major OECD countries – including the European ones – have not been globalized, but continue to be controlled mainly by nationally-owned firms. We have shown elsewhere that these national systems remain very different in technological

---

[10] For one of the few substantial discussions of the problems and possibilities of exploiting foreign linkages, see Solvell, Zander, and Porter(1991).

performance (Patel and Pavitt, 1994b). Some of the differences are in fields of technological specialization, which are beneficial for Europe as a whole since they increase diversity.[11]

However, there has also been divergence between European countries in the levels of investment in business-funded R&D activities, and major differences remain in the education and skills of the workforce (Prais, 1993). Given the patterns we have described above, we doubt whether the autonomous behavior of Europe's large firms will redress the balance: on the contrary, it is in their interest to expand in the countries which have already established strong technological competencies, such as Germany, the United States, and (increasingly in future) Japan. Similarly, we doubt that European-wide programs uniquely concentrating on international collaboration will be effective, since such collaboration tends to be effective only among partners of roughly equal level. Priority in European policy therefore should be given to upgrading the technological competencies in the weaker members of the Union. On this basis, collaboration will emerge as a normal and expanding process rather than as a temporary artefact of policy (Katz and Hicks, 1995).

References

Basberg, B. (1987). "Patents and the Measurement of Technological Change: A Survey of the Literature," *Research Policy*, 16

Cantwell, J. (1992). "The Internationalization of Technological Activity and its Implications of Competitiveness," in O. Granstrand, L. Hakanson, and S. Sjolander (eds.), *Technology Management and International Business*, Chichester: Wiley

Casson, M. (ed.) (1991). *Global Research Strategy and International Competitiveness*, Oxford: Blackwell

Granstrand, O. and S. Sjolander, (1990). "Managing Innovation in Multi-technology Corporations," *Research Policy*, 19

Granstrand, O., L. Hakanson, and S. Sjolander, (eds.) (1992), *Technology Management and International Business*, Chichester: Wiley

Griliches, Z. (1990). "Patent Statistics as Economic Indicators," *Journal of Economic Literature*, 28

Hagedoorn, J. and J. Schakenrad, (1992). "Leading Companies in Network of Strategic Alliances in Information Technologies, *Research Policy*, 21(2), 163–90

Hakanson, L. (1992). "Locational Determinants of Foreign R&D in Swedish

---

[11] We compared the fields of technological specialization of 15 European countries, and found that in only 18 percent of cases were they significantly similar. Given its predominance, Germany's technological specialization was closest to the European average, followed by Switzerland, with both showing relative strength in machinery and chemicals.

Multinationals," in O. Granstrand, L. Hakanson, and S. Sjolander, (eds.) *Technology Management and International Business*, Chichester: Wiley

Katz, J. and D. Hicks, (1995). "Questions of Collaboration," *Nature*, 11 (May)

Patel, P. (1994a). "Strategies of Multinational Firms in the Patent Domain in the US," analysis undertaken for the European Commission (FAST program); Final Report available from Science Policy Research Unit, University of Sussex

(1994b). "Are Large Firms Internationalising the Generation of Technology? Some New Evidence," *IEEE Transactions on Engineering Management*, 43

(1995). "The Localized Production of Global Technology," *Cambridge Journal of Economics*, 19, 141–53

Patel, P. and K. Pavitt, (1991). "Large Firms in the Production of the World's Technology: An Important Case of Non-globalization," *Journal of International Business Studies*, 22(1), 1–21; also published in O. Granstrand, L. Hakanson, and S. Sjolander, (eds.) *Technology Management and International Business*. Chichester: Wiley

(1992). "The Innovative Performance of the World's Largest Firms: Some New Evidence," *The Economics of Innovation and New Technology*, 2(2), 91–102

(1994a). "The Continuing, Widespread (and Neglected) Importance of Improvements in Mechanical Technologies," *Research Policy*, 23, 533–45

(1994b). "Uneven (and Divergent) Technological Accumulation among Advanced Countries," *Industrial and Corporate Change*, 3(3), 759–87

(1994c). "Technological Competencies in the World's Largest Firms: Characteristics, Constraints and Scope for Managerial Choice," *STEEP Discussion Paper*, 13, ESRC Centre on Science, Technology, Energy and Environment Policy, Science Policy Research Unit, University of Sussex

Pavitt, K. (1988). "Uses and Abuses of Patent Statistics," in A. van Raan, *Handbook of Quantitative Studies of Science and Technology*, Amsterdam: North-Holland

Porter, M. (1990). *The Competitive Advantage of Nations*, London: Macmillan

Prahalad, C. K. and G. Hamel, (1990). "The Core Competence of the Corporation," *Harvard Business Review*, 68, 79–91

Prais, S. (1993). "Economic Performance and Education: The Nature of Britain's Deficiencies" *Discussion Paper*, 52, London: National Institute of Economic and Social Research

Rosenberg, N. (1976). "Technological Change in the Machine Tool Industry, 1840–1910," in N. Rosenberg, *Perspectives on Technology*, Cambridge: Cambridge University Press

Solvell, O., I. Zander, and M. Porter, (1991). *Advantage Sweden*, Stockholm: Norstedts

4 Technological entry and diversification in Europe, the United States, and Japan

Franco Malerba and Luigi Orsenigo

Introduction

How relevant are new innovators in Europe compared to the United States and Japan? How many of the new technological entrants in any technology are really *de novo* new innovators, and how many have already innovated in a technology and have then diversified in a different one? How many of these new innovators are occasional innovators, and how many have become persistent innovators? Are there significant differences in the rate of technological entry and exit across technologies? And across countries?

This chapter aims to shed light on these phenomena by examining descriptive evidence on technological entry and on the persistence in inno-vative activities in 49 technological classes using patent data (European Patent Office data) in six countries (Germany, France, the United Kingdom, Italy, the United States, and Japan) for the period 1978–91. The chapter will try to assess whether differences exist between Europe, the United States, and Japan, and among the various European countries.

In recent years, economists have paid a lot of attention to the role of new firms and of exit in industrial dynamics. The availability of panel data and longitudinal micro-data sets has stimulated a lot of empirical investigation in this direction. Dunne, Roberts and Samuelson (1989); Acs and Audretsch (1991), and Baldwin (1995), among others, have shifted the research agenda from cross-sectional analysis of market structure at a given point in time or from case studies of entrants in a specific sector over time to the dynamics of entry and exit across industries over a long period of time. They have shown that industrial evolution is characterized in the aggregate by high degrees of turbulence, with entry and exit accounting for a limited share of sectoral production at the year of entry and exit, but a

We thank Monica Soana for her assistance. This chapter has been written within the Human Capital and Mobility Program of the European Union, Contract no. ERBCHRXCT920002.

large share of production in later years as successful entrants grow and firm population changes. At the sectoral level, they have also found a positive relationship between R&D and entry, but a negative relationship between the share of successful entrants in total entrants and R&D.

Surprisingly, economists have paid limited attention to another phenomenon: new innovators and ex-innovators across sectors and over time. This lack of attention is even more surprising given the abundant scattered empirical evidence on the role of new innovators in affecting the rate and direction of technological change in an industry. Several case studies of specific new technologies (such as autos, computers, semiconductors, and biotechnology, among others) have emphasized the major role of new innovators in the various stages of the development of an industry. In addition, Klepper (1996) and Utterback (1994) have provided several examples of the role of new innovators during the life-cycle of specific industries, particularly in the period following a technological discontinuity. Other studies by Audretsch (1995) and Geroski (1994) have pointed to the relationship between innovation and entry in specific countries (the United States and the United Kingdom). However, the analysis of the role of "new" innovators across several countries and for several technologies has been largely neglected.

This chapter aims to shed light on this topic. We define technological entry ("new" innovators) in terms of firms which innovate for the first time in a given technology, and technological exit ("ex"-innovators) as previous innovators which do not innovate any more in a given technology. Note that new innovators may be firms that have been in existence for quite some time. What do we know about "new" innovators and "ex"-innovators? Not much. Basically research has found that new firms are not necessarily new innovators. Only a minority of new firms are created because of the launch of an innovation: most new firms rather use established production processes and do not have very innovative products.

In this chapter we introduce a novel distinction: we divide technological entry and exit into "real" and "lateral". When analyzing various sectors (and not the economy as a whole), we consider as "real" entrants those firms which innovate in the period under consideration but did not innovate previously in any one technological class and "real" exiters those who were innovators in previous periods but are not in the period under consideration. Some of these real entrants are "newly established" firms. We consider as "lateral" entrants and exiters those firms which innovated in the past in a different technology. These firms are "established" innovators engaged in a process of technological diversification. As a consequence of this diversification, some of these firms may exit from the technological classes in which they were previously active. Others may keep their technological diversification quite broad and continue also to innovate in other technological classes.

We also propose that a key factor affecting the rate of "gross" innovative natality and mortality is the specific nature of a technology. Elsewhere (Malerba and Orsenigo, 1990, 1993, 1995, 1996), we suggested that the relevant *technological regime* – defined as a combination of (technological) opportunity, appropriability and cumulativeness conditions, and the specific features of the knowledge base underpinning innovative activities in an industry is a major factor that affects the sectoral patterns of innovation and, consequently, innovative entry. In this chapter we extend the reasoning by including exit. We may expect that high (technological) opportunity conditions, low appropriability conditions, and low (firms') cumulativeness are conducive to high rates of innovative entry and exit. On the contrary, high appropriability conditions and high (firms') cumulativeness reduce drastically the rate of innovative exit. In addition, a knowledge base that is simple, or system-specific and codified, may generate high entry of specialized producers. On the contrary, a knowledge base that is tacit and complex may reduce the rate of entry of new innovators. If the major dimensions of technological regimes are different across technologies but invariant across countries, one should expect consistent differences in the patterns of innovation across technological classes but strong similarities across countries in the same sectors. This is what Malerba and Orsenigo (1995, 1996) found for technological entry as well as for other dimensions of the patterns of innovative activities.

But what are the key factors affecting "real" and "lateral" entry and exit? The major conjectures advanced here are that while technological regimes affect both "real" and "lateral" technological entry and exit, lateral entry and exit are also affected by technological proximity and by the pervasiveness of a technology. These two additional conjectures are based on two types of evidence. Analyses on a selected sample of firms regarding their technological diversification and corporate coherence (see Dosi, Teece and Winter, 1991; Patel and Pavitt, 1997) show that firms move into technologically-related sectors and they cluster around inter-related technologies. We may expect therefore that lateral entry and exit are driven by the relationship between technologies, defined by their inclusion in the same macrotechnological class. In addition, work on pervasive technologies (Patel and Pavitt, 1994; Bresnahan and Trajtenberg, 1994) shows that some technologies are more pervasive than others. We may therefore expect that technological diversification into a technology or away from a technology, may be related to its degree of pervasiveness.

This chapter is organized as follows. After presenting the data-set and the methodology, we assess the technological relevance of new innovators and ex-innovators, by distinguishing between real new entrants and lateral entrants, and real exiters and lateral exiters. We examine the patterns of survival of entrants (how long they continue to innovate after entry and how much their innovative activities increase with age). We then examine similarities and differences in the patterns of technological entry and exit at the sectoral level. We next look at the inter-sectoral patterns of lateral entry and exit (from which technological classes lateral entrants come, and to which technological classes lateral exiters go). We then look at country differences. Finally, we briefly address the question of the relationships between the patterns of entry and exit and technological growth and specialization.

Data

Our analysis is based on patent data. Criticisms of the use of patent data are well known. Here only a brief discussion is presented (see Griliches, 1990, for a more detailed discussion). Not all innovations are patented by firms. Patents cannot be distinguished in terms of relevance unless specific analyses on patent renewals or patents citations are made. Finally, different technologies are differently patentable, and different types of firms may have different propensities to patent. However, patents represent a very homogeneous measure of technological novelty across countries, and are available for long time series. They also provide very detailed data at the firm and technological class level. As a consequence, they are an invaluable and unique source of data on innovative activity.

This chapter has used European Patent Office (EPO) data for the period 1978–91. The data refer to EPO patent applications by firms and institutions of various countries, with the exclusion of individual inventors.[1] Patents that are applied for by more than one firm (co-patents) have been attributed to each one of the co-patentees (and therefore have been counted as many times as the number of co-patentees).

The EPO database has been elaborated at the firm level (excluding individual inventors) for six countries: the United States, Germany (Federal Republic), France, the United Kingdom, Italy, and Japan. As far as the United States is concerned, 133,475 patents and 11,476 firms have been

---

[1] Although some of these individual inventors work for a firm or an institution, the majority of individual inventors include individuals who do not work in firms or institutions, and owners of small firms who record the patent in their name. The exclusion of individual inventors thus means an under-estimation of the innovative activities of smaller companies. The share of the patents held by private individuals is usually larger in technological classes and countries where the role of small firms is higher. In the chapter we will use the term "firms" for both firms and institutions. Institutions such as universities and research centers, however, have a small share of total patents in the six countries considered.

considered; for Germany, 108,118 patents and 8,495 firms; for France, 43,986 patents and 5,671 firms; for the United Kingdom, 35,175 patents and 6,055 firms; for Italy, 15,175 patents and 3,803 firms; and for Japan, 81,217 and 3,990 firms. The small number of Japanese firms compared to the United States and Germany may imply that the data concerning this country have to be considered with great care. Relatedly, German firms are a very large number and therefore may be over-represented in the sample because the EPO is in Germany and firms located in Germany may patent more frequently than firms of other countries. However, since our aim is not to discuss technological performance but the structure of innovative activity at the industry level, we think that Japanese under-representation and German over-representation does not create serious distortion in our results. In addition, for the four European countries, data on the economic size of the innovating firms has been gathered. The economic data cover 56 percent of the German patenting firms, 49 percent of the French firms, 34 percent of the British firms and 51 percent of the Italian firms. Economic data on firms applying for patents concerns size in terms of employees in 1991. A bias may therefore be present in the analysis in favor of firms active during the early 1990s. Firms that are part of business groups have been treated in the present analysis as individual companies.

49 technological classes related to sectors of activity are considered in the analysis. These classes have been created starting from the various sub-classes (4 digits) of the International Patent Classification (IPC) and grouping them according to specific applications.[2]

This data set is likely to provide an overestimation of the rates of entry. Given the novelty of the EPO, several firms have only recently begun to patent there. Many firms thus appear as new innovators in the database, although they might appear as persistent innovators in other datasets (for instance, US patents). Moreover, the EPO system is quite similar to the German system. Thus, in the early years, German patents constitute a significant share of total European patents, while in the following periods other countries have begun to catch up. This would result in lower rates of entry for Germany as compared to other countries, and hence the values of entry rates should be considered with great care. For this reason, we have divided the data set in two sub-periods (1978–86 and 1987–91), which correspond, roughly, to an equal number of patents in each sub-period.

However, the extent of the bias discussed above should have limited importance because we are more interested in the relationships that exist between the various indicators of entry and exit across sectors and across countries, rather than to their absolute values. Finally, comparisons with

---

[2] Details on the procedures of construction of the classification are available on request.

similar data computed on the OTAF–SPRU database for US patents (Malerba and Orsenigo,1995), while confirming that the absolute values of the measures of entry are somewhat lower as compared to the EPO data, suggest also that the sectoral and country differences between EPO and USPO patent data are quite small. In other words, the bias operates in a similar way across most sectors and countries.

The turbulence of innovators

Gross technological entry and exit

The description of the patterns of innovative birth and death begins with the measurement of the average birth and death rates across the 49 technological classes for the six countries considered in this study. Table 4.1 reports the average values for the measures of innovative birth.

The data suggest that innovative birth in terms of *firms* (number of firms that patented for the first time in technological class i in the period 1987–91) over the total number of firms patenting in 1987–91) (*ER*) is a significant phenomenon in the six countries. A large proportion of innovators patent for the first time in the period 1987–91: the average rate of innovative natality varies from 0.63 in Germany to 0.80 in Italy. The technological relevance of the new innovators in terms of share of total patents (patent held by firms patenting for the first time in technological class i in the period 1987–91 over total number of patents in the period 1987–91) (*PESH*) is much smaller but still substantial, varying from 0.30 in Germany to 0.61 in Italy (see table 4.1).

This suggests that new innovators are much smaller than incumbents in terms of patents. Indeed, the relative size of the new innovators (compared to persistent innovators) in terms of patents (average size in terms of patents of entering firms relative to average size in terms of patents of persistent innovators) (*PERS*) ranges from 0.32 in the United States to 0.51 in Italy. The firms that patent for the first time in the period 1987–91, however, are not necessarily small firms. Indeed, the economic size of new innovators measured in terms of employment (relative economic size in terms of entrants in terms of employees in 1991 compared to the economic size of persistent innovators in terms of employees in 1991) (*SERS*) is still less than the size of incumbents, but is much larger than the relative size of new innovators in terms of patents. This data is available only for the four European countries: it is around 0.75 of incumbents' average economic size for Germany, France, and Italy. Only in the case of the United Kingdom are new innovators much bigger than the average incumbent (1.7) (see table 4.1).

Table 4.1. *Technological entry*

	Germany	France	United Kingdom	Italy	United States	Japan	Average	Std dev.
Technological entry in terms of number of firms								
Entry rate (*ER*)	0.63	0.69	0.70	0.80	0.67	0.69	0.70	0.05
Lateral entry/gross entry (*LER*)	0.46	0.38	0.35	0.26	0.38	0.52	0.39	0.05
Technological entry in terms of patents								
Entrants' share (*PESH*)	0.30	0.40	0.43	0.61	0.32	0.38	0.41	0.11
Patents of lateral entrants/patents of entrants (*PLESH*)	0.48	0.42	0.41	0.31	0.43	0.59	0.44	0.09
Average size of entrants in terms of patents relative to incumbents								
Entrants' relative size (*PERS*)	0.35	0.39	0.40	0.51	0.32	0.35	0.39	0.09
Lateral entrants' relative size (*PLERS*)	0.41	0.58	0.65	0.98	0.46	0.53	0.60	0.21
Real entrants' relative size (*PRERS*)	0.26	0.32	0.35	0.48	0.24	0.29	0.32	0.07
Average size of entrants in terms of number of employees relative to incumbents								
Entrants' relative size (*SERS*)	0.73	0.73	1.70	0.75			0.98	0.48
Lateral entrants' relative size (*SLERS*)	0.90	4.19	4.01	1.56			2.91	1.38
Real entrants' relative size (*SRERS*)	0.25	0.21	0.08	0.51			0.26	0.18

Innovative mortality (see table 4.2) reveals a pattern remarkably similar to innovative natality. Death rates (number of firms that patented in technological class i in the period 1978–86 and did not patent in that same class in the period 1987–91) (XR) are of the same magnitude as birth rates, varying from 0.53 in Japan to 0.74 in the United Kingdom. In each country, except Italy and Japan, death rates are almost equal to birth rates. Again, the share of patents held by firms which have ceased to innovate in the second period (1987–91) (patents held by firms that patented in technological class i in the period 1978–86 and did not patent in that same class in the period 1987–91) ($PXSH$) is smaller as compared to all patenting firms (ranging from 0.26 in Japan to 0.49 in Italy). Their relative size in terms of patents (average size in terms of patents of exiting firms relative to average size in terms of patents of persistent innovators) ($PXRS$) varies from 0.33 in Germany and the United States to 0.52 in Italy. The values of both these indicators are strikingly similar to those of the corresponding birth variables. Again, exiters are not necessarily small firms. Indeed, they are slightly bigger than new innovators in terms of employment (relative economic size of exiters in terms of employees in 1991 compared to the economic size of persistent innovators) ($SXRS$) (except in the United Kingdom): in France and Italy they are even larger than the average incumbents (see table 4.2).

In sum, technological activities (as measured by patents) are characterized by high degrees of turbulence. The population of innovators changes substantially over time, through birth and death processes. Entrants are slightly smaller firms than incumbents in economic terms, whilst exiters are sometimes bigger. Both entrants and exiters, however, are relatively small innovators in terms of patents.

Lateral and real entry and exit

The previous result would seem to suggest that innovative birth and death occur in the "fringe" while a stable "core" of larger and persistent innovators accounts for the bigger share of technological activities. However one has to consider that entrants in any one technological class may well have innovated before in a different technological class. Similarly exiters may well start (or continue) to innovate in a different technology. Thus, gross entry (exit) has to be decomposed in two components: "real" entry and exit and "lateral" entry and exit.

Lateral entry is usually less relevant than real entry in terms of firms and patents. In terms of firms lateral entry (LER) accounts on average for 0.39 of gross entry (ranging between 0.26 (Italy) and 0.52 (Japan)) and a marginally larger fraction of the patents of gross entrants (0.44) (see table

Table 4.2. *Technological exit*

	Germany	France	United Kingdom	Italy	United States	Japan	Average	Std dev.
Technological exit in terms of number of firms								
Exit rate (XR)	0.62	0.70	0.74	0.67	0.68	0.53	0.65	0.07
Lateral exit/gross entry (LXR)	0.45	0.36	0.32	0.26	0.40	0.55	0.39	0.10
Technological exit in terms of patents								
Exiters' share (PXSH)	0.27	0.46	0.47	0.49	0.34	0.26	0.38	0.10
Patents of lateral exiters/patents of entrants (PLXSH)	0.46	0.40	0.36	0.28	0.45	0.56	0.42	0.10
Average size of exiters in terms of patents relative to incumbents								
Exiters' relative size (PXRS)	0.33	0.47	0.43	0.52	0.33	0.39	0.41	0.08
Lateral exiters' relative size (PLXRS)	0.39	0.66	0.66	0.64	0.51	0.40	0.55	0.13
Real exiters' relative size (PRXRS)	0.24	0.38	0.34	0.44	0.27	0.32	0.33	0.07
Average size of exiters in terms of number of employees relative to incumbents								
Exiters' relative size (SXRS)	0.83	1.29	1.33	0.73			1.04	0.31
Lateral exiters' relative size (SLXRS)	1.76	8.08	2.22	1.66			3.43	3.11
Real exiters' relative size (SRXRS)	0.07	0.12	0.17	0.50			0.21	0.19

4.1). Lateral entrants are thus larger innovators than real new entrants in terms of patents (although they remain considerably less important than the average incumbents). In general, lateral entrants are firms of large economic size as compared to the average innovator: when size is measured in terms of employees (*SLERS*), the size of the average lateral entrant is 2.91 the size of the average innovator and 18.81 the size of the average entrant.

Conversely, real new entrants are essentially firms of small economic and innovative size (see table 4.1). On average in terms of employment entrants are 0.26 the economic size of incumbents (*SRERS*) and have 0.32 of patents (*PRERS*). Italy is a major exception, with rates, respectively, of 0.51 and 0.48.

Again, the patterns of lateral and real exit are quite similar to the patterns of lateral and real entry (see table 4.2). In each country, the ratio of lateral exit over gross exit is almost the same as the corresponding ratio calculated for entry, both in terms of number of firms (*LXR*) (on average, 0.25 of incumbents) and in terms of patent shares (*PLXSH*) (on average, 0.15 of patents by incumbents). Similarly, lateral exiters are much bigger than real exiters in economic terms (on average, 23.32) and in patent terms (on average, 1.16). They are also bigger than the average patenting firm in terms of employment (*SLXRS*) (on average, 3.43) but smaller in terms of patents (*PLXRS*) (on average, 0.55). Real exiters are smaller firms in terms of patents and employment than the average patenting firm and the lateral exiter. In addition, they are smaller than real new entrants in terms of patents, but not necessarily in terms of employment (see table 4.2).

Turbulence as a composite phenomenon

The turbulence of innovators is thus composed of four types of actors: real new entrants, lateral entrants, real exiters, and lateral exiters. These actors show some features that are similar (net entrants and net exiters; lateral entrants and lateral exiters) and some features that are different (real new entrants/exiters and lateral entrants/exiters). Real new entrants and exiters are usually firms of small economic size with few patents each. Real new entrants generate more patents than are lost by the real exiters. Lateral entrants and exiters are usually firms of large economic size engaged in a process of technological diversification, expanding the range of technologies in which they are active and eventually abandoning old technologies.

Survival of the new innovators: persistent or occasional innovators?

In assessing the performance implications of the entry of new innovators, it is important to know whether new innovators are occasional or persistent innovators. We need to explore whether, and for how long, they continue to patent after entry, and whether they tend to increase or decrease their technological performance over time.

A large fraction of the new innovators ceases to innovate soon after entry and survival decreases in the latest-entry cohorts. This has been shown by examining the survival of firms in various periods: 1978–82, 1983–5, 1986–8, and 1989–91 (data are not reported here). Here, country differences matter. For example, the survival rates of the firms that patented in the period 1978–82 and were still patenting in the period 1989–91 range between 48.2 percent in Japan and 20.7 percent in the United Kingdom.[3] As a result of the processes of entry and exit, the age distribution of innovators is strongly skewed towards the youngest and the oldest cohorts. Data concerning the patent shares of firms that survived after entry confirm these results: the patent share of each entry cohort declines over time in each period and in each country. These results suggest that indeed a large fraction of new innovators is composed of *occasional* innovators. They represent a large fraction of the whole population of innovators, but not necessarily of the total number of patents at any given time.

However, another fraction of entrants survives and grows larger in terms of patents as time goes by: they become *persistent* innovators. These older firms who continue to patent represent an important contribution to total patenting activities in any period. This is a clear indication of the presence of *cumulativeness* in technological knowledge and the process of building up of technological capabilities and competitive advantages by those firms that are able to survive. These capabilities and advantages generate a continuous stream of innovation by surviving firms.

Sectoral differences in the patterns of entry and exit

Patterns of correlation among the indicators of natality and mortality across technological classes

The average statistics examined above obscure the substantial diversity of the patterns of natality and mortality across technological classes. Despite

---

[3] The decline in survival rates in the latest-entry cohorts may be biased because some of the exiters in the latest periods may well patent again in the future. However, preliminary investigations seem to show that the probability of innovating again after three years of the last patent is quite low, and it tends to decrease with the length of the gap.

this diversity, the entry variables and the exit variables are systematically related to each other within any one technological class. In particular, all the indicators measuring the importance of innovative natality are positively correlated to each other and to the corresponding indicators of mortality (data are not reported here). In other words, technological classes characterized by high natality rates are also characterized by a high patent share of entrants, high relative size (in terms of patents) of entrants as well as high mortality rates, high patent share of exiters, and large size of exiters in terms of patents. In other words, natality and mortality occur simultaneously in each technological class.

In addition, across technological classes gross entry and exit are negatively correlated with lateral entry and exit. High lateral entry is associated with low gross entry and exit rates and patent shares, low relative size (in terms of patents) of exiters (in particular, lateral exiters), and net entrants and exiters. Conversely, high lateral entry (on gross entry) is positively correlated with high lateral exit (on gross exit) and the relative size in terms of patents of lateral entrants. No correlation is observed with the relative size of entrants. That is to say, technological classes characterized by high turbulence show simultaneously and consistently a lower relative role of lateral entry and exit.

In sum, two different types of technological classes emerge.
(a) One group is composed of *turbulent classes*: high gross entry and exit with most of the entry generated by totally new innovators and most of the exit by firms which stop patenting.
(b) A second group is composed of *stable classes*: low gross entry and exit with entry and exit mostly associated to processes of technological diversification – in these technological classes, lateral entrants tend to be relatively big (and real new entrants small); conversely exiters (especially real exiters) tend to be smaller innovators.

Stable and turbulent technological classes

In order to control for the robustness of these results, we performed principal components' analysis for each of the six countries for which we have the data. In each country, a first principal component emerges which captures a large proportion of the variance (0.61 in Germany, 0.49 in France, 0.58 in the United Kingdom, 0.37 in Italy, 0.60 in the United States, and 0.54 in Japan). In all countries, this first component discriminates between technological classes characterized by high (low) lateral entry and exit and high (low) relative size (in terms of patents) of lateral entrants as compared to total entrants, and low (high) patent shares and low (high) relative size in terms of patents of gross entrants and exiters.

Moreover, in most countries turbulent and stable technological classes tend to be the same: 21 technological classes are consistently stable and 12 classes tend to be consistently turbulent.[4] 16 remaining classes show more variation across countries or do not fit neatly into these two categories. The stable group comprises most of the chemical and electronic technologies, vehicles and aircraft; the turbulent group includes mechanical technologies, traditional technologies (e.g. furniture), and agriculture. This broadly confirms the more general findings related to the similarity of the Schumpeterian patterns of innovation for a given technological class across countries (Malerba and Orsenigo, 1995, 1996).

We claim that the sectoral patterns of innovative natality and mortality are remarkably similar across countries, because there are technology-specific factors which are rather invariant across countries and which are major determinants of the ease and modalities of entry and exit. One of these factors is the *technological regime* defined (as above) in terms of opportunity, appropriability, and cumulativeness conditions and the characteristic of the knowledge base. In a related paper (Breschi, Malerba and Orsenigo, 1997) we provide an econometric test of this relationship for three European countries (Germany, the United Kingdom, and Italy). We show that in the case of technological regimes characterized by high opportunity, low appropriability, and low cumulativeness, gross technological entry is high, while in case of high appropriability and cumulativeness gross technological entry is low.

Lateral entry and exit: the patterns of technological diversification

In this section, we discuss the sectoral sources and destination of lateral entry and exit. We ask from which technological classes new innovators that begin to patent in a technological class come, and in which technological class firms that cease to patent in a specific technological class continue their innovative activities: we inquire about the patterns of technological diversification of entrants and exiters.

---

[4] The stable classes are: gas, hydrocarbons, oil; inorganic chemicals; organic chemicals; macromolecular compounds; new materials; adhesives, coatings, synthetic resins; biochemicals, bio and genetic engineering; drugs; metallurgy; vehicles, motorcycles, other land vehicles; aircraft; measurement and control instruments; laser technology; optics and photography; computers, data-processing systems; other office equipments; electrical devices and systems; electronic components; consumer electronics; telecommunications; multimedial systems; nuclear technology. The turbulent classes are: furniture; agriculture; medical preparations; natural and artificial fibers, paper; machine tools; industrial automation; railways, ships; materials handling apparatus; civil engineering, infrastructures; mechanical and electric technologies; lighting systems; decorative and figurative arts, sports and toys; others.

Matrices of lateral entry and exit

We constructed matrices of lateral entry and exit for 49 technological classes (not reported here). The 49 technological classes have also been regrouped in eight macro-classes: "traditionals," chemicals, mechanicals, electricals, electronics, transport, instruments, and a residual class (others). Table 4.3 provides the details of the composition of each macro-class.

The patterns of technological diversification within and among macro-classes have then been examined. We constructed matrices of lateral entry and exit for the eight macro-classes: "traditionals," chemicals, mechanicals, electricals, electronics, transport, instruments, and a residual class (others). Matrices are to be read as follows (table 4.4). As far as the entry matrices are concerned, rows (i) indicate the technological classes of origin and columns (j) the technological classes of destination. Each cell a (ij) reports the "diversification events" in terms of number of firms diversifying in a technological class j. Thus an (ij) is the percentage of firms in the class of destination j who have patented previously in the class of origin i. Since lateral entrants often patent in many different technological classes, firms are counted as many times as the number of technological classes in which they patent. In other words, the cell a_{ij} tells us that in technological class j, x percent of the total number of firms that started to patent in that technological class j patented before in technological class i. Thus, the sum by column j is calculated with reference to the total number of "diversification events." For example, in table 4.4 in Germany we have that in chemicals 6.2 percent of "diversification events" are from traditional technologies, 37.3 percent from chemical technologies, 31.2 percent from mechanical technologies, and so on.

Mortality matrices are constructed in the same way (see table 4.5). Columns j indicate the technological class of origin and rows i the class of destination. Cell a_{ij} thus shows the "diversification events" in terms of the percentage of firms that ceased to patent in class j but have continued to patent in class i. Again, firms are counted as many times as the technological classes in which exiters have continued to patent in the period 1986–91.

Patterns of technological diversification

The elements along the main diagonal indicates the pattern of diversification within macro-classes. In a sense, the main diagonal identifies those macro-classes in which *technological proximity* is a main rationale for diversification. Chemicals, mechanicals and electronics are the macro-classes with the largest amount of within-macro-class diversification. This diversification is therefore driven by *technological proximity*.

Table 4.3. *Composition of each macro-class*

| 1 "Traditionals" | 1 Food, tobacco
2 Clothing, shoes
3 Furniture
4 Agriculture
5 Mining
17 Natural and artificial fibers, paper
46 Decorative and figurative arts, sports, toys | 3 Mechanicals | 22 Machine tools
23 Industrial automation
24 Industrial machinery and equipment
25 Agricultural machinery
29 Materials handling apparatus
30 Civil engineering, infrastructures
31 Engines, turbines, pumps
32 Mechanical engineering
33 Mechanical and electric technologies |
| 2 Chemicals | 6 Gas, hydrocarbons, oil
7 Inorganic chemicals
8 Organic chemicals
9 Macromolecular compounds
10 New materials
11 Adhesives, coatings, synthetic resins
12 Biochemicals, bio and genetic engineering
13 Miscellaneous chemical compounds
14 Chemical, analytical physical processes
15 Drugs
16 Medical preparations
18 Chemical treatment of natural or artificial fibers and paper
19 Agricultural chemicals
20 Chemical processes for food and tobacco
21 Metallurgy | 4 Electricals

5 Electronics

6 Transport

7 Instruments

8 Others | 34 Household electric appliances
35 Lighting systems
41 Electrical devices and systems
37 Laser technology
39 Computer, data processing systems
40 Other office equipments
42 Electronic components
43 Consumer electronics
44 Telecommunications
45 Multimedial systems
26 Vehicles, Motorcycles and other land vehicles
27 Aircraft
28 Railways, ships
36 Measurement and control instruments
38 Optics and photography
47 Ammunitions, weapons
48 Nuclear technology
49 Others |

Table 4.4. *Matrices of lateral entry*

i \ j	Percentages of the total number of "diversification events" in each technological class							
	Traditional	Chemicals	Mechanicals	Electricals	Electronics	Transport	Instruments	Others
Germany								
"Traditionals"	7.21	6.22	6.50	5.67	4.24	6.14	6.00	4.94
Chemicals	30.31	37.26	26.03	25.26	25.50	19.02	24.87	24.72
Mechanicals	29.55	31.21	34.73	34.08	28.51	38.02	33.19	31.97
Electricals	7.83	5.42	7.73	4.05	7.65	5.91	8.20	7.56
Electronics	9.96	6.58	8.35	14.20	13.64	10.08	14.75	14.83
Transport	4.97	3.63	6.03	4.93	5.85	7.23	5.19	4.36
Instruments	7.2	7.97	8.26	8.97	11.79	9.87	5.47	10.46
Others	2.97	1.71	2.37	2.84	2.82	3.73	2.33	1.16
Lateral entry	100.00	100.00	100.00	100.00	100.00	100.00	100.00	100.00
France								
"Traditionals"	5.93	5.59	5.94	4.64	4.07	3.76	4.05	5.34
Chemicals	24.78	42.77	24.19	26.09	24.25	18.24	26.52	26.72
Mechanicals	31.32	24.12	28.98	32.92	22.98	34.59	31.02	29.01
Electricals	7.16	4.43	8.54	3.66	8.58	6.93	8.76	5.73
Electronics	12.92	9.03	12.78	15.86	19.48	16.98	15.28	16.41
Transport	6.11	3.03	6.23	4.39	5.79	5.04	7.42	5.73
Instruments	8.73	8.11	10.12	10.48	12.42	9.12	4.71	8.39
Others	3.14	2.92	3.22	1.96	2.43	5.34	2.24	2.67
Lateral entry	100.00	100.00	100.00	100.00	100.00	100.00	100.00	100.00

Table 4.4. (cont.)

i	Percentages of the total number of "diversification events" in each technological class							
j	Traditional	Chemicals	Mechanicals	Electricals	Electronics	Transport	Instruments	Others
United Kingdom								
"Traditionals"	7.76	5.86	6.81	3.38	4.84	6.06	5.67	2.31
Chemicals	36.37	39.83	28.26	25.75	25.37	24.74	32.24	27.74
Mechanicals	26.04	22.88	30.63	32.49	22.72	36.36	28.61	27.17
Electricals	4.96	5.51	6.14	5.06	9.02	5.54	6.71	5.79
Electronics	10.34	10.24	11.91	15.18	17.86	10.12	15.46	16.76
Transport	3.98	3.39	5.67	5.06	2.99	5.06	3.86	4.63
Instruments	7.16	10.32	8.32	12.24	15.86	10.61	5.16	12.14
Others	3.39	1.97	2.26	0.84	1.34	1.51	2.29	3.46
Lateral entry	100.00	100.00	100.00	100.00	100.00	100.00	100.00	100.00
Italy								
"Traditionals"	5.05	3.21	5.42	1.64	2.51	0.00	1.13	4.35
Chemicals	31.32	53.95	22.04	31.15	29.38	14.02	45.75	34.77
Mechanicals	31.32	18.67	34.42	25.41	18.13	42.12	24.29	17.38
Electricals	4.03	2.65	9.68	6.56	11.86	7.00	5.66	2.18
Electronics	11.09	9.62	12.17	18.04	21.26	15.80	15.82	17.38
Transport	6.06	2.65	6.77	6.56	3.74	3.50	3.95	6.53
Instruments	8.10	7.74	8.32	9.82	12.49	15.80	2.82	15.22
Others	3.03	1.51	1.18	0.82	0.63	1.76	0.58	2.19
Lateral entry	100.00	100.00	100.00	100.00	100.00	100.00	100.00	100.00

United States

"Traditionals"	6.28	6.31	5.54	5.69	4.84	7.17	4.55	6.22
Chemicals	42.45	54.84	36.33	33.97	28.70	28.70	36.06	39.43
Mechanicals	21.79	17.09	20.92	22.28	19.67	26.95	21.18	20.24
Electricals	4.11	3.09	6.08	3.39	6.46	6.87	5.89	4.63
Electronics	12.82	8.82	15.51	19.00	21.92	14.03	21.86	15.44
Transport	2.18	1.48	3.12	2.59	2.77	2.87	3.08	2.67
Instruments	7.84	6.55	10.05	10.29	13.29	9.57	5.76	10.12
Others	2.53	1.82	2.45	2.79	2.35	3.84	1.62	1.25
Lateral entry	100.00	100.00	100.00	100.00	100.00	100.00	100.00	100.00

Japan

"Traditionals"	3.84	4.06	3.68	4.81	4.05	2.75	4.07	4.04
Chemicals	41.23	45.75	39.52	35.68	39.18	34.12	43.79	40.29
Mechanicals	21.01	18.42	21.53	24.77	20.63	29.46	24.83	21.97
Electricals	5.56	5.29	6.89	2.11	7.28	6.35	7.06	6.23
Electronics	14.47	13.88	14.65	17.48	13.93	14.40	11.32	14.66
Transport	3.21	2.09	3.04	3.17	2.93	2.54	2.88	2.93
Instruments	9.04	9.07	9.48	10.09	10.85	8.05	5.36	9.52
Others	1.64	1.44	1.21	1.89	1.15	2.33	0.69	0.36
Lateral entry	100.00	100.00	100.00	100.00	100.00	100.00	100.00	100.00

Notes:
i: class of entry.
j: class of origin.
Source: CESPRI/EPO.

Table 4.5. *Matrices of lateral exit*

i j	Percentages of the total number of "diversification events" in each technological class							
	Traditional	Chemicals	Mechanicals	Electricals	Electronics	Transport	Instruments	Others
Germany								
"Traditionals"	6.74	5.47	6.39	6.19	5.92	6.01	4.37	4.67
Chemicals	38.09	35.68	29.76	26.79	26.11	21.38	30.22	29.51
Mechanicals	28.34	30.56	32.34	32.16	25.64	34.53	32.63	30.37
Electricals	5.87	5.26	6.62	4.02	8.62	7.36	8.31	5.52
Electronics	9.22	10.47	10.41	15.42	16.03	14.69	15.41	14.02
Transport	4.62	3.96	4.74	4.69	4.26	4.89	4.08	6.15
Instruments	5.94	7.82	9.03	9.55	12.13	9.58	4.23	8.70
Others	1.18	0.78	0.71	1.18	1.29	1.56	0.75	1.06
Lateral exit	100.00	100.00	100.00	100.00	100.00	100.00	100.00	100.00
France								
"Traditionals"	5.35	5.94	6.94	7.72	5.01	5.64	6.73	8.19
Chemicals	32.45	36.19	26.01	19.68	20.99	13.08	27.73	22.41
Mechanicals	30.29	24.44	28.81	32.98	23.24	36.39	27.17	34.42
Electricals	4.93	6.39	8.01	4.25	11.69	6.72	8.96	5.47
Electronics	11.71	11.18	11.86	15.96	19.88	15.91	17.09	11.47
Transport	4.30	3.46	5.98	6.39	3.89	6.37	5.61	6.01
Instruments	6.78	9.86	9.66	9.56	11.54	10.59	4.19	12.03
Others	4.09	2.54	3.63	3.46	3.76	5.30	2.52	0.00
Lateral exit	100.00	100.00	100.00	100.00	100.00	100.00	100.00	100.00

United Kingdom

"Traditionals"	7.15	3.47	6.43	2.93	2.44	7.60	6.14	4.34
Chemicals	28.56	53.25	21.85	22.06	24.39	26.58	24.57	26.08
Mechanicals	42.84	18.19	28.49	36.76	29.27	37.98	25.44	21.75
Electricals	4.75	4.96	7.61	7.37	14.64	8.86	10.52	4.34
Electronics	11.91	9.74	16.14	10.29	14.02	7.59	21.94	21.74
Transport	0.00	1.52	8.32	8.82	3.05	1.26	4.38	4.35
Instruments	2.39	8.00	8.31	10.29	12.19	7.59	2.63	13.05
Others	2.40	0.87	2.85	1.48	0.00	2.54	4.38	4.35
Lateral exit	100.00	100.00	100.00	100.00	100.00	100.00	100.00	100.00

Italy

"Traditionals"	7.16	3.47	6.42	2.93	2.44	7.60	6.13	4.34
Chemicals	28.56	53.25	21.85	22.06	24.39	26.58	24.57	26.08
Mechanicals	42.84	18.19	28.49	36.76	29.27	37.98	25.44	21.75
Electricals	4.75	4.97	7.60	7.37	14.63	8.86	10.52	4.34
Electronics	11.91	9.74	16.14	10.29	14.03	7.59	21.94	21.74
Transport	0.00	1.51	8.32	8.82	3.05	1.26	4.38	4.35
Instruments	2.39	8.00	8.32	10.29	12.19	7.59	2.64	13.05
Others	2.39	0.87	2.86	1.48	0.00	2.54	4.38	4.35
Lateral exit	100.00	100.00	100.00	100.00	100.00	100.00	100.00	100.00

United States

"Traditionals"	5.19	5.16	5.43	6.44	5.36	7.09	4.21	8.01
Chemicals	41.28	46.10	39.77	39.03	34.86	32.18	44.37	37.48
Mechanicals	22.64	19.17	20.88	21.94	19.71	27.72	18.86	21.44
Electricals	4.46	4.88	6.26	2.95	6.28	5.28	7.33	5.08
Electronics	12.77	11.29	13.05	14.77	17.25	12.71	15.94	15.38

Table 4.5. (cont.)

j	i Traditional	Chemicals	Mechanicals	Electricals	Electronics	Transport	Instruments	Others
	Percentages of the total number of "diversification events" in each technological class							
Transport	3.05	2.25	3.41	3.06	2.81	3.64	2.84	3.27
Instruments	8.04	9.04	9.48	9.60	11.36	9.24	4.39	7.53
Others	2.57	2.11	1.72	2.21	2.37	2.14	2.06	1.81
Lateral exit	100.00	100.00	100.00	100.00	100.00	100.00	100.00	100.00
Japan								
"Traditionals"	7.15	5.11	5.26	6.62	4.72	5.76	4.47	4.84
Chemicals	43.87	44.69	37.58	35.39	35.04	34.01	37.15	41.79
Mechanicals	18.09	17.21	21.08	21.54	19.49	21.61	22.07	19.77
Electricals	5.53	5.31	5.92	3.52	7.57	6.92	6.43	6.72
Electronics	13.54	14.87	16.24	19.68	18.61	19.02	19.82	13.44
Transport	3.04	2.55	3.51	2.69	2.37	2.02	2.51	3.36
Instruments	7.59	8.99	9.18	9.52	11.32	8.93	6.43	9.71
Others	1.19	1.27	1.23	1.04	0.88	1.73	1.12	0.37
Lateral exit	100.00	100.00	100.00	100.00	100.00	100.00	100.00	100.00

Notes:
i: class of exit.
j: class of diversification.
Source: CESPRI/EPO.

Technological pervasiveness can be observed in several ways from our matrices. As far as the matrices composed by 49 classes are concerned, five technologies are the main sources of entry into most of the other classes: chemical, analytical and physical processes, industrial machinery and equipment, measurement and control instruments, materials handling apparatus, and electrical devices and systems. This holds for all the countries examined. As far as the eight macro-classes are concerned, chemicals, mechanicals, and electronics are the main macro-classes' sources of lateral entry into the other macro-classes[5] (see table 4.4).

Matrices of exit (both with 49 technological classes and with nine macro-classes) show a very similar behavior. Lateral exiters diversify into chemicals, mechanicals, and electronics. A large fraction of exit ends up in net exit – i.e. firms do not patent any longer in any technological class.

Three types of macro-classes

In sum, three types of technological macro-class may be identified.
(a) *Highly turbulent macro-classes with high rates of real entry/exit:* traditionals and transport. They are characterized by high turbulence, with high rates of both gross and net entry and exit, but little diversification into other technologies.
(b) *Stable macro-classes with high rates of lateral entry/exit:* chemicals and electronics. In these macro-classes persistently innovative firms constitute the main source of innovation (entry by net entrants is difficult and net exit occurs relatively infrequently) and diversify into all other technologies.
(c) *Highly turbulent macro-classes, with high rates of both real and lateral entry/exit:* mechanicals and instruments. They are a major source of technological diversification, but real entry and net exit are an important phenomenon, too.

Country differences

Despite these similarities, are European countries significantly different from the United States and Japan in the patterns of technological natality and mortality?

At the aggregate level, some country-specific differences are indeed visible. Inspection of tables 4.1 and 4.2 reveals that Germany and Japan are

---

[5] These macro-classes, however, also have the largest number of firms. One way to have a measure of pervasiveness at the macro-class level which also takes into account the size of each macro-class is to weight each class for the relative number of firms in it. This last measure is not provided in this chapter.

"stable" countries: birth and death rates are relatively low, the patent share and the relative sizes of entrants and exiters are small, while the role of lateral entry and exit is significant. At the other extreme, Italy is a "turbulent" country, with a lot of "real" entry and limited "lateral" entry and exit. The other countries fall in between these two extremes, although the United States is not too different from Germany and Japan. Inspection of the patterns of survival confirm these results. Again, Germany, Japan, and the United States are characterized by high rates of survival and high relative size of the "oldest" firms and Italy by low rates of survival and low relative size of the "oldest" firms.

The matrices of technological diversification (lateral entry and exit) (tables 4.4 and 4.5) show also remarkable similarities across countries. They confirm, however that in general in Germany and Japan (and to a lesser extent in the United States) technological change proceeds relatively less through the entry and exit of new innovators than through processes of technological diversification and lateral entry and exit.

Similarities across countries in the sectoral patterns of natality and mortality are evident. At a disaggregated level, we performed correlation analysis for each of the indicators of the patterns of innovative natality and mortality across the six countries. That is to say, we investigated how variations in the value of each indicator over the 49 technological classes were correlated across the other countries. Results (not reported here) show significant differences across countries (i.e. small values of the correlation coefficients) only in relation to the variables measuring lateral mortality and the relative size of net entrants. Japan and Italy, however, appear to diverge relatively more frequently than other countries from the general patterns of correlation: for many variables the values of the correlation coefficient of these two countries are lower than those of the other four countries. However, no systematic differences in the patterns of mortality and natality appear.

Finally, specific technological classes show a different behavior across countries. For example, food and tobacco is a "stable" sector only in the United Kingdom and Japan; clothing and shoes is a stable sector in Italy and the United States; mining is a stable sector in France and Japan; agricultural machinery is a turbulent sector in the United Kingdom and United States; household electric appliances do not show any consistent pattern.

In sum, countries seem to be grouped into:
(a) *countries with high stability, high survival rates, and high diversification processes*: Germany, Japan, and, to a lesser extent, the United States
(b) *countries with high turbulence, low survival rates, and limited diversification processes:* Italy, and, to a lesser extent, France and the United Kingdom.

Entry, exit, and technological performance

So far, the data suggest that the patterns of entry and exit are technology-specific – and, to a lesser extent, country-specific – phenomena. One might ask, however, whether countries' technological performance is in some way related to "stability" or "turbulence." On the one hand, high rates of innovative activities might be systematically linked to the entry of new innovators who displace ex-innovators unable to keep up with the pace of technological change and the emergence of new technological trajectories. On the other, technological performance might be linked to the existence of a stable core of persistent innovators, who master a complex and differentiated knowledge base and on this basis are able to diversify into new technological fields and "jump" into the new emerging technologies.

At this stage, we cannot provide a complete answer to this question. We have performed simple correlation analysis between indicators of the patterns of entry and exit and indicators of technological growth and specialization RTA (i) for each technological class i of country c.[6]

As far as *technological growth*[7] is concerned, the more dynamic among the 49 technological classes are the ones with a high entry rate and a low exit rate, together with a positive relevance of lateral entry and a negative relevance of net entry. The average size of entrants is positively related to the rate of growth of patents. Interesting differences emerge between the turbulent and the stable technological classes. In the *turbulent* technological classes the role of gross as well as net entry and net exit is positive.[8] On the other hand, in the *stable* technological classes, the role of gross entry is positive and gross exit negative, while lateral entry and lateral exit are positive and significant. This indicates that technological growth in turbulent classes occurs through new innovators, with a very limited role for technological diversification both in entry and in exit.

For the 49 classes, *technological specialization* (as expressed by RTAs) is associated with a lot of net entry and exit. A closer look at turbulent and stable technological classes, however, shows a more complex and differentiated picture. In *turbulent* classes, technological specialization takes place with a lot of gross entry and also of net entry and exit, indicating that

[6] Revealed technological advantages RTAic are expressed by the world patent share of country c in technology i with respect to total world patent share of country c (for all technological classes). RTA provides an indication of the degree of specialization of a country in a specific technology.

[7] Measured in terms of the rate of growth of patents of country c in technological class i between the period 1978–85 and 1986–91.

[8] From the construction of the index of lateral entry *PEDSH* (share of patents of lateral entrants on total patents of entrants), a significant and positive value of the index of lateral entry means a significant and negative value of net entry.

new innovators are a major source of specialization. On the other hand, in *stable* classes, specialization takes place with limited gross entry and exit, indicating that established innovators within that technological class are the major source of specialization. These established innovators are also major innovators, because they are much larger in terms of patents than new innovators and ex-innovators. (see table 4.6)

Conclusions

This chapter has shed light on the features and dynamics of technological entry and exit in Europe, the United States, and Japan in 49 technological classes. Twelve main conclusions can be drawn from the present analysis:

(a) In Europe, as well as in the United States and Japan, innovative activities are characterized by high degrees of turbulence. The population of innovators changes substantially over time, through birth and death processes. Entrants are slightly smaller firms than incumbents, whilst exiters are sometimes bigger. Both entrants and exiters, however, are relatively small innovators.

(b) The turbulence of innovators in a given technology is a composite phenomenon of net and lateral entry/exit. Innovative birth and deaths are composed of totally new innovators and ex-innovators (net entry/exit) and by established innovators coming from, or moving into, other technological classes (lateral entry/exit). In particular:

 – *net entry/exit* generates high turbulence, while lateral entry/exit is usually associated with lower turbulence

 – *lateral entrants/exiters* are usually large firms engaged in a process of technological diversification into new technologies; net entrants/exiters are conversely small firms (with few patents), and net entrants generate more patents than the ones lost by the exiters.

(c) Lateral entry and exit may be driven by technological *proximity* as well as by technological *pervasiveness*. This is particularly true in chemical, mechanical, and electronics technologies.

(d) A large fraction of new innovators in terms of firms is composed of *occasional innovators*. They also constitute a significant part of the whole population of innovators.

(e) Only a fraction of these entrants, however, survives and grows larger (in terms of patents) as time goes by. Older firms who survive and continue to patent represent an important contribution to total patenting activities in any period.

(f) *Persistent innovators* therefore generate a major share of patents in each technology.

Table 4.6. *Correlation coefficients between natality and mortality indicators and indicators of patent number (PT), patent growth (GP), and specialization (RTA).*

	49 classes			Turbulence			Stable		
	PT	GP	RTA	PT	GP	RTA	PT	GP	RTA
Entrant share (ESH)	-0.51**	0.26**	-0.10	-0.49**	0.26*	0.17	-0.54**	0.39**	-0.51**
Entry rate (ER)	-0.41**	0.28**	-0.01	-0.38**	0.43**	0.20	-0.36**	0.32**	-0.33**
Lateral entry rate (PEDSH)	0.08	0.20**	-0.32**	-0.09	-0.22*	-0.16**	0.07	0.23**	0.00
Entrant relative size (PERS)	-0.41**	0.23	-0.14	-0.36**	-0.08	0.09	-0.41**	0.39**	-0.41**
Exiter share (PXSH)	-0.46**	-0.05**	-0.04	-0.49**	-0.05	0.09	-0.51**	0.10	-0.43**
Exit rate (XR)	-0.31**	-0.32	0.06	-0.41**	-0.17	0.13	-0.30**	-0.46**	-0.17*
Lateral exit rate (PXDSH)	0.06	0.04	-0.26**	-0.09	-0.24*	-0.45**	-0.02	0.25**	-0.01
Exiter relative size (PXRS)	-0.42**	0.10	-0.10	-0.44**	0.12	0.03	-0.45**	0.07	-0.34**

Notes:

** = significant at 99 percent.

* = significant at 95 percent.

(g) The sectoral patterns of innovative natality and mortality are remarkably similar in Europe, the United States, and Japan.

(h) This result suggests that technology-specific factors, which are rather invariant across countries (such as technological regimes), are important determinants of the ease and modalities of entry and exit.

(i) In all sectors, gross entry and gross exit, as well as net entry and net exit, are positively related, while gross and net entry/exit are negatively correlated with lateral entry/exit.

(j) Technological classes can be grouped according to their degree of turbulence into:
  - *turbulent* technological classes, in which most of the entry is composed of new innovators and most of the exit is composed of firms which stop patenting
  - *stable* technological classes, in which entry and exit are associated with processes of technological diversification; in these technological classes, lateral entrants tend to be relatively large.

(k) Country-specific differences however are also detectable:
  - Germany and Japan are *stable countries*: birth and death rates are relatively small, the patent share and the relative sizes of entrants and exiters are small, whilst the role of lateral entry and exit is significant
  - Italy is a *turbulent country*, with small lateral entry and exit
  - France and the United Kingdom as well as the United States, fall in between these two extremes.

(l) The degree of turbulence is related to technological growth and technological specialization:
  - in *turbulent* technological classes *technological growth* is associated with high gross entry as well as high net entry and net exit, while in *stable* technological classes it is associated with high gross entry and low gross exit, and with high technological diversification in terms of lateral entry and lateral exit; this indicates that technological growth in turbulent classes occurs through new innovators, while in stable classes it takes place through established innovators coming from other technological classes
  - in *turbulent* technological classes *technological specialization* takes place, with high gross entry and also high net entry and net exit, indicating that new innovators are a major source of specialization; on the other hand, in *stable* classes technological specialization is associated with limited gross entry and exit and high cumulative advancements of large established innovators within that technological class.

References

Acs, Z. and D.B. Audretsch (1991). "Technological Regimes, Learning and Industry Turbulence," Berlin, mimeo

Audretsch, D.B. (1995). *Innovation and Industry Evolution*, Cambridge, Mass.: MIT Press

Baldwin, J. (1995). *The Dynamics of Industrial Competition*, Cambridge: Cambridge University Press

Breschi, S., F. Malerba, and L. Orsenigo (1997). "Technological Regimes and Schumpeterian Patterns of Innovation," *CESPRI Working Paper*, 93

Bresnahan, T. and M. Trajtenberg (1994). "General Purpose Technologies: Engines of Growth?," *Journal of Econometrics*, 65, 83–108

Dosi, G., D. Teece, and S. Winter (1991). "Toward a Theory of Corporate Coherence," in G.Dosi, R. Giannetti, and P. Toninelli (eds.) *Technology and the Enterprise in a Historical Perspective*, Oxford: Oxford University Press

Dunne, T., M.J. Roberts, and L. Samuelson (1989). "The Growth and Failure of US Manufacturing Plants," *Quarterly Journal of Economics*, 104 (November) 671–98

Geroski, P. (1994). *Market Structure, Corporate Performance and Innovation Activity*, Oxford: Clarendon Press

Griliches, Z. (1990). "Patents Statistics as Economic Indicators: A Survey," *Journal of Economic Literature*, 28(4), 1661–1707

Kamien, M. and Schwartz, N. (1982). *Market Structure and Innovation*, Cambridge: Cambridge University Press

Klepper, S.(1996). "Entry, Exit, Growth and Innovation over the Product-life Cycle," *American Economic Review*, 86(3), 562–83

Malerba, F. and L. Orsenigo (1990). "Technological Regimes and Patterns of Innovation: a Theoretical and Empirical Investigation of the Italian Case," in A.Heertje and M. Perlman (eds.), *Evolving Technologies and Market Structure*, Ann Arbor: University of Michigan Press, 283–306

(1993). "Technological regimes and Firm Behavior," *Industrial and Corporate Change*, 2(1), 45–71

(1995). "Schumpeterian Patterns of Innovation," *Cambridge Journal of Economics*, 19(1), 47–66

(1996). "Schumpeterian Patterns of Innovation are Technology Specific," *Research Policy*, 25(3), 451–78

Patel, P. and K. Pavitt (1993). "Technological Competencies in the World Largest Firms," *STEEP Discussion Papers*, 13, Science Policy Research Unit, University of Sussex

(1994). "The Continuing, Widespread (and Neglected) Importance of Improvements in Mechanical Technologies," *Research Policy*, 23, 533–45

(1997). "The Technological Competencies of the World's Largest Firms: Complex, Path-dependent but not too much variety," *Research Policy*

Schumpeter, J.A. (1912). "Theory of Economic Development," *Harvard Economic Studies*, Cambridge, Mass (published in 1934)

(1939). *Business Cycles,* New York: McGraw-Hill
(1942). *Capitalism, Socialism and Democracy*, New York: Harper & Bros
Utterback, J. (1994). *Mastering the Dynamics of Innovation*, Cambridge, Mass.:
    Harvard University Press

5 Spatial patterns of innovation: evidence from patent data

Stefano Breschi

Introduction

The last few years have witnessed a renewed and increasing interest on the part of economists in the geographical dimension of economic phenomena. Such revived attention in issues of economic geography rests ultimately upon the recognition of the essential importance of knowledge externalities and "spatially-bounded" increasing returns in promoting the spatial concentration of economic activities and growth (Krugman, 1991a, 1991b; Romer, 1986, 1990; Grossman and Helpman, 1991; Arthur, 1990).

Based upon such theoretical developments, several empirical studies have attempted to measure the extent to which knowledge spillovers take place and to explore the fundamental question of whether, and to what extent, knowledge externalities are spatially localized. A striking result of Jaffe (1986, 1989b) was that firms' innovative and economic performance depend not only on their own investment in R&D, but that they are also strongly affected by the R&D spending of other firms and universities. On the other hand, Jaffe, Trajtenberg, and Henderson (1993) found evidence that knowledge spillovers, as measured by patent citations, are most likely to occur within geographically-bounded areas rather than flowing freely across regions.

These results have quite obvious and fundamental implications for the economic theorizing of technical change and innovative processes. In the first place, firms' efforts to advance technology do not generally proceed in isolation, but are strongly supported by various external sources of knowledge: public research centers, universities, industry associations, and other firms (Nelson, 1993; Kline and Rosenberg, 1986; von Hippel, 1988). If the ability to innovate is affected by the spatial proximity to external sources of relevant knowledge, one should then observe wide differences in innovative capabilities among firms located in different geographical areas (Lundvall, 1993; Storper, 1992). In the second place, innovative activities also have a strong cumulative nature. This implies that firms located in innovative areas will find themselves in a more favorable position for the next round of innovation as compared with firms located in less innovative regions (Feldman, 1994). Moreover, firms which have successfully innovated will tend to grow relatively faster than non-innovators and new innovative firms will be attracted towards innovative regions because of the availability of essential knowledge inputs. Both these factors (the "local" nature of knowledge externalities and the cumulative character of technical change) are likely to give rise to a virtuous and self-reinforcing process by which past innovation breeds future location of innovative activities within selected areas, eventually leading to the spatial clustering of innovative activities (Arthur, 1990; Feldman, 1994).

Building upon such arguments, the basic claim of this chapter is that, while innovative activities tend in general to agglomerate within specific locations, the intensity of the geographical concentration and the spatial organization of the innovative processes may differ remarkably across sectors. For example, in some industries one may find few very large firms which compete at the global level and hold the largest share of total innovations. In other industries innovative activity is dispersed across a large number of small and often new firms scattered geographically. In yet other industries several firms located in specific regions are involved in intense processes of knowledge exchange: competition here takes place among regions rather than simply among firms. From such a perspective, the claim which is put forward is that the spatial clustering of innovation should be explicitly modeled as emerging from the interaction between learning, competition, and selection processes which take place among firms and geographical areas. In turn, the nature and the intensity of such processes are ultimately shaped by technology- and sector-specific conditions, summarized by the notion of a "technological regime" (Malerba and Orsenigo, 1990, 1993; see also chapter 4 in this volume). "Technological regimes" are broadly defined by the level and type of opportunity and appropriability conditions and cumulativeness of technical knowledge and by the nature of knowledge and the means of knowledge transmission and communication.

With such a theoretical background, the aim of this chapter is to identify some broad empirical regularities in the spatial distribution of innovative activities across sectors. In addition, an attempt is also made to explore the possible relationship between sectoral and spatial patterns of innovation and to test the role played by spatial cumulativeness in explaining regions' technological performance.

The chapter is organized as follows. A broad conceptual scheme is proposed for interpreting the spatial dimension of technical change. The notion of technological regime is introduced and discussed, and the basic mechanisms through which the specific properties of each technology can affect the geographical patterns of innovation investigated. The data source used for the

Table 5.1. *The relevant dimensions of technological regimes*

Opportunity (1)	Appropriability (2)	Cumulativeness (3)	Knowledge Base (4)
Level: Ease of innovating for any given amount of money invested in search	*Level:* Effectiveness of various means of protecting innovations from imitation	*Level:* Degree of persistence or serial correlation among subsequent innovations	*Nature* Tacit vs. codified Complex vs. simple System-specific vs. independent
Sources: Universities Public research centers Users and suppliers Competitors	*Means:* Patents Secrecy Lead time Continuous innovation Complementary assets	*Dimensions:* *Firm:* ability to innovate strongly dependent on accumulated competencies of specific firms *Sectoral:* relevant knowledge diffused widely across firms in a sector *Spatial:* existence of spatially localized knowledge externalities	*Means of transmission:* *Formal:* publications, formal teaching, licenses, reverse engineering *Informal:* interpersonal contacts, on-the-job training, mobility of personnel

empirical analysis is briefly described and a wide array of empirical indicators explored with the aim of identifying spatial patterns of innovation and the possible relationships between sectoral and spatial organization of innovative activity. Finally, there is a summary and some concluding remarks.

Spatial dimensions of technical change

Technological regimes: some notions

The notion of a "technological regime" dates back to the contributions of Nelson and Winter (1982) and Winter (1987), and provides a very general description of the technological environment in which firms operate. In broad terms, a technological regime can be defined by the particular combination of four fundamental factors, whose relevant dimensions are reported in table 5.1:

(1) Opportunity conditions reflect the probability of innovating for any given amount of resources invested in a search. More precisely, two basic

dimensions of technological opportunities – *level* and *sources* – are considered here.

(2) Appropriability conditions summarize the possibilities of protecting innovations from imitation and of reaping profits from innovative activities. Two fundamental dimensions – *level* and *means of appropriability* – characterize a regime of innovative protection.

(3) Cumulativeness of technological knowledge can be formally defined as the degree of serial correlation among innovations. It represents the probability of innovating at time $t+1$ conditional on innovations at time t or the amount of innovations generated in previous periods. In more general terms, cumulativeness denotes a technological environment characterized by *continuities* in innovative activities and in the accumulation of technological capabilities. From these definitions, one can identify three different levels of cumulativeness – *firm*, *sectoral*, and *spatial*.

(4) Nature of the relevant knowledge base refers to the properties of the knowledge upon which firms' innovative activities are based. Two major characteristics of the knowledge base – *the nature of knowledge* and *the means of knowledge transmission and communication* – are considered here.

In recent years, the effects of technological regimes have been thoroughly explored by several authors (Malerba and Orsenigo, 1990, 1993; Cohen, 1995; Cohen, Levin and Mowery, 1987). The major conclusion of such contributions is that industry-specific conditions (i.e. technological regimes), by shaping modes of learning, competition, and selection processes, ultimately determine the number and types of innovative actors and the overall organization of innovative activities across sectors. In this vein, recent empirical studies have demonstrated that the patterns of innovative activities differ systematically across sectors, but are remarkably similar across countries for each sector, and that technology-related factors (i.e. technological regimes) play a major role in determining the specific patterns of innovative activities of a sector across countries (Malerba and Orsenigo, 1995 and 1996). Two particular groups of sectors have been identified, in which innovative activities are structured and organized in different ways. The former represents a widening pattern and comprises most mechanical and traditional sectors: concentration of innovative activities is low, innovative firms are mostly of small size, stability in the ranking of innovative firms is low and entry of new innovative firms is high. The latter represents a deepening pattern and includes chemical and electronic sectors: concentration of innovative activities is high, innovative firms are mainly of large size, stability in the hierarchy of innovative firms is high, and entry of new innovative firms is low.

Building upon such results, the basic claim here is that the specific properties defining a technological regime not only affect the way innovative activities are differently structured and organized across sectors, but that they may also have consequences at the geographical level. In fact, it may be argued that the effects of technology-specific conditions are not uniformly distributed across locations. Rather, they tend to have quite different impacts on units located in different geographical areas. If this is so, one can then argue that the processes of learning, competition, and selection do not act simply on firms, but also upon geographical areas and firms located in different regions, and this may determine different levels of geographical concentration of innovative firms. Moreover, if the sectoral organization of innovative activities greatly differs across industries, one should then expect such differences to have a major impact on the organization of the same activities at the spatial level. In other words, the sectoral and spatial patterns of innovation should be very intimately related, being two faces of the same coin.

The rest of this section will be devoted to exploring this issue. In particular, the way the specific features of each technological regime, by affecting innovative activities, competition, and selection processes, can also affect the spatial distribution of innovative activities, will be discussed.

Technological regimes and spatial patterns of innovation

As a first step, the role each individual dimension characterizing a technological regime plays in affecting the spatial distribution of innovative activities is briefly sketched.

Knowledge base
The nature of the knowledge base and the related means of knowledge communication and transmission strongly affects how firms can effectively get access to the pool of innovative opportunities and knowledge externalities, thus contributing in a crucial way to determining the geographical location of innovators. In other words, they crucially affect the spatial boundaries within which firms can search for new knowledge inputs. In this respect, one can very briefly note what follows. The more the knowledge base is tacit, complex, and part of a larger system, the more geographically concentrated the population of innovators will be. Under such circumstances, in fact, the available "transport" mechanisms of knowledge have an informal nature: interpersonal contacts, "face-to-face" talks, on-the-job training, mobility of personnel, and so on. The spatial proximity among agents may therefore be of paramount importance in facilitating the transmission of knowledge, both within and across different organizations (Hägerstrand, 1966; Pred, 1966; Winter, 1987). Conversely, the more knowledge is codified, simple, and independent, the more important are formal means of knowledge communication – formal teaching, publications, licenses, and so on. In such circumstances, one can argue that

geographical proximity does not play a crucial role in facilitating the transmission of knowledge across agents (Lundvall, 1993).

Opportunity

As far as technological opportunities are concerned, two dimensions appear to be important for a spatial interpretation of technical change: *level* and *sources*.

Ceteris paribus, technological regimes marked by high levels of innovative opportunities are expected to lead to high degrees of sectoral – and, therefore, also geographical – concentration of innovative activities. High technological opportunities, by allowing successful innovators to gain a substantial edge in their relative competitiveness, are in fact associated with strong selective pressures (Nelson and Winter, 1982). In such a case, the evolution of industrial structures is likely to exhibit a strong tendency towards sectoral concentration, and therefore a low number of innovators. Selection on firms is here likely to dominate selection on geographical areas.

The sources of innovative opportunities strongly affects where such opportunities are available and effectively transmitted to firms, thereby shaping the spatial location of innovators (Feldman, 1994). More particularly, in those sectors in which the sources of opportunities are related to R&D activities, universities, and public research institutions, one may expect a noticeable concentration of innovators within a few regions and especially metropolitan areas. The availability of qualified human capital, the location of universities and firms' headquarters, and more generally the existence of a dense network of interactions drives the spatial agglomeration of innovative activities (Howells, 1989; Malecki, 1980). On the other hand, where suppliers and users represent fundamental sources of new knowledge, the spatial clustering of innovators may arise because geographical proximity plays a crucial role in facilitating the establishment of stable and durable relationships among agents, upon which the effective transfer of knowledge is based (Lundvall, 1993; von Hippel, 1988).

Appropriability

Ceteris paribus, high degrees of technological appropriability are likely to lead to high levels of sectoral – and, therefore, also geographical – concentration of innovative activities. In fact, by limiting the extent of knowledge spillovers and by allowing successful innovators to maintain their acquired competitive advantages, high degrees of technological appropriability are expected to result in a lower number of innovators and therefore a relatively higher level of spatial concentration of innovative activities. Conversely, by determining a wider diffusion of knowledge across firms, low appropriability conditions may lead to a relatively more spatially diffused base of innovators. In this case, the effect on the geographical distribution of innovators will crucially depend on the extent to which knowledge spillovers are spatially localized.

Cumulativeness

The effects of technological cumulativeness on the spatial patterns of innovation may differ, depending on what the relevant dimension of cumulativeness is.

If cumulativeness at the firm level is high (therefore also indicating high degrees of appropriability), one would expect to find a rather high degree of stability in the hierarchy of innovative firms and low rates of innovative entry. In such circumstances, the selection process favors existing technological leaders. Existing innovators accumulate technological knowledge and capabilities and build up innovative advantages which play an important role in affecting their competitiveness and act as powerful barriers to entry of new innovators. In this case, selection on firms is rather stronger than selection on locations, and high levels of spatial concentration are typically associated with high levels of sectoral concentration of innovations.

On the other hand, if cumulativeness at the sectoral level is high (therefore indicating the existence of widespread knowledge externalities), the effects on the geographical distribution of innovative activities will crucially depend on the nature of such knowledge externalities, and on the extent to which they are spatially localized. In this regard, one could say that the more knowledge is tacit, complex, and systemic, the more likely it is that geographical proximity will play an important role in capturing the benefits of knowledge spillovers, thus pushing towards the spatial clustering of innovative activities. Conversely, the more knowledge is standardized, relatively simple, and independent – and, therefore, quite easily transferable over long distances – the less spatial proximity is helpful or even necessary in order to get access to the relevant knowledge.

Finally, "spatial cumulativeness" refers to the degree of persistence with which the accumulation of innovative capabilities takes place within specific geographical areas. High cumulativeness at the spatial level therefore indicates the importance of spatially localized knowledge externalities and innovative capabilities accumulated by local firms and institutions. In such a case, one may expect to observe high levels of spatial concentration of innovators within a few regions. More precisely, location here "matters" and the spatial clustering of innovative activities is the outcome of competition and selection processes which take place among regions and firms located in specific areas, rather than simply among firms.

Towards the identification of some regularities

A crucial point which must be stressed is that sectoral and spatial patterns of innovative activities are essentially determined by the specific combination of each of the above-mentioned variables, and not by each dimension considered individually. The task of identifying an exhaustive taxonomy of all possible combinations is beyond the scope of this chapter. In this section, the more limited task of sketching a few theoretical cases emerging from the specific combination of the variables defining a technological regime is carried out. More specifically, three major cases can be identified:

> (1)   *Deepening and concentrated pattern*
>   *Sectoral pattern:* high concentration, large size, low entry, high stability (deepening).
>   *Spatial pattern:* high and persistent concentration (concentrated).

A first important case refers to a combination of high opportunity, appropriability, and cumulativeness (at the firm level). Under such a technological regime, the Schumpeterian dynamics of innovators is characterized by the emergence of a restricted "core" of large oligopolistic firms. In particular, high cumulativeness at the firm level implies that technological capabilities accumulated by firms within their own boundaries constitute the fundamental basis upon which present innovative activities take place. This factor, coupled with very high opportunity and appropriability conditions, accelerates the pace with which less successful firms are selected out, thus leading to the market dominance of few innovators. With respect to the geographical distribution of innovative activities, one should similarly expect a high concentration of innovators within a few regions (and especially metropolitan areas), where some of the essential knowledge inputs are located. In other words, the spatial concentration of innovators in these sectors is likely to follow to a large extent the sectoral one: the selection process on firms is of first-order with respect to the selection on geographical areas. Moreover, if cumulativeness at the firm level is high, one can expect sectoral and spatial concentration of innovative activities to persist over time.

> (2)   *Widening and concentrated pattern*
>   *Sectoral pattern:* low concentration, small and medium size, high entry, low stability (widening).
>   *Spatial pattern:* high and persistent concentration (concentrated).

A second possible case refers to a combination of medium opportunity, low appropriability and high cumulativeness (at the sectoral and the spatial level) and to a knowledge base characterized by high degrees of tacitness and system-specificity. Under such a technological regime, the Schumpeterian dynamics of innovators is likely to lead to a rather large and fragmented population of innovators. In fact, low appropriability and low cumulativeness (at the firm level) conditions are such that firms' competitive advantages are neither lasting enough nor entirely appropriable to generate dominant market positions. In a spatial perspective, however, rather high levels of geographical concentration of innovative activities may be expected. Since technical change here requires the mastery of tacit and specific know-how and expertise (not easily codifiable, nor entirely embodied in general-purpose equipment), the communication and transmission of these mainly tacit and application-specific cognitive assets can take place only through a set of informal mechanisms, whose effectiveness sharply increases with spatial proximity. The establishment of common codes of communication developed through spatial proximity and extensive processes of knowledge exchange among firms located within specific regions generates knowledge externalities and technological cumulativeness within spatially bounded areas and drives the spatial clustering of innovators in a few selected locations. It may be also argued that the selection processes in these sectors do not operate only upon individual firms, but also upon clusters of firms located in different geographical areas.

(3) *Widening and diffused pattern*
  Sectoral pattern: low concentration, small and medium size, high entry, low stability (widening)
  Spatial pattern: low concentration (diffused)

A third possible case refers to a combination of low opportunity, appropriability and cumulativeness (at the firm level) and to a relatively codified and generic knowledge base. In such a technological regime, which prevails in most traditional sectors, selection forces are quite reduced, and a large population of innovators with low degrees of concentration is likely to emerge. In fact, given the low appropriability and (firms') cumulativeness conditions, any possible competitive advantage is likely to be quickly eroded by other competitors, thus leading to a rather fragmented industrial structure. The spatial pattern of innovation is likely to be characterized by relatively high degrees of geographical dispersion of innovators. The relatively simple and codifiable nature of technological knowledge underlying the innovative process is such that spatial proximity does not play an important role in facilitating the transmission of knowledge among firms. Moreover, the low opportunity, appropriability and (firms') cumulativeness conditions strongly limit the possibility of concentration owing to the growth of firms located within specific areas. A scattered and almost randomly distributed spatial pattern of innovation is therefore likely to be the norm, rather than the exception, in such sectors.

It must be stressed again that the examples briefly sketched do not exhaust all possible cases. Rather, they are functional to the empirical analysis of the spatial patterns of innovative activities across sectors which is carried out in the following sections.

Data sources

This chapter has used the EPO–CESPRI[1] database which is based on European Patent Office (EPO) data for the period 1978–91. For a detailed description of the EPO–CESPRI database, see Malerba and Orsenigo's chapter 4 in this volume. As far as the spatial unit of observation is concerned, Nomenclature of Statistical Territorial Units (Nuts) level II has been adopted here. According to the definition provided by the European Office of Statistics (Eurostat), Nuts level II refers to: "regions," for France and Italy, "counties," for the United Kingdom, and "Regierungsbezirken," for Germany.[2] Using the data set just described, patents have been attributed to the geographical area in which the *establishment* responsible for the development of the innovation is located.[3]

Two final remarks are needed. In the first place, the shortcomings of patents are well known. However, patents provide an invaluable source of data for the spatial analysis of innovative activity because, by containing the address of applicants, they permit us to trace the spatial evolution of technologies with a level of detail which no other indicator to date has been able to provide. In the second place, the choice of administrative regions as spatial units of observation is not entirely satisfactory. Knowledge flows and functional linkages are likely to differ across sectors and the ideal unit of observation may range from the world to the industrial district and the town. Moreover, there are rather large differences across countries in the definition of the boundaries of political jurisdictions. As a consequence, the above mentioned choice has been mainly suggested by the need to compare rather homogeneous areas across countries. In any case, it represents a first proxy which can improve our understanding of the spatial dimension of technical change.

[1] Center for Research on Internationalization (CESPRI) (Bocconi University, Milan).
[2] There are 20 "regions" for Italy, 22 "regions" for France, 32 "counties" for the United Kingdom, and 31 "Regierungsbezirken" for Germany.
[3] Since patents can be filed by subsidiaries, divisions or establishments of companies with head-quarters in other geographical areas, even within the same country, the database distinguishes between the location of the innovating establishment and the location of the larger, parent company. Of course, there remains a potential source of bias in the data due to the widely diffused practice of firms' headquarters to patent inventions which have been developed by divisions and establishments. The resulting bias consists in an over-estimation of the spatial concentration of innovative activities in urban and metropolitan areas within each country, where most head-quarters are located. While there are not easy solutions to this bias, it must be also pointed out that this problem is likely to create some distortions only in sectors where large, multi-plant firms are important. Moreover, as long as patents can be considered as products flowing from basic research activities, which are conducted in laboratories located close to firms' headquarters, the extent of the distortion can be further lessened.

Spatial patterns of innovative activities

The aim of this section is to identify some broad empirical regularities in the geographical organization of innovative activity. Patterns of spatial concentration of patenting activity are explored, both within each country and for the four countries as a whole. The purpose here is to assess the extent to which innovative activities tend to cluster in a few geographical areas. Inter-industry differences in the intensity of geographical concentration of innovations are also explored. The second objective is to investigate the relationship between the sectoral and the spatial organization of innovative acitivities. In particular, the analysis aims to evaluate the extent to which the spatial concentration of innovations is caused by the industrial concentration of innovative activities or, conversely, the extent to which it can be attributed to a large population of small and new firms located in a few areas. Finally, a rough measure of spatial cumulativeness is introduced and its implications for explaining regions' technological performance discussed.

The spatial concentration of innovative activities

Table 5.2 provides a broad picture of the regional distribution of innovative activity among the European regions.[4] At this aggregate level, the empirical evidence suggests the existence of a strong concentration of innovative capabilities among a restricted number of regions. Of the total number of patents filed to EPO in the period 1985–91 almost 42 percent was recorded in just four leading regions: the Ile-de-France (Fra), South-East (UK), Oberbayern (Ger), and Darmstadt (Ger). In addition, it should be also observed that among the 10 most innovative regions, seven are German, suggesting that the real "core" of European innovative capabilities is located in such an area. Moreover, as the value of the Entropy Index seems to indicate, a high dispersion of innovative shares characterizes the "fringe" of less innovative areas. By and large, the empirical evidence thus supports a picture of Europe's technological landscape as divided into three broad areas: a "core" that carries out the bulk of the European innovative effort, a "satellite" that substantially contributes to the process of advancing technology, and a "fringe" of marginal regions whose innovative performance is negligible. Furthermore, the Spearman rank correlation coefficient indicates a very high stability over time in the ranking of innovative regions, in spite of the fact that the spatial concentration appears to slightly decrease.

Table 5.2 also reports the regional distribution of patenting activity for five

---

[4] In table 5.2, Nuts level I has been used to identify regions in the United Kingdom. For the other three countries, Nuts level II has instead been used.

Table 5.2. *Spatial distribution of patenting activity among European regions, 1985–1991 and percentage change, 1978–1984 to 1985–1991*

Four countries, five technological macro-classes

Regions	All sectors		Regions	Traditional sectors		Regions	Mechanical sectors	
	1985–91	Δ%		1985–91	Δ%		1985–91	Δ%
Ile-de-France (Fra)	16.7	−2.9	Ile-de-France (Fra)	14	0.0	Ile-de-France (Fra)	13.8	−18.3
South-East (UK)	9.6	−15.0	South-East (UK)	8.5	−23.4	Düsseldorf (Ger)	6.8	6.2
Oberbayern (Ger)	8.6	−11.3	Darmstadt (Ger)	7	−13.6	Oberbayern (Ger)	6	13.2
Darmstadt (Ger)	6.8	−13.9	Düsseldorf (Ger)	5.8	−17.1	Stuttgart (Ger)	5.7	42.5
Köln (Ger)	5.9	−31.4	Lombardia (It)	5.2	48.6	Köln (Ger)	4.7	−42.7
Düsseldorf (Ger)	4.5	−2.2	Rhones-Alpes (Fra)	3.6	−2.7	South-East (UK)	4.7	−7.8
Lombardia (It)	3.7	94.7	Oberbayern (Ger)	3.3	26.9	Darmstadt (Ger)	4.7	−6.0
Rheinessen-Pfalz (Ger)	3.6	−21.7	Köln (Ger)	3.2	−33.3	West Midlands (UK)	3.7	−7.5
Stuttgart (Ger)	3.6	38.5	Veneto (It)	3.2	113.3	Karlsruhe (Ger)	3	3.4
Karlsruhe (Ger)	2.6	13.0	Stuttgart (Ger)	2.6	36.8	Lombardia (It)	3.1	63.2
Other regions	34.4	17.4	Other regions	43.6	4.3	Other regions	43.8	8.7
Total	100.0	–	Total	100.0	–	Total	100.0	–
No. of regions	84	3.7	No. of regions	81	5.2	No. of regions	81	3.8
Entropy Index	3.36	5.7	Entropy Index	3.58	2.3	Entropy Index	3.60	5.9
Spearman rank coeff.	0.98		Spearman rank coeff.	0.92		Spearman rank coeff.	0.96	

Table 5.2 (cont.)

Transport sectors			Chemical sectors			Electronic sectors		
Regions	1985–91	Δ%	Regions	1985–91	Δ%	Regions	1985–91	Δ%
Ile-de-France (Fra)	21.5	−0.5	South-East (UK)	14.1	15.6	Ile-de-France (Fra)	20.9	−6.7
Oberbayern (Ger)	10.4	−5.5	Ile-de-France (Fra)	13.2	−9.6	Oberbayern (Ger)	16.8	−23.3
Stuttgart (Ger)	7.2	148.3	Darmstadt (Ger)	11.9	−9.8	South-East (UK)	11.6	2.7
Piemonte (It)	5.4	68.8	Köln (Ger)	11.2	−33.3	Darmstadt (Ger)	4.7	−7.8
West Midlands (UK)	5.1	−23.9	Rheinessen-Pfalz (Ger)	9	−18.2	Stuttgart (Ger)	4	−4.8
South-East (UK)	4.3	−15.7	Düsseldorf (Ger)	5	−2.0	Karlsruhe (Ger)	3.1	10.7
Köln (Ger)	4	−24.5	Lombardia (It)	4.8	77.8	Lombardia (It)	3.1	210.0
Düsseldorf (Ger)	3.1	−43.6	Oberbayern (Ger)	3.9	−4.9	Freiburg (Ger)	2.9	16.0
Darmstadt (Ger)	3.1	24.0	Karlsruhe (Ger)	2.2	46.7	Köln (Ger)	2.5	−19.4
East Anglia (UK)	3	−6.3	Münster (Ger)	2	−13.0	Hamburg (Ger)	2.5	56.3
Other regions	32.9	−0.3	Other regions	22.7	37.6	Other regions	27.9	26.2
Total	100.0	–	Total	100.0	–	Total	100.0	–
No. of regions	77	2.6	No. of regions	82	5.1	No. of regions	78	4.0
Entropy index	3.22	1.5	Entropy Index	3.04	9.7	Entropy Index	3.02	7.4
Spearman rank coeff.	0.90		Spearman rank coeff.	0.95		Spearman rank coeff.	0.95	

Note:
– = not available.
Source: EPO-Center for Research on Internationalization (CESPRI) (Bocconi University) database

technological macro-classes in which all patents can be classified. A remarkable concentration of patenting activity among a few regions characterizes the chemical–pharmaceutical and the electrical–electronic macro-classes and, to a lesser extent, the transport sector. On the other hand, lower degrees of spatial concentration can be found in the traditional and mechanical macro-classes. The leading innovative regions vary across technological macro-classes, even though the Ile-de-France (Fra), South-East (UK) and several German regions always dominate the innovative scene. Furthermore, the value of the Spearman rank correlation coefficient for each of the five technological macro-classes suggests the existence of a remarkable stability over time in the hierarchy of innovative regions, in spite of the fact that the spatial concentration appears to decrease in all sectors (with the partial exception of transport).

Table 5.3 comes closer to the central interest of this chapter. It reports, for each country and for each of the 49 technological classes in which patents have been aggregated, the value of the Herfindahl Equivalent Index (HEI) calculated in the period 1985–91, and its absolute change with respect to the period 1978–84. It therefore provides a measure of the spatial concentration of innovative activities within each country. An inspection of the data suggests two main points:

(1) *Existence of significant differences across technological sectors in the degree of spatial concentration of innovations.* Within each of the four countries, the Herfindahl equivalent index takes relatively high values (therefore indicating relatively high degrees of spatial diffusion and broad similarities among regions in innovative capabilities) in mechanical and especially in traditional sectors. On the other hand, it takes consistently lower values (therefore indicating low degrees of spatial diffusion and large asymmetries in regions' innovative capabilities) in most chemical and electrical–electronic sectors. Moreover, a cross-country comparison based on Pearson–Spearman rank correlation coefficients provides evidence of remarkable similarities across countries in the absolute level and in the ranking of the 49 technological sectors according to the rate of spatial concentration of innovations (table 5.4). This suggests that the degree of spatial concentration of innovative activities differs systematically across technological classes, but is remarkably similar across countries within each technological class. This result thus provides support for the hypothesis that technology-specific factors (i.e. technological regimes), relatively invariant across countries, can play an essential role in affecting the intensity of spatial concentration of innovative activities.[5]

[5] For each country and for each of the 49 technological classes, the Spearman rank correlation coefficient between the ranking of innovative regions in the period 1978–84 and the period 1985–91 has been also calculated. The results (for brevity not reported here) show, generally, very high degrees of stability in the ranking of innovative regions over time. This result therefore indicates the importance of spatial and firm cumulativeness.

Table 5.3. *Spatial concentration of innovative activities (Herfindahl Equivalent Index, HEI)*

1985–91 and absolute change 1985–91 to 1978–84, 49 technological classes, four countries

Technological classes	United Kingdom		France		Germany		Italy	
	HEI	Δ	HEI	Δ	HEI	Δ	HEI	Δ
1 Food and tobacco	1.7	−0.6	4.3	0.8	14.0	7.4	3.5	0.4
2 Clothing and shoes	13.6	7.9	5.3	−1.3	9.4	−0.2	2.0	−0.1
3 Furniture	11.2	2.2	4.3	0.5	13.8	−3.4	3.7	−0.2
4 Agriculture	11.1	0.6	8.3	1.0	12.5	−0.1	7.3	3.0
5 Mining	6.5	−1.7	1.2	−0.7	11.6	4.1	2.9	1.9
6 Gas and hydrocarbons	2.3	0.6	1.2	−0.1	5.9	−0.2	2.0	−0.2
7 Inorganic chemicals	3.3	1.6	1.2	−0.1	6.6	2.0	2.5	0.1
8 Organic chemicals	1.8	0.3	1.3	0.0	5.1	0.6	2.2	0.5
9 Macromolecular compounds	2.0	0.0	1.2	0.0	4.4	0.1	1.7	0.3
10 New materials	5.8	2.1	1.4	0.2	8.2	−0.3	3.4	0.1
11 Adhesives and resins	2.2	0.0	1.5	0.3	5.3	0.8	3.4	1.8
12 Biochemicals	2.9	1.1	1.7	−0.1	8.2	0.4	2.8	0.8
13 Misc. chemical compounds	1.3	−0.3	1.7	0.3	2.3	0.0	2.2	0.6
14 Chemical processes	3.7	0.8	1.7	0.1	10.7	1.8	4.2	1.2
15 Drugs	2.2	0.7	1.6	−0.1	8.5	0.6	3.0	1.3
16 Medical preparations	5.2	1.2	3.5	1.2	7.7	0.3	5.0	0.3
17 Natural, artificial, fibers	11.6	1.9	3.7	0.2	11.1	1.3	2.7	0.5
18 Chemical processes for fibers	6.5	2.6	3.3	0.5	7.5	2.3	4.5	1.7
19 Agricultural chemicals	4.2	1.7	2.8	0.5	5.8	2.5	3.1	1.5
20 Chemical processes for food	2.8	0.1	4.1	−0.4	10.4	4.0	4.0	−1.3
21 Metallurgy	4.1	1.1	1.4	0.0	6.2	0.2	4.0	−0.7
22 Machine tools	5.2	−0.2	1.5	0.4	6.3	−1.5	4.8	0.5
23 Industrial automation	10.9	2.2	2.1	0.2	10.2	0.6	4.7	0.5
24 Industrial machinery	12.5	3.6	2.8	0.4	12.7	0.3	5.5	0.4
25 Agricultural machinery	8.1	1.4	3.8	−1.3	4.4	−5.0	4.1	−0.1
26 Vehicles	7.1	−2.1	1.7	0.1	8.5	−1.1	2.6	0.0
27 Aircraft	2.9	−1.1	1.2	0.1	6.0	2.6	2.4	−1.2
28 Railways and ships	6.0	−0.9	2.4	0.0	9.4	3.4	5.7	1.7
29 Materials handling appliances	11.3	2.4	3.5	0.3	16.5	1.7	5.3	−0.3
30 Civil engineering	17.5	4.8	3.4	0.7	15.3	0.6	5.3	0.6

Table 5.3. (*cont.*)

1985–91 and absolute change 1985–91 to 1978–84, 49 technological classes, four countries

Technological classes	United Kingdom		France		Germany		Italy	
	HEI	Δ	HEI	Δ	HEI	Δ	HEI	Δ
31 Engines, turbines, pumps	5.9	−1.9	1.3	−0.1	7.4	0.3	4.4	0.6
32 Mechanical engineering	9.1	−2.1	1.7	0.1	13.2	0.1	4.1	0.6
33 Mechanical, electrical technologies	8.1	2.5	1.5	0.0	9.6	−0.9	5.9	−0.3
34 Household. electrical appliances	9.2	3.5	3.6	0.7	11.5	0.4	4.6	−0.9
35 Lighting systems	5.7	0.4	1.5	−1.1	4.7	1.9	3.0	−0.5
36 Measurement instruments	5.3	1.0	1.5	0.1	8.7	2.0	3.8	0.2
37 Laser technology	2.3	−0.9	1.1	0.0	3.8	−0.5	3.4	2.2
38 Optics and photography	2.6	0.1	1.2	0.1	7.3	0.9	4.0	−1.4
39 Computers	3.2	−1.4	1.2	0.0	4.6	0.9	2.6	1.4
40 Other office equipment	3.2	−1.7	2.2	0.8	7.7	0.9	1.2	0.1
41 Electrical devices	4.3	1.2	1.7	0.2	7.0	1.6	3.5	−0.7
42 Electronic components	3.1	0.5	1.4	0.0	4.0	1.0	1.8	−1.7
43 Consumer electronics	2.6	0.0	1.2	0.1	7.6	0.8	2.8	−3.0
44 Telecommunications	3.0	0.3	1.1	0.0	3.7	1.0	2.8	0.3
45 Multimedial systems	1.1	0.1	1.4	−1.1	3.7	0.7	2.1	1.1
46 Arts, sports, toys	6.1	0.1	4.0	−1.5	13.8	−1.6	4.7	0.7
47 Weapons	2.2	−1.5	1.3	−0.2	6.5	2.4	1.8	−2.8
48 Nuclear technology	2.3	0.4	1.1	0.0	3.6	−2.5	3.3	2.3
49 Others	8.5	3.9	3.0	−0.4	16.3	3.9	5.0	1.6

Source: EPO–CESPRI database.

(2) *Existence of significant differences across countries in the geographical concentration of innovations.* Besides sectoral differences, one also observes significant differences across countries in the spatial concentration of innovative activities.[6] In this respect, France can be described as a "centralized" national system, showing the lowest levels of HEI in most technological

---

[6] Innovative activities are in general highly concentrated within each country in a single leading region. On average, in the period 1978–91, the region Ile-de-France holds more than 80 percent of total patenting activity in France, whereas Lombardia holds slightly more than 40 percent of all Italian patents, Greater London more than 45 percent of British patents, and Oberbayern more than 20 percent of all German patents. More generally, innovative activity turns out to be agglomerated within each country in a few "core" regions: the North-West and North-East in

Table 5.4. *Pearson–Spearman correlation coefficient between HEIs*
1985–1991, four countries; $N = 49$

	Pearson			
	United Kingdom	France	Germany	Italy
United Kingdom	1.000			
France	0.582	1.000		
Germany	0.683	0.564	1.000	
Italy	0.551	0.497	0.576	1.000
	Spearman			
	United Kingdom	France	Germany	Italy
United Kingdom	1.000			
France	0.572	1.000		
Germany	0.658	0.650	1.000	
Italy	0.583	0.467	0.573	1.000

Note:
All correlations significant at the 0.01 level.

classes. On the other hand, Germany is characterized by a much wider spatial diffusion of innovative capabilities in most technological classes, while Italy and the United Kingdom stand in an intermediate position.[7] In particular, Italy shows relatively high degrees of regional concentration of patenting activity in traditional sectors (food and tobacco, clothing and shoes, furniture, agriculture, and household electric appliances), and in most mechanical classes. This result therefore suggests that country-specific factors related to the distinctive history of industrial development of each country and to the working of specific institutions and policies can also affect the degree of spatial concentration of innovative activities within each national system of innovation. More precisely, it can be said that, within the constraints imposed by technology-specific factors, country-

Italy (over 80 percent in Lombardia, Piemonte, Emilia Romagna, Veneto, and Friuli), the Southern Länder in Federal Republic of Germany (over 50 percent in Baden-Württemberg, Bayern, Hessen, and Rheinessen-Pfalz), the South-East in the United Kingdom (over 70 percent in Greater London, West–East Sussex, Kent, Oxfordshire, Hampshire, and Buckinghamshire) and the Ile-de-France in France (over 80 percent).

[7] Considering total patenting activity, in the period 1978–91 the HEI was 1.66 for France, 10.30 for Germany, 5.31 for Italy, and 4.29 for the United Kingdom.

specific factors can introduce differences in the overall degree of spatial concentration of innovative activities (without, however, changing the hierarchy of technological classes).

In the next section, inter-industry differences in the spatial concentration of innovations will be related to inter-industry differences in the sectoral organization of innovative activities. In particular, attention will be devoted to exploring the extent to which spatial concentration of innovative activities is related to the sectoral concentration of innovations and to the patterns of localization of new innovative firms.

Spatial and sectoral patterns of innovation

In exploring the relationship between spatial and sectoral patterns of innovation, there are at least two important issues which must be dealt with. In the first place, one needs to evaluate the extent to which inter-industry differences in the geographical concentration of innovations correspond to different patterns of sectoral concentration of innovative activities. For example, a high degree of geographical concentration of innovations in a given sector might be caused by the existence of high rates of sectoral concentration – i.e. the innovative dominance of a few (possibly large) firms. Alternatively, the geographical concentration of innovative activities could be related to the existence of a large population of (possibly small) firms located in a restricted number of areas. In the second place, one needs to evaluate the patterns of localization of new innovative firms and their impact on the geographical concentration of innovative activities. As mentioned above, if knowledge spillovers tend to occur within spatially bounded areas and technical advances have a strong cumulative nature, new innovative firms should be attracted towards innovative regions, thus reinforcing the spatial clustering of innovative activities. On the other hand, in the case where knowledge spillovers flow freely across regions or are internalized within the boundaries of specific firms (i.e. if firm cumulativeness is high), localization of new innovative firms should exhibit an almost randomly distributed pattern.

Table 5.5 tackles the first issue by comparing the degree of geographical and sectoral concentration of innovative activities. More specifically, it reports, for each country and each of the 49 technological classes, the top four regions and the top four firms' concentration ratio for the period 1985–91. This permits us to identify the contribution of the largest innovators to the overall spatial concentration of innovative activities. The empirical evidence seems to suggest the existence of three distinct models of organization of innovative activities, which show remarkably similar features in all countries:

(1) A first model comprises several chemical and electronic sectors. In these technological classes, both the spatial and the sectoral degrees of

Table 5.5. *Spatial and sectoral concentration of innovative activities (C4 regions and C4 firms' concentration ratio), 1985–1991*
Four countries, 49 technological classes

Technological classes	United Kingdom		France		Germany		Italy	
	C4	C4	C4	C4	C4	C4	C4	C4
	Regions	Firms	Regions	Firms	Regions	Firms	Regions	Firms
1 Food and tobacco	91.53	73.73	75.36	25.36	46.12	31.01	87.80	36.59
2 Clothing and shoes	41.07	19.64	73.33	38.10	54.32	24.07	91.55	59.62
3 Furniture	46.73	11.21	72.19	18.34	43.44	10.54	82.01	16.55
4 Agriculture	51.06	21.28	54.29	19.29	44.91	18.56	64.06	14.06
5 Mining	68.48	25.45	97.42	61.80	47.52	13.22	85.29	61.76
6 Gas and hydrocarbons	87.12	57.58	97.30	56.76	67.08	30.17	89.06	60.94
7 Inorganic chemicals	73.50	41.00	94.59	46.72	68.46	34.23	83.33	37.96
8 Organic chemicals	87.70	48.73	96.11	34.40	79.78	67.48	87.07	26.63
9 Macromolecular compounds	83.61	61.70	98.42	52.37	84.45	73.88	92.53	51.04
10 New materials	62.06	25.18	94.78	36.81	61.16	26.88	81.25	30.21
11 Adhesives and resins	79.72	44.06	88.89	34.57	80.04	60.88	84.48	24.14
12 Biochemicals	78.99	34.54	89.18	29.36	59.36	37.66	88.81	44.03
13 Misc. chemical compounds	95.15	88.33	93.94	50.00	90.18	80.10	90.00	45.00
14 Chemical processes	64.87	29.88	88.57	25.64	52.82	15.96	75.37	12.50
15 Drugs	81.52	45.76	92.48	34.40	58.23	28.18	84.79	19.01
16 Medical preparations	60.68	20.11	73.59	14.56	52.88	30.26	78.66	22.53
17 Natural, artificial fibers	48.65	15.32	83.16	24.21	48.80	20.80	85.65	30.00
18 Chemical processes for fibers	68.70	37.39	80.28	19.01	66.87	42.68	81.01	20.25
19 Agricultural chemicals	75.84	47.65	89.16	51.81	75.30	64.33	84.00	36.00

Table 5.5. (*cont.*)

Four countries, 49 technological classes

Technological classes	United Kingdom		France		Germany		Italy	
	C4	C4	C4	C4	C4	C4	C4	C4
	Regions	Firms	Regions	Firms	Regions	Firms	Regions	Firms
20 Chemical processes for food	77.64	49.69	71.77	13.71	50.68	22.60	88.89	33.33
21 Metallurgy	70.63	25.40	96.09	18.62	71.84	22.12	77.94	23.53
22 Machine tools	68.75	33.75	93.33	25.56	69.58	32.92	75.86	41.38
23 Industrial automation	50.97	19.42	86.63	21.22	53.75	13.87	80.57	17.71
24 Industrial machinery	41.91	10.34	77.24	12.62	47.39	11.71	74.85	16.93
25 Agricultural machinery	60.22	38.71	80.18	59.01	67.24	50.29	90.63	43.75
26 Vehicles	61.29	36.93	87.89	38.53	59.22	21.21	92.82	41.37
27 Aircraft	79.26	56.30	98.94	62.96	69.54	41.06	100.00	58.33
28 Railways and ships	62.99	23.62	89.45	40.08	52.27	22.73	67.71	31.25
29 Materials handling appliances	42.93	15.47	74.92	10.01	36.45	7.16	77.36	13.50
30 Civil engineering	35.35	4.58	74.95	11.56	42.04	8.16	74.72	13.08
31 Engines, turbines, pumps	69.58	42.39	94.06	42.52	67.32	22.63	88.55	38.83
32 Mechanical engineering	61.36	34.33	86.32	28.32	46.52	13.10	84.55	21.99
33 Mechanical electrical technologies	57.87	18.52	90.93	21.89	57.26	13.71	71.43	20.41
34 Household electrical appliances	53.57	15.31	71.79	33.93	51.88	19.91	81.54	21.54
35 Lighting systems	60.78	31.37	91.30	55.07	75.14	45.66	97.50	37.50
36 Measurement instruments	59.65	13.65	91.05	18.45	55.20	24.33	85.08	19.15
37 Laser technology	85.71	47.96	100.00	52.63	76.23	50.41	95.45	56.82
38 Optics and photography	82.10	31.66	96.02	33.67	67.37	44.30	81.45	41.94

Table 5.5. (*cont.*)

Four countries, 49 technological classes

Technological classes	United Kingdom		France		Germany		Italy	
	C4	C4	C4	C4	C4	C4	C4	C4
	Regions	Firms	Regions	Firms	Regions	Firms	Regions	Firms
39 Computers	73.86	25.18	96.20	36.23	70.73	54.94	94.44	56.67
40 Other office equipment	79.01	58.02	94.64	48.21	62.15	46.96	100.00	87.50
41 Electrical devices	64.11	15.82	88.74	16.92	53.72	32.11	75.43	20.10
42 Electronic components	74.71	31.29	96.00	37.24	72.33	47.43	91.32	49.58
43 Consumer electronics	78.79	31.52	93.79	36.58	65.69	56.78	90.32	47.10
44 Telecommunications	80.42	35.99	97.33	30.52	75.95	61.85	93.47	47.35
45 Multimedial systems	100.00	83.33	100.00	64.71	86.21	79.31	100.00	87.50
46 Arts, sports, toys	55.24	10.48	80.34	31.03	42.13	11.93	82.67	22.00
47 Weapons	78.47	50.00	96.94	48.98	69.09	57.91	95.92	46.94
48 Nuclear technology	100.00	75.00	99.16	76.69	78.42	65.15	100.00	84.62
49 Others	55.08	18.64	84.44	22.22	39.22	19.83	76.54	18.52

Source: EPO-CESPRI database.

concentration of innovative activities are very high.[8] In such sectors, the spatial clustering of innovative activities finds its explanation in the dominant role played by a few large innovative firms which persistently accumulate over time innovative capabilities within their own boundaries. In other words, one can say that in these sectors selection on firms is a first-order effect with respect to selection on geographical areas, thus driving the process of spatial agglomeration of innovative activities.

[8] More specifically, the sectors which, in all the four countries, present such features are: macromolecular compounds (9), adhesives (11), miscellaneous chemical compounds (13), drugs (15), lasers (37), optics (38), computers (39), electronic components (43), consumer electronics (43), and telecommunications (44). In addition, some sectors related to transport and mechanical technologies also present this combination of high spatial and sectoral concentration of innovative activities: vehicles (26), agricultural machinery (25), engines, turbines and pumps (31).

(2) A second model includes several mechanical engineering classes[9] and is characterized by medium (and, in some cases, high) degrees of geographical concentration and by rather low levels of sectoral concentration of innovative activities. In these technological classes, the accumulation of innovative capabilities takes place at the local level involving a large population of small and medium-sized firms which innovate as a "collective" body. In other words, competition and selection here take place among "clusters" of firms located within specific areas, rather than simply among firms.

(3) Finally, a third model comprises the traditional sectors.[10] In these technological classes, one typically finds a combination of relatively low degrees of both geographical and sectoral concentration of innovative activities, thus indicating that local agglomeration forces are relatively less important.

There are, of course, some exceptions to the patterns just identified. For example, traditional sectors in Italy present relatively high degrees of spatial concentration coupled with rather low degrees of sectoral concentration of innovative activities. As already noted, such deviations demonstrate the important role played by country-specific factors (i.e. national systems of innovation). However, it is also necessary to point out that such national specificities seem to operate always within the directions imposed by sector- and technology-specific conditions.

Table 5.6 deals with the second issue identified above. Focusing on the period 1985–91, patenting firms have been grouped, for each country and each of the 49 technological classes, into "incumbents" and "entrants." The former group comprises those firms patenting in a given technological class in the period 1985–91, which already patented in the same technological class in the period 1978–84. The latter group includes those firms patenting for the first time in a given technological class in the period 1985–91. We have then calculated the contribution of incumbents and entrants to the share of patents held by the top four regions in the period 1985–91 (table 5.6).[11] This allows us to evaluate the extent to which spatial concentration of innovative activities is caused by the geographical agglomeration of new entrants which are attracted by the availability of localized knowledge spillovers – or, conversely, the extent to which

---

[9] In particular, the technological classes that can be included in this group are: metallurgy (21), machine tools (22), industrial automation (23), industrial machinery and equipment (24), materials handling apparatus (29), civil engineering (30), mechanical engineering (32), mechanical and electrical technologies (33), and measurement and control instruments (36).

[10] This group includes: food and tobacco (1), clothing (2), furniture (3), agriculture (4), natural and artificial fibers (17), and household electrical appliances (34).

[11] In other words, for each country and each technological class, the sum of columns relative to incumbents and entrants in table 5.6 measures the share of patents held by the top four regions in the period 1985–91 (reported in table 5.5).

Table 5.6. *Spatial concentration of innovations and the role of incumbents vs. entrants. Percentage share of patents held by the top four regions split according to the contribution of incumbents and entrants*

1985–1991, four countries, 49 technological classes

Technological classes	United Kingdom		France		Germany		Italy	
	Incumb.	Entrants	Incumb.	Entrants	Incumb.	Entrants	Incumb.	Entrants
1 Food and tobacco	72.88	18.64	26.81	48.55	37.21	8.91	25.61	62.20
2 Clothing and shoes	0.00	41.07	29.52	43.81	23.46	30.86	54.93	36.62
3 Furniture	12.15	34.58	11.83	60.36	15.48	27.96	16.55	65.47
4 Agriculture	17.02	34.04	3.57	50.71	11.38	33.53	7.81	56.25
5 Mining	27.27	41.21	45.49	51.93	19.42	28.10	0.00	85.29
6 Gas and hydrocarbons	53.03	34.09	67.57	29.73	56.61	10.47	32.81	56.25
7 Inorganic chemicals	53.50	20.00	55.56	39.03	59.36	9.10	16.67	66.67
8 Organic chemicals	80.84	6.86	76.00	20.11	78.80	0.99	59.28	27.79
9 Macromolecular compounds	74.96	8.64	72.88	25.54	81.86	2.58	61.00	31.54
10 New materials	35.11	26.95	60.58	34.20	52.77	8.38	22.92	58.33
11 Adhesives and resins	52.80	26.92	38.27	50.62	77.89	2.15	17.24	67.24
12 Biochemicals	50.72	28.26	54.08	35.10	54.54	4.82	23.13	65.67
13 Misc. chemical compounds	90.97	4.19	39.39	54.55	82.17	8.01	40.00	50.00
14 Chemical processes	43.74	21.13	57.26	31.30	38.05	14.77	14.71	60.66
15 Drugs	69.24	12.27	54.70	37.78	49.73	8.50	26.24	58.56
16 Medical preparations	32.85	27.83	27.38	46.21	34.58	18.30	13.04	65.61
17 Natural, artificial fibers	20.72	27.93	35.79	47.37	24.20	24.60	53.04	32.61
18 Chemical processes for fibers	53.04	15.65	19.72	60.56	58.94	7.93	2.53	78.48
19 Agricultural chemicals	63.09	12.75	50.60	38.55	66.77	8.54	24.00	60.00
20 Chemical processes for food	46.58	31.06	13.71	58.06	32.88	17.81	7.41	81.48

Table 5.6. (*cont.*)

1985–1991, four countries, 49 technological classes

Technological classes	United Kingdom		France		Germany		Italy	
	Incumb.	Entrants	Incumb.	Entrants	Incumb.	Entrants	Incumb.	Entrants
21 Metallurgy	54.37	16.27	52.41	43.68	52.57	19.27	20.59	57.35
22 Machine tools	25.00	43.75	48.89	44.44	43.75	25.83	17.24	58.62
23 Industrial automation	27.67	23.30	38.66	47.97	33.14	20.61	24.57	56.00
24 Industrial machinery	28.15	13.76	36.28	40.97	33.37	14.02	27.69	47.16
25 Agricultural machinery	23.66	36.56	68.92	11.26	58.00	9.25	25.00	65.63
26 Vehicles	44.94	16.35	62.05	25.84	49.54	9.67	45.95	46.87
27 Aircraft	60.00	19.26	73.54	25.40	50.33	19.21	8.33	91.67
28 Railways and ships	18.90	44.09	30.80	58.65	32.10	20.17	22.92	44.79
29 Materials handling appliances	23.74	19.18	29.41	45.51	19.39	17.06	22.50	54.86
30 Civil engineering	10.15	25.20	30.83	44.12	22.01	20.03	12.20	62.53
31 Engines, turbines, pumps	50.65	18.93	76.37	17.70	52.26	15.05	44.41	44.13
32 Mechanical engineering	45.05	16.32	62.82	23.51	32.62	13.90	26.96	57.59
33 Mechanical, electrical technologies	23.15	34.72	52.66	38.26	35.99	21.27	23.81	47.62
34 Household electrical appliances	17.86	35.71	42.14	29.64	35.58	16.30	28.72	52.82
35 Lighting systems	13.73	47.06	7.25	84.06	45.66	29.48	17.50	80.00
36 Measurement instruments	40.59	19.05	54.25	36.80	44.17	11.03	34.97	50.11
37 Laser technology	52.04	33.67	50.53	49.47	43.44	32.79	25.00	70.45
38 Optics and photography	62.43	19.67	67.73	28.29	58.91	8.46	24.19	57.26
39 Computers	37.41	36.45	59.18	37.03	58.07	12.66	48.89	45.56
40 Other office equipment	16.67	62.35	58.93	35.71	50.61	11.54	81.82	18.18

Table 5.6. (*cont.*)

1985–1991, four countries, 49 technological classes

Technological classes	United Kingdom		France		Germany		Italy	
	Incumb.	Entrants	Incumb.	Entrants	Incumb.	Entrants	Incumb.	Entrants
41 Electrical devices	45.99	18.13	53.06	35.68	44.22	9.49	20.10	55.33
42 Electronic components	56.84	17.86	67.62	28.38	63.53	8.80	60.78	30.53
43 Consumer electronics	52.33	26.46	54.36	39.43	61.36	4.34	29.03	61.29
44 Telecomm- unications	65.48	14.93	64.57	32.76	72.24	3.71	54.69	38.78
45 Multimedial systems	20.00	80.00	29.41	70.59	34.48	51.72	62.50	37.50
46 Arts, sports, toys	10.48	44.76	34.48	45.86	13.45	28.68	8.00	74.67
47 Weapons	56.25	22.22	42.86	54.08	65.55	3.54	18.37	77.55
48 Nuclear technology	62.50	37.50	81.74	17.42	74.27	4.15	15.38	84.62
49 Others	25.42	29.66	8.89	75.56	19.83	19.40	4.94	71.60

Source: EPO–CESPRI database.

such a tendency can be attributed to the continuous (cumulative) innovative effort carried out by incumbents.

Before examining the results reported in table 5.6, it is necessary to point out that empirical evidence (for brevity, not reported here) seems to indicate that entry of new innovators tends to agglomerate quite strongly in a few "core" regions within each country, thus confirming the importance of geographical proximity in mediating the transmission and communication of knowledge. For example, of the total number of "new" patents filed at EPO, slightly more than 41 percent was recorded in Lombardia (It), 61 percent in the Ile-de-France (Fra), 23 percent in Greater London (UK), and 10 percent in Oberbayern (Ger).

Looking at table 5.6, one again finds large differences across sectors in the contribution made by entrants and incumbents to the spatial agglomeration of innovative activities:

(1) The role played by new innovative firms is relatively reduced (with obvious cross-country differences) in most chemical and to a lesser extent electrical–electronic sectors. The share of patents in the top four regions accounted for by entrants is in fact significantly lower than the share held by incumbents, thus confirming that in these technological sectors the

spatial agglomeration of innovations is mainly driven by the (continuous over time) accumulation of technological capabilities which occurs within the boundaries of existing firms. Moreover, this result (coupled with the very low rates of innovative entry characterizing these industries, see Malerba and Orsenigo, 1995) also suggests that innovative natality concerns a "fringe" of firms located in marginal regions.[12]

(2) In most mechanical (and to a lesser extent, traditional) technological sectors, entrants are responsible for a relatively larger share of patents held by the top four regions as compared with incumbents, therefore suggesting that in these technological classes the geographical concentration of innovative activities is mostly determined by processes of accumulation of technological capabilities that take place within a restricted set of regions, and involves a rather large base of innovators.

In summary, these results broadly suggest the existence of large differences across technological classes in both the spatial and the sectoral organization of innovative activities. Such differences can arguably be attributed to the working of sector- and technology-specific conditions (i.e. technological regimes) which structure the way innovative activities are organized at the sectoral and geographical level. On the one hand, the high spatial concentration of innovations characterizing the group of chemical and electrical–electronic technological classes is related to the innovative effort of a few (large) firms which persistently accumulate over time innovative capabilities within their own boundaries. On the other hand, the spatial agglomeration of innovations characterizing the group of mechanical engineering technological classes (and to a much lesser extent, traditional classes) has to do more with the existence of a large population of small and often new firms, localized within a restricted number of regions, which persistently innovate as a collective body and whose hierarchy is ever-changing leaving no room for the emergence of dominant market positions. These differences across sectors can also be related to two different notions of cumulativeness. While in the former group of technological classes cumulativeness at the firm level is likely to play a dominant role (as witnessed by the continuous innovation of a few incumbents who have in their hands the largest share of innovative activities), in the latter group of sectors spatial cumulativeness (i.e. the persistent accumulation of technological capabilities within specific areas which proceeds through the involvement of a large and always renewed base of innovators) is more likely to be the factor responsible for the spatial clustering of innovations.

The role played by cumulativeness in explaining regions' technological performance is briefly explored in the next section.

---

[12] Empirical evidence (not reported here) indicates that, in these technological sectors, new innovators are remarkably more dispersed across geographical areas than the overall population of innovators.

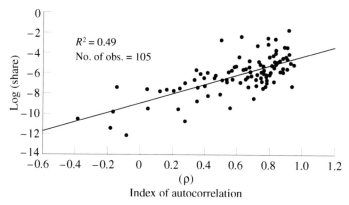

5.1 Spatial cumulativeness and regions' technical performance
Note: First-order autocorrelation coefficient and log share of patents at EPO, 1978–91.

Regions' technological performance: the role of spatial cumulativeness

The previous discussion has pointed out two major factors contributing to the shape of the spatial organization of innovative activities: the "localized" nature of knowledge externalities and the cumulative nature of innovative efforts. Both factors crucially differ across technological sectors, depending on the prevailing technological regime producing different degrees of spatial concentration of innovative activities. However, while there have been attempts in recent times to evaluate the extent to which knowledge externalities are localized (Jaffe, 1989a; Jaffe, Trajtenberg, and Henderson, 1993), no one to date has tried to investigate the extent to which persistence over time in the accumulation of innovative capabilities takes place within specific geographical areas and to link such a phenomenon to regions' technological performance. Indeed, the notion of technological cumulativeness has thus far been analyzed mainly at the technological, sectoral, and organizational levels (Rosenberg, 1976; Nelson and Winter, 1982).

In this section, a very rough measure of spatial cumulativeness is introduced and discussed: the first-order autocorrelation coefficient of patents held by regions. Such measure has been plotted against the share of total European patents held by each region in the period 1978–91, a rough proxy of regions' innovative performance. Actually, the log of regions' share of patents has been represented in figure 5.1 for graphical purposes. The figure can be interpreted as follows: moving from the left-hand to the right-hand side along the horizontal axis, the degree of regional cumulativeness – that is, persistence over time in creative accumulation – increases; on the other hand, moving from the bottom-side to the top-side of the graph along the vertical axis, the regions' share of total patents increases. The data clearly suggest the existence of a significant and positive correlation between the degree of spatial cumulativeness and the regions' technological performance. Higher values of the autocorrelation coefficient are in fact generally associated with higher shares of the total number of patents. This result then implies that regions' technological performance are strongly related to the extent to which firms located there continuously accumulate innovative capabilities over time.

Conclusions

This chapter has focused attention on the spatial dimension of technical change. After a long period during which the subject was largely neglected, several recent contributions have pointed out that geographically "localized" knowledge externalities and the cumulative nature of technical change may generate a strong tendency of innovative activities to cluster spatially. The major claim of this chapter has been that, beside such a common trend, industrial sectors largely differ not only in terms of the degree of spatial concentration, but also in the way geographical clustering is achieved and the relationship with sectoral patterns of innovation. In particular, it has been argued that such differences across sectors can be largely explained by technology-specific factors (i.e. technological regimes).

Four key dimensions of technological regimes have been considered: opportunity, appropriability, cumulativeness conditions, the nature of the knowledge base underpinning firms' innovative activities. Such variables fundamentally determine the influence of space on innovative activities by affecting: (a) the nature and the sources of knowledge, (b) the mechanisms supporting knowledge transmission and communication, (c) the relevance of knowledge spillovers, and (d) the extent to which the accumulation of innovative capabilities takes place cumulatively within specific areas or occurs within the boundaries of specific firms. More generally, it has been argued that different combinations of the above-mentioned variables essentially determine different spatial patterns of innovation across sectors, by affecting competition and selection processes which operate on firms located in different geographical areas. Some simple relationships between these dimensions and possible cases of spatial patterns of innovation have also been discussed.

With such a theoretical background, the present chapter has empirically tested for the existence of different spatial patterns of innovation across sectors. Patent data have been used at the firm and geographical level. The main results which have emerged from the analysis can be summarized as follows:

(1) *Innovative activities are generally characterized by high degrees of geographical concentration and of stability in the hierarchy of innovative regions.* This result seems to provide further support to the hypothesis that "localized"

increasing returns to knowledge play an important role in producing a tendency of innovative activities to cluster spatially. Moreover, an important dimension which has been broadly defined as "spatial cumulativeness" (i.e. the degree of persistence with which regions accumulate technological capabilities over time) emerges as a fundamental explanatory variable of the spatial concentration of innovative activities and regions' technological performance.

(2) *Spatial patterns of innovation appear to systematically differ across technological sectors.* Furthermore, remarkable similarities across countries in the spatial patterns of innovative activities of each technological class seem also to emerge. This result therefore supports the idea that industry-specific and technology-specific factors (closely related to the features of technological regimes and the properties of technical knowledge) play a fundamental role in shaping the spatial patterns of innovation across countries. This result fruitfully complements the findings of recent empirical studies which have demonstrated that "technological imperatives" and sector- and technology-specific factors fundamentally determine the sectoral organization of innovative processes.

(3) *Three major groups of sectors which systematically differ according to the sectoral as well as spatial organization of innovative activities* may be identified:

  – A first group comprises most of the traditional sectors and is characterized by quite a large diffusion of innovative capabilities, across both firms and regions. The relatively simple and codified knowledge base characterizing these technological sectors is such that spatial proximity is not likely to play an important role in affecting the location of innovative units. Moreover, the limited set of available technological opportunities and the low level of appropriability tend to prevent specific firms from gaining a dominant position within the group of innovative firms.

  – A second group of sectors includes most of the mechanical and a few electrical sectors. Such a group of sectors is characterized by a peculiar combination of medium–high degrees of geographical concentration, low degrees of sectoral concentration, a major role played by new innovative firms, and spatially concentrated innovative natality. These results seem therefore to suggest that innovation processes in such sectors tends to have a "collective" and "localized" nature. The high rates of birth of new innovative firms recorded in such sectors, while being diffused among a rather large number of locations, do not actually spread throughout the economic space, but tend to remain within a well defined set of regions. The accumulation of technological capabilities and expertise takes place at a local level through the involvement of a large set of (small and new) firms which persistently innovate as a collective body. Competition and selection here takes place among *clusters* of firms located within specific areas, rather than simply among firms.

– Finally, a third group of sectors includes most chemical as well as electronic sectors. It is characterized by a combination of high degrees of sectoral and spatial concentration, low rates of innovative natality and a dominant role played by a few (large) incumbents. These results suggest that technological competition in such sectors takes place among a "stable" and very restricted number of firms and locations. "Cumulativeness" here refers to a "core" of (large) firms which persistently accumulate innovative capabilities within their own boundaries and which are the real engines of regions' innovative performance.

This chapter has been mainly exploratory and it leaves open several directions for future research. In the first place, more statistical work should be done in order to better assess differences across sectors in the spatial organization of innovative activities. In particular, a more satisfactory measure of spatial as well as firms' cumulativeness should be devised. In the second place, patent data should be coupled with other economic and productive data at both firm and spatial level. This is required in order to control for the extent to which spatial distribution of innovations depends on the location of productive activities. Finally, country-specific factors should be also explicitly included in the analysis in order to grasp the effects induced by the peculiar history of industrial development of each national system of innovation.

References

Arthur, B.W. (1990). "Silicon Valley Locational Clusters: When do Increasing Returns Imply Monopoly?," *Mathematical Social Sciences*, 19, 235–51

Breschi, S. (1995). "La dimensione spaziale del mutamento tecnologico: una proposta interpretativa," *Economia e Politica Industriale*, 86, 179–207

Cohen W.M. (1995). "Empirical Studies of Innovative Activity and Performance," in P. Stoneman, (ed.), *Handbook of the Economics of Innovation and Technical Change*, Oxford: Blackwell

Cohen W.M. and R.C. Levin (1989). "Empirical Studies of Innovation and Market Structure," in R. Schmalensee and Willig R.D. (eds.) *Handbook of Industrial Organization, volume II*, pp.1060–1107. Amsterdam: Elsevier Science Publisher, Cohen, W.M., R.C. Levin and D.C. Mowery (1987). "Firm Size and R&D Intensity: A Re-examination." *Journal of Industrial Economics*, 35(4), 543–65

Dosi, G. (1988). "Sources, Procedure, and Microeconomic Effects of Innovation," *Journal of Economic Literature*, 26, 1120–71

Feldman, M.P. (1994). *The Geography of Innovation*, Dordrecht: Kluwer Academic Publishers

Feller, I. (1971). "The Urban Location of United States Inventions, 1860–1910," *Explorations in Economic History*, 8, 285–303

Grossman, G. and E. Helpman (1991). *Innovation and Growth in the Global Economy*. Cambridge, Mass.: MIT Press

Hägerstrand, T. (1966). *Innovation Diffusion as a Spatial Process*, Chicago: Chicago University Press

Hippel, von E. (1988). *The Sources of Innovation*, New York: Oxford University Press

Howells, J. (1989). "The Location and Organization of Research and Development: New Horizons," *Research Policy*, 19, 133–46

Jaffe, A.B. (1986). "Technological Opportunity and Spillovers from R&D: Evidence from Firms' Patents, Profits, and Market Value," *American Economic Review*, 76, 984–1001

(1989a). "Real Effects of Academic Research," *American Economic Review*, 79, 957–70

(1989b). "Characterizing the Technological Position of Firms, with Application to Quantifying Technological Opportunity and Research Spillovers," *Research Policy*, 18, 87–97

Jaffe, A.B., M. Trajtenberg, and R. Henderson (1993). "Geographic Localization of Knowledge Spillovers as Evidenced by Patent Citations," *Quarterly Journal of Economics*, 63, 577–98

Kline, S.J. and N. Rosenberg (1986). "An Overview of Innovation," in R. Landau and N. Rosenberg (eds.), *The Positive Sum Strategy*, New York: National Academy Press

Krugman P. (1991a), *Geography and Trade*. Cambridge, Mass.: MIT Press

(1991b), "History and Industry Location: The Case of the Manufacturing Belt," *American Economic Review, Papers and Proceedings*, 81, 80–83

Levin R.C., A.K. Klevorick, R.R. Nelson, and S.G. Winter (1987). "Appropriating the Returns from Industrial Research and Development," *Brookings Papers on Economic Activity*, 3, 783–820

Lundvall B.A. (ed.) (1993). *National Systems of Innovation*, London: Pinter Publishers

Malecki E.J. (1980). "Corporate Organization of R&D and the Location of Technological Activities," *Regional Studies*, 14, 219–35

(1983). "Technology and Regional Development: A Survey," *International Regional Science Review*, 18, 89–125

Malerba, F. and L. Orsenigo (1990). "Technological Regimes and Patterns of Innovation: A Theoretical and Empirical Investigation of the Italian Case," in A. Heertje and M. Perlman (eds.), *Evolving Technologies and Market Structure*, Ann Arbor: Michigan University Press, 283–306

(1993). "Technological Regimes and Firm Behavior," *Industrial and Corporate Change*, 2(1), 45–71

(1995). "Schumpeterian Patterns of Innovation," *Cambridge Journal of Economics*, 19(1), 47–66

(1996). "Schumpeterian Patterns of Innovation are Technology Specific," *Research Policy*, 25(3), 451–78

Nelson, R.R. (ed.) (1993). *National Systems of Innovation: A Comparative Study*, Oxford and New York: Oxford University Press

Nelson, R.R. and S.G. Winter (1982). *An Evolutionary Theory of Economic Change*. Cambridge, Mass. and London: The Belknap Press of Harvard University Press

Pavitt, K. (1984). "Sectoral Patterns of Technical Change: Towards a Taxonomy and a Theory," *Research Policy*, 343–73

Pred, A. (1966). *The Spatial Dynamics of US Urban–Industrial Growth, 1800–1914. Interpretative and Theoretical Essays*. Cambridge, Mass.: MIT Press

Romer, P. (1986). "Increasing Returns and Long-run Growth," *Journal of Political Economy*, 94, 1002–37

(1990). "Endogenous Technological Change," *Journal of Political Economy*, 92, s71–s102

Rosenberg, N. (1976). *Perspectives on Technology*. Cambridge: Cambridge University Press

Storper, M. (1992). "The Limits to Globalization: Technology Districts and International Trade," *Economic Geography*, 68(1), 60–93

Thompson, W.R. (1962). "Locational Differences in Inventive Effort and Their Determinants," in R.R. Nelson (ed.), *The Rate and Direction of Inventive Activity*, Princeton: Princeton University Press, 253–72

Winter, S.G. (1987). "Knowledge as Strategic Asset," in D.J. Teece (ed.), *The Competitive Challenge: Strategies for Industrial Innovation and Renewal*, Cambridge, Mass.: Ballinger, 159–84

6 Innovation and the size of industrial clusters in Europe

G. M. Peter Swann

Introduction

One characteristic of the organization of innovative activities is that high-technology industries tend to be concentrated in clusters. This has frequently been observed in the United States, and also in Europe. Two key questions for European strategy towards high technology industries are therefore: (1) Are the forces that have reinforced high-technology clusters in the United States also relevant in the European context? (2) Does the US experience give any clues about the ideal size of these high-technology clusters?

The answers to these two questions are of vital importance for European policy. If the forces generating clusters in US high-technology industries also apply in Europe, then it is reasonable to apply some of the lessons learnt in the US case to the promotion of clusters in Europe. In this case, moreover, we have much to learn from any American experience that sheds light on: (1) the critical mass a cluster has to achieve before it can function effectively; and (2) the size at which a cluster starts to saturate and stops growing. If, by contrast, the forces at work are significantly different, then a different strategy is called for.

This chapter seeks a preliminary answer to these two questions. It is organized in three parts. First, we analyze from a theoretical point of view, under what conditions – and why – industrial clusters would be expected to exhibit a life-cycle. This leads us into a discussion of critical mass and saturation. Second, we summarize some of our recent empirical work on the forces that generate and sustain clusters in high-technology industries in the United States, and see if these are equivalent to those that appear to be at work in Europe. Third, we draw out the implications of evidence on critical mass and saturation in the context of US high-technology clusters

This chapter draws extensively on earlier work by the author, summarized in Swann, Prevezer, and Stout (1998), and uses this to examine the critical mass of clusters in Europe. I am grateful to Martha Prevezer, David Stout, Paul Temple, Simon Shohet, Rui Baptista, and especially Walter Elkan and Morris Teubal for very helpful discussions.

for the European/national balance in policy towards clusters. The second and third sections draw heavily on Swann (1998a, 1998b) and on some results in Baptista and Swann (1998a), but the fourth section is entirely new.

The rise, fall, and revival of clusters

The aim of this first part of the chapter is to describe the life-cycle of the industrial cluster, and the spread of innovative activities between clusters of different vintages.

Much analysis of clusters has focused on the initial formative stages, or what we shall call here the *rise* of clusters. In these stages some form of positive feedback mechanism reinforces the development of clusters. But it is important to remember that this positive feedback lasts only for a limited period. With most clusters, even the most successful, some sort of diminishing returns sets in beyond a certain point – and perhaps even negative feedback. Once again, the clusters that reach maturity do not necessarily then decline into oblivion. A few of them experience a *renaissance* or revival in a new age with a new set of industries.

Such historical episodes have been well documented for a number of cities. Our concern here is less with the historical record than with investigating a class of simple analytical models in which such cycles take place.

The literature on clustering: a very brief introduction

While the work of Porter (1990) and Krugman (1991) has done much to remind economists that geography matters, and to revive interest in the concept of industrial clusters, it must be remembered that work on this theme has a long and distinguished history. Marshall (1920) was perhaps the first economist to analyze the geographical concentration of production activity. It was from observing these "industrial districts" that Marshall developed the concept of external economies. In a famous passage, Marshall observes:

When an industry has chosen a locality for itself it is likely to stay there long: so great are the advantages which people following the same skilled trade get from near neighborhood to one another ... And presently subsidiary trade grows up in the neighborhood, supplying it with implements and materials, organizing its traffic and in many ways conducing to the economy of its material. (1920, 271–2)

For Marshall, the benefits of locating in a cluster (or industrial district) are related to the availability of skilled labor and intermediate goods suppliers, and also to the easy transmission and discussion of new ideas.

But while Marshall's analysis was perhaps the first by an economist, the

phenomenon of clustering was well recognized by historians of the industrial revolution. Mathias (1983, 119–20) gives a fascinating summary of
how the British cotton industry, though initially dispersed, was drawn into
a cluster around Manchester:

the mills concentrated in the more populated regions ... where communications
were easier and cheaper ... The pull of Liverpool and Manchester also became
important as marketing centres, the first for cotton buying, the other for sales. Very
shortly, other external economies developed. ... All these things exercised a cen-
tripetal pull on the cotton industry

Subsequent studies of these phenomena emanate from five distinct traditions. (Here I list only a very few select references. For a much fuller list of
references, I refer the interested reader to a valuable literature review by
Baptista, 1998.)

The first is the important sub-discipline of *urban and regional economics.*
This derives from the pioneering work on location theory by Weber (1928)
and Lösch (1954), and the related theory of *poles de croissance* due to
Perroux (1950). We could perhaps also add to this the tradition of locational models within industrial economics deriving from Hotelling's (1929)
study of ice-cream sellers on a beach.

The second tradition is that of *geography.* Economic geographers have
long been concerned with the phenomenon of clustering, both at an empirical level and at a theoretical level. I cannot do justice to this literature here,
so I refer simply to two reviews – Amin and Goddard (1986) and Conti,
Malecki, and Oinas (1995) – which summarize some of the most important
current issues from the geographers' perspective.

The third tradition is *history.* The magnificent studies of the city by historians and economic historians such as Mumford (1961), Jacobs (1961,
1969), Briggs (1968), Bairoch (1988), and others, capture some of the richness that is sometimes lost in economic analysis.

The fourth tradition can be seen as a development of this historical tradition in that it emphasizes how "history matters" while it is analytical in
style. It might be called the *path-dependent approach* to economics, including the work of Arthur (1990), David and Rosenbloom (1990), Krugman
(1991), Brezis and Krugman (1993).

The fifth tradition is within mainstream economics itself, in what is commonly called "new growth theory" (Romer, 1986, 1990; Grossman and
Helpman, 1992) and in the empirical study of regional spillovers (notably
by Jaffe, 1986, among others).

There are also a large number of empirical industry or technology studies
that have made a substantial contribution to our understanding of clustering as a phenomenon. I will simply list here the work of two authors:

Saxenian (1985, 1994) and Dorfman (1985). This work is interesting because it is able to document the rich complex of socio-economic factors that determine the pattern of clustering observed in high-technology industries, and the relative success of different clusters at different stages of the cluster life-cycle. Saxenian, in particular, shows how a cluster made up of small and medium-sized enterprises having relatively open interaction with each other will be much more vibrant than a cluster made up of a few large vertically integrated multinationals.

The analysis of clustering: an overview

In this section, we describe a simple model with three basic features, which is capable of generating the sorts of cluster life-cycles of interest to us in this chapter. We analyze the growth of clusters in terms of two variables – first, the extent of entry and, second, the growth of incumbent firms in a cluster. The three basic features are as follows:

Agglomeration externalities and positive feedback

It is assumed that firms in clusters grow faster than those in isolation, and/or that clusters attract a higher rate of entry at least during the early and growth phases of the life-cycle for a particular industry. This happens because of agglomeration economies, which impact on entry and growth and hence lead to a form of positive feedback. It is assumed moreover that these effects operate more strongly within a confined geographical area, in part because of the tacit nature of much technological knowledge (Pavitt, 1987).

Congestion effects

It is assumed that the rate of entry and the rate of growth start to tail off (and perhaps even decline) in very large clusters – essentially because the costs of locating in a cluster start to detract from the benefits.

Convergence of technologies

Two technologies, and the industries producing them, are assumed to be *distinct* if the strength of industry A in cluster X has no effect on the rate of growth and rate of entry into industry B at that cluster – and vice versa. The technologies are assumed to be converging when the strength of A in cluster X does have a positive effect on the rate of growth and entry into industry B at that cluster – or vice versa. (We analyze below whether this relationship is likely to be symmetric, and suggest that symmetry is unlikely.)

These three features, and the relative importance of them at different stages of the life-cycle of a cluster, can offer a simple, but we think quite compelling account of the rise, fall and revival of industrial clusters.

Rise, fall, and renaissance

The essence of this cycle is as follows. When a cluster starts to emerge, ahead of other regions, it attracts further entry and firm growth is faster, so it forges further ahead. Beyond a certain size, the costs of locating in the cluster start to rise, but the cluster may still be the preferred location if the benefits are high enough. But as the industry enters its maturity stage, the benefits of clustering start to tail off, and eventually the costs of clustering outweigh the benefits. This is where the second feature of the model starts to dominate.

At this stage, the cluster will be reaching its peak, but will not have entered the decline phase as such. The decline of the cluster starts when the industry itself enters the decline stage of its life-cycle. The cluster is left with large mature firms in a mature industry. These are not, by their very nature, the sorts of organizations that generate significant spillovers, and while the cost of locating at this mature cluster may start to fall, so also do the benefits.

As new industries emerge, firms in those industries may then be faced with location decisions of the following sort. Should they locate in an old cluster, where they have little commonality with incumbents, where the established infrastructure is dated, and where congestion costs are still relatively high, though admittedly declining? Or should they locate in a new cluster where the incumbents, though new and small, are generating the sorts of spillovers that attract entrants, are based in more relevant industries, and where the infrastructure is better? Not surprisingly, many choose the new cluster, and so the decline of the old cluster, based on traditional industries continues, with few firms in new industries to replace the old.

This process could in principle continue until the old cluster disintegrates. But in a few cases the third feature of the model comes into play. Convergence between traditional industries and old industries means that the mature and declining cluster may in fact offer an attractive location for certain types of entrants in newer industries. Computer services' companies, for example, find it attracting to locate near to mature companies in traditional industries, who are starting to exploit the potential of computer technologies in reviving their business. Or, indeed, computer software companies find that the most powerful attractor in locational terms is no longer a strong hardware base in that cluster, but a strong publishing sector with a large stock of intellectual property rights. When old and new technologies converge in this way, then the mature cluster becomes once again an attractive location. And with luck (or planning) the new entrants attracted in this way themselves act as attractors for a new generation of entrants.

This process of convergence is not the only process by which old clusters may be revived. In principle, this could happen simply through the price mechanism. The oldest, derelict, clusters are also the cheapest, and this on its own can attract a wave of new entry. In fact this is not very compelling as an explanation on its own. No doubt the price mechanism plays some role, but so too does technological convergence. Of course, the policy of urban renewal can be seen as an attempt to revive moribund clusters – not always with success, however (Jacobs, 1961).

In the next three sections we explore each stage of this cycle of rise, fall and *renaissance* in more detail.

Rise of clusters

A very simple model, which does however have all the required properties, is in two parts. Let entry of firms into industry i at cluster c be defined as E_{ic} and let the rate of growth of firms in industry i at cluster c be defined as G_{ic}. Then we shall refer to two measures of the *strength* of a cluster $\mathbf{c}$: one is the strength of cluster c in industry i (S_{ic}), and the other is the strength of cluster c in other industries j (S_{jc}). In some of our recent empirical analysis (see p. 115 below) we have used estimates of employment as a measure of the strength of a particular industry in a particular cluster:

$$E_{ic} = f(S_{ic}, S_{jc})$$
$$G_{ic} = g(S_{ic}, S_{jc})$$

A simple case is where $df/dS_{ic} > 0$ and $dg/dS_{ic} > 0$, but $df/dS_{jc} = dg/dS_{jc} = 0$. This means that entry to industry i is higher and firms in i grow faster in clusters that are already strong in i, but the cluster's strength in other industries j does nothing to attract entry or promote growth.

In this case, it is easy to see that when a cluster in industry i gets ahead of rival clusters, it will tend to forge further ahead. Moreover, in the absence of any cross-sectoral effects to attract entry or promote growth, the model will tend to predict that clusters specialize in a single industry. At least, there is no advantage to the cluster in diversifying its industrial base. And while there is no disadvantage either in the model as it stands, it is not difficult to see that if congestion effects are a function of $S_{ic} + S_{jc}$, then there are clear merits in specialization, and clear costs in diversification. To put it simply, if like firms convey benefits on incumbents while unlike firms do not, then if space is limited, it is better to group together with like firms.

Of course this simple case ($df/dS_{ic} > 0$, $dg/dS_{ic} > 0$, $df/dS_{jc} = dg/dS_{jc} = 0$) is not the only possibility. As an empirical matter, the magnitudes (and even the signs) of these derivatives are not likely to be constant. Moreover, the signs and magnitudes are likely to depend on the level of aggregation at which one is operating. We deal with these two points in turn.

One aspect of this is the sort of congestion effect noted above, so that there are diminishing returns to clustering. More subtly, we have found in our research (see p. 118) that the relationship between the strength of the cluster and entry may follow a bell-shaped curve. Below a certain size (the critical mass) the cluster does not attract entry, and the effect of increases in strength on entry (df/dS) are small. But when this critical mass is reached, entry starts to take off sharply (df/dS gets large, and d^2f/dS^2 is maximized). Then as the cluster grows it reaches a point of peak entry, at which $df/dS = 0$. Note that at this point the cluster is still growing, as entry is high. But beyond this point, entry starts to drop off and it then approaches zero.

In short, the magnitudes and signs of these derivatives may be very dependent on the size of the cluster. They may also be dependent on the stage of the industry in its life-cycle. Thus in the formative (introduction and growth) stage of the life cycle, geographical proximity may be critical to tacit technology transfer – which is so essential to industry development – and hence the positive effects are large. But by the maturity stage, the technological knowledge that requires to be transferred is largely codified, so that geographical proximity is no longer such an important issue, and the derivatives used in the model are much smaller.

The second point is that the signs of these derivatives depend on the level of aggregation at which one is working. In one of our recent empirical studies (Baptista and Swann, 1998b) it appears that when one is working at a fairly aggregated level (2-digit SIC industries, for example), there is a clear dichotomy: the effect of strength in "own industry" (i) on growth and entry is positive, while the effect of strength in "other industries" (j) is negative (rather than zero).

When the level of aggregation is much smaller, more subtle effects come into play. In a study of the US computing industry (see p. 116) we have looked at the effect of cluster strength on entry and growth when the industry is broken down into eight sectors (this is at or below the 4-digit level of aggregation). As with the aggregated studies, we find that the effect of other sectors on incumbent growth is negative (though often statistically insignificant), but (in contrast) we find that the effect of other sectors on entry can be positive and rather significant. And moreover, while the effect of own-sector strength on growth is positive (as with aggregated studies), the effect on entry can be negative. This can easily be rationalized by asking, "who would enter a densely populated cluster?"

Why are the results so dependent on the level of aggregation? Consider entry by a firm X. Suppose that companies in related, but not identical, fields to X attract X's entry. On the other hand, suppose that companies that are identical to X may deter X's entry – a little reflection on the Cournot model of oligopolistic competition is enough to convince us that this second assumption is fair. At a *high* level of aggregation, related firms come into the *same* category as identical firms, and so the net effect of own-sector strength on entry may be positive. Conversely, at a *low* level of aggregation, these related firms which attract entry come into a different sector, while the identical firms count as the same sector and deter entry.

Maturity and decline of clusters

The last sub-section showed that positive feedback in the clustering process has its limits. Indeed, beyond a certain point congestion limits the attractiveness of an existing cluster for new entry – particularly if the industry located at that cluster is entering a maturity phase in which geographical proximity is not so important for technology transfer and industrial development.

The maturity of clusters arises (in the language of the bell-shaped entry curve of p. 118) because the cluster has reached a size at which further entry is no longer attracted – and perhaps the growth externality to incumbent firms no longer operates. But this of itself does not explain decline. Entry may stop, and the factors that promote growth may disappear, but that simply implies stabilization at a particular size. It does not imply decline. To explain that, we have to invoke two additional – and we suggest quite common – effects. First, that the industry located at a mature cluster is in the decline stage of its industry life-cycle. And, second, that the cluster fails to attract sufficient new entrants into new industries to compensate for the exit and decline of mature incumbents.

First consider the maturity of industries in mature clusters. We saw above that in some circumstances, clusters would tend to specialize in one industry, and at least during the growth phase of the cluster this specialization is advantageous. Specialization becomes less desirable, however, later in the cluster life-cycle. For if the cluster depends on one industry (or all the industries in the cluster mature at the same time) then maturity and decline – when they arrive – hit the cluster very hard. It is perhaps invidious to single out cities that have suffered especially because of an over-reliance on one industry, but examples (at some stages of their respective histories) include Detroit (cars), Glasgow (shipbuilding), and Manchester (cotton).

Now we turn to the second characteristic required for the decline of clusters: that the cluster fails to attract sufficient new entrants into new industries to compensate for the exit and decline of mature incumbents. The question is "why?" To approach an answer, let me draw an analogy to the Leontief input–output table. This table indicates how growth in sector X generates demand for the output of sector Y. As such, it could be described as a *demand-side* sector-to-sector spillover chart. Imperfect as they may be, input–output tables of this sort exist, and are rather widely trusted. If we had the equivalent *supply-side* sector-to-sector spillover chart, then we would know which industries *attract* which other – where I use the word "attract" to describe attractive forces that derive from the sorts of agglomeration economies defined above. Then we could answer the question.

Our econometric models (see p. 116) map out a set of sector-to-sector supply-side attractive forces: how does strength in sector X attract entry into sector Y? In biotechnology we find few cross-sectoral effects, but in computing these cross-sectoral effects are rather significant. There is no doubt that it would be difficult to calibrate such a matrix on an economy-wide basis. But this matrix would be so helpful in explaining why some clusters have industries which – even if mature – are still capable of attracting successors, while other clusters are dominated by the sorts of industries and firms which are incapable of that.

Some have conjectured that there is a hierarchy of industries on a spectrum between "introvert" at one end and "extrovert" at the other. Some would place the chemical industry at the extrovert end of the spectrum. Indeed, to quote the chapter by Clow and Clow (1958, 230): "The chemical industry is the most polygamous of all industries." In our current frame of reference, this means that the supply-side sector-to-sector spillover chart should show that the chemical industry is unequalled as a suitor – it forms alliances with many other industries, or generates spillovers to many other industries. A cluster strong in this particular industry should be capable of surviving the decline of that industry – essentially because it is good at attracting successor industries to the same location.

Some would place distribution and retailing towards the introvert end of the spectrum – though it has to be said that there is limited evidence for this. The argument is that if (in effect) we knew this invisible supply-side input–output table, it would indicate that while distribution and retailing sectors were undoubtedly successful at absorbing spillovers from manufacturing industry, they were less successful at generating spillovers to the successive generation of entrants.

We can sum up this section as follows. Clusters enter maturity, and can start to decline when the cluster gets large enough to suffer from congestion, when the indigenous industries in that cluster start to decline. The decline is particularly serious when the indigenous industries and firms are ones that do not attract the next generation of entrants into new industries, because they are not generating spillovers that attract entry. The lucky clusters are those that sustain a mix of industries and firms which continue to attract entry – as we see below.

Revival (renaissance) of clusters

We have seen why some clusters enter a phase of unremitting decline. The next issue for our attention is why some clusters – far from entering oblivion – actually recover in a most spectacular way.

Let us start with the example of London. London seems to be an evergreen cluster. Is this because London is a cluster that through luck or design happens to have mature industries which attract the new industries? Or is it simply, as many have put it (including Porter, 1990), that London is a nice place to live? Not, of course, that the latter explanation – London's beneficent industrial archaeology – is independent of its economic history. A city that invests a large share of its (large) economic rents in cultural infrastructure can expect to survive as a "cluster". But I submit that London's success as a cluster also derives from its history of attracting a diverse mix of industries, and its pre-eminent success at exploiting convergence between technologies.

Now let us turn to cities or clusters that recover. Boston is cited as a city that declined as an agricultural center and port, but revived as high-technology center building in some part at least on its retained cultural capital – including its world-renowned universities (Dorfman, 1985).

The theory of business cycles offers some obvious parallels here. The macroeconomy can recover because of the price mechanism: if investment is cheap enough then firms will invest, and investment-led growth will ensue. On the other hand, many macroeconomists following Keynes have cast doubt on whether the price mechanism alone is the key to macroeconomic recovery. Keynes referred instead to the vital role of *animal spirits*. And we can draw a parallel here: just as macroeconomic recovery is related to qualitative business expectations, so also is cluster recovery a function of qualitative factors. The key issue, as we saw on p. 107, is for mature (even moribund) clusters to attract new entry into new industries at that cluster. If the price mechanism won't make this happen, then it must happen through the attractors, or supply-side spillovers.

It seems clear that some entry phases into mature but *renascent* clusters are generated by attractive mature industries. An important concept here is *convergence* between technologies. If two technologies (i and j) are distinct, then however strong a cluster may be in industry i that strength does nothing to attract entry into j – and vice versa. On the other hand, if two technologies (i and j) converge, that means either that a cluster strong in industry A generates spillovers that attract entry into j, or vice versa, or possibly both. (We return to this question of the direction of effects shortly.) If industry i generates spillovers of some value to new entrants in industry j, then the cluster, while an early center for industry/technology i will subsequently become a center for j. Convergence therefore implies a degree of complementarity in the two industries or technologies.

This convergence, as much as movements in relative prices, is the key to cluster revival. It also makes very clear just how important is what I shall call here "industrial archaeology" to the future development of clusters.

Swann (1996) carried out a simulation study of the growth of industrial clusters based on an econometric analysis of entry and growth patterns in computer industry clusters. This found that single-technology clusters, while they might grow faster in the formative stages, did not have the lasting power of diversified clusters. The key concept here is an exceptionally evolutionary one: "Diversity promotes longevity."

The process of convergence

But why and how does convergence happen? And are its effects symmetric (i attracts j and j attracts i) or not?

Let us start with the question of symmetry, because it is easy to answer. There can be no general supposition that convergence has symmetric effects on the two industries i and j. Our computer industry study illustrates this asymmetry. Even if it seems slightly counter-intuitive, software and hardware could be said to "converge" in the sense that clusters with strength in hardware and components are more successful at attracting entry into software. But the attraction is not symmetric: clusters with strength in software do not attract entry into hardware. Indeed, software did not appear to be an attractor in that study. This asymmetry is not surprising given that software grew out of the hardware industry, and this is an important part of the process of "attraction" identified in our US computer industry model. And when we turn to convergence between a mature technology and a new one, symmetry would be most unlikely. The strength of the mature industry at a cluster may start to attract some sorts of entrants into the new industry. But it is unlikely that the strength of the new industry will attract entry into the old – though it may serve to promote growth in the old.

Now let us turn finally to the harder question – indeed the hardest question in this entire field. Why, and how, do technologies – and hence industries – converge? First let us consider an example. One of the most widely quoted examples is the convergence of telecommunications and information technology (IT) (Arnold and Guy, 1986) – though some commentators are skeptical about the real extent of convergence between these two industries. At the simplest level a growing proportion of telephone traffic is in fact in the form of digital messages. At the next level, we find that some computing and electronics companies start to specialize in the branches of technology required to make this interaction happen (modems, communications cards, digital exchanges, etc.). At the next level we start to find that the giants in one industry start to diversify into the other: thus AT&T started to make computers. Systems houses start to offer on-line databases. Alternatively joint ventures start to blossom that cut across the two technologies (Hagedoorn and Schakenraad, 1992).

Indeed, what we have observed with IT recently is that some of these joint ventures (JVs) (notably with multimedia) have cut into a variety of traditional industries. The key to success in multimedia, for example, may be intellectual property rights over software and images rather than technology *per se*. A key component of multimedia strategy is to have the right publisher(s) – with IP rights over a wide range of "software" (images, music, text, poetry, and so on). If geography matters in the multimedia industry, then it seems likely that the leading clusters of this industry will be those with a strong base in the "publishing" industries (broadly defined). It is more plausible to expect the great galleries, recording studios, television-producing communities, and so on to attract computer industry entrants than vice versa.

IT is converging on most industries, in the sense that many industries have created entry opportunities to supply IT applications for that industry. In the quote above, "the chemical industry is the most polygamous of all industries," we should perhaps really replace "chemical" by "IT."

But why does it happen? Is it a technological imperative? Or is it purely a socio-economic construction? This is perhaps one of the unanswerable questions in the philosophy of science. For while technologies – and the convergence between them – are indubitably developed as a product of a socio-economic system, nevertheless technological developments cannot be scientifically arbitrary. The answer to these questions has to be that convergence is not a technological imperative, but neither is it purely socio-economic and technologically arbitrary. Convergence between IT and other industries is not a technological imperative, and it will not happen as a matter of course. But if it can be done, many companies will try to make it happen in the belief that such an alliance will prolong the life-cycle of their products, and hence their growth and profitability. Convergence does not drop on them like "manna from heaven". But they cannot create such convergence out of nothing.

The profitability of convergence depends in part, of course, on the nature of demand for new products that emerges from the convergence of old and new technologies. Almost by definition, the products arising from this convergence will embody characteristics for which there has been no revealed demand in the past. It is always exceptionally difficult to forecast demand for products with new characteristics. Many such products may fail, but some succeed. But the record shows that convergence between traditional technologies and new ones can sometimes yield substantial dividends.

Summary

We can summarize this section by making four observations.

(1) We have seen at least since the industrial revolution that there are a variety of forces that cause clusters to emerge.

(2) While the initial location of a cluster may be a little arbitrary, when it has started to forge ahead it will tend to stay ahead – at least for a while.

(3) When clusters get large, saturation and congestion start to set in. At this stage, the cluster may stop growing, and may even decline if it does not have and cannot attract new industries to replace the old.

(4) Some (perhaps most) clusters never recover, but others *do* recover. While some recovery may derive from the price mechanism, some through urban renewal, and some through the attractiveness of an old city's cultural capital, there is an important role here for convergence between old and new technologies in sustaining recovery of the cluster.

Evidence on clustering forces in the United States and United Kingdom

This section briefly summarizes some of our own findings about the forces that seem to generate and sustain clusters in US high-technology industries. We have not attempted to survey any of the other recent studies in this field. We summarize one study that compares the clustering forces in the United Kingdom and the United States. This finds that while clustering forces can vary significantly between different high-technology sectors, the forces within one sector in the United Kingdom are of the same general form, and strength, as their equivalent in the United States – even if they vary in fine detail. This evidence is in line with arguments elsewhere in this volume (chapter 4, by Malerba and Orsenigo) that inter-sectoral differences in the patterns of innovation are more marked than cross-country differences within a particular sector. Emboldened by this observation, we then summarize the limited evidence we have on critical mass and saturation effects in the US computer industry, which may well be highly relevant to the European setting.

Clustering forces: a review

Swann (1993) analyzed two components of the forces that generate clusters. One is the extent to which strong high-technology clusters attract higher than average entry by new firms. The second is the extent to which strong high-technology clusters promote faster than average growth in the incumbent firms that locate in those clusters. This study examined these factors with particular reference to the computer industry (broadly defined) in the United States.

The main character of the entry results was that strong clusters do attract entry, but tend to attract entry in sectors of computing other than those in which the cluster has strength. So, for example, a cluster that is strong in computer hardware companies and semiconductor component companies is found to attract a disproportionately high amount of entry into the computer software and computer peripherals sectors. But such a cluster does not attract further new entrants into computer hardware and semiconductors.

The main character of the growth results, by contrast, is that a cluster that is strong in a particular sector will tend to promote faster than average growth of the firms in that sector. On the other hand, the cross-sectoral effects here are weak or even negative. Thus a semiconductor company located in a cluster that is strong in all other sectors of the computer industry but not semiconductors will grow less fast than a semiconductor firm located in isolation. These results are described in greater detail in Swann (1998b). They seem to be fairly robust to variations in model specification.

However a rather different picture is found in a study of biotechnology clusters in the United States. In biotechnology, it is the strength of the science base in a cluster that is particularly important in influencing the amount of new entry, though there are a limited number of cross-sectoral effects attracting entry. This naturally leads to a rather different pattern of industrial clustering from that observed in computing. But, once again, the growth of a firm in a particular sector of biotechnology is influenced most by the strength of that sector within the cluster, and again the strength of other sectors has a negligible or even negative effect on the growth of the firm (Swann and Prevezer, 1996).

We have commented elsewhere on possible interpretations of these distinct results (Swann, Previser, and Stout, 1998). One quite appealing explanation is as follows. The high-technology cluster that is strong in a sector (say, i) will generate spillovers that relate especially to the technologies of sector i, but may also be of relevance to sectors other than i. Incumbents belonging to this sector i are likely to be quite adept at exploiting the spillovers generated in these strong clusters, so it is they who benefit, leaving little for new entrants to soak up. This means that firms in sector i will experience faster than average growth, while the cluster will not attract particularly strong new entry.

In contrast, incumbent firms outside sector i are not so likely to be adept at exploiting these spillovers from sector i, since they lie outside their technological competence, so it falls to new entrants, who have greater organizational flexibility, to soak up these spillovers. This means that incumbent firms outside sector i do not grow faster than average, but there can be disproportionately high entry of new firms into these other sectors.

Comparing clustering forces in the United States and United Kingdom

We have performed equivalent studies for the computer industries in the United Kingdom and the United States in an attempt to establish whether clustering forces are of the same type in the United Kingdom, and whether they are of equal strength (Baptista and Swann, 1998a). The same sorts of cross-sectoral effects are found to attract entry in the United Kingdom case, though the precise form of the cross-sectoral effects are different. While in the US case it is the "hard" sectors (computer hardware, semiconductors and computer systems) that attract entry into software and peripherals, in the UK case it is components, hardware, peripherals, and services that seem to do most to attract entry, and this time the induced entry is spread out over a wider range of sectors. These detailed differences may result from the different data sources and approaches used, so they are perhaps of second order. The most important observations about entry are therefore that there are strong cross-sectoral effects, and that they are of comparable strength in the United Kingdom and the United States.

When we turn our attention to the growth of incumbent firms, we find exactly the same results in the UK and US studies. In both cases, own-sector strength promotes growth while other-sector strength does not. The main difference is that the trend rate of growth (independent of the effects of cluster strength on growth) are higher in the United States than in the United Kingdom. The possible reasons for this are discussed in Baptista and Swann (1998a), but may well have something to do with the relative sizes of the US and United Kingdom markets.

Critical mass and saturation effects

Swann (1998b) attempts to identify whether clusters exhibit a critical mass at which entry starts to take off rapidly, and a saturation level beyond which entry starts to tail off. This is done by introducing polynomial terms in total cluster computing employment into the models of entry summarized above.

The character of the results is summarized in figure 6.1, which relates to the US study. These show the level of entry projected by the model as a function of total computer industry employment in a cluster. The general pattern is that entry takes off quite slowly when clusters are small, but when the total computer industry employment is in the thousands then entry

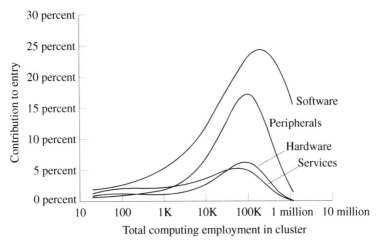

6.1 Cluster strength and entry, US computer industry
Source: Swann (1998b, figure 4.4, 88).

starts to take off in earnest. Entry peaks when total computer industry employment reaches about 100,000 and then starts to tail off in very big clusters.

For each sector, it is quite useful to summarize these critical mass and peak-entry levels of employment. Swann (1998b) does this by defining "critical mass" as the point of maximum acceleration in entry. The rationale for this is from aeronautical analogy: the aircraft takes off when it reaches maximum acceleration along the runway, for that is the point at which the force lifting it off the ground is maximized. Without replicating all the calculations here, our study finds that the take-off point for entry into most computer industry sectors is reached when total computer industry employment in the cluster is about 10,000. And as noted above, the point of peak entry (at which the derivative of projected entry with respect to total computer industry employment is zero) tends to be reached when total computer industry employment in the cluster is around 100,000.

These are only rough estimates, but they can be very useful as a means of classifying clusters in terms of their position in the life-cycle. When, indeed, this classification is compared with the classifications made by industry observers (Herbig and Golden, 1993), there is a remarkable degree of uniformity. Both approaches classify California, New York, and Massachusetts as beyond the point of peak entry, and agree that the "hot spots" for innovative new entry lie in some of the younger clusters (Texas, North Carolina–Virginia, Florida, Oregon, Washington, DC), which are now of a size in between the critical mass and the size required for maximum entry. Further details of this comparison are given in Swann (1998b).

Implications for the national/European balance of policy

If it is fair to assume that these approximate critical mass and peak-entry figures apply also to the European computer industry, then we can draw out some interesting implications for clusters in European high-technology industry. This section reflects briefly on the implications for European and national innovation policy towards high-technology clusters.

The limited evidence summarized on p. 115 was in line with one of the central arguments of the volume – namely, that cross-sectoral differences in patterns of innovation are more important than cross-country differences. Let us assume, for the sake of argument, that this conclusion applies more generally to innovative patterns across Europe. And let us assume, moreover, that the estimates of a cluster's critical mass and saturation employment summarized on p. 118 also apply across Europe. What are the implications of this for policy towards the generation and sustenance of high-technology clusters?

The first conclusion is that the most vibrant clusters will have some diversity. Without that, the cross-sectoral effects that promote entry of innovative new entrants will be reduced, and this entry is essential to ensure a vibrant high-technology cluster. In the US case, the presence of strong "hard" sectors in a computer industry cluster was found to be vital to innovative entry into software and peripherals. In the United Kingdom case, the same sorts of cross-sectoral effects were found, although the strongest effects were between different sectors.

Swann (1996) has used a simulation model developed from the estimated growth and entry equations for the US study to explore the dynamics of cluster growth. This finds that if convergence between technologies is strong (meaning that cross-sectoral effects on entry are strong) then the clusters that ultimately grow to be the largest are those with some diversity of strengths in different sectors of the computer industry. On the other hand, if convergence is weak, the single-technology clusters tend to grow fastest, at least in the short term.

The main policy message, therefore, is that diversity is essential to the long-run growth and vibrancy of the cluster. If a particular region within one country has this diversity, then it can hope to achieve maximum effectiveness as a cluster, subject to scale effects (see below). But if a particular region is too specialized in a few sectors, then it will not have enough diversity on its own to act as a fully self-sufficient cluster.

Perhaps the more interesting conclusions relate to the critical mass and saturation employment in clusters. How many European regions have concentrations of high-technology employment that are large enough to reach the critical mass as identified in the US computer industry study? Is it possible within a single country to assemble a cluster that achieves employment levels in a high-technology industry comparable to those at which the US clusters achieved peak entry? Or is it necessary to coordinate this across several countries? We can shed some very preliminary light on these questions.

The estimates of critical mass and peak entry related to estimates of total computer industry employment in a cluster. The computer industry in this context was defined broadly to include the following eight sectors: computer hardware, systems, peripherals, electronic components, communications equipment, software, services, and distribution. It is important to recognize that these sectors lie in different parts of the ISIC. While the first three (hardware, systems, and peripherals) are included in the ISIC or NACE "Computer and Office Equipment" category 33, components are a part of 345 and communications equipment a part of 344. Software, services, and distribution appear in a quite different part of the ISIC.

Since internationally comparable data by region was readily available only at the 2-digit level, we concentrate in what follows simply on clusters in ISIC/NACE 33 (Computer and office equipment). In this case, we can expect that the employment levels required for critical mass and maximum entry would be below the 10,000 and 100,000 (respectively) required for the computer industry as a whole. The data used for the US computer industry study (Swann, 1993, 1998b) indicate that in 1987 (near the end of the period over which the models were estimated) the three sectors (hardware, systems and peripherals) that are contained within ISIC/NACE 33 would account for about 40 percent of computer industry employment within US clusters. This would suggest that a cluster which is assessed to reach critical mass in terms of overall computer industry employment might have an employment of only 4,000 in these three sectors, and hence in ISIC/NACE 33. By the same logic, a cluster that has reached peak entry in terms of overall computing employment might have about 40,000 in ISIC/NACE 33.

We could therefore use the figures 4,000 and 40,000 as indicators of employment in ISIC/NACE 33 corresponding to overall critical mass in computing. In practice, we have made a small upward adjustment to these indicators, to reflect the fact that part of ISIC/NACE 33 refers to non-computing parts of office equipment that would not be counted as part of the computer industry by the criteria of our US computing study.

Accordingly, we classify any region or country that has 5,000 employment in ISIC/NACE 33 as having reached critical mass in the computer industry, and any that have 50,000 employment in ISIC/NACE 33 as having reached peak entry. Table 6.1 summarizes the position in Europe in 1985. The reason for choosing this early data is that it corresponds roughly to the end of the sample period used for the US computer industry study, and to which the critical mass and peak-entry estimates apply. Table 6.1 presents indices of cluster size or maturity, which are simply the relevant levels of employment divided by 5,000. Thus an index of 1 implies that the cluster has reached critical mass, while an index of 10 implies it has reached the level of employment associated with peak entry.

Table 6.1 shows that Germany (the former Federal Republic), France and Britain viewed as "national clusters" reach or surpass the peak-entry level of employment. Italy nearly reaches this. Within these countries, a number of regions had by 1985 already grown beyond the critical mass – notably Baden–Württemberg, Nordrhein–Westfalen, Bayern (Ger), Ile-de-France (Fra), the South-East (UK), Lombardia and Nord Ovest (including Piemonte) (It). For the Netherlands and Ireland, total employment in the country only just surpasses the critical mass, and according to these estimates, the computer industries in Spain, Denmark and Belgium had not by 1985 reached critical mass.[1]

What can we conclude from this? First, that the EU computer industry employment as a whole represents about five "peak-entry" US clusters. As figure 6.1 makes clear, the rate of entry in a cluster five times the size of the "peak-entry" cluster has fallen back significantly. The implication of this, therefore, is that it is not helpful to think of the European computer industry as *one* cluster. To maximize innovative entry, there should be at least five clusters.

Can we then conclude that the national level is the appropriate level to plan industrial clusters in Europe? Of course from the perspective of countries with small computer industries, the national level is definitely *not* the right level to plan clusters. The national clusters for the Netherlands, Ireland, Spain, Denmark, Belgium, Greece, Luxembourg, and Portugal, are too small to promote sufficient innovative entry. But for the other four countries (Germany, France, the United Kingdom, and Italy), employment is around the "peak-entry" level. Can we conclude that these countries' computer industries are big enough to constitute full-fledged "clusters" in their own right?

While this conclusion might be convenient for the Euro-skeptic, it is not necessarily valid. As we have argued above, the mix of sectors in a cluster appears to be critical for its long-term success. Even if these four national

---

[1] The two Eurostat publications cited made no estimate of the levels of employment in NACE 33 for Greece, Luxembourg, or Portugal.

Table 6.1. *Computer and office equipment index of cluster maturity, 1985*

Index = 1 is minimum size for critical mass; index = 10 is size for peak entry

EUR12	48.8
Germany	15.4
Baden–Württemberg	4.8
Nordrhein–Westfalen	2.8
Bayern	2.8
Niedersachsen	1.4
Hessen	1.4
France	11.4
Ile-de-France	6.0
Méditerranée	1.2
Centre Est	1.0
UK	10.0
South East	4.6
Scotland	1.8
North West	1.2
Italy	8.4
Lombardia	3.8
Nord Ovest	2.2
Netherlands	1.4
Ireland	1.2
Spain	0.6
Denmark	0.4
Belgium	0.4

Source: Author's calculations based on his estimates of cluster size for critical mass and peak entry in US computer industry (see p. 120), and using data from *Eurostat Regions Statistical Yearbook* (1989), *Eurostat Industry Statistical Yearbook* (1988), and *Business Monitor PA330* (1985).

"clusters" are large enough to promote peak innovative entry, we have no evidence to hand that they have the appropriate mix of sectors. The United Kingdom for one (based on the data collected for Baptista and Swann, 1998a) is too light on core hardware and components' sectors. This important question urgently needs some further research, along the lines of our earlier studies for the United States and United Kingdom.

References

Amin, A. and J. Goddard (1986). *Technological Change, Industrial Restructuring and Regional Development*, London: Allen & Unwin

Arnold, E. and K. Guy (1986). *Parallel Convergence: National Strategies in Information Technology*, London: Pinter

Arthur, W. B. (1990). "Silicon Valley Locational Clusters: When do Increasing Returns Imply Monopoly?," *Mathematical Social Sciences*, 19, 235–51

Bairoch, P. (1988). *Cities and Economic Development: From the Dawn of History to The Present*, Chicago: University of Chicago Press

Baptista, R. (1998). "Clusters, Innovation and Growth: A Survey of the Literature," chapter 2 in G.M.P. Swann, M.J. Prevezer, and D.K. Stout (eds.) *The Dynamics of Industrial Clustering*, Oxford: Oxford University Press, 13–51

Baptista, R. and G.M.P. Swann (1998a). "Clustering Dynamics in the UK Computer Industry: A Comparison with the USA," chapter 5 in G.M.P. Swann, M.J. Prevezer, and D.K. Stout (eds.), *The Dynamics of Industrial Clustering*, Oxford: Oxford University Press, 106–23

(1998b). "Do Firms in Clusters Innovate More?," *Research Policy*, 27(5), 527–42

Brezis, E. S. and P. Krugman (1993). "Technology and the Life-Cycle of Cities," *NBER Working Paper*, 4561

Briggs, A. (1968). *Victorian Cities*, London: Pelican Books

Clow, A. and N. L. Clow (1958). "The Chemical Industry: Interaction with the Industrial Revolution," chapter 8 (Part II) in C. Singer, E.J. Holmyard, A.R. Hall and T.I. Williams (eds.), *A History of Technology*, vol IV, Oxford: Oxford University Press

Conti, S., E. Malecki, and P. Oinas (1995). *The Industrial Enterprise and its Environment: Spatial Perspectives*, Aldershot: Avebury

David, P. A. and J. L. Rosenbloom (1990). "Marshallian Factor Market Externalities and the Dynamics of Industrial Localization," *Journal of Urban Economics*, 28, 349–70

Dorfman, N. (1985). "Route 128: The Development of a Regional High-technology Economy," in D. Lampe (ed.), *The Massachusetts Miracle: High Technology and Economic Revitalization*, Cambridge, Mass.: MIT Press

Grossman, G. and E. Helpman (1992). *Innovation and Growth in the Global Economy*, Cambridge, Mass.: MIT Press

Hagedoorn, J. and J. Schakenraad (1992). "Leading Companies in Networks of Strategic Alliances in Information Technologies," *Research Policy*, 21(2), 163–90

Herbig, P. and J. E. Golden (1993). "How to Keep that Innovative Spirit Alive: An

Examination of Evolving Innovative Hot Spots," *Technological Forecasting and Social Change*, 43, 75–90

Hotelling, H. (1929). "The Stability of Competition," *Economic Journal*, 39, 41–57

Jacobs, J. (1961). *The Death and Life of Great American Cities*, New York: Random House

(1969). *The Economy of Cities*, London: Penguin Books

Jaffe, A. B. (1986). "Technological and Spillovers from R&D: Evidence from Firms' Patents, Profits, and Market Value," *American Economic Review*, 76, 984–1001

Krugman, P. (1991). *Geography and Trade*, Cambridge, Mass.: MIT Press

Lösch, A. (1954). *The Economics of Location*, New Haven: Yale University Press

Marshall, A. (1920). *Principles of Economics*, London: Macmillan

Mathias, P. (1983). *The First Industrial Nation: An Economic History of Britain 1700–1914*, 2nd edn, London: Routledge

Mumford, L. (1961). *The City in History*, London: Penguin Books

Pavitt, K. (1987). *On the Nature of Technology*, Brighton: Science Policy Research Unit, University of Sussex

Perroux, F. (1950). "Economic Space: Theory and Applications," *Quarterly Journal of Economics*, 64(1), 89–104

Porter, M. (1990). *The Competitive Advantage of Nations*, London: Macmillan

Romer, P. (1986). "Increasing Returns and Long-run Growth," *Journal of Political Economy*, 94, 1002–37

(1990). "Endogenous Technological Change," *Journal of Political Economy*, 98, S71-S102

Saxenian, A. (1985). "The Genesis of Silicon Valley" in P. Hall and A. Markusen (eds.), *Silicon Landscapes*, Boston, Mass.: Allen & Unwin

(1994). *Regional Advantage: Culture and Competition in Silicon Valley and Route 128*, Cambridge, Mass: Harvard University Press

Swann G. M. P. (1993). "Can High Technology Services Prosper if High Technology Manufacturing Doesn't?," *Working Paper*, 143, Centre for Business Strategy, London Business School

(1996). "Technology Evolution and the Rise and Fall of Industrial Clusters," *Revue Internationale de Systemique*, 10(3), pp.285–302

(1998a). "Towards a Model of Clustering in High-technology Industries," chapter 3 in G.M.P. Swann, M.J. Prevezer, and D.K. Stout (eds.), *The Dynamics of Industrial Clustering*, Oxford: Oxford University Press, 52–76

(1998b). "Clusters in the US Computing Industry," chapter 4 in G.M.P. Swann, M.J. Prevezer and D.K. Stout (eds.), *The Dynamics of Industrial Clustering*, Oxford: Oxford University Press, 77–105

Swann, G. M. P. and M. J. Prevezer (1996). "A Comparison of the Dynamics of Industrial Clustering in Computing and Biotechnology," *Research Policy*, 25, 1139–57

Swann, G. M. P., M. J. Prevezer, and D.K. Stout (eds.) (1998). *The Dynamics of Industrial Clustering*, Oxford: Oxford University Press

Weber, A. (1928). *Theory of the Location of Industries*, trans. C.J. Friedrich, Chicago: Chicago University Press (originally published in German in 1909)

7 "Convergence" and corporate change in the electronics industry

Nick von Tunzelmann

Introduction

There is a widespread feeling that the changes being experienced in many industries, and above all electronics, over the past decade or so, can be thought of as a period of "creative destruction" in the Schumpeterian sense – that is, one in which old ways of corporate thinking and behavior, and the economic framework generally, were subject to drastic restructuring. The "evolutionary" approach to technological change, though claiming a Schumpeterian parentage, however tends to view innovation as proceeding mainly through elaborating on the firm's existing technological knowledge base through applying "routines" (Nelson and Winter, 1982).

A prevailing and probably predominant view expressed over this period has been that the industry would amalgamate through a process of technological convergence, in which digital technology would become the centerpiece of the hitherto somewhat disparate branches of the industry. The most persistent expressions of this attitude concerned the predicted "convergence" between telecommunications and computing, a view that was especially widespread in the mid- and later 1980s. This convergence arose out of the increasing extent to which telecoms switching was becoming based on computerized functions, while on the other side computers were increasingly being interconnected through networking. Such similarities between hardware and function were a major factor underlying a series of attempts by giant corporations at that time to jump from playing a major role in one of these activities to being deeply involved in both. Their fortunes will be discussed below; it is sufficient to state here that the rather unhappy experiences that mostly resulted were enough to deter further such developments.

In the 1990s the theme of convergence has however re-emerged, though directed more at products than at technologies (it still being supposed that digitalization would prove to be a technological commonality). In this view, multimedia or similar developments could combine several product characteristics into the one piece of equipment; "information superhighways" could carry out the telecommunications functions. In this period much more emphasis was being placed on the software rather than the hardware technologies, and much more on users rather than producers of the resulting equipment. The controllers of such developments might prove to be neither equipment producers nor final consumers, as for instance media companies might arrive to dominate the proceedings. The results of this era of innovation are still too recent and uncertain to establish with even the updated database (see below), but they help construct a framework within which the wider questions might be posed.

In looking at the 1980s' developments, partly using pre–1987 patents data and partly looking at commercial indicators, Soete and I (Soete and von Tunzelmann, 1987; von Tunzelmann, 1988) came to the conclusion that there was little hard evidence of success in moving towards a fusion of technologies at the corporate level. This evidence has recently been updated, on the bases of European patents data (from the European Patents Office, EPO) and of a database on strategic alliances maintained at MERIT, by Duysters (1995), who comes to essentially similar conclusions. Basically, communications companies tended to retain their major technological and market strengths in communications, and computer firms in computing.

This chapter focuses on the period since the mid–1980s. It uses data on patents granted in the United States, as compiled in raw form by what used to be called the Office of Technology Assessment and Forecast (OTAF), and processed into usable form by Pari Patel and Keith Pavitt. With extensive help from Patel, I have developed a sub-set of this mass of data which relates to the electronics industry, specifically investigating over 100 electronics multinational companies for the years since 1969. However the turbulence in the industry after 1986 posed awkward problems for continuing the data to cover 1986–92. In this time period there were major restructurings of many of the major parent companies, including their sales or exchanges of whole divisions. It was thus unclear to what extent the concept of the company as the basis of aggregation of the data would continue to be appropriate. In this chapter I look at the companies of each major global region, and then in greater detail at some of the major European electronics companies.

Background: convergence, scale, and scope

The specific issue of communications and computing can be enlarged on in the perspective of wider changes in industry in the late twentieth century, as in figure 7.1 below. In the upper portion, more and more technologies are being incorporated into each particular product – an example being the

a   TECHNOLOGIES

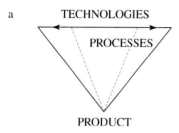

PRODUCT

b   TECHNOLOGY

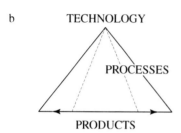

PRODUCTS

7.1 The entrepreneurial problem of scope and scale in the late twentieth century
a Many more technologies to produce a single product.
b Many more products produced from a given technology.

use of microelectronics in modern household appliances or motor vehicles. In the lower portion, each particular technology is being adopted in a wider and wider range of products. For example, a computer firm of recent years has been exposed to diversification of technological frontiers (optical fibers and opto-electronics, superconductivity, neural networks) lying far from traditional strengths in electronics (hardware) and computer science (software). It has also been exposed to a diversification of product range, beginning with the IBM-style mainframes and extending upwards into supercomputers and downwards into minis, micros, laptops, workstations, etc. together with network facilities. Firms require knowledge about the broadening range of technologies and the broadening range of products.

The issue of "convergence", as seen from the perspective of the mid–1980s, was like the bottom half of figure 7.1. Digital technologies based on microelectronics became "pervasive" (Freeman, 1992, 134) and required in an ever-extending number of products. Synergies of technological scope were assumed to be high, so that a telecoms firm developing electronics hardware and software would find little difficulty in spreading into computers, and conversely. The problem implied by the upper half of figure 7.1 was thus thought to be considerably less serious. In the 1990s the situation seems to have been reversed, and the emphasis has come to fall upon uniting wider and wider ranges of technologies into producing specific products, such as for multimedia, as in the upper part of figure 7.1. The reality is that both are involved, and it is combining them which is the crux of the managerial problem confronting the electronics industry (and, indeed, others that have found themselves in this situation, which includes many supposedly lower-tech industries).

The basic difficulty is how to attain and manage the sprawling range of knowledge required. "Bounded rationality" puts a high premium on the ability to diversify ever further at either end, to say nothing of putting all three types of diversification (technologies, products, and processes) together. On the principle of "mental division of labor" (Babbage, 1832) it may prove more efficient to sub-divide the knowledge-generation process in regard to technologies or markets; while on the production side there is a balance to be struck between the principle of the physical division of labor and the throughput attainable from process integration.

For such reasons, firms have been compelled to make choices. Firms which adhered to trying to retain a presence in the full range of products that could be developed from electronics technologies (such as Philips) encountered serious problems and were eventually forced to make choices (Teece and Pisano, 1994). Conversely, specialization in a product without breadth of technological expertise in due course eroded the firm's ability to remain in markets where the technological needs were rapidly advancing (as, for instance, with the United Kingdom firm Amstrad). These problems of "core competencies" were exacerbated by economic pressures. On the one side, R&D costs of successive generations of products were becoming increasingly expensive, as exemplified by central switches in tele- communications exchanges in progressing from electromechanical to fully digital operation (Dang Nguyen, 1985). Additionally, the production costs of technologically-intensive products involved escalating costs – for example, the cost of a factory to produce the Intel Pentium chip was esti- mated at around $1b, while that of the next generation (Pentium II) would be between $1.5b and $1.8b. On the other side, product lives were becom- ing increasingly shortened, thus further and further restricting the time available for recouping the heightening developmental and fixed investment costs. Products were also being threatened by competition from new prod- ucts evolving out of quite different sets of technological competencies (for example, the threat to cables in communications transmission from optical fibers, satellites, etc.).

Our earlier findings therefore attributed the failures of attempted diversification of computer companies into communications, and con- versely, to pressures bearing upon both technologies and markets. On the one side, R&D costs of developing new-generation technologies were rising, at much faster rates than the markets themselves were expanding. Moving laterally into "foreign" technological fields augmented this upsurge of R&D costs, as the price of bringing onstream technologies which lay outside the customary domain of competencies of the firms concerned. On the other side, market structures were quite different as between communications and computing, with the former generally characterized by large (normally parastatal) customers and the latter by dispersed small-scale consumers – this gave rise to major differences in corporate "culture," etc.

Alternatively, one can consider that convergence or divergence was taking place at different levels. Convergence of technologies around digitalization was, temporarily at least, associated with divergence of products, and conversely convergence of products around, say, multimedia was (for the meantime, anyway) associated with divergence of technologies. Assimilation would be long drawn out. Convergence at either end did not necessarily warrant convergence of the firms themselves, because of the costs to them of diversification at the other end. Ultimately, the firm might have to seek alliances or consortia with other producers, with differing competencies, in order to meet the complexity of technologies and/or products; this has been very obvious in the development of multimedia.

Data

Patents prospectively offer some insight into tracking the technological dimension of these changes within and among firms. Although they are by no means perfect as indicators of technological output or productivity, as is well known (see, e.g., Pavitt, 1988), they are organized in such a way as to allow us to draw some parallels with the crucial managerial issues outlined above. It should be emphasized that patents are being used here not to indicate the technological strength of the companies concerned, but to indicate their technological direction. The OTAF classifications, which consist of about 400 main groupings and extremely disaggregated subgroupings, are explicitly intended to be technology- rather than industry-based.[1]

Having developed a classificatory schema, the major corporate restructurings under analysis can then be examined by drawing up matrices which show, for each company, how the percentage of patenting in each class

[1] However detailed examination reveals that a number of the individual codes are as much product- as technology-based (e.g. 84, Music). Only the Canadian patent system makes any attempt to conduct a dual (product and process) classification, and even there the conclusions that can be drawn about mappings between technologies and products are very limited (Ducharme, 1991).

relates to the nature of the patenting organization. The main task in preparing this information is to reconstruct the patenting units as reported by OTAF on a company-by-company basis. The units registered and coded by OTAF could be any laboratory or other sub-unit within the firm. In several of the large European companies the list of sub-units to be scrutinized ran to several hundreds or even thousands, and the number of these which actually recorded patents could be in three figures (largest here was the French firm CGE, with almost 300 patenting units unearthed).

The ownership patterns of companies were established in a number of ways, of which the most important was using volumes of *Who Owns Whom*, which has been published annually or more sporadically for the main regions since 1969. Supplementary information was obtained from the trade press or the companies' own annual reports. The companies are aggregated according to their structure as of the year 1992, by which time the phase of greatest turbulence had subsided. I also consider changes in company structure since my previous aggregation, located in 1986, just before the main upheavals took place.

We can thus proceed to analyze the more substantial corporate changes through comparisons of their patent "profiles," to see whether the changes have on balance led to greater diversification or instead greater specialization. As in previous work, I shall proceed to analyze the technological profiles of the organizations as if the mergers (or demergers, etc.) under scrutiny had prevailed throughout the period. This is therefore a kind of "counterfactual" analysis of the organizations, aimed for the most part at understanding the technological factors which gave rise to the large changes from the mid–1980s.

Results: specialization vs. diversification

The aggregates of companies for each major region are displayed in table 7.1, with the list of companies involved set out in appendix 7.1 (p. 151). For the purposes of this table and section of the chapter, the firms have been allocated to one or other branch of the electronics industry. With most of these firms being multi-product firms, it is often difficult to allocate them just to one branch (e.g., communications, consumer electronics, or instruments), but it is unlikely that plausible changes in thus allocating these firms would make much difference to the results.[2] Those larger companies which spanned broad ranges of the industry were relegated to a residual class of "General electronics" companies.

The first point to note is that these firms are "multi-technology" firms, in

---

[2] Earlier studies also used cluster analysis as a check, and gave generally similar classifications.

the sense we have used elsewhere (von Tunzelmann *et al.*, 1993; Patel and Pavitt, 1994; von Tunzelmann, 1996). Even specialist producers of "single" products, like Wang Laboratories (which concentrated on producing mini-computers) are typically found to have been granted patents in a majority of the 22 technological fields identified below, and which cover the whole field of industrial technologies. That is, these firms conform at least to the upper part of figure 7.1 (many of them, naturally including the "General" companies, also conform to the lower part of the figure).

A common view in the industry is that North American companies are more specialized than European or Japanese firms. The choice of companies and their share in total patents (see appendix 7.1) confirms this at the level of the industry as a whole – that is, there are many more specialist computer or semiconductor firms in the United States than in Europe or Japan, and their share in total patenting is quite significant (by contrast, the only Asian firm included as a "semiconductor" company is Kyocera, which is really a ceramics company). However it is less valid to see the individual US firms as technologically more specialized than those in Europe, once this difference in composition of the industry is allowed for. Table 7.2 briefly recapitulates the data of table 7.1, to contrast the companies of each region in their "heartland" technologies (i.e., of telecoms companies in telecommunications technologies, etc.).

These figures appear to suggest that it was European firms who were the most internally specialized in the telecoms, computer, and semiconductor industries, while the Asian firms (dominated by the Japanese) behave more as expected. The situation is different in consumer electronics, as the European industry's patenting is predominantly that of Philips, which in many respects ought perhaps to qualify as a "General" company.[3] European instruments companies appear to patent relatively little in instrumentation; this is because the leading patentors (Bosch, Lucas) obtain a very high proportion of patents which are here classified as "vehicles", though they are really automotive components.[4]

A more extensive notion of technological concentration can be obtained by calculating the Herfindahl Index from the shares of all patent fields.[5] For present purposes, 22 technological fields have been defined (see appendix 7.2, p. 155). The companies have been aggregated into industrial branches, as already done for table 7.1, and the results of the Herfindahl calculations emerge as figures 7.2–7.4. These have been split into two panels to ease identification. The time paths have been calculated by least-squares regressions

---

[3] Note that the US industry's patenting is almost equivalently dominated by RCA, which as noted below effectively disappeared after 1987.   [4] The high heartland shares of the Japanese companies, Canon and Ricoh, come mainly from photographic instruments
[5] See von Tunzelmann (1996) for more information on this measure.

Table 7.1. *Shares of patent fields, by branch of industry and region,*
1969–1994

Field: Industry	Telecoms (%)	Semicon. (%)	Computers (%)	Image (%)	Laser (%)	Insts. (%)	Total nos.
(A) Europe							
Telecoms[a]	32.41	3.16	11.33	2.66	1.03	12.13	4,961[b]
	+7.34	+0.66	−1.35	−1.53	+0.64	−1.71	−164
	+6.55	+1.83	−2.42	+2.55	+1.15	+6.01	+719
Computers	1.89	0.90	45.07	6.84	0.0	14.09	2,221
	−0.12	+0.40	+24.72	+0.89	–	−4.99	−310
	+1.98	+0.77	+8.48	−3.52	–	−5.36	+208
Semiconductors	4.50	31.20	37.60	2.76	0.0	3.16	1,266
	+5.60	−3.40	+21.83	−16.26	–	−5.54	+102
	−1.28	+13.96	−17.76	+1.47	–	+2.17	+592
Consumer	6.93	7.24	9.41	13.54	0.50	14.76	16,838
	+2.45	−3.03	+2.33	+1.16	+0.02	+1.70	−327
	−0.95	+3.16	+0.50	+3.29	−0.24	+1.79	+1,210
Instruments	1.17	1.14	3.74	3.31	0.02	11.64	9,541
	+0.70	−0.79	+2.35	+3.12	+0.05	+1.32	+204
	+1.06	+1.03	+2.40	−1.13	0.00	+0.59	+83
Military	2.12	0.97	4.87	1.90	0.80	17.70	2,260
	+0.98	−0.04	−2.26	+1.20	+1.86	+1.02	−62
	+3.70	+0.90	+3.37	+0.31	−1.44	+13.37	+106
General	8.02	4.76	7.70	4.81	0.94	17.08	36,094
	+3.58	−1.94	−1.50	+0.59	−0.52	+2.10	+635
	+1.24	+0.73	+1.35	+1.42	+1.17	+0.36	+2,002
All	8.10	4.97	9.39	6.42	0.68	15.19	73,181
	+2.68	−1.54	+0.21	+0.69	−0.14	+1.38	+78
	+1.95	+2.60	+2.42	+1.38	+0.57	+0.85	+4,920
(B) N. America							
Telecoms	20.21	5.78	11.63	4.15	1.72	10.80	27,946
	+0.24	+0.53	−5.13	−2.31	−0.80	−3.23	−2,549
	+6.81	+2.37	−0.30	+0.33	+1.14	+2.79	−34
Computers	4.58	6.24	36.14	9.53	0.49	12.59	31,170
	+1.17	+1.15	+5.08	−0.49	−0.72	−1.41	−1,358
	+2.43	−1.24	+8.10	−0.93	+0.24	−1.91	+4,845
Semiconductors	4.52	22.42	29.66	3.95	0.29	8.09	10,018
	+3.42	+5.45	+18.74	+1.50	−0.75	−4.13	+24
	−1.83	+8.14	+5.59	−2.65	+0.01	+1.24	+2,353

Table 7.1. (*cont.*)

Field: Industry	Telecoms (%)	Semicon. (%)	Computers (%)	Image (%)	Laser (%)	Insts. (%)	Total nos.
(B) N. America (cont.)							
Consumer	6.43	10.61	9.63	30.51	0.98	10.69	9,804
	−0.91	−0.97	−5.89	+6.59	−0.90	−3.88	+313
	−1.83	−10.38	−2.77	+33.08	−0.50	−6.10	−2,035
Instruments	2.00	2.67	14.92	8.28	1.02	39.31	4,306
	−0.01	+0.89	+5.85	+2.73	+0.94	−2.89	−533
	+0.63	+0.82	−4.97	+2.70	−0.47	+5.50	+1,749
Military	4.29	2.86	7.43	1.34	1.82	10.98	18,451
	+3.18	+1.52	+0.44	−0.61	−0.94	−0.75	−1,457
	−2.17	−0.50	+0.31	−0.22	0.00	−1.48	+705
General	5.30	5.94	8.32	2.22	0.38	9.97	43,083
	+1.56	−2.27	+1.10	−2.22	−0.15	+0.57	−2,738
	+6.47	+4.06	+2.13	+0.07	−0.10	+2.12	+3,171
All	7.33	6.58	16.45	6.44	0.91	13.96	158,192
	+0.81	+0.54	+1.53	+0.52	−0.49	−1.35	−8,298
	+1.96	+2.17	+6.09	−1.32	+0.02	+1.66	+10,754
(C) Asia							
Telecoms	14.57	8.82	13.76	4.60	1.41	11.47	4,455
	−2.71	+0.36	−0.49	+4.97	+0.07	+8.18	+307
	−4.68	+5.21	+4.71	−3.93	+0.26	−3.69	+1,448
Computers	9.41	14.70	27.37	5.84	0.73	14.70	5,579
	−4.52	+7.45	+8.87	−7.31	+0.12	+5.04	+619
	+6.18	+3.23	−7.58	+3.57	+1.11	+5.88	+1,752
Semiconductors	2.16	4.58	1.35	2.70	0	22.37	371
	0.00	+6.74	0.00	0.00	−	+5.10	0
	+3.38	−3.29	+1.35	+2.70	−	+9.38	+116
Consumer	4.35	5.18	10.06	24.86	1.13	12.37	25,982
	+1.28	−3.98	+5.15	−1.60	+0.52	+1.45	+1,798
	−0.99	+2.87	+2.09	−0.34	+0.69	+4.25	+7,327
Instruments	1.70	1.50	11.71	14.46	0.61	46.52	16,513
	+0.83	+0.22	+8.28	+2.83	+0.09	−3.05	+1,596
	+1.69	+2.54	+0.88	+11.05	+0.85	−25.22	+4,890
General	4.98	10.29	20.08	10.30	1.12	13.30	46,064
	−1.38	−5.28	+3.61	−0.81	−0.49	+1.16	+3,754
	+1.07	+5.63	+10.09	+1.35	+0.42	+0.81	+14,380

Table 7.1. (*cont.*)

Field: Industry	Telecoms (%)	Semicon. (%)	Computers (%)	Image (%)	Laser (%)	Insts. (%)	Total nos.
All	4.94	7.64	16.11	14.28	1.02	18.63	98,964
	−0.61	−3.07	+5.38	−1.82	−0.04	+3.35	+8,075
	+0.76	+4.29	+5.17	+2.22	+0.60	−2.76	+29,913

Notes:
[a] For each branch of industry: First row shows the average share over the whole period
Second row shows the change in percentage share, 1969–74 to 1980–4
Third row shows the change in percentage share, 1980–4 to 1990–4
[b] In the final column, the second and third rows show change in totals (adjusted for the longer length of the first sub-period).
− = outside range or not calculated.

Table 7.2. *Share of "heartland" technologies in each branch of industry, by region*

Industrial branch	Region	"Heartland" share (%)	All Electronics share (%)
Telecoms	Europe	32.4	64.9
	America	20.2	55.5
	Asia	14.6	50.7
Computers	Europe	45.1	62.1
	America	36.1	64.6
	Asia	27.4	65.7
Semiconductors	Europe	31.2	86.3
	America	22.4	70.9
	Asia	4.6	31.5
Consumer electronics	Europe	13.5	48.8
	America	30.5	70.0
	Asia	24.9	61.3
Instruments	Europe	11.6	16.6
	America	39.3	33.2
	Asia	46.5	32.7

a

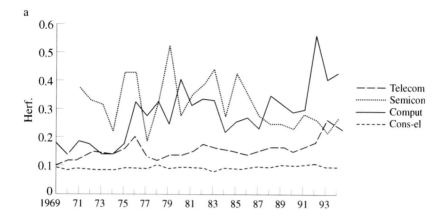

b

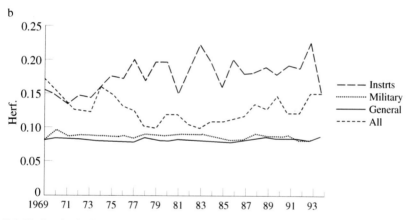

7.2 Technological concentration, European industries

in table 7.3, where I have run linear regressions against time and also quadratic regressions, as a number of the charts in the figures appear to show
U-shaped or other non-linear behavior. The quadratic calculations allow us
to calculate, using simple calculus, the year at which the Herfindahl Index
reached its trend minimum – i.e., the least degree of specialization in technologies (in some cases the patterns were inverse-U-shaped and a
maximum was therefore calculated, while some results failed to provide
either within the time range of the data).

For the European companies in figure 7.2, the upper panel shows a fairly
sustained upward trend – i.e., towards increased specialization, in the telecoms companies and computer companies which are our special concern.

a

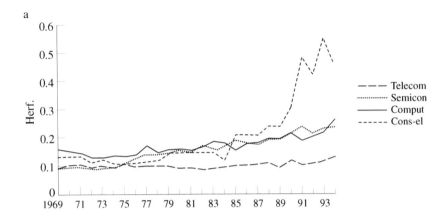

b

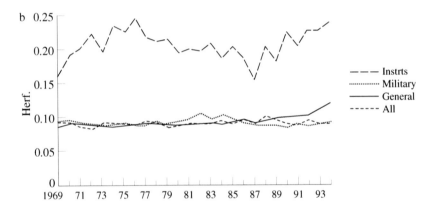

7.3 Technological concentration, American industries

The other patterns from this and the lower panel are less clear to the eye (the jaggedness of the semiconductor curve is because of the small number of patents accruing to SGS–Thomson – or rather its predecessors – in its early years). The table of regression results confirms the strong significance of a linear rise in specialization in the telecoms and computer companies, but also finds a similar result for consumer electronics and instrument companies. The semiconductor branch (composed of just the one company) is the only one to show a significant trend to diversification, though the significance is less than the 5 percent level. Military electronics shows a

a

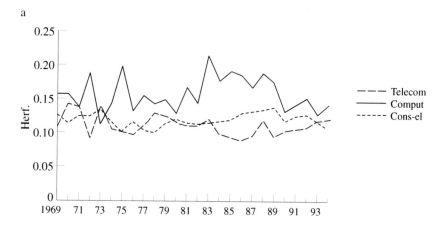

b

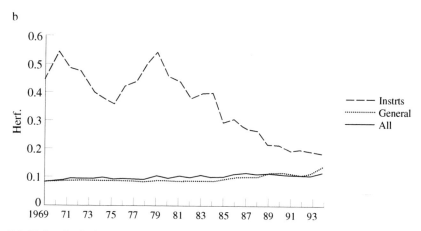

7.4 Technological concentration, Asian industries

significant U-shape in the quadratic equations, as is also obvious to the eye. Instrument companies show a retreat from increased specialization in later years.

For the North American companies (figure 7.3), the graphs show a more consistent picture, with most branches displaying a trend towards increased specialization, most evidently in the later years of the whole period. The linear regressions on time were all strongly significant except for instruments and general companies. For the telecoms and computer companies of our greatest concern, the quadratic results are especially interesting, with

Table 7.3. *Regressions of Herfindahl Index against time*

Industry	Time[a]	Time$_1$[a]	Time^2[a]	Minimum year
Europe				
Telecoms	+4.28***	−0.26	+1.44	1972
Computers	+5.16***	+1.38	−0.07	−
Semiconductors	−1.92*	+1.03	−1.51	−
Consumer	+3.93***	−0.24	+1.32	1972
Instruments	+3.12***	+3.00***	−2.20**	1987[b]
Military	−0.88	−5.57***	+5.42***	1983
General	−1.57	+ 0.13	−0.55	1973
All	+1.90*	−2.33**	+2.99***	1980
N. America				
Telecoms	+2.55**	−2.96***	+3.93***	1979
Computers	+7.89***	−1.16	+3.85***	1973
Semiconductors	+21.92***	+5.00***	+0.62	−
Consumer	+6.67***	−4.38***	+7.90***	1977
Instruments	+0.37	−0.52	+0.63	1980
General	−1.00	+1.27	−1.58	1980
All	+5.86***	−4.43***	+7.42***	1977
Asia				
Telecoms	−1.94*	−1.53	+1.06	1988
Computers	+0.21	+1.57	−1.57	1982
Consumer	+1.29	−1.13	+1.52	1979
Instruments	−8.71***	+0.24	−2.92***	1970[b]
General	+6.46***	−3.50***	+6.47***	1977
All	+8.94***	+3.24***	−0.97	−

Notes:
All figures in table (except years) are t-values.
*** = significant at 1 percent level.
** = significant at 5 percent level.
* = significant at 10 percent level.
[a] Independent variables are:
    Time = time (1969 = 0);
    Time$_1$ = time in quadratic equation;
    Time^2 = time squared in quadratic equation.
[b] = maximum rather than minimum.
− = outside range or not calculated

the trends towards diversification ceasing in the 1970s and thereafter exhibiting a pattern of increasing specialization; a pattern also pursued rather more obviously by consumer electronics (the very high specialization of the latter's final years is, however, largely a result of the segment's decline, as noted below). The instruments branch is not significant in linear or quadratic forms, but the cubic specification (not shown here) gives a significant local trend minimum in 1986.

The Asian companies in figure 7.4 differ much more among themselves. Instruments show a sustained trend to diversification (in part into electronics), supported by the regression results. The general electronics companies show increased specialization, especially in later years, and again in practice into electronics. The telecoms companies show a linear decline but a non-significant rise in later years in the quadratic forms. In general, it seems reasonable to argue that the Asian companies (figure 7.4) show a greater influence of the pervasiveness of the electronics "paradigm." Japanese companies like Fujitsu and NEC make much greater publicity of their efforts towards technological convergence than do Western companies, and the patents data to some extent bear out their claims. However the extent to which they are really bringing about a technological convergence or simply amalgamating two disparate technologies under the one corporate roof remains a matter of dispute.

The Herfindahl Index does not necessarily identify which are the areas of specialization or diversification. A telecoms company, for instance, which had second strengths in computing from an early date, could show increased specialization and yet be exhibiting technological convergence, through building up in these two areas. The next set of regressions made use of all 22 technological fields (as in appendix 7.2) and considered the changes in the percentage of patents in these fields. Two periods were chosen over which to examine such changes: one from the early 1970s to the early 1980s, and the second from the early 1980s to the early 1990s. Quinquennial averages were taken to limit the risk of influence from erratic observations.[6] These changes were regressed against the "revealed technological advantage" (RTA) of the industry. The RTA measure is one that has become familiar from much recent empirical work in this general field – it is comparable to the measure of revealed comparative advantage (RCA) used in analyses of international trade. Here the standard is taken as being set by the aggregate of electronics companies broadly defined, so we are focusing upon the relative differences within the whole sector.

The main concern was to find out the relationship between the changing

---

[6] The average for the early 1970s was actually taken over the six years, 1969–74, and adjusted accordingly.

Table 7.4. *Regressions of patent field share on RTAs,*
1969–1974 to 1980–1984 and 1980–1984 to 1990–1994

Region	RTA, period 1[a]	RTA, period 2[a]
Europe	1.96*	−0.05
N. America	2.69***	3.29***
Asia	−1.80*	−0.20
Total	1.06	0.94

Note:
[a] For significance levels, see notes to table 7.3.

share of a patent field and its overall relative importance, as given by the RTA. A positive association would show that the branch of industry concerned was raising the proportionate amount of its patents that were coming from its overall areas of relative strength. The full range of industry and technology intercept dummies could be included as the number of observations was large. In fact, these made only a modest difference to the significance estimated for the variable of interest, which was the RTA. The full results are too lengthy to report, but a brief resumé is given in table 7.4.

The results show a pattern towards specialization in Europe and an opposite one towards diversification in Asia in the first period, while both average out as being more or less constant in the second period. The North American results show strongly significant trends towards specialization overall in both periods. Disaggregation to the level of the individual branch of industry is likely to show similar results to those already given in table 7.2.

In summary, the results to date indicate that the companies of the various segments of the electronics industry were building on older strengths rather than diversifying into new fields, and their patenting behavior shows little diversification of the kind implied by the notion of technological convergence. At least, this much can be said for the North American and European telecoms and computer industries – for the Asian companies (predominantly Japanese) the situation is more ambiguous.

Organizational change

The next section of the chapter takes the firm rather than the industry as the unit of analysis, and seeks to discover how the corporations themselves were coming to terms with the kinds of problems implied by figure 7.1. This brings us face-to-face with the turbulence in the structure of the industry that took place mainly in the mid- and late 1980s – i.e., during our second specified time period.

From the later 1960s, the governments of a number of Western European countries (and Japan) had sought to respond to fears of American dominance of the electronics industry by trying to forge "national champions," usually by merger of domestic companies and sometimes by bringing in American capital and know-how. Few of these governmental efforts met with any evident success.

By the middle of the 1980s, wider developments such as the globalization of product markets, liberalization of production and marketing conditions, deregulation of industries, and so on, had revealed the inadequacies of attempts to maintain "drawbridge" notions of national champions. Foreign competition was growing inexorably. Moreover, the domestic markets of most countries, even medium-sized ones such as the larger European countries, were still too small to sustain across-the-board strengths in all electronics fields (Arnold and Guy, 1986); and the pressures noted above of rising R&D and investment costs plus product market turbulence rendered this continually less sustainable. The new restructuring thus aimed at greater specialization within particular sub-fields of the electronics industry. The aim had shifted from one of developing national champions to that of advancing "international champions," capable of conducting their own viable foreign operations in a world of product globalization, liberalization, etc. International exchanges of technologies and markets were arranged through a mushrooming of strategic alliances, such as have been widely studied in the literature on management and on innovation. However our main interest in the present chapter concerns the attempted restructuring of some of the major corporations themselves in such a context.

The kinds of changes observed can be roughly grouped as follows:
(a) takeovers of smaller firms (themselves of medium or small–medium size) to compensate for perceived technological weaknesses
(b) takeovers and alliances, intended more for market expansion
(c) mergers or takeovers, for basic survival
(d) cross-takeovers, exchanges and joint ventures (JVs) to reduce complexity
(e) demerging for focus
(f) takeovers and alliances to diversify through technological convergence.

The dividing line between these categories in some cases is a fine one, and some might be classified under more than one of the headings, but there is little to gain at this stage by insisting on a particular taxonomy. There are really two consequences of greater significance that I wish to argue for. The first is that there has been no uniquely successful means by which firms have been able to adjust to the changing technological and institutional environment. Because of the multi-dimensionality of the problem, it seems highly likely that no unique solution will ever be found, and quite likely that there is no "solution" in any case – firms will have to be content with approximating the kinds of organizational structures optimally required.

The second outcome is that attempts to diversify according to the inherent drift of the technologies (situation (f) above) have been least successful of all the strategies to date, on the whole. Of course, this does not refute the notion that ultimately such transformations will be made. At present, the kinds of markets becoming available for the new technological creations are being entered more by start-up firms, especially in the United States, and in more limited areas by established software and media companies. The future of the industries concerned could scarcely be more open.

A number of European examples are chosen for closer analysis here. The first is the case of the French company CGE (Compagnie Générale d'Electricité), now known as Alcatel. Although some of the developments we are analyzing preceded Alcatel's major changes, in a sense it was the maneuvers of this company at the end of 1986 which launched the period of greatest turbulence. The American company ITT was experiencing problems with its European operations in telecoms switching, so CGE/Alcatel seized the opportunity to buy up these operations and focus more tightly on such a field, previously developed within the company through its much older acquisition of CIT (Compagnie Industrielle de Télécommunications). Alcatel NV, with its nominal HQ in the Netherlands, was established in January 1987. The telecoms switching thus became split off from traditional heavy electrical equipment, which became the core business of the segment of CGE that was renamed as Alcatel Alsthom. Subsequently a third, though smaller, strand separated from the others into Alcatel Cable, built around another older acquisition of Les Cables de Lyon, and with its core business in transmission areas of telecommunications. A "counterfactual" reconstruction of the company's patents based on these three broad groupings, which now exist fairly independently of one another, shows the long persistence of their separate technological competencies.

The British equivalent, GEC (General Electric Company plc), came together in something like its present form in 1968, under British governmental blessing, to reduce domestic competition and create a more integrated national production unit. By the 1980s GEC had earned a reputation for having pursued a strategy of profit centers and short-termism, most notoriously under-investing by diverting profits to speculation in City money markets during some years of that decade. In terms of figure 7.1, the company focused fairly exclusively on the product rather than the technology end of the spectrum. Quasi-monopolistic contract-based markets were regarded as the most reassuring, and following them niche markets operating as close oligopolies. GEC continued its strategy of domestic takeover in the interests of reducing competition and accessing rival technologies, including the carve-up of Plessey after 1988; but became increasingly dependent on foreign collaboration for technologies and markets, as in its JV link with Alsthom of France.

Racal was another British company which had grown rather haphazardly through constant merger and takeover from the time of its foundation after the Second World War. From 1988 it decided to hive off the commercially successful mobile phone operations (Vodafone), partly to avoid takeover (at this stage by Cable and Wireless). Eventually in 1991 it split itself into three, mostly to focus upon specific market segments – e.g., to permit Vodafone to compete against its closest rival, Cellnet (linked to British Telecom). At the same time, the security area, based around the acquisition of Chubb Locks and Safes in 1984, was also demerged from the core electronics areas to become Racal Security. The latter has had very few patents over the years in electronics fields, and a relatively high proportion in the machinery and metals fields, linked to its specialization in locks and safes. Conversely Racal Electronics has little presence in machinery and metals, but a considerable one in electronics.

The third British example considered is Standard Telephones and Cables (STC). Until the late 1980s this acted as a subsidiary of the American multinational, ITT, and had few patents of its own. Nevertheless it was very active in developing technologies in this period, and is often regarded as having made the biggest single breakthrough in a journal article published in 1966, demonstrating the feasibility of fiber optics. For this period, the patents granted to ITT which came from United Kingdom sources have thus been reallocated to STC as an approximation of what STC's laboratories achieved. On the other side lay International Computers Ltd. (ICL), created under duress by the same Labour government about the time of the GEC merger, in an attempt to create a "national champion" in the computer industry. These efforts to maintain independence limped on into the 1980s, but from 1980 technological links were made to the Japanese company, Fujitsu, and ICL began to reduce its concentration on computer hardware in favor of a growing attention to software and applications, especially systems integration. The struggling commercial performance of ICL encouraged the Conservative (Thatcher) government to take a kindly view when STC, with a solid market performance behind it, took over ICL in 1984. The then fashionable notions of a "convergence" between communications and computing appeared to give a rationale to this takeover. The fortunes of the two, however, then went in reverse directions.

Under new management and with considerable Japanese impetus, ICL recovered and began making sustained profits. STC waned under indifferent management, and its parent ITT was also experiencing serious problems in its international telecommunications operations (see below). The Canadian firm, Northern Telecom (NT or Nortel), took over some of ITT's equity stake. ICL sought independence from STC, and after some negotiations with European buyers allowed itself in July 1990 to be taken over by Fujitsu, in an operation that caused considerable disquiet more widely in Europe. A few months later STC allowed Northern Telecom to take effective control of itself.

In CGE's French co-champion, Thomson SA, new management in the firm (hitherto Thomson Brandt) in the early 1980s resolved to reduce its six or so product areas to just two, and set about extensive discussions with a variety of partners to conduct the requisite exchanges, sales, and acquisitions, including those with CGE over telecoms. The two remaining nuclei were to be defense electronics, built around Thomson's subsidiary CSF (Compagnie Générale de Télégraphie Sans Fil), and consumer electronics, developed from the subsidiary Thomson Grand Publique, which became known as Thomson Consumer Electronics (TCE). In July 1987, the largest step towards consolidation of this field was taken by agreeing a deal with the US giant, General Electric (GE), over carving up the ailing US firm RCA (Radio Corporation of America), much of which had already fallen under GE's wing. Thomson agreed to buy the consumer electronics sections of RCA in return for selling its medical electronics division to GE. The latter was to be found primarily in Thomson's older acquisition, CGR (Compagnie Générale de Radiologie).

Apart from medical electronics and telecoms (also data-processing), another area Thomson was pruning was components, especially semiconductors. Here the company had to proceed more carefully, because of the obvious threat to dynamism provided by neglecting upstream development in microelectronics. Around 1985 the company had looked across the Atlantic, and sought to revive its semiconductor fortunes by acquiring the specialist chip firm, Mostek, from the rather incoherent US conglomerate, United Technologies.

An alternative was offered more locally within Europe by linking up with the Italian firm, SGS (Società Generale Semiconduttori SpA), which had an enterprising management team but was suffering from restricted technological competencies and market impact. Opinions differ on whether this was a takeover of SGS by Thomson Semiconducteurs or the reverse (or both). Whatever the case, SGS–Thomson became a viable third producer of chips in Europe (after Philips and Siemens). In 1989 it took over the high-tech British firm, Inmos, whose main objective was producing the "transputer" (computer on a chip). Both Inmos and Mostek boosted SGS's base in computing as well as in semiconductors.

The other Italian company included for more intensive study is Olivetti, which also passed into the hands of more dynamic management at the end of the 1970s – in this case, the flair of Carlo de Benedetti, who sought to take Olivetti onwards from its traditional strengths in typewriters to greater possibilities in computers. In the early 1980s, Olivetti struck up a relationship with the US giant telecoms concern, AT&T (American Telephone and Telegraph), which had recently suffered what then was seen as a major reverse on antitrust grounds, of being forcibly separated from its regional operating companies (the "Baby Bells"). However the same judgment had given AT&T greater power to operate abroad, and Olivetti and its computers seemed a suitable prospect for developing notions of "convergence" along lines outlined above. In December 1983 AT&T took a 25 percent stake in Olivetti, and some top Olivetti personnel in the latter were transferred to AT&T. This relationship ran into difficulties as AT&T experienced much greater problems than it had expected in developing computer systems for the US market, and the relationship between the two soured. The data here on technological profiles show that the two were entirely different in their technological profiles, and from this viewpoint it does not seem at all difficult to explain why the synergies were much less than anticipated. AT&T refocused its attention on Italy via STET (Società Finanziaria Telefonica), the parastatal telecoms organization, rather than in computers. Unwilling, however, to abandon notions of "convergence," and pressured by its domestic rivalry with IBM, it acquired the US computer firm NCR (formerly National Cash Registers) at the end of 1990 in a hostile takeover. After massive losses, the latter finally began to fall apart in 1995.

At the same time as it was developing fairly informal links with AT&T, Olivetti was also seeking more formal annexations within Europe. One of the biggest of these was its takeover of the German typewriter company, Triumph–Adler, in 1986. Questions were asked about the takeover on antitrust grounds, but in view of the legal complexities of cross-European links, a blind eye was turned and the takeover went ahead. Examination of the technological fields in greater detail, using annual data, shows a pronounced overlap in office equipment, with even the time patterns having some similarity. The data also show that, despite the internal switch of emphasis under de Benedetti, Olivetti has rather slowed down in the number of computing patents granted in the 1980s and 1990s as compared with the 1970s. Seemingly undiscouraged by the AT&T débâcle, it currently appears to be shifting emphasis back into telecoms, through its own subsidiary Omnitel.

The German company, Siemens, stood out against the trend towards greater specialization. Over its long history, Siemens had developed strengths across the board in electronics and electricals, and has sought to preserve this range up to the present day. By implication, it has faced massive costs for technology development when confronted by such a broad sweep of product markets. The great size of the company – along with Philips, Europe's largest in electronics in terms of turnover, and one of the world's largest private companies in terms of employment – has permitted it to maintain this range. The arguments favoring such a diversified product portfolio, however, ran into problems of commercial sluggishness and some technological deficiencies (e.g., in trying to develop its intermediate semi-electronic switch). Siemens long set its face against aggressive maneuvers such as large takeovers, in which in any case it would probably have faced legal problems on grounds of antitrust, etc. Support was received by linking with other large companies for joint research ventures, and by receiving research assistance from governments, both national and supranational. Despite all this, the leading-edge areas of chips and computers continue to be an area of concern to the company, with a fairly unbroken sequence of losses up to the present. To try to encourage more entrepreneurial attitudes, Siemens restructured its seven or so divisions into about 30 smaller units in the later 1980s, and a considerable portion of its US patenting now emanates from these smaller subsidiaries.

Aside from internal measures, some market expansion was undertaken by takeover of medium-sized companies, regardless of the company's pro-claimed ethos, one case being the dismemberment of Plessey with GEC in 1988, though of greater significance to Siemens itself was the takeover of Nixdorf at the beginning of 1990, as a distress sale. The combined computer activities of Siemens and Nixdorf in SNI (Siemens–Nixdorf Informationssysteme) has thus become Europe's largest indigenous computer firm, though far smaller than the European operations of IBM (Malerba, Torrisi, and von Tunzelmann, 1991). As already pointed out, however, its substantial size has not been sufficient to render it very profit-able, and the time during which this could be explained by difficulties of restructuring the combined operations (i.e., digestion) is now passing.

Tables 7.5 and 7.6 aim to summarize the findings, not only the patterns for the corporations as a whole, but the impact of major takeovers or demergers on the patenting profile. Here we seek to assess whether the cor-porations' principal maneuvers may have widened the range of their com-petencies, or instead aimed at consolidating them.

The data are organized according to two time intervals. The first, drawn from our earlier work (1988, 1993), uses the company structures as of 1986, and considers the time period from 1970 to 1991. This is therefore the situa-

Table 7.5. *Change in Herfindahl Indexes for selected firms, 1970–1991 to 1986–1994*

Company (1)	$H1^a$ 1970–91 (2)	Change[b] (3)	$H1^a$ 1986–94 (4)	Change[b] (5)	Diff.[c] in H1 (6)	$H3^a$ 1986–94 (7)	Change[d] H3 (8)
Alcatel (CGE)	0.0868	−0.0018	0.1061	0.0137	0.0193	0.0296	−0.0010
GEC	0.1480	0.0523	0.1619	−0.0221	0.0139	0.0259	−0.0043
Olivetti	0.1628	0.0862	0.2909	0.1099	0.1281	0.1868	−0.0160
Racal	0.1290	0.0928	0.1896	0.0518	0.0606	0.0623	0.0166
STC	0.1249	0.0625	0.1822	0.0668	0.0573	0.0566	0.0230
Nortel	0.1402	−0.0021	0.1660	0.0876	0.0258	0.0423	0.0127
Siemens	0.0980	0.0177	0.1263	0.0077	0.0283	0.0162	0.0029
Thomson	0.0967	−0.0075	0.1137	0.0553	0.0170	0.0305	0.0257
SGS–Thomson	0.2570	0.0733	0.2996	−0.0092	0.0426	0.0965	0.0089
Wtd. Av.	0.1125	0.0207	0.1434	0.0200	0.0309	0.0327	0.0064

Notes:
[a] H1 and H3 columns show averages for each period for the whole corporations.
[b] "Change" columns show intra-period changes (1970–4 to 1987–91, and 1986–6 to 1992–4, respectively).
[c] "Difference" column shows change in overall H1 from first to second period.
[d] "Change in H3" is for second period only (i.e., 1986–8 to 1992–4).

tion relating to company structures before the main period of turbulence. The results here utilize what we call the "1-digit" Herfindahl Index, essentially based on the list of technological fields given in appendix 7.2 (with slight variations). For the second period, running from 1986 to 1994, I have processed some more detailed data, and am able to compute a "3-digit" Herfindahl Index. This is based on OTAF's classification of patent codes, together with a few more sub-divisions of our own to accord with the "1-digit" breakdown.

Table 7.5 shows the change in the Herfindahl Indexes for each parent company between the two periods. The companies include most of the major European companies that experienced radical corporate change, together with the Canadian firm Northern Telecom, because of its role in taking over STC. The weighted average of Herfindahl Indexes given at the foot of table 7.5 shows a rise in the 1-digit index (H1) from 0.1125 in the first period to 0.1434 in the (partially overlapping) second period (column (4)); thus a rise of 0.0309 as shown in column (6). The latter column shows that indeed every company in this list was more concentrated in the second

Table 7.6. *Effects of corporate changes, for parent company, on Herfindahl Indexes, 1970–1994*

Maneuver	Period[a]	Change in H1 Index[b]	Change in H3 Index[b]
Divisions	1[a]	+0.0401	
	2[a]	+0.0611	+0.0410
Subsidiaries	2	+0.0021	+0.0005
Acquisitions	1	−0.0012	
	2	−0.0019	−0.0020
Takeovers	1	−0.0058	
	2	+0.0031	+0.0007
Joint ventures	1	−0.0059	
	2	−0.0594	−0.0013
Divestments	1	−0.0370	
	2	+0.0022	+0.0034

Notes:
[a] Period 1 = 1970–91 (1986 company structures).
    Period 2 = 1986–94 (1992 company structures).
[b] Figures show the increase/decrease in parent company Herfindahl Index from the specified maneuver

period than in the first, after allowing for the change in the corporate base. The table also shows the "intra-period" change in the H1 index. The weighted average for the first period, which considers the change between a first sub-period (1970–74) and a final one (1987–91) gives a rise of 0.0207 (column (3)), although not all firms showed an increase in concentration over this stretch of time. The change within the much shorter second period was of similar proportions (+0.0200) (column (5)), again with some exceptions for the individual firms. The final column (8) shows the change in the much more disaggregated H3 (3-digit Herfindahl) index. This is considerably smaller in magnitude than in the H1 index, but this is mainly a result of the lower overall index when taken to this level of disaggregation. The change as a percentage of the whole-period average is greater than for H1 (nearly 20 percent as compared with nearly 14 percent). There is thus little indication of diversification even at this more disaggregated level.

These results for the corporations as a whole can be supplemented by examining the specific types of maneuver they carried out. The results are provided in table 7.6. In this table, the types of changes have been aggregated for each of the companies involved – that is to say, we take all of each affected company's acquisitions together, all of their JVs, etc., insofar as they are analyzed in this study (see Appendix 7.3, p. 155). An alternative would be to take each acquisition by itself, but the numbers involved would be large and the effect on the parent company usually fairly small. The results of this sub-aggregation are shown in table 7.6. The figures show the difference between the parent company's index without the type of maneuver and that once the maneuver is allowed for. The results are for the whole of each period (1970–91 or 1986–94), though H3 is not at present available for the former period; as before, they are weighted averages of the parent companies.

Divisionalization had a marked effect on increasing concentration within the new divisions (as compared with the earlier conglomerate form) – this includes demergers like Racal. The effect is particularly marked in the more recent period (for the first period, these are *ex post* counterfactual reconstructions of what the demerged company would have looked like, as previously explained). The proliferation of quasi-autonomous subsidiaries (as, for example, by Siemens) had similar effects for similar reasons, though more muted in their impact because of affecting only a minority of the companies' patents. The remaining maneuvers were somewhat more likely to lead to greater diversification than greater concentration, though both takeovers and divestments slightly enhanced concentration in the second period. (The result for divestments in the earlier period suggests they led to deconcentration, though our earlier findings for a much larger number of companies showed a clear pattern of divestments to encourage focusing on the principal technological fields of the companies.) The finding for JVs is particularly interesting, because it suggests that JVs were indeed being used to seek complementary technologies. An interesting case has been Siemens' use of a JV with Bendix to move into what for Siemens was a new product field – that of automotive electronics – in the mid–1980s. After a short period, Siemens set up its own division in the field, which quickly usurped most of the patenting of the JV. These results thus suggest that JVs are being used productively to maintain or obtain footholds in more peripheral technologies, as indeed much of the recent outpouring of literature on strategic alliances has suggested. However the number of cases analyzed here is small, partly because in general JVs do little patenting, and other results from broader data sets are less encouraging to such a hypothesis (e.g., Duysters, 1995).

Weighted regressions were used to demonstrate the different use of maneuvers to achieve differing technological goals. With size of parent company used as the weight, the $\bar{R}_s^2$ were 0.328 for the changes in H1 and 0.586 for the changes in H3, with all the dummy variables for type of maneuver significantly different at the 1 percent level of significance from that of the basis maneuver (taken to be divisionalization).

The picture that emerges from the study of the electronics companies is thus one of growing technological devolution within companies, growing technological concentration within the companies as a whole, and perhaps some resort to external maneuvers to maintain or enlarge the requisite multi-technology characteristics. Casual evidence from other attempted restructurings that are not covered by these tables – for example, the attempts by Ericsson to diversify into computing or by IBM into communications – seem to back up the results produced so far, and suggest that the provisional findings would be reinforced rather than undermined by taking a larger number of examples into account.

Summary

We may thus summarize the findings of recent experience by suggesting a need for a balance between specialization and diversification. Companies tend to favor greater specialization, on balance, unless they have very deep pockets. In times when expansion is curtailed, this encourages them to rationalize R&D and limit what looks like duplication. However it is out of variety and a multiplicity of approaches that advance most often comes, as the evolutionary school of economists suggests; so the trade-off to be struck here is a rather fragile one. Over-rationalization, such as that conducted by GEC following its 1968 takeovers, is a likely path to decline, at least in competitive leading-edge technologies. Governments, on the other hand, perhaps tend to lean too far towards diversification, as indicated by their support for such takeovers and the creation of (inter-)national champions. One thinks here, for instance, of Mme Cresson's attempt in France in the early 1990s to create a super-company to rival Siemens. The financial sector also has a long history of exaggerating the benefits of greater scale and scope. Again, the balance between these interests will be a rather fine one.

Secondly, our results point to the need for considering "dynamic capabilities" as an on-going process of interaction between the evolution of products, technologies, and processes, as in both the vertical and horizontal dimensions of figure 7.1. In a world in which all of these are proliferating, most have found it unwise to try to track everything, and have sought greater focus or specialization. But firms have resource capabilities which do not necessarily match the ways in which each of these is "drifting" in accord with broader technological and market imperatives. The matching can only be imperfect, as just stated – firms however have to try their best by working to reshape in the face of these external changes by adjusting what they do and how they do it internally. Some of the strategic management literature suggests "sticking to the knitting," which resembles the findings here about incremental adjustment, but does not specify what the "knitting" consists of – is it the products, the processes, or the technologies? In a dynamic and externally evolving context, the main point is to undertake interactive modifications within companies and supportive links outside via JVs, etc.

Thirdly, the analysis implies the restricted extent to which one can rely on "market forces" to carry out such restructurings. Product markets are for the most part competitive, and in them such pressures will no doubt prevail. Other hitherto protected markets within our field of vision are in the process of becoming competitive – for example, telecommunications operators. But markets in technologies are only weakly developed, and arguably ought not to be relied upon even if they were "perfected" in the economist's sense. In any case it seems extremely unlikely that such markets can be greatly "perfected," in view of the major role of information and knowledge in technological accumulation; both of which are exceedingly difficult to express through market mechanisms (von Tunzelmann, 1995, chapter 1). There still remains considerable validity in the view of the Japanese that "market forces" include the process of "forcing markets," in this case by accumulating technological and process competencies.

Finally, we must acknowledge the need to combine this rather limited approach through the patents data with other sources of information. Since the problem is seen basically as one of multi-dimensionality, we must have not only better data on the technologies, but good data on the other dimensions to go with them. Product and market data, in particular, need to be integrated with the technological indicators, in order to develop the "dynamic-capabilities" approach to a point where it becomes applicable in practice, as well as in theory.

Appendix 7.1. *List of companies and industries*

Industry branch	Company[a]	Country[b]	Number of patents
(A) European companies			
Telecoms	ANT Nacht.	DE[c]	119
	Telenorma	DE	22
	Jeumont–Schneider	FR	55
	Ascom	CH	163
	Ericsson	SC	888
	GN	SC	28
	NKT	SC	17
	Nokia	SC	360
	Italtel	IT[c]	47
	STET	IT	318

Appendix 7.1. (*cont.*)

Industry branch	Company[a]	Country[b]	Number of patents
(A) European companies (cont.)			
	BICC	UK	352
	BT	UK	746
	Plessey	UK	1,107
	Racal	UK	440
	STC	UK	299
Computers	Kienzle	DE	237
	Bull	FR	653
	Olivetti	IT	1,031
	ICL	UK	300
Semiconductors	SGS–Thomson	IT/FR	1,266
Consumer electronics	Bosch–Siemens Haus.	DE	107
	Loewe Opta	DE	35
	Philips	NL	14,493
	Bang and Olufsen	SC	13
	Bruel and Kjaer	SC	13
	Electrolux	SC	1,326
	Thorn–EMI	UK	850
Instruments	Robert Bosch	DE	6,151
	Landis & Gyr	CH	208
	Lucas	UK	3,182
Military	MBB	DE	1,395
	Matra	FR	203
	Dowty	UK	242
	Smiths Industries	UK	420
General	AEG	DE	1,910
	Mannesmann	DE	2,195
	Siemens	DE	13,945
	Alcatel	FR	4,332
	Thomson	FR	4,612
	ABB	SC/CH	5,378
	GEC	UK	3,722
(B) American companies			
Telecoms	AT&T	USA	13,444
	GTE	USA	6,227
	ITT	USA	6,476
	Northern Telecom	CA	1,734
	United Telecom.	USA	30
	Western Digital	USA	84
	3COM	USA	14

Appendix 7.1. (*cont.*)

Industry branch	Company[a]	Country[b]	Number of patents
(B) Americans companies (cont.)			
Computers	Amdahl	USA	141
	Apple	USA	223
	Atari	USA	102
	Bolt, Beranek & Newman	USA	52
	Control Data	USA	398
	Commodore	USA	29
	Compaq	USA	242
	Cray Research	USA	115
	Data General	USA	276
	Digital	USA	1,393
	Hewlett–Packard	USA	3,283
	IBM	USA	15,990
	Microsoft	USA	54
	NCR	USA	2,036
	Prime	USA	92
	Silicon Graphics	USA	37
	Sun Microsystems	USA	235
	Tandem	USA	163
	Tandon	USA	21
	Tandy	USA	152
	Unisys	USA	5,917
	Wang Labs.	USA	231
Semiconductors	Harris	USA	1,557
	Intel	USA	814
	LSI Logic	USA	140
	National Semiconductor	USA	1,192
	Texas Instruments	USA	6,020
	VLSI	USA	295
Consumer electronics	RCA	USA	8,247
	Zenith	USA	1,557
Instruments	Dynatech	USA	122
	Honeywell	USA	5,100
	Perkin–Elmer	USA	1,066
	Tektronix	USA	1,595
	Xerox	USA	9,570
Military	Raytheon	USA	2,290
	Rockwell	USA	5,641
	TRW	USA	2,901
	United Technologies	USA	7,619

Appendix 7.1. (*cont.*)

Industry branch	Company[a]	Country[b]	Number of patents
(B) Americans companies (cont.)			
General	General Electric	USA	22,819
	Motorola	USA	8,238
	Westinghouse	USA	12,026
(C) Asian companies			
Telecoms	KDD	JP	456
	NTT	JP	886
	Oki	JP	1,032
	Sumitomo Electric	JP	2,081
Computers	Fujitsu	JP	5,526
	Acer	TW	53
Semiconductors	Kyocera	JP	371
Consumer electronics	Alps Electric	JP	1,502
	Casio	JP	865
	JVC	JP	1,610
	Matsushita	JP	8,341
	Pioneer	JP	2,085
	Sanyo	JP	1,367
	Sharp	JP	3,796
	Sony	JP	5,834
	Lucky-Goldstar	KR	582
Instruments	Canon	JP	11,151
	Fanuc	JP	1,269
	Ricoh	JP	4,093
General	Hitachi	JP	16,549
	Mitsubishi Electric	JP	8,530
	NEC	JP	6,358
	Toshiba	JP	13,083
	Samsung	KR	1,544

Notes:
[a] The above list of companies was a basis for calculating the Herfindahl Indices. Years include: 1969–1994. Not all of the companies are necessarily independent (for example, some are owned by other companies in the list, some others by unspecified parents). The list makes no claims to be comprehensive, but includes most of the major patenting companies.
[b] Country refers to base of activities, not necessarily location of HQ (for example, some locate offshore for tax avoidance).
[c] Country key: CA = Canada; CH = Switzerland; DE = Germany; FR = France; IT = Italy; JP = Japan; KR = Korea; NL = the Netherlands; SC = Scandinavia; TW = Taiwan; UK = United Kingdom; USA = United States.

Appendix 7.2. *List of technological fields*

1	Telecommunications
2	Other communications
3	Semiconductors
4	Computing
5	Electrical devices
6	Image
7	Sound
8	Lasers
9	Instruments
10	Electrical equipment
11	Power
12	Machinery
13	Metals
14	Materials
15	Paper and printing
16	Textiles
17	Biological and agriculture
18	Chemicals
19	Fuels
20	Vehicles
21	Construction
22	Weapons

Note:
Some of the smaller categories have been
combined in analyzing particular firms.

Appendix 7.3. *Company maneuvers analyzed, from the mid-1980s*

Company	Country	Maneuver	New Company	
CGE/Alcatel	(FR)	DVN[a]	Alcatel Cables	after 1987
		DVN	Alcatel–CIT	after 1987
		DVN	Alsthom	after 1987
Alcatel (CIT)	(FR)	DVN	New divisions	after 1987
		ACQ	Alcatel–Thomson	after 1983
		ACQ	ITT acquisitions	Jan. 1987
		ACQ	National Telecom.	Dec. 1989
		ACQ	Telettra	Oct. 1990
Alsthom	(FR)	DVN	New divisions	after 1987
		ACQ	Incoming Alsthom acquisitions	after 1986

Appendix 7.3. (*cont.*)

Company	Country	Maneuver	New Company	
GEC	(UK)	TO	Plessey	Oct. 1987
		ACQ[b]	Outgoing GEC acquisitions	after 1986
		ACQ	Incoming GEC acquisitions	after 1986
		JV	GEC–Alsthom	Dec. 1988
		DMT	Divestments	throughout
Olivetti	(IT)	SUB	New subsidiaries	throughout
		ACQ	Triumph–Adler	Apr. 1986
		ACQ	Smaller acquisitions	throughout
		JV[b]	AT&T	1983/9
AT&T	(USA)	ACQ	NCR	Dec. 1990
		JV[b]	Olivetti	1983/9
Racal Electronics	(UK)	DVN	Racal Security	1991
		DVN	Vodafone	1988/91
STC	(UK)	ACQ[b]	ICL	Jul. 1990
		TO[b]	Northern Telecom	Nov. 1990
Northern Telecom	(CA)	TO	STC	Nov. 1990
Siemens	(DE)	TO	Plessey	Nov. 1988
		ACQ	Nixdorf	Jan. 1990
		SUB	New subsidiaries	after 1987
		JV	New joint ventures	after 1986
Thomson	(FR)	ACQ[b]	CGR	Jul. 1987
		ACQ	RCA	Jul. 1987
		DMT	Thomson Semiconds	throughout
SGS–Thomson	(IT/FR)	ACQ	Mostek (by Thomson)	1985
		DVN	SGS–Ates	Apr. 1987
		DVN	SGS–Thomson	Apr. 1987
		ACQ	Inmos	1989

Notes:
[a] ACQ = Acquisition; DMT = Divestments; DVN = Division; JV = Joint venture; SUB = Subsidiaries; TO = Takeover.
[b] "Failed" maneuver (sale of unit, etc.)

References

Arnold, E. and K. Guy (1986). *Parallel Convergence: National Strategies in Information Technology*, London: Pinter

Babbage, C. (1832). *On the Economy of Machinery and Manufactures*, London: Knight, London; repr. New York: Augustus M. Kelley, 1963

Dang Nguyen, G. (1985). "Telecommunications: A Challenge to the Old Order," in M. Sharp (ed.), *Europe and the New Technologies*, London: Pinter, 87–133

Ducharme, L.M. (1991). "Inter-industrial Technology Diffusion: A Macro Analysis of Technical Change in the Canadian Economy," DPhil thesis, Science Policy Research Unit, University of Sussex

Duysters, G. (1995). *The Evolution of Complex Industrial Systems: The Dynamics of Major IT Sectors*, Maastricht: Universitaire Pers, Maastricht

Freeman, C. (1992). *The Economics of Hope: Essays on Technical Change, Economic Growth and the Environment*, London and New York: Pinter

Malerba, F., S. Torrisi, and, N. von Tunzelmann (1991). "Electronic Computers," in C. Freeman, M. Sharp, and W. Walker (eds.), *Technology and the Future of Europe*, London: Pinter, 95–116

Nelson, R.R. and S.G. Winter, (1982). *An Evolutionary Theory of Economic Change*, Cambridge Mass. and London: The Belknap Press of Harvard University Press

Patel, P. and K. Pavitt (1994). "Technological Competencies in the World's Largest Firms: Characteristics, Constraints and Scope for Managerial Choice," *STEEP Discussion Paper* 13, Science Policy Research Unit, University of Sussex

(1995). "Large Firms in European Technology," HCM workshop, Urbino (February), mimeo

Pavitt, K. (1988). "Uses and Abuses of Patent Statistics," in A. van Raan (ed.), *Handbook of Quantitative Studies of Science and Technology*, Amsterdam: North-Holland

Soete, L. and N. von Tunzelmann (1987). "Diffusion and Market Structure with Converging Technologies," Research memorandum, University of Limburg

Teece, D. and G. Pisano (1994). "The Dynamic Capabilities of Firms: An Introduction," *Industrial and Corporate Change*, 3, 537–56

von Tunzelmann, N. (1988). "Convergence of Firms in Information and Communication: A Test Using Patents Data," Science Policy Research Unit, University of Sussex, mimeo

von Tunzelmann, G.N., with P. Patel and K. Pavitt (1993). "Evolution of Corporate Technology Profiles in IT&T: A Test Study of the Patent Approach," Final Report submitted to Commission of the European Communities, DG III

von Tunzelmann, G.N. (1995). *Technology and Industrial Progress: The Foundations of Economic Growth*, Aldershot: Edward Elgar

von Tunzelmann, G.N. (1996). "Localized Technological Search and Multi-technology Companies," *STEEP Discussion Paper*, 29, Science Policy Research Unit, University of Sussex

8 The dynamics of localized technological change

Cristiano Antonelli and Mario Calderini

Introduction: skill-intensive industries in the European economy

The notion of localized technological change seems especially appropriate to understanding the dynamics of innovation in much of European industry, heavily characterized by so-called "traditional sectors," such as the mechanical engineering sector or textiles and garments. Still, in many traditional industries technological change, as measured in terms of productivity growth, is intense and rapid. Indicators such as R&D intensity or patent-counting fail to appreciate the innovative capability of most traditional industries: technological change in fact is mainly based upon learning-by-doing and tacit knowledge rather than conventional R&D activities.

The distinction between traditional industries and high-tech industries in fact seems less and less appropriate when the dynamics of endogenous technological change based upon bottom-up processes of accumulation of technological knowledge plays a role. When the dynamics and the sources of technological change are analyzed according to the distinction between generic and localized knowledge, it seems clear that much of the European industry seems to fall into the new category of skill-intensive industries.

The notion of localized technological change makes it possible to implement the well known distinction elaborated by Pavitt (1987) between science based, supplier-dominated, specialized suppliers, and scale-intensive industries based upon the direction of the flows of technological information across industries. In the Pavitt classification, science-based industries are viewed as the main source of technological innovations that are eventually transferred to the rest of the economic system, embodied in capital goods and intermediary inputs.

A five-pronged classification which integrates the skill-intensive industries makes it possible to appreciate the dynamics of technological changes that are based upon localized technological knowledge. This differs significantly from the top-down process which views technological innovations as spurred on by scientific discoveries eventually implemented by R&D activities conducted by firms on which Pavitt's classification clearly relies. In these industries, the internal bottom-up learning process based upon the improvement of design and technological processes plays a major role in feeding the continual introduction of technological and organizational innovations.

The internal organization of companies and the relationship between production departments and marketing activities; the structure of internal labor markets and hence the wage structure and the role of seniority and efficiency wages, the integration of user–producer relations into the decision process of firms and in the accumulation of tacit knowledge; the creative and timely adoption of new capital goods and intermediary inputs; the implementation of technological changes by means of parallel changes in the organization of companies; the close interaction between changes in processes and products in terms of design are all aspects that play a major role in skill-intensive industries as a source of technological knowledge, and consequently of technological changes. Besides the specific nature of technological change and the high rates of total factor productivity (TFP) growth, complementary characteristics of skill-intensive industries are the small size of firms, the high levels of regional concentration, the high levels of wages and the low levels of capital intensity, and the tight web of cooperative agreements among firms.

The dynamics of localized knowledge

Standard Arrovian microeconomics suggests that technological information should be considered a public good, in that its use is non-excludable and non-rival and its production and use are characterized by high levels of indivisibility, it can also be easily transferred and learned at little cost. Thus, it cannot be appropriated by innovators but it can be applied to a wide variety of uses. In the traditional approach; the generation of technical knowledge is the result of a deductive chain that utilizes scientific discoveries and general methodological procedures developed mainly in pure research, and is then applied to the specific activities of each firm. The flow of technological information is considered to be a spontaneous aspect of economic systems. Intellectual property rights can increase appropriability but reduce the scope for the socialization of innovation benefits. The basic trade-off between appropriability regimes is that they offer incentives to innovate through patents and secrecy. There are, however, also losses because of the duplication of research efforts, delays in diffusion, and obstacles to the recombination of knowledge.

This traditional view of technology as information is being increasingly challenged by recent developments of the Schumpeterian approach, which stress the distinction between information and knowledge – for information is an input in the production of knowledge. Technological knowledge is "localized" in tacit learning processes that are related to the background and experience of the innovator. Hence, it is largely excludable and its use is partly rivalrous. In fact, technological knowledge tends to be highly localized in well defined technical, institutional, regional, and industrial situations. As localized technological knowledge is firm-specific, it is costly to use elsewhere. The transfer and adaptation of localized technological knowledge from one firm to another involves specific costs which according to many empirical analyses amount to almost the same sum as the original cost of introducing new technology. The localized character of technical knowledge increases its appropriability but reduces its spontaneous circulation in the economic system (Antonelli, 1995 and 1999).

Technological change is inherently localized in that it consists of changes in the technical capability of the production process and the structure of organization that are limited to a well defined set of characteristics, in terms of size, age, location, industrial specialization, levels of integration and diversification, mix of complementary and inter-related inputs, cumulated competence, skills, factor and output market strategies of firms. Localized technological change builds upon two different forms of knowledge: the generic and the tacit. The former is based upon scientific and structured information that as a public good is available to everybody with low costs of imitation and acquisition. The latter is the result of lengthy learning processes, is highly idiosyncratic and specific to the business environment of the firm. Technological change can be more or less localized according to the mix of generic and tacit knowledge it relies upon, but neither is disposable.

The approach to localized technological knowledge as a quasi-private good elaborates on recent understanding about the origins and flows of the generation process of technological knowledge within organizations and in the relations among organizations:

(1) *technological knowledge is embedded in the "circumstances" in which the firm operates* – hence technological change is localized in the techniques currently used by each firm, in the markets in which each firm operates, in the existing information channels among firms and customers, in the organizational structure of firms, and in the informational space in which each firm operates.

(2) *The traditional distinction between new technologies and existing technologies appears much less strong.* In fact, relevant search costs are necessary to acquire information and command of techniques different from those currently used, even if they are part of an existing technol-

ogy. Conversely, the generation of new technologies can rely on the knowledge acquired by means of learning-by-doing and learning-by-using in the spectrum of techniques currently used.

(3) *The generation of technological knowledge is the result of a joint process of production, learning and communicating* of which R&D activities should be considered only as a part. Consequently, R&D activities cannot and should not be considered the sole factors in the generation of new technological knowledge, and should not be separated from the current flow of activities within the firm and the relations between the firm and its environment.

In this approach, the generation of new knowledge is mainly the outcome of the efforts of innovators that draw on learning processes highly localized and specific to the history and experience of each innovator (David, 1993a, 1993b).

R&D expenses defined as the resources allocated in the specific activity of experimenting and developing new products and new processes are only an aspect of a more general process of learning and capitalizing on the experience acquired. The introduction of localized technological changes rests upon the availability of localized knowledge, which consists of highly specific and tacit bits of technological information featured by strong specific and idiosyncratic characters. Localized technological knowledge in turn emerges from daily routines and from the tacit experience acquired in using capital goods, in producing and manufacturing, and in interacting with customers and other manufacturers. Localized technological knowledge can also be viewed as the product of a systemic bottom-up process of induction from actual experience which contrasts sharply the individualistic top-down process of deduction from general scientific principles on which the received theory of knowledge as a public good formerly rested.

In this context, there is a growing consensus that technological knowledge, which is generated by firms, draws on a combination of four factors: internal and external codified knowledge and internal and external tacit knowledge. The generation of technological knowledge is, in fact, heavily dependent on the appropriate mix of learning processes which leads to the accumulation of tacit knowledge and formal R&D activities which enable codified knowledge to be gathered, processes of collective learning to be built up, and informal exchanges of information and experience among firms to develop along with forms of formal cooperation among firms which have their own R&D laboratories. In such a complex mix, each element is indispensable. However, the role played by each component evolves over time during the technology life-cycle (see table 8.1).

In fact, firms rely upon varying mixes of tacit and generic knowledge in order to generate localized technological innovations. The extent to which

Table 8.1. *The dynamics of the four dimensions*
of technological knowledge

	Tacit	Codified
Time		
Internal	Learning	R&D
External	Socialization	Recombination
	Time	

a firm can rely more on tacit and technological than on generic and scientific knowledge seems itself a variable that is influenced by the evolution of the characteristics of the economic and technological environment. Hence the study of the determinants of the innovation capability of firms must take into account the architectural characters of the innovation system into which each firm is embedded and more specifically three classes of factors:

(1) the amount of resources devoted to implementing the accumulation of tacit knowledge by each agent in the system

(2) its receptivity to technological knowledge generated by third parties; and

(3) the properties of the system in terms of connectivity and distribution of receptive agents.

New technological knowledge in fact emerges also from the daily interaction of learning firms among themselves and with other scientific institutions. In such interaction, communication and trading of information play a major role. The structure of inducement forces that pushes firms to introduce new localized technological innovations deserves careful analysis.

Role of demand-pull forces in the dynamics of localized technological change

Localized technological change is generated by the interplay between different mechanisms of inducements. When attrition forces such as elastic barriers (David, 1975) and switching costs, relevant information costs such as search costs and learning processes that, combined with R&D expenditures, make it possible to change the technology are all taken into account, the notion of localized technological change becomes pertinent. Localized technological change is the endogenous outcome of the interplay between substitution costs and learning processes (David, 1975; Atkinson and Stiglitz, 1969; Stiglitz, 1987). In fact, all changes in the levels of demand, input costs and relative competitivity for each firm engender substitution costs for switching both sizes and techniques (Antonelli, 1995 and 1999).

Changes in factor costs push firms to change their production techniques and hence to face emerging switching costs, especially in terms of search, firing, and scrapping so that, once more, firms may want to explore the opportunity to capitalize on their experience acquired by means of learning-by-doing and learning-by-using, with appropriate levels of R&D expenditures, so as to be able to increase their factor productivity and increase the TPF of the current mix of production factors without changing the factor intensity.

Changes in demand imply that firms are induced to make efforts to cope with the in(de)creased levels of their output by in(de)creasing the levels of their inputs: this, however, is subject to dimensional switching costs that push firms to mobilize all their learning capabilities so as to capitalize on the experience acquired and hence introduce innovations that make it possible to adjust output to the desired levels without changing their input levels.

The literature on demand-pull explores the determinants of the rates of introduction of technological change. Here the basic assumption is that firms are pushed to introduce technological innovations by the pressure of demand (Rosenberg, 1974). In fast-growing markets the rates of return to innovation are larger so as to trigger accrued innovative efforts of firms and independent inventors that eventually lead to the generation of faster rates of innovation (Schmookler, 1966). Kaldor provides a framework for analyzing this dynamic at the aggregate level. In fact, Kaldor makes explicit the hypothesis of a positive relationship between the growth of output and the growth of labor productivity in industries, countries, and regions, but not at the firm level, based upon the accelerated introduction of technological innovation triggered by the rates of growth of output (Kaldor, 1957; Kaldor and Mirrless, 1962).

The rate of growth of output is thus endogenously determined by the growth of labor productivity and the growth of capital productivity, both driven by technical invention or innovation in that more capital per worker available entails the introduction of superior techniques which embody technical progress and increased labor productivity assumes the use of more capital per person with increased efficiency (Kaldor, 1957). The underlying assumption here is one of increasing returns, which contribute to the reduction of the average unit costs and to a faster rate of economic growth if irreversibility in internal economies is also assumed. This effect is well known as the Kaldor (1957) principle and it is common to all firms.

Recent developments in evolutionary theory have nevertheless shown that cumulative causation and path dependency of economic processes not only apply to firms or industries as a whole (Kaldor, 1960), but that they are also at the core of selection mechanisms between competitive firms and technologies (Metcalfe, 1994). "Selection" in this context is based on the notion of variety in behavior as the essential driving force to produce change. Competition is no longer seen only as the result of differences in the rates of growth, but also as the rate of change of the market share of each individual firm – that is, comparative efficiencies of rival firms are strongly associated with their relative market position (Metcalfe, 1994). It follows that the process then is fully endogenous so that, in the presence of increasing returns, either the process of selection among behaviors in a given distribution or the actual distribution are endogenously determined.

The result is a strong interdependence between selection and variety. Increasing returns can be thought of as deriving from fairly diverse processes. Dynamic economies accumulate as a function of current output and are related to the learning processes of the firms – that is, to the knowledge and experience the firm has acquired over the years. This type of economy can be both internal and external if knowledge spillovers take place and if the firm is able to benefit from them. Static internal economies hoard as a function of the growth rate of output and depend only upon the range of output of each firm. Static external economies depend on the output of the industry and accumulate in proportion to its growth rate, but also depend on the relative position of each firm with respect to the mean industry growth rate. Hence firms which are expanding their market shares will be able to benefit more fully and at an accelerated pace from external economies. The Kaldor–Verdoorn effect takes into account only the average growth rate of the industry, while the Fisher principle accounts also for diversity of behavior and rate of improvement in average behavior. Hence, when adding the Fisher principle to the treatment of economic growth, one is able to stress the importance of both competitive selection across variety and the endogenous process generation of variety itself.

The Schumpeterian literature provides another set of explanations for understanding the role of demand in determining the rates of introduction of innovations. The Schumpeterian literature privileges the analysis at the firm level in out-of-equilibrium conditions where the variation between firms is taken to be the leading characteristic of the market-selection process. In the Schumpeterian literature the basic incentive to innovate is provided by market entropy (Metcalfe, 1989, 1992). The larger the time variance in market shares, the larger the efforts of firms to introduce innovations, for two contrasting and yet complementary reasons. Fast-growing firms that have increasing market shares, and hence larger levels of output, have larger mark-ups so that they can rely on larger cash flows, retain larger shares of them to fund internally risky projects, and hence invest larger amounts of resources in R&D activities (Metcalfe, 1995). Declining firms that on the contrary see both their market shares and their profits, and, hence, their output – shrinking are now induced by the emerging failure to fund R&D activities aggressively in order to survive and meet the adversity with the introduction of both product and process innovations (Antonelli, 1989). In sum, it should be clear that because of the attention paid to the variance in market shares the Schumpeterian literature stresses also the role of the demand at the firm level in assessing the amount of incentives for firms to introduce technological innovations.

Basic hypotheses

In the general context of our approach to the dynamics of localized technological change, the process of introduction of demand-pulled localized technological changes plays a major role. Firms facing the pressure to accommodate their size to the new levels of their demand – both generated by aggregate changes (as in post-Keynesian tradition), and by the increasing share of a given market (as in the Schumpeterian tradition), will face the trade-off between increasing their size either by means of extensive growth based on the increase in the levels of input, or by means of an intensive growth based upon the increase of the levels of general efficiency of their production technology.

The introduction of demand-pulled localized technological changes will be larger the larger is the increase in the demand levels, the larger the dimensional switching costs, and the larger the opportunities to generate innovations based upon the experience and local knowledge acquired by means of learning-by-doing and learning-by-using and R&D activities.

The overall increase of demand levels and the rightward shift of the demand curves has one more important effect in terms of the inducement of accelerated rates of diffusion of previous waves of technological innovations. Higher levels of investments, necessary to adjust output to the new desired levels, in fact make it possible for firms to adopt technological innovations that had been delayed by the sunk costs of existing fixed capital. All additional investments can be used to purchase new capital equipment that embody the new technologies. The diffusion of new capital goods embodying technological innovations reinforces the rates of productivity growth of the system and feeds further increases in real wages and the height of the demand curves.

In sum it should be clear that a strong positive relationship between the growth of TFP and the increase in the demand for the products can be expected at the firm level.

Empirical analysis

The empirical validation of the hypotheses specified in previous sections is based upon evidence about the mechanical engineering industry. Technological change in this industry, in fact, is characterized by the relevance of learning processes, both external and internal, creative recombination of existing knowledge, as well as standard R&D activities. Regional clustering of SMEs specialized in narrow yet complementary market niches plays a major role in enhancing connectivity and receptivity so as to make the circulation of the knowledge fast and effective. The data set includes 136 manufacturing firms in a time span of six years (1988–94). Such choice finds its motivations in the peculiar evolution of the discrete-parts manufacturing industry in that period, which is believed to be particularly representative of localized dynamics of technological change. In these years, the industry recovered from the crises of the late 1980s and experienced a fast growth fueled by the demand for capital goods after 1991, with an increase in added value, and – most important – TFP.

In a strict sense, the past decade has been characterized, in the medium and large mechanical firms, by the attempt to optimize production capabilities via an increase of efficiency in the production function in a strict sense, where the latter refers to the actual manufacturing line where parts are manufactured. A large amount of capital assets has therefore been devoted to the automation of production lines, with the specific purpose of maximizing productivity in terms of mere volumes. However, conscious of the tough challenge imposed by a new market scenario characterized by product diversity, emphasis on differentiation, shorter life-cycles, and pressure on time to market, mechanical industry placed a great deal of trust in flexible manufacturing paradigms, which were deemed to be able to reproduce economies of scale on a quite heterogeneous production mix. It is beyond the scope of this chapter to investigate the reasons for the substantial failure of the flexible paradigm, which had virtually closed the automation-rush by the end of the decade. Hopes to substantially increase productivity were consequently diverted to other aspects of manufacturing activities, which on the contrary were beginning to show increasing degrees of repetivity in industrial operations and were therefore indicated as potential sources of consistent productivity increases. Specifically, the product design function was granted the role of productivity-booster, which in the previous years had been granted to the manufacturing function *stricto sensu*. (Calderini and Cantamessa, 1997).

This paved the way, in the mechanical engineering industry, for the so-called "integration age," dominated by the paradigm of Computer Integrated Manufacturing (CIM). The core of this paradigm was the integration (basically via information technologies) of different operations which are at the boundaries of the manufacturing process. The frequency of product design operations, but also process design, machine tools programming and set-up, and production scheduling, became such as to require automation and integration of activities which were previously entirely committed to workers.

The nature of capital assets needed for this purpose is quite peculiar, as well as the knowledge that is necessary to trigger and sustain the innovative momentum. Technologies for integration are typically not on the shelf. The specificity of the capital investment required is such as to virtually prevent the existence of a defined set of available techniques or at least make it quite obscure. The value of computer aided techniques is not intrinsic, whereas the substantial contribution to productivity and added value is given by mutual relationships among old and new technologies. Actually, the task of implementing a CIM environment is largely an empirical, trial-and-error process, where firms are forced to rely heavily on their own knowledge resources and experience. The nature of the problem – namely, the non-availability of ready-to-use capital assets and formalized knowledge – is such as to discourage imitative behaviors, and patterns of innovation are deeply influenced by localized knowledge and learning-by-doing. The profile of capital investments in the mechanical engineering industry over the years 1988–94 clearly reflects such aspects.

Integration is also a task which, by definition, simultaneously involves several different assets, which have to be adapted, interfaced, and flexibly devoted to different manufacturing activities. In this context, sunk costs related to pre-existing fixed assets assume a consistent relevance, and the problem of indivisibility involves not only single items but also the entire set of physical assets in aggregate. As a final remark, it is quite evident, on these bases, that a set of technologies whose explicit task is to integrate other technologies (often pre-existing) is highly path-dependent, and dimensional switching costs can be a heavy burden.

These few lines should have sketched the environment in which shifts in the demand curve of firms within the mechanical sector (systematically occurring from 1988 to 1992), have triggered innovation processes characterized by localized knowledge, learning-by-doing and learning-by-using, and tacit knowledge. The data set described below has allowed us to reinforce these considerations with some empirical evidence.

Empirical evidence

In order to search for empirical evidence about the causal relationship between demand shocks and localized technological change we have to tackle the problem of estimating the firm-level efficiency of production units and to correlate it to different patterns of demand. The framework of analysis is fairly simple and is based on the notion that there exists a relationship of dependence between the trend in efficiency increase and the trend in demand, in the form of:

$$\eta = a_0 + a_1 x + a_2 x^2 + a_3 x^3 + \ldots + a_n x^n \tag{8.1}$$

where,

$$\eta = \frac{d\varepsilon_{it}}{dt} \text{ trend in efficiency of firm } i \text{ at time } t,$$

and

$$x = \frac{\left(\dfrac{dFATT_{it}}{dt}\right)}{FATT_{it}}$$

with $FATT$ = total gross revenue at time t.

The variable x represents the percentage increase/decrease of demand for firm i in the unit of time, whilst the dependent variable η is the average increase of efficiency for firm i in the unit of time.

The functional specification of (8.1), which is expressed in a generic polynomial form, allows us to take into account both symmetrical (n even) and asymmetrical (n odd) responses to demand shocks and has been selected on the basis of the empirical evidence which was available to us. For the sake of simplicity, we have limited our analysis to a cubic model, in the form:

$$\eta = a_0 + a_1 x + a_2 x^2 + a_3 x^3. \tag{8.2}$$

We have evidence for a symmetrical response to demand shocks (both positive and negative shocks either increase or decrease firms' efficiency), when the coefficient a_3 is not statistically different from zero, while if we can reject the null hypothesis $a_3 = 0$ we have an evidence of asymmetrical responses to demand shocks (positive/negative demand shocks originate positive/negative efficiency shifts). The estimation procedure is therefore in two steps: first, we have to estimate efficiency trends of single firms over the years considered, second, we regress efficiency trends against demand shocks, as in (8.2).

The first part of estimation could be based on the study of residuals of a classic Cobb–Douglas form,

$$Y = A \cdot K^\alpha \cdot L\beta \tag{8.3}$$

where Y is a measure of production level, K is a measure of capital assets, L is a measure of labor, while A is the level of general efficiency.

Equation (8.3) can be studied with standard econometric techniques on the basis of fairly restrictive assumptions. Nevertheless, given the dynamic nature of the phenomenon to be studied, we would rather avoid any assumption concerning the constancy of parameters over time. Moreover, for the purpose of our study we are looking for a relative measure of the efficiency trend, as measured with reference to the efficiency trend of the sector on aggregate. Specifically, we are looking for a rank measure of firm's efficiency within the sector. We argue that the non-parametric technique DEA (Data Envelopment Analysis) is appropriate to this purpose. The output of this technique is in fact a measure of efficiency that is relative to the maximum efficiency within the sector over the years and is not conditional upon any parametric restriction, not setting up any *ex ante* hypothesis about the elasticity of substitution of factors. DEA is well suited to studying dynamic efficiency trends and avoids the limitations classic to standard parametric techniques as far as dynamic variety in the population of firms is concerned. The use of DEA is legitimated by the consideration that firms in our sample are fairly homogeneous, manufacturing small discrete parts on a medium to large scale.

The framework of analysis proposed (Sengupta, 1995) is based on a multi-input/single output problem, which considers a linear production function in the form of:

$$Y = \lambda_0 + \sum_{i=1}^{n} \lambda_i X_i \tag{8.4}$$

which is a more general expression for (8.3). In (8.4) Y is the output factor, λ is a set of weights to be determined and X is a generic input factor. In our specific case, we use added value as a measure of production level (Y), total net production assets for capital input (K), and total labor costs for labor input (L).

Of course, a dynamic version of (8.4) can be written, in the form of:

$$\Delta Y = \Delta \lambda_0(t) + \lambda'(t) \Delta X(t) + \Delta \lambda'(t) X(t). \tag{8.5}$$

This dynamic specification (8.5) decomposes the output change into three parts: the shift in the production function ($\Delta \lambda_0$), the input changes weighted by the parameters, and the parameters changes weighted by the inputs. In macrodynamic models of economic growth, the shift component $\Delta \lambda_0$ is called the Hicks' neutral technology indicator, the second component indicates that part of the output growth which can be accounted for by input growth at a constant marginal productivity, and the third component specifies the remaining part of output growth explained by changes in input parameters at a constant level of input application.

Expression (8.5) sets the general framework for the basic problem in dynamic efficiency analysis, which is how to specify and measure the dynamic production frontier corresponding to the production function (8.4), when time-series data are available for a cross-section of firms. With a two-period horizon one could set up the following DEA model in order to test the dynamic efficiency of the kth firm:

$$\min \Delta h_k = y' z_k$$

$$s.t. \ \gamma' z_j \geq \Delta y_j; \ j = 1, 2, \dots, N \qquad (8.6)$$

$$\lambda \geq 0$$

where $\gamma' = (\Delta \lambda_0, \lambda', \Delta \lambda')$ and $z'_j = (1, \Delta i'_j(t), z'(t))$.

The concept of (8.6) is to obtain the best possible efficiency for each of the firms in the sample – which, since the observed output value is fixed, is obtained via the definition of input weights which minimizes the total input factor, constrained to the condition that no firm would achieve a level of efficiency

$$\varepsilon = \frac{\Delta y_{kt}}{\gamma' z_{it}} > 1.$$

The model in (8.6) can easily be generalized to the case of multi-periods, as for the data set investigated:

$$\min \sum_{t=0}^{T-1} \gamma(t) z_k(t)$$

$$s.t. \ \gamma'(t) z_j(t) \geq \Delta y_j(t); \ j = 1, 2, \dots, N \qquad (8.7)$$

$$\lambda(t) \geq 0 \ t = 0, 1, \dots, T - 1.$$

The expression above leads us to define a set of firms' efficiencies over the years considered, which form the panel of data that we would use as a dependent variable in our model of demand-shock-induced technological change. We would try to test to which extent trends in efficiency (increases) are explained by demand shocks by means of (8.2). Our hypothesis is that demand shocks should have an effect on efficiency trends within two years since the time of the shock itself. Therefore, we have used as a proxy of x the average trend of demand over the two years preceding the demand shock:

$$x = \frac{FATT_t - FATT_{t-2}}{FATT_{t-2}} \qquad (8.8)$$

and

$$\eta = \frac{\varepsilon_t - \varepsilon_{t-1}}{\varepsilon_{t-1}}. \qquad (8.9)$$

Table 8.2. *Estimation of equation*

Non-linear regression summary statistics			Dependent variable EFF	
Source	DF	Sum of squares		
Regression	4	26,67280		
Residual	676	20,33293		
Uncorrected total	680	47,00573		
(Corrected total)	679	45,90285		

$R^2 = 1 -$ Residual SS / Corrected SS $= 0.5645$

			Asymptotic 95 % confidence interval	
Parameter	Estimate	Asymptotic std. error	Lower	Upper
a_0	0.006177613	0.008651380	−0.010809194	0.023164419
a_1	−0.047238666	0.099953120	−0.243494563	0.149017232
a_2	1.685745938	0.216374870	1.260898327	2.110593549
a_3	−0.528505406	0.083797979	−0.693041016	−0.363969796

Results from the estimation are listed in table 8.2. Such a table provides evidence that the coefficient of the cubic term (a_3) is significantly negative, while the quadratic term a_2 is significantly positive, suggesting that there exists a direct proportionality relationship between demand shocks and efficiency shifts.

We interpret these results as a first piece of evidence – although not conclusive given the relatively low level of R^2 – of a dependency relationship between demand shocks and efficiency trends in the mechanical engineering sector.

Conclusions

Technological knowledge can be considered a highly impure public good with relevant elements of excludability and rivalry that relies upon a continuum of specifications of different forms of knowledge: at one extreme one finds the notion of generic and scientific knowledge, at the other the notion of tacit knowledge. Localized technological change is based upon a mix of generic and tacit knowledge (Antonelli, 1995).

Tacit knowledge has a high degree of idiosyncrasy as it emerges from daily routines and from the experience acquired in using capital goods, in producing and manufacturing, and in interacting with customers and with other manufacturers. Tacit knowledge consists of highly specific pieces of technological know-how acquired by means of lengthy processes of learning-by-using and learning-by-doing. Tacit knowledge incorporates the experience and the skills of manpower, as well as the opportunities of improving products and production processes generated by highly circumstantial factors and events. Tacit knowledge is consequently specific with respect to the full set of environmental and complementary factors that shape the learning process, and its process of accumulation is highly path-dependent in that it reflects the specific learning opportunities each firm has come across over time. In sum, it seems possible to assume explicitly that tacit knowledge is likely to be stylized as a "by-product" of other necessary activities such as production and sales and that the generation of this knowledge is therefore an externality in the ordinary conduct of business that requires low levels of additional "dedicated" expenditure.

Generic knowledge consists of general scientific principles that are germane to a variety of uses and users. Generic knowledge is based upon tacit and technological knowledge as it emerges from tacit learning procedures, but requires broad efforts to be fully articulated and codified. Firms that are able to generate generic knowledge have high levels of requirements of formal training for their employees. Generic knowledge is the outcome of formal R&D expenditures that elaborate upon the tacit knowledge which is drawn on as a "by-product" by other activities and is the outcome of learning processes but requires high levels of additional expenditure and the command of scientific information that implies the access to qualified academic and research institutions. Hence we can assume that generic knowledge requires a longer and more costly accumulation process.

In the generation of localized technological change, firms rely on both tacit and generic knowledge. The generation of new knowledge is the result of a joint process of production, learning, and communicating, of which R&D activities should be considered only one part. Consequently, R&D activities cannot and should not be considered the sole factors in the generation of new technological knowledge and should not be separated from the current flow of activities within the firm and in the relations between the firm and its environment. R&D expenses – defined as the resources allocated in the specific activity of experimenting and developing new products and new processes – are only an aspect of a more general process of learning and capitalizing on the experience acquired (Nelson, 1987).

The generation of new knowledge is mainly the outcome of the interplay between the institutionalized efforts of innovators that draw on generic knowledge and learning, processes highly localized and specific to the history and experience of each innovator. The generation of localized technological knowledge can therefore be viewed as the product of a systemic bottom-up process of induction from actual experience, which integrates the top-down process of deduction from general scientific principles on which generic knowledge is built. In this context, the capability to innovate successfully appears to be conditioned by learning opportunities that are both internal and external to each firm. In so doing, it seems possible to highlight the systemic character of technological knowledge and the role of externalities and interdependence in the introduction of a new technology.

The development of knowledge within industries is strongly influenced by the network structure of relations among firms. Firms relying on localized knowledge can implement their technological capability not only by means of R&D expenditures and internal learning, but also through the systematic absorption of technological and scientific externalities available in their environment.

The methodology of special interaction becomes extremely relevant in this context. Special interaction can be studied in physics as the outcome of two classes of forces termed *connectivity* and *receptivity*. The former measures the number of connections in place among the agents in the network and the latter the capability of each agent to absorb the information received. The generation of localized knowledge is viewed as the outcome of a collective undertaking strongly influenced by the characteristics of the system in terms of connectivity and receptivity which shape the availability of information and communication channels among learning agents. In fact, the capability of firms to generate technological innovations rests upon the continual effort to keep open all the information and communication channels that parallel the flows of goods.

As the results of our empirical analysis suggest, a macroeconomic environment characterized by fast rates of growth is most conducive to stimulating the innovative capability of firms in skill-intensive industries such as mechanical engineering, where technological change rests upon high levels of competence based upon tacit knowledge, rather than top-down scientific discoveries. The dynamics of localized technological change supply new microeconomic evidence to the Kaldorian relationship between rates of output growth and rates of productivity growth. It seems in fact clear that the faster is the output growth, the larger are the stimulations to capitalize on acquired tacit knowledge and the faster is the rate of introduction of localized technological innovations. The generation of new localized technological change in turn makes it possible to increase TFP, hence to reduce market prices, and to increase market share and output, feeding a recursive virtuous cycle of growth (Antonelli, 1998).

The notion of localized technological change and the related implementation of the original Pavitt classification in the new class of skill-intensive sectors characterized by fast rates of introduction of technological innovations and high levels of TFP growth but low levels of R&D and patent intensity, has important effects for both the European economics of innovation and a European innovation policy. Too much importance has been paid by innovation economics and policy to R&D activities, as if they were the unique source of knowledge for firms and the only factor of technological accumulation in order to generate technological innovations. Many small firms rely almost exclusively on tacit localized knowledge and yet are fully able to generate important innovations. An innovation policy oriented to push the innovative capability of skill-intensive sectors should pay attention to feeding all the processes of learning, implementing technological cooperation among firms and between firms and research institutions, and to the processes of on-the-job training of the workforce. The creation of industrial technological centers specifically designed to sustain the localized processes of technological change so as to socialise the technological know-how specific to each industry might play a major role in this context.

References

Antonelli C. (1989). "A Failure-inducement Model of Research and Development Expenditures: Italian Evidence from the early 1980s," *Journal of Economic Behavior and Organization*, 12, 159–80

(1994). "Localized Technological Change and the Evolution of Standards as Economic Institutions," *Information Economics and Policy*, 6, 195–216

(1995). *The Economics of Localized Technological Change and Industrial Dynamics*, Dordrecht and Boston: Kluwer Academic

(1999). *The Microdynamics of Technological Change*, London: Routledge

Atkinson, A.B and J.E. Stiglitz (1969). "A New View of Technological Change," *Economic Journal*, 79, 573–8

Binswanger, H.P., V.W. Ruttan *et al.* (1978). *Induced Innovation,* Baltimore: Johns Hopkins University Press

Calderini M. and M. Cantamessa (1997). "Innovation Paths in Product Development: An Empirical Research," *International Journal of Production Economics*, 51, 1–17

Cantner, U. and G. Westermann (1998). "Localized Technological Progress and Industry Structure," *Economics of Innovation and New Technology*, 5

David, P.A. (1975). *Technical Choice, Innovation and Economic Growth*, Cambridge: Cambridge University Press

(1993a). "Path-dependence and Predictability in Dynamic Systems with Local Network Externalities: A Paradigm for History Economics," in D. Foray and C. Freeman (eds.), *Technology and the Wealth of Nations,* London: Pinter Publishers

(1993b). "Knowledge Property and the System Dynamics of Technological Change," in *Proceedings of the World Bank Annual Conference on Development Economics*, Washington, DC

Dixit, A. (1992). "Investment and Hysteresis," *Journal of Economic Perspectives*, 6, 107–32

Kaldor, N. (1957). "A Model of Economic Growth," *Economic Journal*, 67, 591–624

Kaldor, N. and J. Mirrlees (1962). "A New Model of Economic Growth," *Review of Economic Studies*, 29, 174–92

Malerba, F. (1992). "Learning by Firms and Incremental Change," *Economic Journal*, 102, 845–59

Metcalfe, J.S. (1989). "Evolution and Economic Change," in A. Silberston (ed.), *Technology and Economic Progress*, London: Macmillan

(1992). "Variety Structure and Change: An Evolutionary Perspective on the Competitive Process," *Revue d'Economie Industrielle*, 59, 46–61

(1994). "Competition, Fisher's Principle and Increasing Returns to Selection," *Journal of Evolutionary Economics*, 4, 327–349

(1995). "The Design of Order: Notes on Evolutionary Principles and the Dynamics of Innovation," PREST and School of Economic Studies, University of Manchester, mimeo

Nelson, R. (1987). *Understanding Technical Change as an Evolutionary Process*, Amsterdam: North-Holland

Pavitt, K. (1984). "Sectoral Patterns of Technical Change: Towards a Taxonomy and a Theory," *Research Policy*, 13, 343–74

(1987). *On the Nature of Technology*, Brighton: Science Policy Reseach Unit, University of Sussex

Phillips, A. (1970). "Structure Conduct Performance and Performance Conduct Structure," in J.W. Markham and G.F. Papanek (eds.), *Industrial Organization and Economic Development, Essays in Honor of E.S. Mason*. Boston: Houghton-Mifflin

(1971), *Technology and Market Structure*, Lexington: Lexington Books

Rosenberg, N. (1974). "Science Invention and Economic Growth," *Economic Journal*, 84, 90–108

(1976). *Perspectives on Technology*, Cambridge: Cambridge University Press

Salter, W.E.G. (1966). *Productivity and Technical Change*, Cambridge: Cambridge University Press

Schmookler J. (1966). *Invention and Economic Growth*, Cambridge, Mass.: Harvard University Press

Sengupta, J.K. (1995). *Dynamics of Data Envelopment Analysis*, Dordrecht: Kluwer Academic

Steindl, J. (1947), *Small and Big Business*, Oxford: Basil Blackwell

(1952). *Maturity and Stagnation in American Capitalism*, Oxford: Basil Blackwell

Stiglitz, J.E. (1987). "Learning to Learn: Localized Learning and Technological Progress," in P. Dasgupta and P. Stoneman (eds.), *Economic Policy and Technological Performance*, Cambridge: Cambridge University Press

Stoneman, P. (1983). *The Economic Analysis of Technological Change*, Oxford: Oxford University Press

Sutton, J. (1991). *Sunk Costs and Market Structure*, Cambridge, Mass.: MIT Press
Sylos Labini, P. (1984), *The Forces of Economic Growth and Decline*, Cambridge, Mass.: MIT Press
Young, A. (1928). "Increasing Returns and Economic Progress," *Economic Journal*, 38, 527–42

Part II
Inter-firm collaboration and research networks

9 Inter-organizational collaboration: the theories and their policy implications

Patrick Llerena and Mireille Matt

Introduction

Since the 1980s, many empirical studies have focused on cooperation and have underlined the increasing use of that strategy by firms, especially in high-tech industries (telecommunications, biotechnologies, new materials, chemistry, etc.). During that same period, many European countries and the European Union have played an essential role in financing private technological development through large cooperative R&D programs (see Geuna, chapter 15 and also Garcia-Fontes and Geuna, chapter 14 in this volume). In Japan, MITI has organized such programs and has long supported part of the research costs. On the contrary, the US position concerning cooperation does not match that of Japan and Europe. The US policy allows organizations to form R&D agreements but does not deliberately stimulate them through subsidies by virtue of antitrust legislation. Consequently, inter-organization agreements represent an extending private strategy, but they do not convince all policy-makers that they are a relevant policy tool. Facing this diversity of conceptions and facts, which policy should in fact be adopted? Should the state prevent cooperation because of social inefficiencies? Should it simply relax antitrust laws? Or should the policy-maker stimulate R&D agreements between organizations?

The main purpose of this chapter is to provide a theoretical analysis of the rationale of a public policy oriented towards the development of inter-firm (or, more generally inter-organization) collaborations in R&D. The basic argument is that the rationale depends on the perspectives adopted by policy-makers. These perspectives can be characterized in two ways: (1) a static or a dynamic analysis of inter-firm agreements; (2) organization as an information or a knowledge-processing unit. The two perspectives are obviously linked but have different analytical implications.

If the perspectives are based on a static analysis of the effects of inter-firm agreements, the policy is designed as an "exception" to competition, because of the specificities of R&D activities (public good, uncertainty, asymmetries of information, spillovers, etc.). The stability of the agreement is considered rather low, and cooperation is rather unusual in a spontaneous way. The agreement is then essentially considered as a transitory phase before a merger (through acquisition) or a return to a competitive situation (see, for example, transaction cost analysis). If dynamic effects are considered, new aspects come into consideration: intertemporal learning (both individual and collective or organizational), lock-in effects (positive or negative), indirect effects, and spillovers towards other activities (see Sharp and Senker, chapter 12 in this volume). The policy objectives have then to cope with the implementation of a new organizational scheme, to improve the coordination between different activities and/or competencies.

If organization is considered as a solution to the specific problem of information-processing (unequal distribution of information, etc.), in a context of resource allocation the agreement appears only as a particular organizational solution to this kind of problem. On the other hand, if organization is conceived as a "processor of knowledge," then an agreement should be seen as a means to create, diffuse, and distribute knowledge.

These different perspectives shed different, but complementary, lights on the policy implications of these theories.

Inter-organization collaboration in static approaches

Analytical tools

We attempt here to emphasize important aspects of collaboration in a neoclassical context. Broad questions such as the emergence of an agreement between firms (i.e. the private incentives to cooperate), the stability conditions and the welfare considerations are addressed. Transaction-costs arguments are also considered. These questions are very important in order to develop a first rationale for technological public policies.

Tacit or explicit collusion

Cooperative behaviors are often presented as situations emerging in oligopolistic market structures. The emergence and the stability of an agreement between firms is usually studied in a situation of explicit collusion with a formal and constraining contract, or in a context of tacit collusion without a formal contract. Explicit collusion corresponds to the creation of a cartel where firms maximize the sum of their individual profits (cooperative game). Collaboration is tacit when a non cooperative equilibrium strategy that guarantees the collusive profit to the firms emerges.

In game theory, the tacit collusion case is represented by the "prisoner's dilemma" (i.e. the non-emergence of a tacit collusive behavior in a non repeated game). Many contributions have tried to solve this dilemma and to find conditions favoring cooperation between self-interested agents – for instance game repetition during an infinite number of periods. Under such conditions, particular strategies will induce cooperative behaviors. Friedman (1971) demonstrates that the "trigger strategy" allows cooperation to emerge under specific conditions. Axelrod (1984, 1992) considers self-interested heterogeneous agents with imperfect rationality and shows that the "tit-for-tat" strategy constitutes a solid way to solve the dilemma when the horizon is infinite and the probability of meeting again is high. But two firms linked by tacit relationships could be incited to pursue their collaboration in a more explicit way. For example, Clarke (1983) underlines the fact that firms share information only inside formal structures.

The simplest way to formalize a cartel is to consider two firms which jointly decide the quantity to be produced in a cooperative game. In case of identical firms and perfect information, the conclusion of an agreement is quite easy: the cartel's profit equals the monopoly's and the firms' individual decisions are symmetric. In case of heterogeneous firms (product differentiation and/or heterogeneous cost functions), the joint profit maximization proves more difficult. Side-payments are often presented as the most efficient way to obtain successful cooperation. However, the solution often remains unstable. Instability is mainly explained by the difficulty of negotiating and by opportunistic behavior of the partners. This phenomenon is increased under uncertainty, but this instability problem can be solved under specific conditions. For example, in an economy with n firms, d'Aspremont et al. (1983) suggest simply letting the deviating firms join the competitive fringe. The authors show that with a finite number of firms it is always possible to find a stable cartel in the economy.

It seems that cooperative behavior (tacit or explicit) may emerge and remain stable under very particular conditions. What about welfare considerations? In the prisoner's dilemma, the cooperative equilibrium represents the single Pareto-optimum. In the general equilibrium approach, joint decisions about price and/or quantity are often perceived as anti-competitive strategies. Cooperative behavior entails an economic welfare loss and consequently a sub-optimal solution. Antitrust legislations are based on such arguments.

Cooperative behavior and welfare implications: the R&D case
Introducing R&D activities into the analysis might change the general results presented above. The specific properties of R&D (i.e. indivisibility, uncertainty, and inappropriability) induce sub-optimal resource allocation by the market. The price system fails to coordinate the decentralized

agents' innovative activities and market failures appear. Intellectual property rights, public subsidies, and cooperation in R&D are considered as the main tools for reducing market imperfections.

The literature concerning R&D collaboration is extremely large and contains many types of modelization (De Bondt, 1995). To remain consistent with the dynamic part of this chapter and because the welfare analysis is relatively clear, we will present only the general results of multiple-stage models which consider strategic interactions between research and production.

D'Aspremont and Jacquemin (1988) pioneered this analysis based on R&D spillover hypotheses. Many subsequent models have been built on their structure, but differ in some detail. Roughly speaking, all these contributions suppose that in a first stage firms choose R&D investments either cooperatively or non-cooperatively and that in a second step they compete to produce the improved output. For instance, De Bondt, Slaets, and Cassiman (1992), De Bondt (1991), De Bondt and Veuglers (1991), and Kamien, Muller, and Zang (1992) examine the effect of product differentiation. Others include information-sharing aspects (Motta, 1992; Vonotras, 1994). They all consider exogenous spillovers, but do not formalize them in exactly the same way. The different situations can be summarized as follows:

- Spillovers are perfectly symmetric – i.e. all firms (cooperating or not) possess the same spillover parameter.
- Spillovers are differentiated – i.e. only cooperative firms share all the information and the spillover factor equals one. The latter is below one when firms compete in R&D.
- In these first two cases cooperation can take place only between all the firms of the industry.
- Spillovers are differentiated – i.e. cooperative firms share more information than non-cooperative ones. These models introduce the possibility that only a part of the firms cooperate, while the others remain in the competitive fringe. The former absorb the results generated by the partners of the agreement (voluntary spillovers) *and* the information generated by the non-cooperative firms (involuntary spillovers, smaller than the voluntary ones). The latter benefit only from involuntary spillovers. Thus, two different groups of homogeneous agents (cooperative and non-cooperative) exist.

In the first two cases, firms always have incentives to cooperate in R&D as their individual collusive profits are higher than the non-cooperative ones. Moreover, in the case of a high spillover parameter, economic welfare is higher under cooperation than under competition. The third situation provides unclear profit and welfare results.

When each firm is characterized by a different spillover (i.e. by differences in the absorptive capacity and/or upstream vs. downstream R&D), cooperative behavior is modified. In a duopoly configuration, Matt (1996) shows that cooperation emerges in only two situations: (1) when spillovers are symmetric (small or high coefficient), and (2) in some cases of heterogeneity. In other words, diversity (i.e. heterogeneous spillovers) increases the difficulty for a firm to reach an R&D agreement. This result has important implications in terms of public policy. The welfare analysis highlights the fact that the economy is better off under cooperation than under competition when one or both spillovers are relatively high, i.e. when leakage of information is important. Moreover, in case of high spillovers, firms have incentives to internalize their R&D decision in an agreement, and to invest more.

Finally, the recognized advantages of R&D cooperation over competition in terms of welfare are higher R&D investments, better diffusion of results, elimination of wasteful duplication of efforts, and access to new markets. Nevertheless, these relationships also often remain unstable because of information asymmetries, opportunistic behavior, or high negotiation costs. These reasons for instability (opportunism, negotiation costs) correspond to factors included in the concept of transaction costs that will be studied below in order to underline additional characteristics of cooperation.

Transaction costs and flexibility

The approaches considered up to now have been exclusively market oriented and suppose substantially rational agents. In institutional or neo-institutional perspectives the coordination of economic activities is analyzed in a market–hierarchy opposition. The economy is compared to a nexus of contracts between two or more agents; within this nexus, institutions emerge and correspond to zones where decentralized market mechanisms are replaced by a centralized system of specific contracts. This perspective assumes modified hypotheses concerning behavior, the nature of transactions, and the economic environment.

Williamson (1985) considers opportunistic agents with limited rationality. Under these assumptions, organization becomes a means to ease information acquisition and transmission that could not be conveyed by the price system because of high costs and/or complexity. It becomes also a good way to reduce opportunistic behavior as it allows the establishment of conflict-reducing procedures and the generation of structures dominated by power-based relationships. Another central concept in the existence of transaction costs is the notion of asset-specificity. This notion is related to the degree of redeployment and complementarity: stopping a relationship containing weakly redeployable assets entails high costs; assets are complementary when using them together (in collaboration) generates a quasi-rent compared to using them separately.

According to Williamson, limited rationality, opportunism, uncertainty, and asset specificities explain the existence of particular contracts compared to those of the standard theory. They are characterized by a governance structure resulting from monitoring procedures, power-based relationships, and incentive schemes. Different types of transaction are associated with particular governance structures characterized by specific costs and competencies. Williamson identifies three different governance structures:

- The *market* is the appropriate mode of coordination of non-specific investments and occasional transactions – i.e. of situations where the price contains the information necessary to describe the environment.
- The *hierarchy* is appropriate in the case of recurrent transactions involving idiosyncratic assets and is able to adapt in a highly perturbed environment. Administrative procedures are important and considered to be efficient.
- The *hybrid forms* are characterized by an intermediate position in all attributes: intermediate asset specificities (not idiosyncratic), recurrent or occasional transaction frequency, autonomy of actors, intermediate administrative procedures, and medium adaptation capability. Cooperation is seen as an unstable form of coordination because in the case of increased uncertainty or more specific assets hierarchy becomes more advantageous.

This has common features with the option-value approach in terms of flexibility (Wolff, 1992). Here, cooperation is characterized by an intermediate degree of flexibility. Cooperation is less flexible than the market (but more than integration) in terms of future actions, but involves more sunk costs (but less than integration). Nevertheless, collaboration contains a greater informational flexibility than the market (but less than hierarchy), which means that the agreement allows the partners to achieve specific informational learning. The instability of this coordination form remains high, for the reasons mentioned above.

To sum up, static approaches explain the emergence of collusive private behavior in terms of individual profit maximization and of transaction-cost minimization. In the pure market oriented analysis, decrease of R&D risks, economies of scale, and information-sharing are the main private advantages of cooperation. The neo-institutional perspective completes the analysis by considering the creation of asset specificities, adaption ability, and to some extent greater informational flexibility. In both approaches, firms are considered as economic units which have to cope with strategic behavior under incomplete or imperfect information. They have to find out the most efficient contract or transaction, taking into account the informational structure of the environment. Agreements appear as intermediate cases which, by definition, can only be unstable: the incentives are linked to the self-interest of each firm involved in the cooperation and the "repressive" scheme has a loose form. More basically, the problem is to compare the efficiency of different organizational forms to solve some specific informational issues: under uncertainty, information is considered as the central element of the resource-allocation issue.

Moreover, private behaviors are not necessarily consistent with social requirements. The next section will focus on the policy implications of cooperative behaviors. It will define some factors explaining the policy-maker's behavior, partly based on a social-private comparison.

Policy implications

The previous section described the behavior of firms in terms of collusive strategy and presented some welfare implications. Facing this analysis, what kind of policy should the policy-maker adopt concerning inter-organization collaborations?

Market approach

In a pure market approach, public authorities have to correct market failures and to preserve the economy near a Pareto-optimal situation. The policy-maker has to assess the welfare of the economy with and without cooperation and to compare the results with actual private strategies. If private strategies are in harmony with public interests, the authorities will not intervene. If, however, there is a conflict between the private and the public interests, the policy-maker will apply an active policy. For instance, if firms cooperate spontaneously and welfare under cooperation is smaller than that under competition, the policy-maker will apply antitrust legislation. If firms do not cooperate spontaneously and welfare under cooperation is higher than that under competition, the policy-maker will stimulate agreements between organizations.

For simplicity's sake, we will consider only two dimensions of a formal agreement, each characterized by two possibilities:
• the objective of the agreement: R&D – price and/or quantity (without R&D activities)
• the characteristic of the partners (costs, products, etc.): symmetric – asymmetric.

When *symmetric or asymmetric firms* manage to decide price and/or quantity jointly (without conducting any R&D activities), cooperation is generally considered welfare-inconsistent. Under such conditions, the policy-maker adopts antitrust legislation. In very specific cases, cooperation could be welfare-improving and the policy-maker just relaxes the legislation.

Based on the strategic investment literature, the R&D cooperation case is somewhat more critical. When *firms are symmetric*, whatever the amount of spillovers they always have incentives to cooperate. The analysis of the different contributions underlines the fact that in the case of small spillovers, welfare would be better under R&D competition. As mentioned above, the policy-maker should preclude collusive behavior. In the case of high spillovers, private and public interests are consistent, and the policy-maker has no reason to intervene.

The existence of large R&D cooperative programs supported by the state is explained only when *firms benefit from asymmetric* spillovers. In this case, cooperation emerges spontaneously in very specific spillover configurations. Under such a hypothesis, marginal situations exist where asymmeric firms remain competitive in R&D when cooperation would Pareto-improve the economy. In that specific case only, the policy-maker adopts an active policy that subsidizes R&D cooperation involving partners characterized by different research or absorptive capacities. It is important to emphasize that the emergence of a need for an R&D agreement policy arises when there is a certain degree of diversity between firms (different spillovers). This policy uses incentive mechanisms and allows a market failure reduction.

Transaction-costs approach

In the transaction-costs theory, the public policy-maker is characterized by limited rationality and no efficiency criterion exists which permits a clear decision. The Pareto-criterion is replaced by what Williamson (1993, 131–2) calls "remediableness." His efficiency conception is radically opposed to that of the standard theory. He makes no reference to an ideal situation and supposes that "an existing condition is held to be efficient unless a feasible alternative can be described and implemented with net gains". Efficiency is never absolute but always relative. State intervention could then be justified by the fact that:

• economic agents cooperate but market or hierarchy is more efficient
• firms are unable to reach spontaneously an agreement considered as the appropriate organizational form.

In the first case, the policy-maker has two possibilities. On the one hand, she considers competition as the alternative solution because it is more flexible in terms of future actions or more efficient in terms of transaction-costs savings. In that case, the policy-maker decides to adopt antitrust legislation.

On the other hand, she considers hierarchy to be the alternative coordination means and decides to integrate the economic activities in the form of either a public firm (administration), or a private regulated firm.

But according to the features of the agents and the environment, it would not be surprising to assume that economic actors are unable to coordinate all their activities spontaneously and efficiently. A firm might look for specific competencies and for a partner to develop a new product or process or to start a research project. But this search process could prove difficult because the firm is unable to find the right partner because of a lack of information and the existence of many barriers precluding the contractors from agreeing (opportunism, information asymmetries, lack of guarantees, etc.). Consequently, the main objective of public policy is to influence the level of transaction and searching costs so as to modify the balance between the costs and advantages of hybrid forms. But what could be the motivation of a policy-maker to stimulate R&D cooperation between private agents?

One important element is certainly the pursuit of social goals that agents would not spontaneously undertake because of high R&D costs or risks, and also because the profitability is judged too weak or negative. These social goals are related to such domains as health, aerospace, public transportation, telecommunication, or other improved public goods. The policy-maker decides to spend large amounts of money in those cooperative programs because she supposes that the results will lead globally to positive economic impacts that are greater than all the costs incurred. In other words, she supposes that the economic situation after the specific program will be better than without it or under an alternative situation.

Another argument concerns the possibility to generate new – socially valuable – private assets that could not emerge without the conclusion of an agreement. Here, the policy-maker decides to establish contractual procedures, conflict-resolution possibilities, and to subsidize part of the innovation expenses so as to stimulate cooperation between agents that would not have met without public intervention. The main effect is to provide the initial conditions for implementing an efficient organizational form generating net gains in terms of new assets. The argument is reinforced by the fact that hybrid forms can also be considered as a flexible coordination means in terms of information creation and spreading.

In the static approaches, the objectives of public policy are based on optimization procedures. In the pure market analysis, the policy-maker has to maximize the social welfare of an economy, or in other words to reduce market failures. The neo-institutional implications are related to the minimization of transaction and searching costs. The public policy-maker has to implement the most efficient organizational form by using opportunity-cost arguments. This objective is to provide either public technologies or specific assets that would not have occurred without her active participation. In both cases, the procedures involved to implement the policy are incentive oriented. In the pure market approach, the policy-maker designs an incentive scheme that maximizes the public objectives under incentive and individual rationality constraints. For the neo-institutional conception, public policy supplies pre-established contractual agreements and subsidies that reduce transaction costs.

In addition, both approaches (pure market and transaction-costs analysis) have a common feature which is to limit the coordination and incentive problems to an informational problem (asymmetries, etc.). In an evolutionary perspective, it is mainly this fundamental assumption which is relaxed.

Inter-organization collaboration in an evolutionary perspective

Dynamic aspects of inter-organization collaboration

In the static analysis described above, the decision to cooperate depends on the agents' optimization behavior and on the definition of bilateral contracts between them: the agents have given cognitive capabilities and the main objective is to maximize the allocation of resources. These approaches consider a weak form of learning that mainly corresponds to the accumulation of information without any cognitive evolution. What we would like to emphasize in the present section is that the essential feature of technological development relies on the creation of competencies and knowledge, based on a continuous cognitive process. This is the reason why in an evolutionary perspective, the firm must be "conceived as a processor of knowledge" (Cohendet et al., 1996) where learning (individual or organizational) constitutes a central process of creation and accumulation of knowledge and competencies. We will first underline the fact that cooperation should be seen as an organizational means particularly relevant for the development of new technologies. We will also stress the conditions favoring the emergence of inter-firm agreements and more precisely those favoring the creation of an organizational rent inside the cooperation. Finally, we will underline the factors influencing the partners' organizational learning.

Inter-organization agreements as a learning strategy

In an evolutionary perspective, "technology," broadly defined as the combination of knowledge, skills and artefacts (Metcalfe, 1993), moves along trajectories delimited by the innovation possibilities frontiers, themselves determined by a paradigm (Dosi, 1988). Technological development is characterized as a selective, cumulative, and path-dependent process involving complex and uncertain activities. Innovative activities are often conducted in a perturbed environment that firms must master in order to survive. In that context, one essential hypothesis concerns the rationality of agents. Economic agents are perceived as limited in their knowledge, and in their capability to foresee future events and to solve complex problems. Their rationality is contingent upon their cognitive, research, and information-processing capabilities, but also upon the experience and the context in which decisions are taken. Rationality is then specific to each agent. To innovate in a successful way, economic actors have to understand the evolution of the environment and the interface between them and the world in which they act and take decisions: they have to *learn*. In that perspective, "learning" means discovering, and corresponds to a process of creation of new logical structures or mental maps which will be modified, but also added to or eliminated from the memory. Learning constitutes a central concept because it generates new knowledge and opportunities.

The organization then represents a means to ease the acquisition, transfer and creation of knowledge that could not be exchanged by the price system and that is too complex to be processed by isolated agents. The organization becomes a way to stock available knowledge and a favorable place for agents to learn, thus inducing organizational learning. One important consequence of the characteristic of individual rationality and the existence of learning processes is the emergence of endogenous diversity – and, more precisely, cognitive diversity. The organization could be represented as a set of agents characterized by their own representations or images of the theory in use in the organization but also by different knowledge and skills. Organizational learning corresponds to a collective cognitive process that enables us to capitalize, filter, and create competencies and knowledge by mobilizing existing skills through specific coordination procedures (routines, rules, interpretation frameworks, etc.). If organizational learning depends on the number and the diversity of individual interpretations and their diffusion inside the organization, it depends also on the creation of links between existing competencies, and consequently on the existence of a common knowledge base. Coordination allows the members to share, confront and articulate their interpretations and skills – agents learn through interactions with others, but they also have to learn how to interact in order to learn. This last form of learning – i.e. deutero learning (Argyris and Schön, 1978) – becomes crucial inside an organization to gain better internal coherence, but it also constitutes a new learning strategy for the firms that decide to cooperate.

Inter-firm cooperation then turns out to be a specific coordination means allowing individual firms to ensure the coherence of innovative activities in a new organization. Cooperation also favors the exchange of complementary and diverse knowledge and competencies firms did not possess inside their knowledge base; it also favors the organizational learning of each partner ("learn to interact in order to learn"). The basic principle behind the process of learning which is specific to an inter-firm agreement is the need to cope with increased complexity of the environment and consequently the necessity to find, use, and develop a larger range of different competencies. An agreement between different organizations, and especially between firms, becomes an interesting way of developing new technologies and products. The exploitation of the existing diversity (in terms of knowledge and competencies) then becomes a complementary action to the exploration of new solutions (i.e. new diversity-creation) generated during the collaboration. Agreements are viewed as a specific tool for this exploitation as well as for exploration and creation. Individual firms could consider a given agreement as an efficient way to *explore* new technological solutions, by interacting with a complementary knowledge base; for the policy-maker, agreements essentially represent a specific tool for the *exploration and exploitation* of knowledge-base diversity.

Evolution of agreements and partners' organizational learning
Consequently, in this section, cooperation is no longer studied as a solution that reduces market imperfections, but as an organizational form particularly relevant for technological development. The emergence of cooperation between diverse organizations is not only motivated by profit but for firms it becomes a way, on the one hand, to create an organizational rent inside the agreement and, on the other, to strengthen internal organizational learning, provided they are able to extract a part of the rent. The focus of this approach is the creation of competencies and knowledge favoring the internal learning processes of each partner. We will not analyze in great details the organizational dynamics of the agreement itself as it is studied by Bureth, Wolff, and Zanfei (1998) (chapter 10 in this volume).

According to many studies, and in particular to Wolff (1992), the key factors influencing the creation of an asset specific to the agreement or of an organizational rent can be sub-divided into two stages: the *definition-specification* stage and the *implementation* stage. The definition-specification phase allows organizations to determine the degree of commitment of each partner and the nature and intensity of their interaction. The implementation phase of an agreement is the effective carrying out of the agreement, characterized by the emergence of trust, the transfer of knowledge, and the creation of a specific asset or of an organizational rent. Transfers of know-how and trust should favor the emergence of interactive learning and the creation of novelty and/or of a specific asset.

In terms of dynamics, it is possible to add a third stage that corresponds to the evaluation of the agreement and the decision to continue or to stop the cooperation (see Bureth, Wolff, and Zanfei, 1998). If a specific organizational asset has emerged, the learning effects and the evolution of the relations necessarily create some lock-in phenomena. Moreover, if the created asset is non-appropriable by the different partners but is integrated in the collective knowledge of the agreement, the stability of the cooperation increases. In that situation, bilateral interdependence between organizations becomes durable; cooperation could even become autonomous. In the case of stable relationships and more appropriable results, the stability often induces the reinforcement of the existing agreement or the creation of a new contract containing new objectives. The different partners will then begin with the first stage of the cooperation – i.e. the definition stage – and renew the dynamics.

Finally, we emphasize some complementary conditions favoring the success of an agreement and the reinforcement of the learning capability of the members themselves. This last point more precisely concerns agreements which settle from the start the duration of the contract, as is often the case for R&D cooperations. Partners agree on a common goal but carry on their own personal objectives. In such situations, one of the incentives to enter into a collaboration is to benefit from the organizational rent developed in the cooperation and to transfer the knowledge into one's own company. But extracting a part of the rent supposes the existence of links between the results generated by the agreement and the competencies of the firm. This extractive ability depends in particular on the absorptive capability of the organization. The latter is built upon the structure of interfaces between the firm and its environment, the channels of transfer of knowledge, and the distribution of knowledge inside the company. It corresponds to a balance between a certain homogeneity of the knowledge base necessary for the cohesion of the organization and a certain diversity necessary to exploit and explore external knowlege. Cohen and Levinthal (1990) underlined the fact that a central aspect of the absorptive capability is the existence of R&D investments. Internal R&D should not be considered as a substitute for external R&D, but as complementary or even as essential to exploit external results. Beside the absorptive capability, other factors influence the extractive capacity of the firm. Bureth, Wolff, and Zanfei (1994, 1998) distinguish three other elements: the appropriability regime, the negotiation ability, and the negotiation power. The extraction of results is regulated by contractual relations governed by conventions. The appropriation of results must be regulated by formal rules established at the beginning of the cooperation: intellectual property rules, licenses, etc. These rules are of greater importance when different organizations of the agreement are characterized by different institutional conventions – for example, universities and firms. During the definition of the contract, the ability and the practice of negotiation will have a positive impact on the extractive possibilities. But this ability should be used in favor of the agreement and not detrimentally to the partners who might retaliate. Finally, according to that extractive ability, firms will be able to acquire new competencies and knowledge and to improve their organizational learning processes in different domains such as scientific and technological know-how, management of R&D projects, management of cooperation and relations with partners, and improvement of the critical mass or the human capital of the organization.

Policy implications

In an evolutionary perspective, the policy implications should be analyzed under at least two aspects: the coordination of the diversity of competencies and of firm trajectories, and the incentives for knowledge creation. The determining element of the analysis, compared with the neoclassical view, is not the time dimension but the dynamic characteristics of learning processes: cumulativeness, irreversibilities and lock-in, knowledge creation, and the selection mechanism. The policy should be justified by the necessity to correct some limits inherent in the development of new technologies and its design should tackle the complexity of the evolutionary process of technological change. These limits correspond to evolutionary failures (CESPRI, 1996) – i.e. to a lack of adaptation of some mechanisms that stimulate technological change and evolution. These failures are different from the market ones which emerge for inappropriability, indivisibility, and uncertainty reasons.

Our presentation will be in two stages: the first will consider the correction of evolutionary failures (coordination, competence accumulation, lock-in, selection, etc.) and the second the incentive and organizational aspects.

Incentive policy towards cooperation as a means to correct evolutionary failures

The main arguments we would like to emphasize are linked to the need not only to coordinate at one point in time the diversity of existing competencies in order to create new ones, but also to have a tool to escape lock-in or to explore new research avenues, especially those based on inter-disciplinary competencies. Moreover, when the competencies and their evolution are at the center of the conceptual framework, new forms of "risks" appear. The most obvious of these are: the risk to be locked in an inefficient routine; the risk of an insufficient level of exploration and/or of a rigid exploitation routine; the risk of cumulating knowledge which becomes obsolete with the emergence of a new trajectory.

In an evolutionary approach, we can consider that "diversity drives evolution and evolution generates diversity" (Cohendet, Llerena, and Sorge, 1992). The existence and the creation of diversity at different levels of aggregation (competencies, technologies, behavior, institutions, systems of innovation, etc.) generate costs but also advantages resulting from learning processes and from new knowledge. The different forms of diversity (in particular, technologies and competencies) give a broader knowledge base and a spectrum of learning activities which, in principle, should make more rapid economic growth possible and give a better ability to quickly react and keep pace with changing environmental parameters. It also allows a maximum number of options to be kept available and applicable. The key characteristic of being able to survive in such a diverse and perturbed environment is the ability to learn. The value of diversity depends consequently on how the processes of learning function and are organized. However, a system of broader diversity also requires more information to be described, and this leads to additional costs. Thus the valorization of diversity does not mean that all differences are a "good thing," or that they must be maintained, or that options must be preserved at any cost. According to the central role played by diversity in the process of innovation and in the evolution of the economic system, an incentive policy towards cooperation is justified by the necessity to valorize the diversity of an innovation system. This policy has to coordinate diversity so as to overcome different evolutionary failures that have a negative influence on the virtuous cycle "diversity–evolution–diversity" (cf. figure 9.1). Elsewhere, we present some failures that underlie the rationale of a public policy oriented towards the development of inter-organization agreements.

Lock-in failures   The systemic feature of innovation implies a co-evolution of organizations, institutions, and technologies. This co-evolution entails a diversity of local and national systems of innovation characterized by specific technological development, standards, networks, and institutions. Such an interactive and cumulative process could induce negative lock-in phenomena at the different levels. These negative lock-in phenomena could then be the origin of a reduction of diversity that entails diminishing learning possibilities and consequently reduces the pace and the variety of innovation. A technology policy towards cooperation could correct these failures at least at two levels: the organization and the technology.

Organizations may have accumulated knowledge and competencies that become obsolete because they were driven by the success of their trajectory

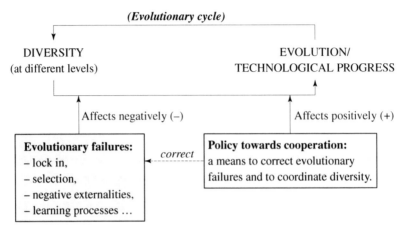

9.1 Incentive policy towards cooperation: an evolutionary approach

and have forgotten to explore new alternatives. A networking policy (see also David, Foray and Steinmueller (1998, chapter 13 in this volume) should ease and create the transition conditions towards new trajectories. The encounter of new theories in action and the interaction with new partners (coming from different sectors, institutional frameworks, etc.) opens the possibilities of new research alternatives. In that case, the coordination of diversity induces the identification of new "open windows" in order to leave the obsolete technology and create a new paradigm.

At the level of a technology, the valorization of diversity through a policy-inducing cooperation depends on the maturity of the technologies (Cohendet and Llerena, 1997). If we consider a technology after the starting-up stage – i.e. at the stage of auto-organization (Willinger and Zuscovitch, 1993) where new principles arise owing to knowledge accumulation – many mechanisms can introduce path-dependency in the creation and use of the technology. These mechanisms will increase the costs of interacting if some features of common organization are not present to reduce the global operating costs of developing the technology. A policy towards cooperation allows a reduction of the costs of interaction and creates the necessary conditions to reach a common language to exploit the potential use of the new technology and to diminish the risk of incompatibility between different local experimentations. When technologies enter a more mature phase, the main costs of diversity are the risk of duplication of mature processes of production and therefore the lack of economies of scale which could prevent the economic systems as a whole from being competitive. However, the benefit of diversity and its coordination through cooperation should not be under-estimated. The coordination of diversity on the one hand eases the transition towards new – potentially "better" – technologies, and on the other, develops "sub-technologies" and products that are components of the mature technologies.

Selection failures The origin of diversity and the nature of selection represent two important concepts of an evolutionary framework. Selection occurs in each environment where agents interact in order to choose technological options. Selection thus occurs in the market, but also inside organizations; we will concentrate on the latter only. Organizations manage and select their innovation development in directions that they consider relevant to the anticipated evolution of the environment. Their anticipations are related to the context (institutions, external relationships, etc.) in which they evolve, and the internal selection of technological alternatives are thus characterized by a social and external dimension. In that perspective, cooperative agreements allow firms to build their technological and economic anticipations with their partners and to avoid too early irreversible choices based only on personal anticipations. Cooperation then constitutes a way to organize and to socialize selection between organizations, each having their own vision of the world. An incentive policy towards cooperation could have at least two impacts (Matt, 1996). First, the policy-maker could channel the choices because she is able to influence the anticipation context of firms. This kind of policy creates adequate conditions to explore new alternatives, based on the coordination of existing diversity and this in a shorter time than without networking structure. Second, some existing interactions between organizations could last too long and homogenize their anticipations. In this case, the policy-maker should widen the cooperation possibilities in order not to root anticipations (and therefore selection mechanisms) in a relationship based on rigid exploitation routines instead of exploration ones.

Negative externality failures Every process of knowledge creation generates two types of externalities: positive and negative. If positive externalities favor knowledge diffusion, sharing and communication, the negative ones reduce knowledge creation and reinforce the inefficient lock-in phenomena inherent in the co-evolution mentioned above.

The reduction of negative externalities and the stimulation of positive feedbacks by a policy based on inter-organization agreements should be effective at the institutional level. When an innovation system is characterized by norms leading to negative externalities (rules of knowledge restriction), an active policy is necessary to change mentalities towards the generalization of a social model based on knowledge diffusion. When a system is characterized by norms favoring the creation of positive externalities, an active policy based on cooperation makes it possible to maintain these norms in the sense that defection could rapidly lead the system towards social norms based on knowledge restriction.

This may have important consequences for the valorization of diversity at the level of a technology. When considering a technology at the starting-up stage, diversity has a specific value for the policy-maker, in the sense that different local experiments involving multiple trials and errors could inform the policy-maker and the other organizations rapidly about possible developments and practices of the technology, or at least about which misuses or misconceptions could be avoided. The main costs of diversity at this early stage result from information diffusion: each local unit needs to be able to communicate with other units through interactive learning, and to abstain from purely private modes of appropriation. A policy that favors cooperation is then able to create an adequate environment for interactive learning between different local units and to provide incentives to exchange information about the different experimentations.

Under the dynamic perspective, the incentives to cooperate become at the same time a way to manage the risk by opening up the set of opportunities viable for the firms and by using a flexible organizational form as a remedy for the consequences of the risks listed above. For example, by spreading the risk (not only financial risk) over partners and public authorities, a technology policy based on inter-firm agreements could be a tool to cope with insufficient exploration routines, emerging spontaneously from the behaviors of firms. In particular, some of the research programs launched by European authorities such as the European Union or European Space Agency (ESA) should be evaluated in these terms.

Incentive and organizational structure concerning inter-firm cooperation

We should also consider that the policy-maker has to design new incentive mechanisms because, contrary to the neoclassical analysis, asymmetries of information and opportunism can lead to efficiency in a dynamic context (Cohen, 1984). In this perspective, incentive mechanisms should be able to maintain certain kinds of asymmetries so as to favor dynamic efficiency by allowing "creative tensions." More precisely, one of the objectives of a policy that stimulates cooperation is to ease local learning processes – i.e. firms or local systems of innovation – by minimizing transaction and communication costs and by favoring positive externalities and learning processes. From this point of view, incentives could be in a monetary form, providing for diminished transaction costs and completed by organizational or institutional considerations favoring knowledge diffusion, communication and creation.

According to Axelrod (1992), one of the means to stimulate heterogeneous agents to cooperate is to modify the benefits of organizations. The first possibility is to punish defection so that cooperation becomes the best short-term strategy, whatever the others' decisions. The second option is to subsidize cooperation so that the motivation to cooperate in the long term is stronger than a short-term defection strategy. But these monetary incentives could be insufficient to promote cooperation and to stimulate knowledge and skills creation. In this case, it is necessary to modify institutional norms and to stimulate agreements that favor learning objectives.

These modifications are especially relevant when cooperating organizations are characterized by different institutional rules and theories of action that could be incompatible and block the transmission and creation of knowledge. Institutional incompatibility concerns more specifically university–firm relationships, as they are governed by different divulgation rules (Dasgupta and David, 1994; Geuna, 1998, chapter 15 in this volume). During an agreement, it could be difficult to decide which part of the created knowledge or technology should be submitted to the university rules (entire divulgation) or to the firm rules (secrecy). The role of the policy-maker is then to implement the following tools and organizational arrangements:

- To place contractual tools at the partners' disposal to allow them to establish the rules of intellectual property rights and their applications.
- To stimulate cooperations involving research centers that are characterized by institutional rules halfway between those of firms and those of universities and that could be considered as mediators. Universities could also play this role in case of agreements containing a high proportion of firms identified by different theories of action. These differences could entail some tensions which universities could solve by focusing and orientating the research on the bases of scientific knowledge on which firms could federate.

These measures, which enable different organizations to find agreement, could stimulate firms to cooperate and to benefit from high learning potentialities.

At a more global level – i.e. national or international – some studies underline the fact that inter-organizational relationships are often local and that consequently organizations do not exploit knowledge potentially available elsewhere. In order to enlarge the field of exploitable knowledge, the policy-maker should encourage specific agreements:

- containing members that never collaborate; this allows different organizations to meet other partners and to benefit from their networks
- between industrial sectors that do not usually exchange knowledge

- containing universities specialized in scientific disciplines arrived at maturity in order to favor technological transfers and industrial applications
- in new emergent technological domains where networking structures are not yet established.

These conditions not only favor a better exploitation of existing knowledge, but also stimulate the exploration of new research avenues based on new interdisciplinary combinations. They allow the correction of some evolutionary failures and improve the valorization of diversity.

Conclusion

In this chapter, we have provided a theoretical analysis of the rationale of a public policy towards inter-organization agreements using two approaches: the market and organizational perspectives. These two approaches provide different but complementary arguments concerning the relevance and the means of implementing a technology policy towards cooperation. The differences and complementarities could be synthesized as follows:

(1) Diversity is a central concept that explains the need to implement a technology policy leading to cooperation in the two approaches, but the concept has different meanings. In a *static perspective*, diversity – or, more precisely, heterogeneity – is exogenous. Agents are characterized by given cognitive capabilities and learning mainly corresponds to the accumulation of information without any cognitive evolution. The main issues are thus to find solutions in order to reduce asymmetries and unequal distribution of information. In a *dynamic perspective*, diversity is endogenous to technological development. Diversity drives evolution which drives diversity. Organizations are considered as "processors of knowledge" where learning, based on a continuous cognitive process, creates competencies and knowledge. Valorizing and coordinating diversity is thus at the center of the analysis of innovation.

(2) In the *market approach*, state intervention in favor of cooperation happens only in situations where agents are heterogeneous. The policy-maker subsidizes only R&D cooperations involving partners characterized by different research or absorptive capacity. The intervention is based on the existence of a conflict between private and public interests – i.e. in situations where firms do not cooperate and the social welfare would be better under cooperation. State intervention and private decisions are both based on optimization procedures. In the evolutionary perspective, state intervention is explained by the need to coordinate and valorize diversity in order to improve knowledge and competencies creation – i.e. learning processes. The difference between private and

public interests is justified by limits inherent in the evolution of local systems of innovation. These limits correspond mainly to evolutionary failures: negative lock-in phenomena and selection mechanisms, and existence of negative externalities.

(3) In the static approaches, incentive mechanisms towards cooperation correspond to *financial structures* (neoclassical perspective) and *pre-established contractual agreements* (neo-institutional conception) that reduce market failures or transaction costs. The subsidy represents an incentive reward scheme allowing the state to reduce agency phenomena and to stimulate agents to provide the expected effort. The coordination and incentive aspects are limited to an informational problem. In the dynamic perspective, the means of intervention correspond to the modification of the institutional system (from a system dominated by negative externalities to a system dominated by positive ones, for example). The policy-maker implements instruments and rules (organizational aspects) inducing new cooperations that favor a better exploitation of existing diversity and stimulation of new research avenues (exploration) – i.e. higher learning potentialities. Finally, these instruments may provide a better management of inefficient lock-in phenomena.

References

Argyris C. and D.A. Schön (1978). *Organizational Learning: A Theory of Action Perspective*, New York: Addison-Wesley

Axelrod, R. (1984). *The Evolution of Cooperation*, New York: Basic Books

(1992). "Donnant, donnant: théorie du comportement coopératif," Paris: Editions Odile Jacob, Sciences Humaines, French translation of R.A. Axelrod, *The Evolution of Cooperation*

Bureth, A. S. Wolff, and A. Zanfei (1994). "Inter-firm Collaboration, Commitment and Learning. The Formation and Evolution of Cooperative Agreements in the European Electronics Industry," Eunetic Conference. "Evolutionary of Technological Change," (Strasbourg), (6–8 October)

(1998). "Cooperative Learning and the Evolution and Stability of Inter-firm Agreements in the European Electronics Industry" chapter 10 in this volume

CESPRI (1996). "Literature Survey on Public Policy in the Evolution of Industrial Sectors from a System of Innovation and Evolutionary Perspectives," *Draft Report for the European TSER program, ISE,* PL 95 1029, Milan: Bocconi University (September)

Clarke, R.N. (1983). "Collusion and Incentives for Information Sharing," *Bell Journal of Economics,* 14, 383–94

Cohen, M.D. (1984). "Conflict and Complexity: Goal Diversity and Organizational Search Effectiveness," *American Political Science Review,* 78, 435–51

Cohen, W.M. and D.A. Levinthal (1990). "Absorptive Capacity: A New Perspective on Learning and Innovation," *Administrative Science Quarterly*, vol. 35, 128–52

Cohendet, P. and P. Llerena (1997). "Learning, Technical Change and Public Policy: How to Create and Exploit Diversity," in C. Edquist (ed.); *Systems of Innovation: Technologies, Institutions and Organizations*, London: Pinter, 223–41

Cohendet, P., F. Kern, B. Mehmanpazir, and F. Munier (1996). "Knowledge Coordination, Competence Creation and Integrated Networks in Globalized Firms," EMOT Workshop (European Science Foundation). "Learning and embeddedness: Evolving Transnational Firm Strategies in Europe (27–29 June)

Cohendet, P., P. Llerena and A. Sorge (1992). "Technological Diversity and Coherence in Europe: An Analytical Overview," *Revue d'Economie Industrielle*, Special Issue, 59, 10

Dasgupta, P. and P. David (1994). "Towards a New Economics of Science," *Research Policy*, 23, 487–521

D'Aspremont C. & Jacquemin A. (1988) : "Cooperative and noncooperative R&D in duopoly with spillovers", *American Economic Review*, 78, 1133–37

D'Aspremont C., A. Jacquemin, J. Gabszewiz, and J. Weymark (1983). "On the Stability of Collusive Price Leadership," *Canadian Journal of Economics*, 16, 17–25

David, P.A., D. Foray, and W.E Steinmueller (1998). "The Research Network and the New Economics of Science: From Metaphors to Organizational Behaviors," chapter 13 in this volume

De Bondt, R. (1991). "Cost-reducing Strategies with Spillovers," in J. Thepot and R.A. Thietart, *Microeconomic Contributions to Strategic Management*, Amsterdam: Elsevier Science Publishers, 33–50

(1995). "Spillovers and Innovative Activities," 22nd Annual meeting of the European Association for Research in Industrial Economic (EARIE) (Juan les Pins) (3 September)

De Bondt, R. and R. Veuglers (1991). "Strategic Investment with Spillovers," *European Journal of Political Economy*, 7, 345–66

De Bondt, R., P. Slaets and B. Cassiman (1992). "The Degree of Spillovers and the Number of Rivals for Maximum Effective R&D," *International Journal of Industrial Organization*, 10, 35–54

Dosi, G. (1988). "Sources, Procedures, and Microeconomic Effects of Innovation," *Journal of Economic Literature*, 26, 1120–71

Friedman, J.W. (1971). "A Noncooperative Equilibrium for Supergames," *Review of Economic Studies*, 38, 1–12

Geuna, A. (1998). "Patterns of University Research in Europe," chapter 15 in this volume

Kamien, M.I., E. Muller, and I. Zang (1992). "Research Joint Ventures and R&D Cartels," *American Economic Review*, 182, 1293–306

Matt, M. (1996). "Politiques technologiques et accords de coopération en R&D: théorie et application à des programmes européens," Thesis for Doctorate of Economic Science, Université Louis Pasteur, Strasbourg

Metcalfe, J.S. (1993). The Economic Foundations of Technology Policy: Equilibrium and Evolutionary Perspectives," Department of Economics and PREST, University of Manchester

Motta, M. (1992). "National R&D Cooperation: A Special Type of Strategic Policy," *CORE Discussion Paper,* 9202, Louvain-La-Neuve, (January)

Richardson, G.B. (1972). "The Organization of Industry," *Economic Journal,* 82(327), 883–96

Sharp M., and J. Senker and I. Galimberti (1996). "Co-operative Alliances and Internal Competencies: Some Case Studies in Biotechnology," Science Policy Research Unit, University of Sussex, mimeo, see also chapter 12 in this volume

Teece, D.J. (1986). "Profiting from Technological Innovation: Implications for Integration, Collaboration, Licensing and Public Policy," *Research Policy,* 15, 285–305

Vonotras, N. (1994). "Inter-firm Cooperation with Imperfectly Appropriable Research," *International Journal of Industrial Organization,* 12, 413–35

Williamson, O.E. (1985). *The Economic Institutions of Capitalism. Firms, Markets, Relational Contracting,* New York: Free Press

(1989). "Transaction Cost Economics," in R. Schmalensee and R.D. Willig (eds.), *Handbook of Industrial Organization I,* Amsterdam: Elsevier Science Publishers, 136–82

(1993). "Transaction Cost Economics and Organization Theory," *Industrial and Corporate Change,* 2, 107–56

(1994). *Les institutions de l'économie,* Paris: InterEditions, French translation of *The Economic Institutions of Capitalism*

Willinger, M. and E. Zuscovitch (1993). "Efficience, irriversibilités et constitution des technologies," *Revue d'Economie Industrielle,* 65, troisième trimestre, 7–23

Wolff, S. (1992). "Accords inter-entreprises et flexibilité : éléments théoriques et application au secteur des télécommunications," thesis for Doctorate of Economic Science, Université Louis Pasteur, Strasbourg

10 Cooperative learning and the evolution of inter-firm agreements in the European electronics industry

Antoine Bureth, Sandrine Wolff, and Antonello Zanfei

Inter-firm alliances, learning and commitment: the stability issue

Technological inter-firm agreements have received considerable attention in recent years. This is notably true for EU policy-makers, whose concern for the technological implications of alliances has been increasing since the early 1980s, giving rise to a pragmatic relaxation of legal, competitive and antitrust constraint, on the one hand, and to the organization of specific industrial meetings and task forces to promote pro-competitive cooperation on the other.[1] Under specific circumstances, alliances are thought to represent an important way to reinforce industrial competitiveness, by giving firms access to external, technological or commercial complementary resources, or by achieving scale and scope economies. The competitiveness-enhancing role of alliances is even more pronounced in the electronics industry, since they may contribute to the European entrance into the "information society," which represents a further priority of the Union's industrial policy.

This view is based on the reasonable assumption that the formation of inter-firm alliances can generate new, economically useful knowledge, thus increasing firms' ability to compete in high-technology industries (Teece 1992, Robertson and Langlois, 1995; Lazaric and Marengo, 1997). However, in order to better understand the likely competitive impact of technical alliances, a deeper inquiry is needed into factors affecting the evolution and stability of technical alliances over time.

Recent contributions on inter-firm agreements have addressed the stability issue. Some authors have highlighted the inner instability of alliances

Funds from the European Union under the Human Capital and Mobility Program (contract no. ERBCHRXCT920002) are acknowledged. Zanfei also thanks the Italian National Research Council, CNR (contract no. 96.0197.CT11) for additional financial support.
[1] For instance, see the special issue on EU industrial policy of the *Revue du Marché Commun et de l'Union Européenne* 396 (March 1996).

due to the weakness of incentive structures that are associated with these organizational modes, especially under circumstances of high and increasing uncertainty (Aoki 1990; Kogut, 1989). On the one hand, firms will be interested in increasing ownership control of other firms, in order to reduce the risk of opportunistic behavior in their transactions with them. On the other hand, by doing so they will run the risk of reducing their counterparts' incentives to invest, learn and innovate (Vaccà and Zanfei, 1989; Meschi, 1995). The difficult balance between these tensions may explain why a number of inter-firm agreements and joint ventures are relatively short-lived and unsuccessful. Other scholars have emphasized the "experimental nature" of alliances: in each period, partners obtain an outcome of the cooperative experiment, and that becomes the basis for further action (Mody, 1993; Doz, 1996). By collaborating, firms accumulate knowledge on their partners' characteristics, about the domain of cooperation, and about environmental opportunities, and are enabled to take decisions about whether, and how, to continue collaborating in a more informed way.

In this chapter we suggest that two further aspects of learning-by-collaborating should be considered in order to explain firms' decisions to continue or discontinue cooperation over time. On the one hand, learning by cooperating will *negatively* affect the stability of alliances to the extent that new assets are created which can be used outside the specific relationship that has generated it. Firms in a better position to gain access to, and utilize, such redeployable assets will increase their bargaining power within the network. This will possibly reduce the other party's incentives to invest in the agreement. The alliance may then collapse because a party loses ground in the distribution of rents and either defects from the partnership, or reduces its contribution to rent-creation.

Furthermore, regardless of how asymmetric access to and use of redeployable assets is, firms may utilize such assets competitively against each other. This may occur through direct rivalry in the same market where partners are active, or through the formation of other alliances with possibly conflicting outcomes. Under these circumstances, the alliance may break up because firms fear or experience their partners' opportunistic use of resources generated through cooperation.

On the other hand, learning by cooperating *positively* impacts on the stability of inter-firm agreements because it is a commitment-intensive process. Two factors are at work here. First, commitment is a *pre-condition for learning*. In fact firms tend to use commitment as a means to reduce uncertainty and create a more stable condition for learning. By sustaining highly irreversible investments that are specific to the agreement, firms will signal their actual availability to cooperate, and they will reveal their preferences and skills. As agents have limited capacity to detect, select, and treat information, their cooperative behavior will be heavily influenced by these signals (Simon, 1957, 1976). In other words, commitment will fix some "relational parameters," reducing environmental variety and variability and creating an environment that is more conducive to cooperative learning.

Moreover, learning by cooperating requires specific investments devoted to absorption, adaptation, and use of assets contributed by the different parties. Specialized workers and managers must be devoted to these functions acting as gatekeepers, and new skills must be formed for this purpose. Particularly in the case of collaboration between firms that are (at least partly) autonomous, this coordination process cannot be simplified through the mere imposition of one party's communication procedures, behavioral norms, and conventions. It requires a mutual effort of firms to deal with, and connect to, different cultures, competencies, and organizational structures.

Second, part of the outcome of learning is also *specific to the collaborative venture*, and tends to reinforce commitment. Routines and communication procedures are generated, tested in the process of cooperation, modified and eventually replaced. New specific competencies are accumulated by personnel devoted to cooperation. Partners get to know each other, and trust will eventually emerge. Mutual acquaintance and trust may represent key assets, but they are scarcely redeployable in contexts different from the collaborative venture that generated them. Thus they also increase the costs the parties would sustain in case of contractual breach, and contribute to stabilizing the venture.

In sum: decisions to continue or discontinue cooperation will depend on the balance between the allocation, use, and generation of knowledge and other resources that are redeployable and guarantee flexibility, and the allocation, use, and creation of assets that are specific and will favor inertia of collaborative ventures.[2] A key implication is that stability of collaborations cannot be considered a value *per se*. Continuity of cooperation over time may signal a successful interaction that partners are willing to perpetuate; but it could also reflect lock-in phenomena (David, 1985; Arthur, 1989; see also chapter 9 in this volume). Partners may in fact be induced to maintain existing linkages because they have sustained irreversible investments, and because non-redeployable assets were produced, in spite of the fact that the results of collaboration were well below their expectations.

Conversely, the break-up of an agreement does not necessarily mean that partners failed to attain the objectives that were defined *ex ante* or during the process of cooperation. The alliance may also end because some, if not all, partners realize that "the mission is over," satisfactory results have been

---

[2] This is consistent with the idea that irreversibilities are a source of both opportunities and of rigidities, as developed by Gaffard (1990), Dosi and Metcalfe (1991), and Foray (1991).

attained, and there is no reason to continue interaction for the time being. This will most probably occur when cooperation has generated valuable assets that firms may effectively utilize on their own or with different partners in different contexts.[3] Under these circumstances, discontinuing cooperation is not equal to failure, because new, redeployable assets have been generated through the venture.

In the following sections we shall discuss our analytical framework in greater detail, using illustrative evidence from case studies of inter-firm agreements in the European electronics industry. We are perfectly aware that using historical examples, such as those examined in this chapter, does not generally "demonstrate" anything. However, they can draw the scholar's attention to the role played by some key variables, whose impact on collaborative behavior may not be effectively detected through more quantitative analyses. This is especially useful when considering such complex phenomena as collaborative ventures occurring in a very turbulent environment such as the European electronics industry, in which some of the events that are shaping the evolution of the industry are often difficult to measure; when measurable, they might not be statistically relevant but might signal the initial stages of some astonishing change. (Who would have forecast the extent of diffusion of semiconductors, of personal computers, or of cellular telephony when examining statistical data of their market penetration in their early stages?) From this perspective, our reflections on case studies are meant to be a useful complement for other theoretical and empirical work that is being carried out on this subject.

The chapter is structured as follows. We briefly illustrate some of the findings of previous empirical analyses based on data banks, highlighting the increasing recourse to alliances in European high-technology industries. This will pave the way for the focus on the results of our own survey of case studies of alliances in which European electronics firms were involved. Using this illustrative evidence, we examine the role of commitment as a pre-condition for learning in collaborative alliances. We then consider how learning can produce both redeployable and non-redeployable assets. We illustrate some cases in which important tensions emerged between forces leading to network stability and forces leading towards instability, and concludes by discussing the interdependencies between redeployable and non-redeployable assets and drawing some policy implications from the analysis. The basic features of the empirical evidence, on which our reflections are based, will be described in the appendix (p. 231).

---

[3] Participating firms need not agree on the consideration that "the mission is over." Some parties may reach this conclusion before the others and decide to utilize redeployable assets in a way that undermines the very existence of a given alliance – e.g. commercializing those assets competitively or setting up alliances with previous partners' competitors.

Inter-firm agreements in European high-technology industries

Over the past two decades, three important aspects of the general phenomenon of inter-firm alliances have emerged: an increasing recourse to cooperative strategies, their primarily technological dimension, and the prevalence of the so-called "Triad" (United States–European Union–Japan) as a geographical focus of the resulting networks.

In terms of industrial organization, the growth of inter-firm cooperation is an important feature of the last 15 years. Several studies conducted in the 1980s[4] highlighted this trend. During the whole 1980–89 decade, the total number of agreements recorded by Merit's CATI database has more than doubled to more than 10,000 operations. Focusing only on information technology (IT), the increase is most apparent: they have grown by a factor of 3.5 in the same period. Furthermore, as their progression appears to have begun earlier and to have occurred at a higher rate than in other sectors, agreements in IT also constitute a major share of total alliances in high-technology industries (41.2 percent in 1989, according to Hagedoorn and Shakenraad, 1991).

The increasing recourse to agreements is the more interesting since the majority of them associate potential competitors acting in the same – or at least interconnected – markets (Jacquemin, Lammerant, and Spinoit, 1986; Morris and Hergert, 1987). At the same time, they concentrate in high-technology industries, and they very often cover R&D activities. This can be interpreted as a sign of the fact that technology acquisition and exchange is at least as important an objective as benefiting from wider markets.

The nature of technological alliances can be better qualified if we observe the "geography" of agreements. According to most studies, the share of alliances including partners from the most advanced areas of the world (the Triad) is the highest (above 80 percent, according to the CATI database). As partners originate from countries characterized by comparable development levels, it appears that these alliances have little to do with technological catching-up or with the transfer of mature technology. Cooperation is most frequently the way to keep up with the technological frontier: by associating complementary resources and competencies, it makes it possible to explore and exploit new technological opportunities.

Focusing on European firms' cooperative strategies in IT, it appears that international alliances tend to be very frequent, particularly with US partners. Delapierre (1991) conducted a survey of different empirical sources, and highlighted that approximately half of European companies' agreements involved a US firm, whereas the proportion was below one third

---

[4] Cf. Jacquemin, Lammerant, and Spinoit (1986); Morris and Hergert (1987); Larea–Cerem (1986), Hagedoorn and Schakenraad (1991); D'Orazio et al. (1992).

when other EU companies were involved. A very small share of agreements involved Japanese partners. Most notably, however, intra-European agreements devoted to R&D and innovation occurred more often than in the case of EU–US alliances, the latter being more focused on commercialization objectives (Duysters and Hagedoorn, 1996). This mostly intra-regional orientation of technical alliances suggests that cultural homogeneity as well as institutional barriers to entry are probably playing an important role in shaping the direction of inter-firm cooperation anyway.

In spite of the drawbacks which appear to affect any database on joint ventures, drawing from press information,[5] the evidence we have reviewed paves the way to our analysis of factors influencing the evolution (and continuity) of alliances over time. Among others, Hagedoorn and Schakenraad (1992) found out that for a certain number of core technologies, the growth pattern of alliances stabilized or even declined towards the end of the 1980s. IT industries are no exception to this rule.[6] The authors explain this evolution in terms of the experience companies accumulate, leading them to dissolve alliances whenever cooperation does not yield satisfactory results. In other words, firms *learn* through experience whether it is advantageous or not to continue cooperating, and some ability to select partners may be attained over time.

Kogut (1989) addresses the stability issue even more directly. Using a sample of 92 joint ventures contacted by mail questionnaires, he found out that the "hazard rate" (ratio of terminated ventures to all agreements that survive at a given moment in time) increases from 5.4 percent to 15.2 percent in the first three years of the alliance life-cycle. While observing that a part of this venture mortality rate is due to successful completion of the cooperative task, he highlights the important role of *incentive structures* of partners involved in a collaborative alliance. Using his own words:

Instability of the venture should increase the greater the competitive incentives among partners, and the lower the degree of commitment to the overall relationship. (Kogut, 1989, 185).

The two studies we have just mentioned provide highly complementary explanations of the topic we are focusing on in this chapter: the evolution and

---

[5] Data are seldom available concerning the monetary values and the strategic importance of recorded agreements; press information frequently reflects marketing and advertising objectives of the firms involved; coverage of large firms is higher than for small ones; the role of Asian companies is usually under-estimated in databases drawing from the English-language international press; joint venture failures are not reported as accurately as joint venture formation; large databases are hard to update and are frequently subject to change in the methodology of data collection over time. See Mariti and Smiley (1983); Delapierre (1991); D'Orazio *et al.* (1992); Duysters and Hagedoorn (1996).

[6] Similar results appear in the study conducted by Cainarca *et al.* (1989).

stability of alliances. Both learning (about partners, technologies, environmental conditions and how to manage a venture) and incentives (to deviate from or to behave consistently in the agreement, to capture rents from cooperation, to control or share knowledge) play a key role in firms' decisions to continue or discontinue collaboration over time. As anticipated in the previous section, it is by the interaction of learning with commitment/incentive structures that the stability of ventures is primarily affected. In other words, learning requires some degree of commitment to occur; and learning processes themselves generate some commitment as well. To the extent that learning is commitment-intensive, alliances will be stable. To the extent that knowledge generated through cooperation is generic, re-usable, and can be utilized competitively by partners, this will reduce stability of cooperative ventures.

Using evidence from case studies, let us focus our attention first on the linkage between commitment and cooperative learning.

Evolution of inter-firm alliances: learning needs commitment

Whereas learning through inter-firm cooperation has recently been emphasized in the literature about strategic alliances (see, for instance, Crossan and Inkpen, 1995; Levinson and Asahi, 1995; Child, 1997), its relationship to commitment and stability issues remains largely to be explored.

As anticipated earlier, learning by cooperating requires that firms mobilize resources, that will be at least partially lost in the case of a break-up of the alliance. This is because of two basic reasons. First, commitment helps reduce the variety and variability of the contexts in which cooperation takes place, thus creating "stable windows" within which agents can learn. Second, firms need to irreversibly invest in communication skills, procedures, and facilities in order to absorb and utilize the assets exchanged and shared with partners.

Some initial, *ex ante* commitment is necessary to get cooperation started. However, further investments appear to be necessary during the life-cycle of inter-firm agreements to sustain cooperative learning processes. We shall argue that the distribution of such investments over time will depend on the partners' evaluation of two factors: (1) how effective cooperation was during the previous period; (2) how one party's commitment is being reciprocated by the others.

Uncertainty, stable windows, and cautious learners

In a number of industries, including electronics which we consider more closely here, firms face (and contribute to generating) a high uncertainty in terms of variety and variability of technology, markets, and organizational modes. Firms entering a new business in this field may hardly know what technological trajectories will look like, or have a limited perception of the real size of the market they will be entering. In some cases, market opportunities are systematically under-estimated as the width of alternative applications is unpredictable (as the experience of telematics and value-added services reveals). In other circumstances they are over-estimated, because important factors such as customer acquaintance, switching costs, and user abilities are not properly evaluated (as in the case of artificial intelligence or network management services). Even in more consolidated business areas within the electronics *filière*, new and converging technologies are affecting and revolutionizing existing trajectories (as in the case of opto-electronics applied to central office switching or superconductivity applied to computer industry). These technological transformations introduce largely unpredictable complexities in development and commercialization processes which in some circumstances may increase costs beyond the limits that would be compatible with actual and potential market size.

Uncertainty is a major force spurring firms to enter inter-firm cooperation. When dealing with frequent and unpredictable changes of technology and markets, even the largest firms can hardly tackle all the challenges and opportunities by means of internal growth or mergers and acquisitions. In fact, environmental complexity increases time and resource constraints. Firms will generally prefer to experiment with new and uncertain activities through alliances as these require a lower and less binding organizational and financial burden than mergers and acquisitions. From this perspective, a cooperative venture permits us to isolate specific areas of collaboration where and only where there is a need for complementary assets or a larger scale of activities must be attained. By maintaining – at least partially – firms' independence, cooperation also enhances creativity, and increases the probability of success when tackling new problems and opportunities. Last but not least, collaborative ventures generally allow the partners some degree of freedom in the development of further alliances, thus leaving the door open to the exploitation of a wider range of learning patterns.

The considerations we have just recalled help to understand the diffusion of inter-firm agreements in industrial contexts subject to technological and market uncertainty. A further point to be stressed here is that uncertainty is also *endogenous* to the cooperative process itself. Part of this endogenous uncertainty originates from the coordination problems with which co-operative networks are generally associated.[7] It is frequently assumed that

---

[7] We assume that firms will not generally be able to precisely evaluate coordination costs before eventually entering a relationship with an external party. We therefore consider such costs more as a consequence of the decision to grow than a factor motivating the choice between alternative modes of external growth.

inter-firm alliances have a weaker incentive structure than more hierarchical forms of organization. This may give rise to higher risks of cheating and opportunism. Even when the incentive problem is adequately addressed within inter-firm agreements, firms may sustain an organizational burden that exceeds their management capabilities. Companies joining large networks may not be able to effectively coordinate their efforts with their partners. Especially when no clear leadership emerges within an alliance, a likely result would be a high dispersion and duplication of innovative activities. Firms with limited ability to select market and technological opportunities may also run the risk of expanding the range and scope of alliances beyond their needs and abilities to effectively manage and utilize them.

Endogenous uncertainty also stems from the fact that firms do not know in advance what their partners are really like. They do not know exactly what resources they really have, whether they are actually complementary to their own, and what is likely to be their real contribution of skills and assets to the venture. Furthermore they do not know how their partners will behave, with what priorities and objectives they will join a network, and how responsive their participation to the alliance will be to changes in their general strategies. Firms will generally base their expectations on their partners' competencies and behavior on very incomplete and imperfect *ex ante* information. Important sources of such information are: previous direct experience of cooperation with the same or other partners, reputation of potential partners, and other firms' collaborative action with demonstrative effects in the same and related fields. These sources will reveal a limited amount of information that can be re-used when setting up new ventures. In a context of high technological complexity, a firm may quickly lose ground or acquire new valuable competencies in a given research area, and some of its commercial strengths may be eroded or significantly changed. Moreover, when dealing with large firms, it is often impossible to penetrate all its "secrets" with a single agreement, and only a fraction of the relevant information concerning other firms' collaborative alliances will be public or accessible. As a general statement, one may thus conclude that firms can hardly reach a satisfactory level of information concerning their partners' actual rent-creation and rent-extraction abilities in a given area of business before experiencing rather long periods of cooperation in that area (Bureth, Wolff, and Zanfei, 1994).

In sum: on the one hand firms will attempt to face uncertainty with the flexible tools of inter-firm agreements and cooperative learning. On the other, they will have to deal with further uncertainty stemming from the cooperative process itself.[8] Such (endogenous) uncertainty will ultimately

---

[8] This assumption makes sense only from an evolutionary perspective. The acquisition of information reduces uncertainty, but the way by which information is obtained and processed is in turn itself subject to uncertainty.

concern the actual efficiency (cost-effectiveness) of activities carried out cooperatively, their potential outcome, and the distribution of rents among partners.

The discussion above introduces our main argument here: we suggest that firms may be willing to increase their degree of commitment to a venture as a means to lower the level of uncertainty that is associated with collaboration. By so doing, firms will eventually create more favorable conditions for learning.

Irreversible investments may reduce uncertainty (and enhance learning) in three main ways. First, by committing to a venture, a firm will provide a clear signal of how determined it is to cooperate, and will attempt to influence the partners' behavior consistently with the choice made. This is the basic intuition behind the idea of "commitment to sacrifice" – i.e. irreversible and risky actions that can be taken by one company to alter the outcomes of cooperation. Gulati, Khanna, and Nohria (1994) exemplify this with the case of a firm signing a long-term contract with a supplier outside the venture to gain access to materials needed for the alliance: the firm makes it clear to partners that it will not credibly choose a non-cooperative strategy, because this would imply a net loss of irreversible investments (Dixit, 1980). A possible effect of such a choice (especially but not necessarily under the assumption that decisions are repeated indefinitely) is that of removing the partner's doubts about adopting a cooperative behavior (e.g. sharing technology):

commitment to sacrifice something in the event that a less desirable outcome emerges, can be sufficient to ensure that this outcome does not emerge in the first place. (Gulati, Khanna, and Nohria, 1994, 64).

This use of commitment to signal determination to cooperate was apparent in some of our case studies. The 1987 agreement between the Italian subsidiary of the US computer manufacturer, DEC, and the software producer for office automation, Formula, is illustrative. At the beginning of cooperation, Formula was interested in taking advantage of DEC's reputation, commercialization strength, and linkages with manufacturing automation, an area that was complementary to the one in which Formula was more active (office automation). Besides, it felt that an alliance with DEC would reduce its dependence on IBM as a platform. In order to signal its motivation to cooperate with DEC, Formula eventually decided to unilaterally commit to the venture by setting up a specific unit to commercialize DEC's products. This appears to have increased DEC's interest in Formula and led to a stronger collaboration, with DEC funding Formula's investment in the development of a UNIX version of packages for office automation.

Second, commitment reduces uncertainty by clarifying firms'

preferences concerning the domain, object, and goals of cooperation. When irreversibly investing in a specific activity (e.g. a given technology or application) within a venture, a firm will demonstrate its conviction that the business is worth entering. In a context of high complexity of technology and markets, some firms may also have limited information on the steps that are most likely to be profitable when handling relatively new technology or penetrating scarcely known markets. Those who have the lowest acquaintance with the new business will then be available to act consistently with the direction indicated by a partner that is perceived to be better informed, because it is the only known path in a very uncertain environment.

For instance, one can consider the 1987 ABB–IBM agreement aimed at the development of an expert system to monitor and guide the maintenance of electric engines. This was a completely new, and unknown, application market for IBM, nor had ABB an adequate experience in the field of artificial intelligence to go it alone. The domain and objectives of collaboration were clearly defined when ABB provided an explicit signal of commitment to the new and promising field. Precise assignments were given to a small but highly motivated team of technicians to provide IBM software and artificial intelligence experts with all the information they needed about the actual functioning of engines. This led to the definition of a complex set of hypotheses connecting specific (likely) causes and flaws to correct. Part of the results of this valuable work done by ABB technicians was not re-deployable in case of the break-up of the alliance, as applications were framed into an "electronic environment" (the so-called "shell") supplied by IBM, so that the transfer to a different environment would have implied (and actually did imply) a considerable adaptation cost. However, the decision to commit to this specific research direction helped IBM identify its partner's preferences and reassured it about the profitability of the business when entering a radically new field of endeavor.

Third, commitment reduces uncertainty by *constraining the behavior* of partners. One way to constrain behavior is the institutionalization and routinization of some key joint activities. Firms entering cooperation often find it useful to agree on certain rules of behavior and reporting that guarantee to joint action a desirable level of "accountability and reliability" over time.[9] Such organizational bodies and procedures are the result of a collective effort of partners, and are largely non-re-usable in different collaborative contexts. The 1989 agreement between AT&T–General Business Communications Systems and Italtel Telematica helps illustrate this argu-

---

[9] This idea goes back to Nelson and Winter (1982) who noted that routines are "the source of continuity in the behavioral pattern of organizations." On the linkage between the search for accountability–reliability and inertia of organizations, see Hannan and Freeman (1984).

ment. Two formal mechanisms governing the alliance were established by contract. The first one was a so-called "Overside Board", which was supposed to meet twice a year and ensure the general monitoring of the entire alliance, governing all the different modules of the agreement. The second one, called "Technical and Commercial Management Board" was meant to be more operational and was designed differently for each of the operative modules of the venture, and was thus more specialized in nature.

We have described three different ways by which commitment helps reduce uncertainty for firms participating in a network. It is quite apparent that by reducing uncertainty, commitment will also favor (cooperative) learning. In fact:

- When technology and markets are largely unknown and subject to rapid change, it is helpful for firms to stabilize some "relational parameters" – i.e. it is reassuring for them to know that certain actions will or will not be taken by their partners owing to their irreversible investments in the alliance. A party will then be more available to transfer information to the other if the recipient firm's commitment is high enough to cause it a significant loss in case of contractual breach.

- Once "relational parameters" are fixed, firms can divert resources from monitoring activities, and devote more time and assets to different and more productive cognitive activities, such as exploring and exploiting innovative trajectories. This may be more urgent than monitoring each other's behavior, because it may reveal that a trajectory is not worth exploring or exploiting further, so that cooperation can be broken before the parties get too involved.

- If partners increase their commitment over time and signal their determination and reliability, it is most likely that mutual trust will also increase, and this will contribute to creating better conditions for learning.

- Finally, as we argued earlier, commitment may signal a party's interest in a specific field of endeavor or may be a way to constrain the activity of partners in following a specific behavior for a given amount of time. Especially at the beginning of cooperation, this may help define a precise research agenda.

A remark is needed with reference to the last point. While having a precise research agenda may induce firms better to focus their learning efforts, the importance of maintaining a rigorous and pre-defined set of objectives to pursue should not be over-emphasized. Entering an agreement may open up a wide spectrum of exploratory possibilities that are not predictable *ex ante*, giving rise to unexpected learning as well (Kanter, 1994). Our case studies highlight the importance of these unexpected outcomes of cooperation, resulting from learning patterns that were not defined *ex ante* in a specific collaborative agenda. During the ABB–IBM venture the "electronic shell" supplied by IBM proved to be inadequate, and a different supplier for this part of the project was eventually chosen, with subsequent changes in the working methodologies and software. The 1987 joint venture between Olivetti and Canon is another case in point. The agreement was originally focused on the incremental development of a copying machine designed by the Japanese company and ameliorated through joint research efforts. Eventually, developments were made possible for a number of applications that were not defined at the moment the two firms entered collaboration, ranging from fax, cash registers, and word-processing.

Initial commitment thus provides a valuable basis for the first stages of collaboration. It is from this basis that further developments, and even radical deviations, can take place.

An important qualification is needed at this point. Commitment may indeed favor learning, therefore generating higher rents from cooperation. From this perspective, unilateral commitment can be a fundamental element in the rent-creation process. However, by the same token, the partner unilaterally increasing its commitment to the venture will see its rent-extraction ability reduced. In other words, it will contribute to generating greater revenues by favoring joint and individual learning, but it may well be able to appropriate a smaller share of these revenues (Bureth, Wolff, and Zanfei, 1994). In fact, if one (and only one) party makes non-redeployable investments, it might then be locked-in to the relationship and its bargaining power will be reduced relative to its partner. The latter can then extract as much of the rent generated through the agreement as the loss the former would bear in case of contractual breach. The investing party may thus be forced to continue cooperation (because of the lock-in effect) in spite of the fact that its own rent-extraction capabilities are diminishing (because of the bargaining-power effect). So asset-specificity asymmetry can cause severe investment-incentive problems. In order to avoid lock-in effects, the investing party would be well advised to ask the other to give her some guarantee of good behavior, immediately thereafter, by transferring a bond or a hostage (Williamson, 1983). In other words, unilateral commitment can be a very transitory substitute for trust, whereas only *bilateral commitment* will generate the incentives to invest in the creation of knowledge, and favor the appropriate exchanges of information.

From this perspective, one can also explain one of the most recurrent characteristics of cooperative behavior, that is, firms' preference for a gradual involvement into collaborative ventures on a "step-by step" basis.[10]

---

[10] The idea of a "step-by-step" involvement is further developed in Wolff (1996). Doz (1996) also provides interesting insights on this point.

Through unilateral commitment a firm spends (and risks) its own resources with the aim to get cooperation and learning started. If and only if: (1) a process of (individual and/or collective) learning actually starts, (2) such process is evaluated as satisfactory in terms of actual and expected revenues, and (3) commitment is eventually reciprocated, thus introducing a better balance in the bargaining power position of partners within the alliance, will the firm which has acted as a first-mover be available to increase its own commitment and get more involved in the venture. In several circumstances, firms explicitly express, from the very beginning of cooperation, their willingness to proceed on a step-by-step basis, leaving the door open for the possibility of modifying their level of commitment according to the results of cooperation over time. Hewlett-Packard's 1988 minority participation into the Italian supplier of telecommunications network components NECSY entailed a sort of checkpoint after four years of cooperation which would have enabled both firms to evaluate the results and decide whether to increase commitment or dissolve cooperation. Similarly, in many of Alcatel's alliances, the French firm's equity participation plays the role of an option to increase its involvement over time, usually leading to a full acquisition or majority participation in the venture's capital structure. This is, for instance, the basic agreement made when the Alcatel–US Sprint joint venture was signed in 1993, aimed at the development and commercialization of broad-band "asynchronous transfer mode" (ATM) technology: Alcatel was expecting to extend its original share into the venture after five years, acquiring Sprint's 49 percent shares in case of success of the joint venture. In some other cases, such as the 1990 Alcatel–Chorus alliance which we shall discuss later in greater detail, full acquisition did not occur because the cooperative process revealed that such a solution would spoil the partner's incentive structure, possibly reducing its contribution to the venture. Nevertheless, in this case, involvement also occurred on a "step-by-step" basis: after the agreement was applied to, and experimented with, as a part of Alcatel's activities (leading to the adaptation of an advanced version of UNIX technology to Alcatel's private business exchanges), it was eventually extended to other activities within Alcatel, and subsequently (in 1993) to the whole of the Alcatel Alsthom group.

Organizing the absorption and transfer of assets

A conceptually different reason why commitment favors learning is that absorption, exchange, and use of assets must be organized, and this implies highly non-redeployable investments (Arrow, 1974). In general terms, this takes us to the heart of a typical evolutionary argument: the exploitation of diverse and specialized (knowledge) assets requires coordination, and this implies that some of the assets are shared and homogeneous. As Marengo (1993, 2), posits it:

> Some shared knowledge is necessary to make any form of coordination of decentralized decisions possible; but, if all decision makers shared the same knowledge, no learning could actually take place. When agents differ with regard to their representations of environment and their capabilities, there must exist an organizational body of knowledge which guarantees the coherence of the various learning processes.

Such an "organizational body of knowledge" can take the form of a set of codes, information packages, interfaces, routines, and/or common languages, which may partially or totally rely on skilled people acting as "gatekeepers" between different information providers. Gatekeepers will generally be endowed with important abilities to absorb, "de-contextualize," and "re-contextualize" knowledge for alternative uses (Cohen and Levinthal, 1989; Di Bernardo and Rullani, 1990; Arora and Gambardella, 1994; Cohen et al., 1996). Setting up such an organizational body of knowledge does not reflect the need of stabilizing the context within which collaborative activities (and learning) take place. It (primarily) corresponds to a different need: building the *knowledge blocks* and *communication channels* that allow the absorption and exchange of assets, in order to enhance both individual learning (at the level of each firm or unit involved) and collective learning.

Two points must be made here. The first concerns the costs of setting up such an organizational body of knowledge. We submit that these costs tend to be particularly high, especially when firms from different nationalities are involved. Organizational bodies of knowledge will have to be constructed collectively, by mediating different corporate cultures,[11] merging different technological and organizational competencies, matching incentive structures and integrating pre-existing languages. Our case studies provide evidence of the high investment that has to be sustained to set up collective knowledge and effective communication channels.

An interesting example is Hewlett-Packard's agreement with NECSY, a specialized supplier of network elements to the Italian telecommunications manufacturers and carriers, mentioned above. NECSY provided its knowledge of telecommunications technology in general, some expertise in the emerging area (at the time) of network quality measurement and network management devices. Hewlett-Packard, which had not entered the tele-

---

[11] Cremer (1990, 54) defines corporate culture as the "stock of knowledge that is common to a substantial portion of the employees of the firm, but not to the general population from which they are drawn."

communications business, offered its more general competence in measurement-instrument and information-processing technology, its marketing expertise, and its internationally widespread distribution network. Translating technical languages was not the biggest problem in this case, although personnel from NECSY had to be transferred to the Hewlett-Packard labs in the United States for a long period in order to adapt the design of products to technical quality standards required by the US company. The most costly and time-consuming problem was that of matching NECSY's technical expertise with Hewlett-Packard's marketing culture. Hewlett-Packard commercialization channels were not used to selling measurement devices with such a high degree of systemic complexity as those for telecommunications purposes. Illustrating technical characteristics of such products to customers requires new skills and more detailed documentation. More sophisticated commercialization capabilities were also required because of the greater role played by the customization process. As unit costs of equipment were significantly higher (from 10,000–30,000 dollars for traditional instruments, to over 500,000–1 million dollars for the new measuring systems), the decision-making level is usually located higher in the customer firm's hierarchy, thus changing the nature of the negotiation process. Finally, as a result of these factors, the product selling cycle is much longer (up to two years, as opposed to a maximum of three months in the case of traditional instruments) and the risk run by sellers is higher. In order to solve these problems, both partners had to invest heavily in communication. Four experienced Hewlett-Packard managers were used as interfaces to transfer know-how on technical documentation and after-sale support services, and long training was necessary both at NECSY and at Hewlett-Packard. A high-level manager from Hewlett-Packard had also to be seconded to coordinate these activities. The whole process required over four years, from the beginning of the venture until an order for the new product line had been successfully placed, and communication problems had not been completely solved even by that time.

The second issue refers to the reversible–irreversible nature of such investments. We have shown that setting up information packages, interfaces, and communication channels is a very costly investment. But how much of these investments can be recovered if the alliance breaks up? The answer to this question is complicated by the fact that, when setting up communication channels, the irreversibility of investment largely depends on re-usability of outcomes. In other words, investing in communication is part of the learning process: one can hardly separate the moment at which the investment is made and that in which learning occurs. Take the Hewlett-Packard–NECSY case we have mentioned. In order to communicate, both

firms had to invest time and personnel in finding a way of mutual understanding. The investment consisted in re-allocating resources from existing
uses with the explicit aim of building a body of collective knowledge that
would have made it possible to adapt NECSY's technology to the needs of
Hewlett-Packard's distribution channels, and vice versa. But this collective
knowledge is, in itself, the result of information exchanges and processing
which eventually leads to a commonalty of ideas and methods. These
common ideas and methods are in turn important to proceed in the mutual
adaptation of manufacturing (on NECSY's part), and commercialization
(on Hewlett-Packard's part). The construction of this collective knowledge
could then be considered as the production of a sort of "intermediate good"
that is necessary for further learning. The problem is then evaluating how
redeployable this intermediate good is. Given the high specificity of what
was actually learned in this preliminary phase, one is tempted to say that
the degree of re-usability of this "product" is low (NECSY's personnel who
got acquainted with the details of Hewlett-Packard's distribution facilities,
product portfolio and commercialization procedures will not be able to
utilize the same knowledge to collaborate with another distributing
company. What is at least partially re-usable, interviewed officers said, is a
methodology adopted in the R&D, manufacturing, or commercialization of
the products that eventually proved successful. But this should probably be
considered one of the "final" outcomes of the learning processes.

Things change if the collective body of knowledge firms need in order to
communicate is represented by information packages and organizational
devices that are "general and abstract" in nature.[12] In this case, investing for
the construction of such an organizational body will be much less commitment-intensive. Given the generic nature of knowledge contributed, this
can be easily re-used elsewhere at any moment. As we shall see when discussing the outcomes of learning (p. 219), re-usability of assets contributed
to a venture combined with the lower degree of protection that is guaran-
teed by patenting systems induces a high potential instability to collaborations based on the sharing of generic knowledge. A possible
counter-balancing factor, reducing the destabilizing effect of generic

---

[12] Following Arora and Gambardella (1994), we can identify "abstract" knowledge with the
ability to represent phenomena in terms of a limited number of "essential elements,"
making abstraction from the specific context in which such phenomena were originally
observed; and "general" knowledge with the ability to relate the outcome of a particular
experiment to the outcomes of other experiments that may be distant from a historical, geographical, or even logical point of view. Arora and Gambardella have emphasized that the
use of general and abstract knowledge in industrial research has received a great impulse
from scientific advances, which increased the theoretical understanding of problems, and
from the complementary evolution in the field of instrumentation, particularly computers
and communications devices.

knowledge, is represented by the fact that exploitation of such assets often needs to be associated with costly, indivisible infrastructures, such as complex research labs and expensive scientific instrumentation. If all participants to a network have sustained such high and irreversible investments, *de facto* committing themselves to the cooperative venture, they are forced to continue cooperating until the fixed costs are fully recovered. This will occur in spite of the fact that each party will run the risk that the knowledge generated be used competitively by the other. To illustrate, we shall consider the case of the 1990 alliance between CNET and SGS–Thomson. The objective was to pool resources in order to jointly develop manufacturing processes for Application Specific Integrated Circuits (ASIC) for telecommunications and videocommunications purposes. CNET is more active in basic research, a complement to SGS–Thomson's applied and development activities, while SGS–Thomson is a supplier of components for telecommunications uses, a key field of interest for CNET (presently owned by France Telecom). Firms looked for, and eventually found, a common ground in the expertise they both had in a rather generic field of integrated circuit technology, and put together some 150 researchers with a certain degree of inter-changeability. The collective body of knowledge the two firms built was thus characterized by a rather generic content, so that reversibility was ensured. However, the development of so-called "submicron" technologies required the availability of a costly technological environment (called a "white room") and sophisticated equipment. The initial investment required, which is proportional to the miniaturization of processes, amounted to 1 billion francs (approximately $180 million). A "heavy" investment like this acts as a powerful binding factor. As a result, learning was favored both by the ease of communication stemming from a shared body of (largely general and abstract) knowledge, and by the stabilizing effect of large material investments.

Learning and generation of redeployable and non-redeployable assets

So far, we have discussed how the degree of partners' engagement in a collaborative venture can help the development of the learning processes. The irreversibility of the commitment was described as exerting a positive impact on learning and on the stability of cooperation. But one of the outcomes of learning is the emergence of (knowledge) assets that are endogenous to collaboration. Let us now consider the nature of these assets and the degree of commitment that is attached to them. Three categories of assets stemming from cooperation can be defined: relational, methodological and technological assets.

Relational assets refer to all the knowledge and information attached to the relationship with specific partners. We find here the increase of information about the true competencies and bargaining power of the partner, the routines, the common codes and languages set up to work together, the object of cooperation, the abilities to detect and to exploit environmental opportunities. Trust also belongs to this category of relational assets. The main feature of this class of assets is that they are not transferable. They belong to a specific cooperative venture, and will be lost as soon as the relation stops. Even if each of them can be considered as a sunk cost, they have different values in terms of irreversibility.

There seems to exist a threshold of mutual knowledge accumulation beyond which breaking up an alliance (and switching to other partners) becomes very costly, even if the existing relation is not fully satisfactory. Hewlett-Packard and NECSY are probably close to that threshold. Acquaintance between partners is considered a fundamental asset by both, preventing them from withdrawing from the venture in spite of several drawbacks characterizing their experience. In 1992, a date that was decided as a checkpoint at the beginning of the venture in 1988, the record of the agreement's performance was dismal. However, the partners decided to continue cooperation because they had both significantly committed to the venture. Hewlett-Packard had invested a lot in terms of setting up interfaces, training salesmen and organizing new organizational units to coordinate activities related to the venture. NECSY had sustained 65 percent of the costs of a very expensive experiment (35 percent was the equity share of Hewlett-Packard, and costs were shared pro rata). Moreover, an intangible, collective, specific asset had been created through the process: the development of a common language and conventions which were shared by most members of NECSY and divisions of NECSY concerned in the agreement.

Let us now turn our attention to trust. It is immediately apparent that it is much more volatile an asset. There is a form of asymmetry in the accumulation of this asset: a party's trust in another member of an alliance will generally increase gradually as a result of acquaintance and of the observation of that member's cooperative behavior. As trust grows and becomes mutual, this will reinforce the relationship between the partners. But if one of them deviates from the agreement, trust will immediately be eroded – in other words; trust is much harder to build than to lose. If opportunistic behavior can undermine trust, technical reliability can reinforce it. It is important to stress the role of reliability because, while it strengthens trust and therefore stability, it also increases the reputation a firm can rely upon outside the venture. This latter effect may lead to different results in terms of stability. On the one hand, a firm's reputation of high reliability increases collaborative opportunities, including relationships with competitors, with potentially negative effects on stability. On the other hand, new collaborative ventures induced by reputation can be a way for partners to learn more and attain dynamic efficiency advantages. This latter appears to have been the prevailing effect in the case of the 1990 technology transfer agreement between Alcatel Business Systems and its French supplier Chorus. Alcatel conducted in-depth tests of the quality and reliability of Chorus as a supplier of real-time software technology, to be applied to PBXs. In order to do so, the telecommunication manufacturer sent a team to work at Chorus for over nine months, and eventually reached the conclusion that the partner was reliable. After a few months, the reputation of Chorus' system had spread to a number of purchasers and increased the potential for applications, which has actually reinforced Alcatel's interest in the venture.

To sum up, relational assets are obtained through a costly and discontinuous process of learning. Irreversibility is strong, and can hardly be reduced. But the relational assets provide the basic information for the development of a second category of assets, which we name "methodological assets."

Methodological assets include the outcome of second-order learning processes (learning to learn): how to get information about the partner, how to manage an agreement, how to spot and to extract strategic competencies, etc. They contribute to the functioning of the agreement but are totally encoded in the organizational routines of each partner, albeit in different proportions. To the extent that firms assimilate such learning-to-learn abilities, they increase their possibilities to enter new ventures and extract economic value from them. It follows that methodological assets are often easily transferable to other situations of cooperation. Methodological assets may also help in increasing the efficiency of a given alliance, as organizational routines can be improved and embodied in specialized units devoted to the management of inter-firm agreements. Methodological assets determine the ability of a firm to cope with different partners, possibly in different fields.

Examples of methodological learning can be observed in several of our cases. An important outcome of the long collaboration between ABB and IBM in the field of expert systems for the monitoring and self-maintenance of electric engines was the development of a methodology that IBM can reuse in different applications of its technology. Generally speaking, the procedure consists of a number of logically inter-connected steps of interaction between a software expert and an expert of the specific application domain, which can be easily adapted to different contexts. Learning to cooperate was also an important result of the Alcatel–Chorus alliance. This venture represents a turning point in Alcatel's attitude towards external growth strategies; in fact, it had never signed significant alliances in technologically strategic areas before, as it had always preferred to acquire 100 percent or majority participation in the target firms. This corresponds to a significant change in management style, which is also reflected in the formal procedures that Alcatel is now following when having recourse to "outsourcing," especially in the field of software.

The third category is *technological assets*. In the case of alliances with some technological content, such as the ones we have studied, the production of these assets is a key outcome of the learning processes. Examples are: joint learning-by-doing or learning-by-user–producer interaction, concerning a product or process on which the collaboration is focused. Some of these assets have more or less the same features as relational assets in terms of specificity, except that they do not embody a volatile component (such as trust in the case of relational assets).

However, firms appear to be more and more involved in the effort to increase their abilities to "convert" specific knowledge assets, conceived for application to specific contexts, into more general and abstract knowledge that can be more easily transferred and applied to different contexts. This appears to be consistent with a more generalized process that has received a great impetus from advances in the areas of science, instrumentation, and computational capabilities. Evidence of this tension can be found in several of our examples. For instance, the ABB–IBM collaboration on expert systems, after several years' joint activity and information exchange, led firms to develop general-purpose knowledge from a very specific application. A general methodology was created for the design of intelligent monitoring systems that could be re-used in different fields. Similarly, Chorus' agreement with Alcatel–BS focused first on the very specific application of the former firm's technology to the latter's PBX. But, as Chorus expanded its collaborative activity and learned to cooperate, it developed some general competencies for application of its system outside the Alcatel environment. The interest of firms in re-usability of their technology often combines with an attempt to avoid being locked-into alliances, as this will reduce potential learning and market exploitation, as well as partners' bargaining power. The DEC–Formula agreement for the development and commercialization of office automation software is illustrative. Formula was interested in the alliance with DEC because it reduced its dependence on IBM technology; once it perceived the danger of being identified with DEC technology too closely, it strove and eventually succeeded in sharing the costs of the development of products aimed towards a multi-client environment (based on UNIX).

In the case of agreements focused on basic or pre-competitive research, which already tends to be generic and abstract in nature, the wide usability of knowledge generated is in itself a factor reducing irreversibility and potentially inducing instability. Let us consider the ECRC joint research venture involving three large computer manufacturers (Siemens, Bull, and ICL) for advanced projects in artificial intelligence. Here, each firm had the big rent-extraction problem of pushing R&D conducted by the research center in a direction that was more useful to its own applications needs. It was a bargaining-power problem because it entailed being able to impose one specific research direction instead of another, given a certain budget. In order to exert this bargaining power, each partner had to set up interfaces between its own applications needs and the joint research center. Such interfaces were basically represented by each firm's manufacturing engineers and R&D labs. The most efficient of such interfaces appears to be ICL's: the more flexible and less hierarchical organizational structure of this firm, as compared to Siemens' and Bull's, seems to have favored more effective contacts with the very informal and academic oriented research environment of ECRC. As a result, ICL was able to exploit eight out of the 15 projects carried out by the joint research center since the beginning of its existence. This significant asymmetry in rent-extraction abilities caused conflicts among participants to the venture, as Siemens and Bull were less and less interested in continuing to fund research that was being taken advantage of primarily by ICL.

Tensions between stabilizing and destabilizing forces

Cooperative learning implies that the parties irreversibly invest in the alliance, and some reciprocation is needed between partners in order to stabilize cooperation. Part of the outcomes of the learning process may reinforce the parties' commitment to the venture, while other assets generated through cooperation may actually be highly redeployable, thus increasing firms' incentives to exit and exploit them outside the relationship that generated them. The stability of alliances will then depend, *inter alia*, on the balance between the allocation, generation, and use of specific, non-redeployable assets, and the allocation, generation, and use of generic, redeployable assets. Our case studies show this tension between forces leading towards stability and forces leading to the dissolution of inter-firm agreements. Table 10.1 summarizes the results of our research. Table 10A.1, reported in the appendix (p. 231) provides further descriptive information on the type and content of the partnerships we have analyzed. Of the 14 cases included in the list, nine appear to have demonstrated a rather high "stability," as the relationship is steadily continuing as such, with no significant foreseeable change of this condition in the near future. The remaining five cases in our sample either refer to alliances that have been discontinued (as the AT&T–Italtel agreement or the ABB–IBM venture),

Table 10.1 *Commitment, learning, and stability of inter-firm alliances: evidence from case studies*

	Unilateral commitment	Reciprocity	Redeployable assets	Non-redeployable assets	Use of redeployable assets	Stability
Alcatel–BS–Chorus	Alcatel	High	High	Low	Cooperative/Competitive	High
Alcatel–Sprint	–	High	High	Low	Cooperative/Competitive	High
Automa–Geotop	Automa	Low	Low	High	Cooperative	High
AT&T–Italtel.	Italtel	Low	High	High	Competitive	Low
DEC–COMAU	COMAU	Low	High	Low	Competitive	Low
DEC–Formula	Formula	High	High	High	Competitive	High
ECRC (Bull–Siemens–ICL)	–	Low	High	Low	Co-operative/Competitive	Low
Metelliana (Engineering–Credito Tirreno)	–	High	High	High	Independent	High
IBM–ABB	ABB	Low	High	Low	Independent	Low
IBM–Fiat	–	High	High	High	Cooperative	High
NECSY–Hewlett-Pacard	NECSY	High	High	High	Cooperative	High
Olivetti–Canon	–	High	High	Low	Cooperative	High
Olivetti–Conner	Olivetti	High	High	Low	Cooperative	Low
SGS–Thomson–CNET	SGS-Thomson	High	High	Low	Cooperative/Competitive	High

Source: Authors' interviews 1994–1995

or represent examples of collaborative ventures with some degree of instability, that might determine, or is already determining, the break-up of the existing relationship or a significant modification of it (some partners could exit or be substituted as in the ECRC venture, or a previous cooperative relationship could turn into a full acquisition, as in the case of Olivetti–Conner).

It may be worth recalling that, consistently with our premises, "stable" ventures should not be considered more efficient than the others. Nor do we mean that all partners involved in one group are more satisfied than the others with the outcomes of cooperation. We shall come to this more qualitative aspect later (p. 229). We have so far only been interested in the issue of continuity, no matter whether this is desirable for all or any of the parties. We are not suggesting that the variables we have identified above and whose impact we discuss below, are the only relevant ones to explain stability, but it seems to us that, in most of our cases, they may nonetheless help in firms' decisions to continue or discontinue cooperation. There are indeed some cases that cannot be fully explained in terms of the balance between redeployable and non-redeployable assets. In these circumstances, we shall attempt to identify some further factors to underpin our explanation.

One important feature emerging from the study is that, in most cases we considered, one of the partners had taken the risk of unilateral commitment, to get cooperation started. In order to signal its interest in the alliance, COMAU unilaterally decided to transfer to the joint venture formed with DEC, the whole of its internal division devoted to software development for factory automation, a total of 50 employees. For similar reasons, Olivetti provided some 120 of its employees, originally in charge of a unit specialized in the design and development of electronic disk drivers, and a financial contribution of over 2 million dollars, for the start-up of the joint venture formed with Conner. In the initial, exploratory phases of cooperation with Chorus, Alcatel supplied half a dozen experienced engineers, who spent two months' full-time at Chorus to transfer their skills concerning uses and applications of UNIX technology. Afterwards, they kept frequent contact and participated in a number of technical meetings with Chorus personnel over the following seven months.

We could continue with examples. However, it may be more interesting to observe that when this unilateral commitment is *not* adequately reciprocated the alliance almost invariably reveals a low stability. In the case of the ABB–IBM alliance, ABB sustained the largest share of irreversible costs. It paid for IBM machinery, "shell" and expert systems, for the technical assistance of the IBM software experts, for the set-up and maintenance of a specialized team to work in collaboration with the IBM consultants. In the end, it was easy enough for the US computer company to draw back from the alliance when some problems eventually emerged with commercial exploitation. The AT&T–Italtel agreement was characterized by a comparable asymmetry, with Italtel showing a much greater engagement in the strategic alliance than its US partner. This is not so much the case with the sub-set of this alliance we analyzed more closely (which referred to private business systems only), but it appears to be so with regard to the general agreement, which covered all segments of the telecommunications equipment market. As the US company gradually lost interest in the equipment business in favor of the more profitable service activities, it was ready to exit with limited costs (Zanfei, 1994).

These examples are perfectly consistent with the argument we developed above concerning the potentially destabilizing effect of unilateral commitment, if not reciprocated. What these examples reveal is that, if no reciprocation occurs, alliances may break down not only because the investing party is not reassured by the other party's action, and decides not to continue committing to the venture, but also because the non-investing party may more easily leave if circumstances become adverse.

In most cases, examining the initial commitment and the subsequent reciprocation is not enough to draw conclusions on the likely or actual stability of a venture. Perhaps it is not sufficient even to explain the two cases we have just cited. One should also observe how decisions to commit to a venture interact with the generation and use of redeployable and non-redeployable assets. In the majority of our cases, cooperation appears to have led to the generation of some redeployable assets, whereas half of our sample is made by alliances in which there is a very limited generation of highly-specific, non-redeployable assets. A case in which the creation of redeployable assets is high, and the generation of specific assets rather limited, is the Alcatel–Sprint joint venture (JV). This alliance is characterized by valuable, general-purpose developments in the field of Asynchronous Transfer Mode (ATM) technology, while limited irreversibilities are present, and the contractual provisions are not too constraining for either party. Another case in point is the ECRC joint research venture involving Siemens, ICL, and Bull. Here the object of cooperation is pure research on artificial intelligence, and downstream applications are beyond the scope of the alliance; hence, specificity of assets generated through cooperation is very limited.

In three out of the five cases in which the alliance has been discontinued or is undergoing significant pressure for change, all destabilizing factors are present: a low reciprocation of initial commitment, a high generation of redeployable assets together with a limited creation of non-redeployable assets. Apart from IBM–ABB and ECRC, this is, for instance, what happened in the DEC–COMAU venture. In this case, the initial provision of 50 employees by COMAU was never reciprocated, as the rest of the personnel were hired from the labor market. The output of cooperation is mainly represented by the development of a project for software integration, based on a multi-client technology (UNIX), which is therefore characterized by a low specificity. As a result, centrifugal pressures prevailed, and the alliance faced severe difficulties in the early 1990s.

By contrast, one may observe that stability may be assured, in spite of a high generation of redeployable assets, if these assets are not used competitively. When partners show some degree of market complementarity, or when they agree to jointly commercialize at least part of the resources generated through cooperation, then the destabilizing nature of redeployable assets may be counter-balanced. The IBM–Fiat case is illustrative. The two firms started cooperating for the development of value-added services for the use of the Italian car manufacturer and its supplier and eventually developed skills and network infrastructures that can be exploited outside the captive market. They agreed to transfer to the "Intesa" JV all of their activities in this field, and commercialize their services cooperatively. The NECSY–Hewlett-Packard venture has some similarities, although a higher irreversibility of investments characterizes the development of this relationship and helps to explain its stability over time. In this case a cooperative attitude in the commercialization of part of the products jointly developed was also helpful in avoiding conflicts and stabilizing the venture. As observed earlier, these companies have actually invested a lot in the development of common standards and procedures to make NECSY's products suitable for commercialization through Hewlett-Packard's channels. Even more straightforward is the case of Metelliana. Here, a software designer and system integrator (Engineering) set up a joint venture (called Metelliana) with an Italian bank, Credito Commerciale Tirreno, to take care of the customer's IT needs and commercialize EDP services outside the captive market. A clear complementarity of markets emerged, with Credito Tirreno interested in the exploitation of cooperative solutions in the captive market only, and Engineering more interested in the commercialization of similar solutions for other banks. This helps avoid conflicts over the use of redeployable resources generated through cooperation, and stabilizes the venture.

Finally, a few words on two cases that cannot be easily explained in terms of our interpretive scheme alone: Automa–Geotop, and DEC–Formula. The former is characterized by a high asymmetry in the level of commitment, with a small-sized manufacturer, Automa, taking care of the whole development of a new electronic measurement device that a specialized reseller, Geotop, commercialized in the niche market of designers. No reciprocation is assured to Automa's efforts, the output is highly specific and can be commercialized in a very limited market. In terms of our interpretive scheme, we observe both destabilizing factors (no reciprocation), and stabilizing factors (high specificity of output). The outcome appears to be one of considerable stability. The agreement is not formalized at all, with the reseller imposing conditions unsatisfactory for the supplier. Automa asked for changes in the conditions and a more precise normalization of the agreement, but no modification was obtained.

The DEC–Formula case is also characterized by a peculiar mixture of destabilizing and stabilizing factors. After heavily committing to a partnership with DEC, the Italian software house realized that it would be better off increasing its independence while keeping one foot in the venture. It rejected DEC's offers to buy equity shares into its capital. It took advantage of the reputation obtained thanks to the alliance with DEC and increased the range of clients it served, at times acting competitively against its partner. Again, stabilizing factors (high, reciprocated commitment) coexisted with destabilizing factors (generation of redeployable assets and competitive use of them). Here, too, the outcome was one of stability. Formula not only avoided being acquired, and obtained maintenance of the existing structure of the agreement. It also received funds from the US company to finance research for UNIX applications – i.e. a multi-vendor technology that enhanced its independence from DEC.

Why did stabilizing factors prevail over destabilizing factors in these cases? These two experiences, albeit rather different in nature, highlight the key role played by an important factor that has been only marginally considered so far, and should be integrated into our scheme. That is the role of partners' *bargaining power* in firms' decisions to continue or discontinue cooperation. In both cases one of the partners was willing to destabilize the venture. DEC wanted to increase its control over Formula by means of equity participation; Automa would have liked to change the rules of the game and formalize the contract with Geotop. As we have shown, they both had good reasons to do so, in terms of our framework. In the DEC–Formula case, the generation of redeployable assets was high and there was a continuous risk of competitive use to be overcome; in the Automa–Geotop case, the supplier's commitment was not being reciprocated, the results of cooperation and the distribution of rents were not satisfactory for Automa.

However, in both cases the other party appeared to enjoy a higher bargaining power, which prevented any change in the conditions of cooperation. Such changes in bargaining conditions are at least partially exogenous with respect to the cooperative process itself. Geotop controlled the access to the market. When designing the product, it was a skilled technician of Geotop who was able to translate the specific user requirements into the technical jargon used by the specialized supplier. Had Automa controlled this "interface" between technical aspects of production and user needs, it could have exerted a greater bargaining power in the alliance because it might have switched to another distributing company.

In the other case, Formula enjoyed a high bargaining power for two reasons. First, it was active in a field – software design and development – that is by definition horizontal, multi-purpose, and multi-client. This *per se* increased Formula's outside options and augmented its bargaining power. Second, as a consequence of the deep changes occurring in the computer and office-automation market, DEC realized that it was in its own interest that a key supplier increased its applications capabilities and its acquaintance with different electronic platforms and with multi-client technology.

Conclusions and policy implications

The stability of collaborative alliances is heavily influenced by firms' individual and collective learning processes. Decisions to continue or discontinue cooperation over time will depend – *inter alia* – on the balance between irreversible assets and redeployable resources that are being used and generated through cooperation over time. Significant interdependencies exist between these categories of assets, and two such interdependencies may be highlighted here.

First, methodological assets, that are highly redeployable, are positively influenced by the accumulation of relational assets (which tend to be highly irreversible). Such relational assets as shared languages and collective routines that are generated through collaboration between specific partners may constitute a basis for the development of more general-purpose languages and routines, which will eventually increase a firm's ability to cooperate with third parties as well. This generalization process may be very costly: extrapolating a general rule from a specific collaborative experience in order to adapt it to a different collaborative activity may indeed turn out to be more difficult (and costly) than elaborating new ad hoc relational assets. However, transforming specific relational assets into more general-purpose, second-order abilities (learning to cooperate) may have significant increasing returns, with higher advantages the larger the number of collaborative ventures a firm is willing (or forced) to enter. From this perspective, there appears to be a strong endogenous mechanism leading firms to increase the number of agreements they are involved in, as this is a way to justify their investment in the generalization of highly specific, non-redeployable assets generated through cooperation. (To use a metaphor, this would spur firms to depart from monogamy to attain increasing promiscuity in inter-firm relations.)[13]

---

[13] We are indebted to Paul David for this metaphor.

Second, the use of redeployable assets (e.g. generic technology developed through cooperation) will influence the value of non-redeployable assets (e.g. trust), thus exerting an indirect impact on cooperation stability. To the extent that redeployable assets are used competitively against partners, this will immediately erode trust and reduce effectiveness of collective routines governing the venture. When deciding how to utilize the redeployable assets stemming from cooperation, firms will then have to evaluate the trade-off between the possible gains from opportunistic behavior and the likely loss it will suffer (in terms of possible collaborative rent streams it will have to give up) from the break-up of an existing alliance that may occur as a consequence of such behavior.

Firms' intentional moves in the direction of more opportunistic uses of general-purpose assets, as well as their decisions to try and generalize some of the more specific outputs stemming from cooperation, will negatively influence the stability of a given collaborative venture over time. However , important environmental factors will also affect the balance between stabilizing and de-stabilizing behaviors. One that has frequently emerged from our analysis, and which is probably playing a key role in determining the evolution of cooperation over time, is the increasing importance of general and abstract knowledge as a competitive asset. In all fields where such a fundamental trend can be observed, it is more likely that firms will be forced to increase their efforts to generalize specific assets stemming from cooperation, and this could increase the inherent instability of collaborative ventures over time.

Should this be a worrisome development? A policy implication of our research is that stability is not *per se* a relevant measure of the quality and effectiveness of technological alliances. In order to evaluate the "social benefits" of collaborations, if any, one should thus know the amount and value (net of costs) of redeployable and non-redeployable resources generated through cooperation.

There are two further implications of our analysis and of the likely trend we have highlighted towards greater use of general and abstract knowledge in industrial activities. First, to the extent that collaborations are increasingly focused on the generation and use of general and abstract knowledge, it is more and more likely that part of this knowledge will be disseminated and become available outside the research labs of large companies. Second, the more inter-firm alliances are used as flexible and reversible tools to handle new challenges and opportunities in high-technology industries, the higher the *exploratory* nature these ventures will show, and the lower the possibility that technological trajectories are fully *exploited*, especially when dealing with complex technologies. Whether this development is likely, and whether it should be considered socially desirable or not, is subject-matter for future research.

Appendix *Empirical evidence and research methodology*

This work is primarily based on case studies. In-depth interviews with strategic planning and R&D managers of 16 firms were carried out in 1993 and 1994 in order to analyze their decision-making process and experience in 21 cases of collaboration (including: two cases of cooperation and two acquisitions made by Engineering, and two cases in which Automa was involved) (see table 10A.1, p. 233). This list also includes two cases of 100 percent acquisitions which, by definition, are not to be considered as agreements. These two cases were considered only to obtain some elements for comparison, particularly concerning the reasons why cooperation did not take place instead.

The ventures examined cover a variety of different fields of IT: application-specific integrated circuits; artificial intelligence; expert systems for engine maintenance; software design and system integration; factory and office automation; value-added services and networks; electronic measuring devices; telecommunications-network management; and private branch exchanges. Cases were selected according to the following three, rather broad, criteria.

First, they had to have some *technological content*, either as a primary focus of cooperation or as a non-trivial side-effect of collaboration when they pursued other objectives. Agreements that had only financial purposes were excluded *a priori*, and we looked very carefully into cases that appeared to have mere manufacturing or marketing content, and considered them if they either implied the sharing of technological resources or had clear implications for innovative capacity of one or all partners involved. This occurred in at least three of our cases out of our sample (DEC–Formula, Automa–Geotop, Engineering–Metelliana). The option in favor of collaborations with some technological content is due to analytical reasons. In fact, we are primarily interested in the complex problem of the generation, sharing and transfer of knowledge. In our view, explicit (formal and informal) agreements between firms are a primary way through which they can focus on the production of specific assets and exchange information linked with technological purposes, and can therefore increase their efficiency in the generation and use of knowledge. Particularly in the case of tacit knowledge, the lack of any measurement makes market transactions ineffective, and compels firms to build a common frame in which information can be valued by each participant in the exchange. At the same time, the internalization of transactions may not be a solution to this problem in a context of technological complexity (as that characterizing the electronics industry), as the variety and variability of relevant information required to handle technical problems is beyond the scope even of very large firms. In sum, examining agreements with technological content means entering into the black box of the exchange of knowledge by the main door.

Second, we were interested in *"spontaneous" agreements* – that is, ones that are not the direct result of national or transnational research programs stimulating inter-firm cooperation, as is the case of Sprint or Eureka in Europe. We did consider two cases of collaboration involving firms which had previously got into contact within an Esprit program (the CNET–SGS–Thompson alliance and the ECRC joint research venture involving Siemens, ICL, and Bull). However, in both cases the Community's incentives were not the primary factor affecting the decision to enter or continue cooperation. Instead, one of the experiences we examined (the Social Security Network consortium headed by Sovak of Holland and Italsiel of Italy) did have its origin within the framework of a European research funding program (the European Nervous System program of DGXIII). As in the cases of acquisitions, this experience was considered with the primary aim of highlighting the similarities and differences with the other cases of spontaneous cooperation.

Third, the selected agreements had to have a "history": we attempted to evaluate not only factors affecting the decision to cooperate, but also those that *influenced the effects of cooperation* – and, among these, learning and stability effects in particular. In a limited number of cases it was possible to reconsider and update case studies that were previously carried out with different research aims (the experiences of IBM–ABB, DEC–Formula, IBM–Fiat, and NECSY–Hewlett-Packard were studied in 1989 by A.Tunisini (1990) within the framework of a previous research conducted at IEFE, Bocconi University, and reconsidered here). This helped to create a historical perspective, and appreciate the differences between expected and actual results of cooperation.

Appendix

Table 10A.1 *Basic information on the sample firms*

Partners	Year of agreement	Field of agreement	Type of agreement
DEC, Italian subsidiary of the US computer manufacturer COMAU, factory automation subsidiary of Fiat, Italy	1985	Development and commercialization of integrated systems in factory automation	50–50 JV called SESAM
DEC, Italian subsidiary of the US computer manufacturers FORMULA, Italian software house	1987	Adaptation and joint marketing of software in office management	Non-equity agreement
IBM, Italian subsidiary of the US computer manufacturer FIAT, Italian car manufacturer	1987	Supply of value-added services and networks	50–50 JV called INTESA
AUTOMA, Italian small engineering firm, GEOTOP, Italian reseller of measuring systems	1987	Commercialization of electronic data recording systems	Informal agreement
IBM, US computer manufacturer ASEA BROWN BOWERY (ABB), Italian subsidiary of the Swiss-Swedish conglomerate	1987	Development and commercialization of artificial intelligence systems applied to electric engines	Non-equity agreement

Table 10A.1 (cont.)

Partners	Year of agreement	Field of agreement	Type of agreement
NECSY, Italian medium sized telecom equipment supplier HEWLETT-PACKARD, US computer and electronics manufacturer	1988	Adaptation and commercialization of network management systems	OEM and minority equity participation of HP
AT&T GBCS, private equipment branch of the US telecommunications company ITALTEL Telematica, specialized branch of the Italian Telecom manufacturer in the field of private networks	1989	Adaptation and commercialization of AT&T's PBX technology	Part of a larger alliance implying exchange of minority equity shares
BULL, French computer manufacturer, ICL, British computer manufacturer now belonging to Japan's Fujitsu, SIEMENS, German Electronics manufacturer	1982	Basic R&D in the field of IT	JV, called ECRC
SGS-THOMSON, French–Italian microelectronics manufacturer CNET, Research center of France Telecom, French network operator	1990	Applied R&D in ASIC circuits	JV 50–50, called CROLLES
ITALSIEL, software subsidiary of Italy's IRI Several partners of different EC countries	1992	Feasibility study and first implementation of a European social security network	EEC joint R&D program called SOSENET
ENGINEERING, Italian software house and system integrator		Portfolio of agreements	JVs and acquisitions

Partners	Year	Objective	Structure
ALCATEL BS, private telecom branch of French equipment manufacturer CHORUS systems, French software house	1990	Adaptation of UNIX technology to Alcatel's PBX	OEM plus technology transfer
ALCATEL CIT, French telecom manufacturing company US SPRINT, US long-distance service carrier	1993	Development and commercialization of Broad Band ATM	JV, 51% Alcatel 49% US SPRINT
OLIVETTI, Italian electronics manufacturer CONNER PERIPHERALS INC., US peripheral supplier	1988	Design, development and commercialization of new disk drivers	JV, 51% Olivetti 49% Conner
OLIVETTI, Italian electronics manufacturer CANON Italy, Italian subsidiary of the Japanese electronics manufacturer	1987	Development and application of image production technology	50–50 JV

Source: Authors' interviews and case studies (1994–5)

References

Aoki, M. (1990). "Towards an Economic Model of the Japanese Firm," *Journal of Economic Literature*, 28(1), 1–25

Arora, A., and A. Gambardella (1994). "The Changing Technology of Technological Change: General and Abstract Knowledge and the Division of Innovative Labour," *Research Policy*, 23, 523–32

Arrow, K. (1974). *The Limits of Organization*, New York: W.W. Norton

Arthur, W.B. (1989). "Competing Technologies, Increasing Returns and Lock-in by Historical Events," *The Economic Journal*, 394(99), 116–31

Bureth, A., S. Wolff, and A. Zanfei (1994). "Interfirm Collaboration, Commitment and Learning. The Formation and Evolution of Cooperative Agreements in the European Electronics Industry," Eunetic Conference on "Evolutionary Economics of Technological Change," (Strasbourg) (October)

Cainarca, G.C., M.G. Colombo, S. Mariotti, C. Ciborra, G. De Michelis, and M.G. Losano (1989). *Tecnologie dell'informazione e accordi fra imprese*, Milan: Edizioni Comunità

Child, J. (1997). "Learning through Inter-organizational Cooperation," communication to the Final EMOT Programme Conference, ISTUD (Stresa) (11–14 September)

Cohen, M.D., R. Burkhart, G. Dosi, M. Egidi, L. Marengo, M. Warglien, S. Winter, and B. Coriat (1996). "Routines and Other Recurring Action Patterns of Organizations: Contemporary Research Issues," *Industrial and Corporate Change*, 5(3), 653–721

Cohen, W., and D. Levinthal (1989). "Innovation and Learning: The Two Faces of R&D," *Economic Journal*, 397(99), 569–96

Cremer, J. (1990). "Common Knowledge and the Coordination of Economic Activities," in M. Aoki, O.E. Williamson, and B. Gustaffson (eds.), *The Firm as a Nexus of Treaties*, London: Sage

Crossan, M.M. and A.C. Inkpen (1995). "The Subtle Art of Learning through Alliances," *Business Quarterly*, 60(2), 68–78

David, P. (1985). "Clio and the Economics of QWERTY," *American Economic Review*, 2(75), 332–7

Delapierre, M. (1991). "Les accords inter-entreprises: partage ou partenariat? Les stratégies des groupes européens du traitement de l'information," *Revue d'Economie Industrielle*, 55, 135–61

Di Bernardo, B., and E. Rullani (1990). *Il management e le macchine*, Bologna: Il Mulino

Dixit, A. (1980). "The Role of Investments in Entry Deterrence," *Economic Journal* (March), 95–106

D'Orazio, A., A. Gambardella, L. Pontiggia, S. Torrisi, S. Trenti, and A. Zanfei (1992). "Growth through External Linkages in the European Electronics Industry," in *The Economics of Scientific and Technological Research in Europe*, final report prepared for the European Commission, DGXII (December)

Dosi, G. and J.S. Metcalfe (1991). "Approches de l'irréversibilité en théorie économique," in R. Boyer, B. Chavance, and O. Godard (eds.), *Les figures de l'irréversibilité en économie*, Pans: Editions de l'EHESS

Doz, Y.L. (1996). "The Evolution of Cooperation in Strategic Alliances, Initial Conditions or Learning Processes," *Strategic Management Journal*, 17, 55–83

Duysters, G. and J. Hagedoorn (1996). "Internationalization of Corporate Technology Through Strategic Partnering: An Empirical Investigation," *Research Policy*, 25, 1–12

Foray, D. (1991). "The Secrets of Industry are in the Air: Industrial Cooperation and the Organizational Dynamics of the Innovating Firm," *Research Policy* 20(5), 393–405

Gaffard, J.L. (1990). *Economie industrielle et de l'innovation*, Paris: Galloz

Georgescu-Roegen, N. (1971). *The Entropy Law and Economic Process*, Cambridge: Cambridge University Press

Gulati, R., T. Khanna and N. Nohria (1994). "Unilateral Commitments and the Importance of Process in the Alliances," *Sloan Management Review* (Spring), 61–9

Hagedoorn J. & Schakenraad J. (1991). "The Role of Interfirm Cooperation Agreements in the Globalization of Economy and Technology," CCE, *Fast Occasional Paper* 280 (November)

(1992). "Leading Companies in Networks of Strategic Alliances in Information Technologies," *Research Policy*, 21(2), 163–90

Hannan, M. and J. Freeman (1984). "Structural Inertia and Organizational Change," *American Sociological Review*, 49, 149–64

Jacquemin, A., M. Lammerant, and B. Spinoit (1986). "Competition Européenne et cooperation entre entreprises en matiere de Recherche et Developpement," CEE, *Document de Travail* B080

Kanter, R.M. (1994). "Collaborative Advantage," *Harvard Business Review* (July–August) 96–108

Kogut, B. (1989). "The Stability of Joint Ventures: Reciprocity and Competitive Rivalry," *Journal of Industrial Economics*, 2(38), 183–98

LAREA–CEREM (1986). "Les stratégies d'accords des groupes de la CEE: Intégration ou éclatement de l'espace industriel européen," Programme Europe Industrielle et Technologique, Commissariat Général au Plan, Paris (October)

Lazaric, N. and L. Marengo (1997). "Towards a Characterisation of Assets and Knowledge Created in Technological Agreements," *DRUID Working Paper* (September)

Levinson, N.S. and M. Asahi (1995). "Cross-national Alliances and Interorganizational Learning," *Organizational Dynamics*, 24(2), 50–63

March, J.G. (1991). "Exploration and Exploitation in Organizational Learning," *Organization Science*, 2, 71–87

Marengo, L. (1993). "Knowledge Distribution and Collective Learning: On Some Social Aspects of the Exploitation vs. Exploration Trade-off," paper presented to the seminar on "Institutional Change and Network Evolution," (Stockholm) (June)

Mariti, P. and R.H. Smiley (1983) "Cooperation Agreements and the Organization of Industry," *Journal of Industrial Economics*, 4, 437–53

Meschi, P.X. (1995). "Structure and Organizational Performance of International Joint Ventures," in R.Schiattarella (ed.), *New Challenges for European and International Business*, Urbino: EIBA–Confindustria

Mody, A. (1993). "Learning Through Alliances," *Journal of Economic Behavior and Organization*, 2(20), 151–70

Morris, D., & M. Hergert (1987). "Trends in International Collaborative Agreements," *Columbia Journal of World Business* (Summer), 15–21

Nelson R.R., and S. Winter (1982). *An Evolutionary Theory of Economic Change*, Cambridge, Mass. and London: The Belknap Press of Harvard University Press

Powell, W.W., K.W. Koput, and L. Sith-Doerr (1996). "Inter-Organizational Collaboration and the Locus of Innovation: Networks of Learning in Biotechnology," *Administrative Science Quarterly*, 41, 116–45

Robertson, P., and R. Langlois (1995). "Innovation, Networks and Vertical Integration," *Research Policy*, 24, 543–62

Simon, H.A., (1957). *Models of Man*, New York: Wiley

(1976). "From Substantive Rationality to Procedural Rationality," in S. Latsis (ed.), *Methods and Appraisal in Economics*, Cambridge: Cambridge University Press

Teece, D.J. 1992. "Competition, Cooperation, and Innovation: Organizational Arrangements for Regimes of Rapid Technological Progress," *Journal of Economic Behavior and Organization*, 2(18), 1–25

Tumisini, A. (1990) "Accordi di Cooperazione tra imprese nel settore delle tecnologie informatiche: Complementarità, chiarezza e trasparenza," *Economia e politica industriale*, 65, 43–69

Vaccà, S. and A. Zanfei (1989). "L'impresa come sistema aperto a rapporti di collaborazione," *Economia e politica industriale*, 64, 47–89

Williamson, O.E. (1983). "Credible Commitments: Using Hostages to Support Exchange," *American Economic Review*, 73, 519–40

Wolff, S., (1996). "La dynamique des accords inter-entreprises dans le secteur des télécommunications. Une approche en termes de flexibilité et d'apprentissage," in J.L. Ravix (ed.), *Coopération entre les entreprises et organisation industrielle*, Paris: CNRS–Éditions

Zanfei, A. (1994). "Surviving Competition Through Cooperation," *Journal of Industry Studies*, 2, 65–76

11 Firm specialization and growth: a study of the European software industry

Salvatore Torrisi

Introduction

This study compares internal corporate changes (new subsidiaries and other reorganizations) and external links (mergers and acquisitions, minority stakes, joint ventures, and other collaborative agreements) of European and US software firms. The chapter has two main purposes. First, to show the main objectives of external and internal growth and, second, to analyze the relationship between firm specialization in 1983 and the patterns of firm growth and diversification in the period between 1984 and 1992.

Why is the software industry an interesting case study in this field? Software is a "pervasive" technology that is produced in many different sectors. Software users produce a significant share of their software programs in-house. According to some estimates, internally developed software represents about 60 percent of software expenditures in the largest European markets (Germany, France, the United Kingdom and Italy), while packaged software (acquired from specialized software firms) and outsourcing (custom software and services contracted to independent contractors) accounts for 40 percent of total software expenditure (IDC, 1990).

Despite the importance of non-traded software activities, an independent software industry has emerged since the 1970s as a consequence of "vertical disintegration" from different business organizations and the entry of many new firms. This process of vertical disintegration is similar to that of mechanical engineering during the second half of the last century, which led to the spin-off of machine tools' factories from many different industries, including firearms, bicycles, and automobiles (Rosenberg,

The author thanks the participants in the Workshop "The Economics of Scientific and Technological Research in Europe," University of Urbino (February 24–25, 1995) for useful comments on an earlier version of this chapter. Iolanda Schiavone and Alfredo Volontè provided valuable research assistance. The European Commission (Human Capital and Mobility Program, DGXII), CNR, and MURST provided financial support.

1976). Today, many large suppliers of computer software and services have spun off from established electronic and computer firms (e.g. GSI from Générale Electricité and Sterling Software from Sterling Electronics) and from non-electronic firms (e.g. EDS from General Motors, Scicon from British Petroleum, and Istel from British Leyland–Rover Group). The entry of innovative start-ups has also contributed to the rapid growth of the software industry during the 1980s. This has mostly occurred in packaged software compared with computer services.

The specialization of software activities has been promoted by two main factors. First is the progress of hardware technology and the pervasiveness of software technology – that is, its use as an input for many economic sectors. The number of software packages for minicomputers and larger systems in the US market increased from about 5,000 in 1979 to 6,200 in 1982 while the suppliers rose from 900 to 2,000 (Gotlieb, 1985, 208). The introduction of personal computers, workstations, and distributed computer networks (local area networks or LANs) in the 1980s created new windows of opportunities for software firms. Large opportunities for economies of scale emerged in the production of software packages as a result of network externalities produced by the emergence of standard platforms for personal computers (IBM PC, IBM–Microsoft's MS-DOS, and Microsoft's Windows) (Steinmueller, 1996). This has encouraged vertical disintegration of software activities from hardware manufacturing. During the 1980s most computer manufacturers reduced their in-house production of software and services. Moreover, the diffusion of compatible personal computers favored the "portability" of software packages on a large installed base of computers from different producers and accounted for the fast growth of firms which entered the market in this period, such as Lotus (electronic spreadsheet), Microsoft (operating systems and office applications), Ashton–Tate (database management systems), and Novell (LAN operating systems). In Europe, the high market fragmentation, caused by linguistic and cultural barriers across countries, reduced the opportunities for economies of scale and scope in software packages. Market fragmentation is one of the factors, including the early entry and market pre-emption by US firms, that hampered the start-up of a European industry of packaged software (cf. Malerba and Torrisi, 1996; Torrisi, 1998). Most European firms have thus specialized in services and customized software, a market segment populated by many small and medium-sized firms, each serving a few large customers.

The second main factor that has influenced the evolution of this industry is the "unbundling" of software sales from those of computers, a practice introduced by IBM in 1969 in the United States and followed by its main competitors world-wide. The unbundling effect has reinforced the technological change effect described above in that it has stimulated vertical disintegration of hardware manufacturers and the entry of many specialized computer software and services firms independent of hardware manufacturers.

As a consequence of these factors, the market for software and services has increased at a rapid rate over the last decade and the average net profits in software activity have been high compared with other information technology (IT) market segments, including computers. Software as a share of total revenues of the largest world IT companies classified in *Datamation* increased from 8.6 percent to 11.6 percent between 1988 and 1992. The share of computer services (excluding computer maintenance) increased over the same period from 8 percent to 15.6 percent. By contrast, the share of hardware products (excluding data communication equipment) of these companies remained stable in this period (rising from 34.2 percent to 34.8 percent of total revenues). The growth of software and services revenues was mainly accounted for by specialized software firms. Most hardware manufacturers reduced software and services revenues as a share of their total revenues – for instance, Digital Equipment Corporation's (DEC) software and services share declined from 25 percent in 1981 to 17 percent in 1992. Hewlett-Packard's share declined from 29 percent to 8 percent in 1992.[1] Moreover, the profitability of software firms is high compared with that of computer firms. *Datamation* has compared three samples of firms selected from the world's largest IT companies. The returns on sales of software firms fell from 12.4 percent in 1988 to 10.1 percent in 1992 while service firms' returns on sales remained largely stable (falling from 6.7 percent to 6.3 percent). Hardware firms showed a 10.5 percent return on sales ratio between 1988 and 1990, which fell to 3 percent in 1992 (*Datamation*, June 15 1993, 12–15).

The progressive reduction of margins from hardware sales and the rising importance of open standards have spurred hardware manufacturers towards software and services. Some of these have tried to re-enter the software market through mergers and acquisitions (M&As). In 1995, IBM acquired Lotus Development, one of the largest US producers of software packages, and software increased significantly as a share of total sales for IBM, from 17 percent in 1990 to 26 percent in 1992. For other hardware manufacturers software also increased as a share of total revenues – Unisys (from 16 percent to 26 percent), Amdhal (from 2 percent to 20 percent), and Hewlett-Packard (from 3 percent to 8 percent) (*Datamation*, June 15 1991 and June 15 1993). Moreover, the largest European software

---

[1] IBM represents an exception to this trend towards vertical disintegration of software and services. Its share of software and services increased from 17 percent to 28 percent between 1981 and 1992 (*Datamation*, June 15 1982 and June 15 1993).

firms have recently resorted to large capital partners: Istel was acquired by AT&T from British Leyland, Cap Gemini sold 34 percent of its shares to Daimler–Benz Interservices (Debis), and Finsiel tried to merge with Olivetti's software division.[2] These strategic alliances were encouraged by a reduced growth of the software market during 1992–4 and the lack of financial and managerial resources showed by many large European software firms.

However, this process does not seem to bring about a complete re-integration of software activities by hardware manufacturers or users. Hardware manufacturers that have increased their software and services activities face a strong competition from firms such as Microsoft, Computer Associates, and Andersen Consulting, which are not integrated in hardware manufacturing. These firms have strong service and organizational capabilities that are important to coordinate the activities of many sub-contractors and to serve international markets. Moreover, most software firms have grown within the software sector or have diversified towards related activities (e.g. telecommunication services), whereas they have not diversified into hardware. This suggests that there are no significant economies of scope between hardware and software activities which justify their integration.

The chapter is organized as follows. We describe vertical disintegration and diversification in the economic literature, and illustrate the data. We then discuss the main empirical results: inter-firm linkages, internal restructuring, and the trajectories of software firms' growth. Finally, we summarize the main results.

Industry specialization and firm diversification: a survey of the literature

Economists and economic historians have explained specialization and the division of labor among firms by focusing on different factors, including market size and economies of scale, technological change, diseconomies of scope, and contract incompleteness. Drawing on the classical contributions of Adam Smith, Stigler (1951) set out the reasons why market extent for individual final products results in "vertical disintegration" of upstream activities. Young industries internalize most phases of their production activities for several reasons, among which is the lack of reliable supply of materials, components, and machinery. By contrast, maturing industries rely on a larger market for their goods and externalization of upstream activities becomes attainable because they enjoy economies of scale or economies of specialization (due to learning-by-doing etc.; see also chapter 10 in this

---

[2] The latter agreement has not been concluded for various reasons, including Olivetti's serious financial difficulties since 1991.

volume). Thus, the economies enjoyed by the suppliers of inputs depend on the market size for final products. However, the market size for a single final product explains only in part the division of labor among industries. Another explanatory factor is represented by technological external economies. Rosenberg (1976) has argued that in the second half of the last century the American machine tool industry spun off from many industries which utilized various machine tools for two main reasons: economies of specialization and "technological convergence". By the latter Rosenberg meant the process by which the skills and techniques for handling and shaping metals or for sewing fabrics became widespread among many different industries: the machine tool industry has thus enjoyed both internal economies of scale and the external economies arising from technological spillovers.

Patel and Pavitt (1994) have measured the importance of technological convergence and vertical disintegration of technological activities, showing that technological capabilities in the field of mechanical engineering (and, to a lesser extent, others such as chemical and instrumentation engineering, computers, materials, and biotechnology) are spread across a wide range of industrial sectors. This level of technological diffusion indicates that firms specialized in mechanical engineering may have access to a large pool of knowledge and benefit from technological externalities produced by different sectors. Malerba and Orsenigo (1996) have studied the organization of technological activities for different technologies, showing that in mechanical engineering the concentration of innovative activity is low, the average size of innovators is small, the hierarchy of innovators is relatively unstable over time, and the rate of entry of new innovators is high (see also chapter 4 in this volume).

These studies show that the characteristics of the knowledge underpinning technological activities, including its pervasiveness, vary across sectors, affecting the organization of innovative activities and the evolution of industry structure. A low concentration of innovative activities in mechanical engineering is associated with a low market concentration compared with other industries (such as electronics and chemicals), characterized by a high technological and market concentration.

Another stream of the literature explains vertical disintegration and division of labor among industries by focusing on diseconomies of scope among different stages of the production chain or "economies from doing a limited set of activities" (Perry, 1989, 232). Finally, the transaction costs' economics and the theory of the firm as "incomplete contracts" explain vertical disintegration by pointing out asset-specificity, contract-incompleteness, and residual rights of control over specific investments (Williamson, 1975; Grossman and Hart, 1986).

The literature on the division of labor and vertical disintegration, however, is not clear as to what the implications of market size, transaction costs and technological regimes are for the direction of firm growth and diversification. After the stage of take-off, an industry will enter a stage of development and maturity. Some scholars suggest that with maturation the firms which are active in the industry begin to diversify their business activities to exploit their excess financial, technological and managerial resources (Penrose, 1959). However, this is not the case with mechanical engineering firms, which seem not to have taken advantage of their knowledge and expertise to diversify into new businesses. Similarly, most established software firms maintain a high degree of specialization or diversify in businesses closely related to their core activities. Why they do not diversify, for instance, in to computer hardware or telecommunications equipment, despite the technological relatedness among these industries?

The economic literature highlights several factors which limit diversification. First, there are increasing returns to specialization which are linked to learning-by-doing and dynamic economies of scale. Second, related diversification allows the achievement of economies of scope from the exploitation of "excess resources" or quasi-public inputs in similar sectors. Third, coordination costs increase with the variety of lines of business – there are diminishing returns to diversification caused by managerial bottlenecks in the exploitation of excess resources (Montgomery and Wernerfelt, 1988).[3] Fourth, the incentive to diversify varies with the industry life-cycle. Firms from mature industries, endowed with excess financial resources, are more likely to diversify compared with firms operating in new, fast-growing industries. The latter give firms greater opportunities to invest "excess resources." Fifth, business relatedness (or a narrow business portfolio) facilitates the implementation of incentives schemes, as demonstrated by Rotemberg and Saloner (1994). Finally, there are the firms' limited cognitive resources and capabilities. The learning process is characterized by cumulativeness, path-dependency, idiosyncracy, and inertia which affect firms' ability to try unknown avenues of R&D and growth (Nelson and Winter, 1982; Pavitt, 1991; Teece et al., 1994; Rumelt, 1995). As a consequence, when expanding their activities, firms attempt to do "more of the same" or "more of something closely related, something of which the firm has some degree of relevant knowledge" (Winter, 1993, 190–1).

In order to diversify their business, firms may rely on internal growth (e.g. new subsidiaries or divisions) or external growth (M&As, joint ventures

---

[3] The separation between propriety and control may cause excessive diversification. To maximize their utility function, managers may push diversification beyond the level which is optimal for firm's profitability (Jensen and Meckling, 1976).

(JVs) and other collaborative agreements). This chapter does not focus on the factors which affect the choice between internal or external growth. However, in theory, external growth may be thought of as a natural channel of diversification. Through external linkages, firms may gain access to the scientific or technical knowledge required to develop new products. In a world of rapid technical change and increasing knowledge multi-disciplinarity, it is difficult for a single firm to develop internal capabilities in many different fields. Thus, firms are encouraged to set up linkages with external sources of knowledge, including the acquisition of firms endowed with specific capabilities. Moreover, firms seek to reach new markets through agreements or M&As with the aim of enjoying increasing returns to scale and scope from the use of their "excess resources," especially intangible ones. In this case, the choice of external linkages as an alternative to internal growth may reveal the need to reduce the time and the costs for the accumulation of complementary capabilities (e.g. sales and post-sales service networks). The choice between non-equity agreements (or minority stakes) and M&As may also depend on the level of idiosyncrasy and market-specificity of complementary capabilities. Assume that there are economies of scope at the level of R&D activities but not at the level of commercialization or post-sales services. In these circumstances, a firm will probably merge its R&D activity with that of another firm to take advantage of "synergy." However, the same firm will rely on non-equity agreements to commercialize its products.

Data and methodology

The analysis of firm external linkages and corporate reorganizations in this chapter focuses on 18 European firms specialized in software and computer services. The growth strategies of these firms were compared with those of 20 American software and computer-services firms. My analysis draws on a database containing 994 operations concerning the sample firms. Integrated software and hardware firms (e.g. IBM, Siemens, and Olivetti) are not included in the database. The operations were conducted by the sample firms during the period between 1984 and 1992:

- 638 of these operations are *external linkages* – (JVs), minority participation, licensing agreements, other collaborative agreements, and M&As.
- 274 operations refer to *internal corporate changes* – creation and shutdown of new subsidiaries, and other internal reorganizations (e.g. the merger of two divisions, jobs cuts, or organizational improvements).
- 82 operations concern the stipulation of new contracts (mostly with large customers).

Firms were selected from the International Data Corporation (IDC) classification of the largest European and North American software and services firms operating in Europe in 1989. The sample includes the largest European firms in 1990, such as CAP–Gemini–Sogeti (France), Finsiel (Italy), SD–Scicon (United Kingdom–France), and Software AG (Germany) from six EU countries – France, Germany, Italy, the Netherlands, Sweden, and the United Kingdom. As table 11.1 shows, European firms are specialized in computer services, except for SAP and Software AG which specialize in packaged software. Finally, the sample includes the largest US firms such as Microsoft, Computer Associates, Oracle and Lotus. In contrast with their European counterparts, US firms specialize in packaged software – only five sample firms specialize in computer services.

The data on firms' growth were collected from the Predicasts F&S database, which is based on information drawn from press sources (see references on pp. 267–8). Firms for which information is provided are classified by Predicasts according to their main business area. The sample firms were classified under the SIC codes 7372 (packaged software) and 7370 (computer and data-processing services, excluding 7372). Each operation is also classified by Predicasts according to SIC classification. This allows the comparison between the firms' area of business and the business sector of each operation. Finally, Predicasts provides information about the partner(s), its nationality (although not systematically), and a brief description of the operation. On the basis on this qualitative information, a database was set up. This provides the following data: 4-digit SIC code of the operation, year to which each operation refers, type of operation (M&A, JV, etc.), country of the partner (or the new subsidiary), number of citations in the press, content (R&D, Production, Marketing, Financial). These qualitative, nominal-level data were then transformed into quantitative, ratio-level data. When possible these data have been integrated with other information from annual reports concerning other structural features of the firms' economic activities (e.g. sales).

Unfortunately, in the case of software firms, data on R&D and annual revenues are avaliable for only few firms and some years. This represents a major constraint on the possibility of accounting for firm-specific fixed effects.

Revenues in computer software and services in 1989 (or 1990) were utilized as an indicator of firm competencies in software technology (cf. table 11.1). Data provided by *Datamation* and IDC allow us to separate software and services revenues from total revenues. Software and services represent over 50 percent of total revenues for all sample firms, except for McDonnel Douglas, which drew only 2.45 percent of its total revenues from services (system integration), and Mentor Graphics, a hardware–software

Table 11.1 *Sales and total external linkages of sample firms*

Firm (1)	Revenues ($ million) (2)[a]	External linkages (3)[b]	New sub (4)[c]	Home country (5)	Core business (6)
Europe					
CAP–Gemini–Sogeti	889.20	51	18	France	Services
Finsiel	628.90	15	1	Italy	Services
SD–Scicon	431.50	11	1	UK	Services
Sligos	400.70	24	1	France	Services
Sema Group	378.60	36	0	UK	Services
Concept	288.20	7	0	France	Services
Datev	285.10	1	0	Germany	Services
Hoskyns	277.10	17	0	UK	Services
GSI	267.00	4	1	France	Services
Programmator	259.10	2	0	Sweden	Services
Volmac	256.50	7	0	Netherlands	Services
Logica	225.40	32	7	UK	Services
Telesystèmes	212.00	13	0	France	Services
Thorn–EMI Software	209.20	2	1	UK	Services
SAP	183.10	6	2	Germany	Software
CGI	166.30	11	0	France	Services
Istel	166.20	10	1	UK	Services
Software AG	154.20	11	3	Germany	Software
Total Europe		260	36		
USA					
Microsoft	1,323.00	67	9	USA	Software
Computer Associates	1,310.70	35	0	USA	Software
Oracle	1,002.00	11	12	USA	Software
Lotus Development	664.00	49	11	USA	Software
D&B Software Services	539.00	1	0	USA	Software
WordPerfect	452.40	4	1	USA	Software
McDonnell Douglas	398.00	20	3	USA	Services
Novell	388.00	67	5	USA	Software
Policy Management	272.00	3	0	USA	Services
American Management	261.90	2	2	USA	Services
ASK Computer Systems	249.70	4	0	USA	Software
SAS Institute	240.00	3	1	USA	Software
Autodesk	237.90	12	4	USA	Software
Ashton-Tate	230.50	17	2	USA	Software
Pansophic Systems	228.80	14	0	USA	Software
Cadence Design Systems	178.00	15	2	USA	Software
Mentor Graphics	170.00	21	6	USA	Software

Table 11.1 (*cont.*)

Firm (1)	Revenues ($ million) (2)[a]	External linkages (3)[b]	New sub (4)[c]	Home country (5)	Core business (6)
USA (cont.)					
Computer Sciences	160.00	3	0	USA	Services
Sterling Software	155.00	12	0	USA	Software
Computer Services	–	18	1	USA	Services
Total USA		378	59		

Notes:
[a] 1989 or 1990 revenues.
[b] External links include M&As, JVs, minority stakes, licensing agreements, and other inter-firm agreements.
[c] New subsidiaries.
– = not available.

manufacturer which has focused its business on software and services – these represented 39 percent of its total revenues in 1990 and 74 percent in 1992 (*Datamation*, June 15 1993). Moreover, many established packaged software producers rely on one or a few products. For instance, Ashton–Tate in 1990 drew 74 percent of its revenues from its dBase, a database-management system and Cap Gemini over 95 percent of its revenues from professional services. To analyze firm specialization, I also compared 1990 revenues with the 1983 stock of subsidiaries classified by SIC code by Predicasts Thesaurus (see references on p. 267).

Although, in general, revenues or the SIC code of corporate subsidiaries are not direct measures of technical competencies, these can be used as a proxy of technical capabilities for several reasons. One is the lack of other reliable indicators, such as patents and copyright, particularly for firms specialized in services, which do not make substantial use of these instruments for the protection of their innovations. Even large software package producers rely on other means for appropriating the rents of innovations, such as lead time (to reach the market first with an innovation), continuous product improvements and, to a lesser extent, copyright (Torrisi, 1998).

Another reason for using sales specialization as an indicator of technological capabilities is linked to the nature of software production. In general, firms specialized in a given business sector may have to accumulate technological capabilities in upstream activities (e.g. componentry). However, this is not the case with software because these activities are mostly a process that produces "software by means of software." A software producer or a system integrator may have to develop new software development tools to improve its production, but they are unlikely to develop competencies in, for instance, solid-state physics or chemicals. The number of computer science graduates, system engineers, and mathematicians in theory provides a more accurate measure of the firm's technological competencies. But this indicator also has some important drawbacks – including the fact that, for instance, mathematicians or system engineers can be employed in purely commercial activities, where their scientific and technological capabilities are not fully exploited.

Firm growth, restructuring, and diversification: empirical evidence

Relative importance of internal and external growth

Table 11.1 shows the total number of new external linkages (M&As, JVs, minority stakes, and other agreements) and new subsidiaries activated by the sample firms during the period 1984–92. The sample includes large producers of packaged software such as Microsoft, Computer Associates and SAP, and service providers such as McDonnell Douglas and Cap Gemini. Over the period under consideration, the 18 European firms included in the sample set up on average about 1.6 linkages per year against about 2.2 for the 20 US firms, as indicated by column (c) of table 11.1. This difference is related to the different average size of the two groups of firms – there is a positive correlation between the number of links and firm size (OLS coefficient $= 0.45$; $t = 4.50$).

There are no significant differences across firms with different specializations in terms of the propensity to become involved in inter-firm linkages.[4] Among the firms with a propensity significantly above the average there are both service providers, like Logica and Sema-Group, and firms specialized in software packages, like Novell and Ashton–Tate.

Relevant differences emerge between European and US firms in terms of the geographical horizon of their linkages. About 63.3 percent of the linkages set up by European firms involved foreign partners (either other European firms or non European ones), against 31.4 percent of the linkages devised by US firms. This can be easily explained by the large US domestic market compared with the fragmentation of the European market.

---

[4] At this level of the analysis I refer to "total external linkages" for the sake of simplicity. Later, the differences between different types of external linkages will be explored. The chi-square test shows that there is no significant association between firm specialization and external linkages. Chi-square statistics were also calculated for agreements, M&As and new subsidiaries. Finally, chi-squared statistics indicate no association between the nationality of the firm (European or US) and the variables mentioned above.

Moreover, some large US firms such as Andersen Consulting and Microsoft probably established long-term relationships with foreign partners before the period under examination. Furthermore, for many European software firms external linkages have represented an important strategy for reaching a "minimum" efficient scale that is required for competing with the larger US firms. Considering the limited size of the European national markets, international linkages may represent an important way to increase the size of business activities.

Table 11.2a shows the evolution of different types of external links made by European firms over the period under examination. Agreements (JVs, minority participation, licensing agreements, and other agreements) represent 60 percent of total external operations, against 40 percent of M&As. Total external operations have increased over this period, showing that the sample firms increasingly rely on external sources of technical and market-specific knowledge. Table 11.2b shows a similar pattern for US firms. However, these relied more on M&As than agreements until 1989, while their European counterparts mostly focused on agreements (cf. figures 11.1a and 11.1b).

These differences reflect the different specialization of US and European firms. As mentioned above, a large domestic market and other factors have prompted US firms to specialize in packaged software. In this market segment firm size is particularly important to achieve economies of scale and scope, as compared with services and customized software. Thus, US firms, a large share of which specialize in packaged software, tried during the 1980s to increase their size through M&As. It is worth noting, however, that the number of collaborative agreements is larger than M&As for both European and US firms. Compared with collaborative agreements, M&As have a strong impact on the firm's organization, which has a limited ability to manage an increasing number of different business units.

Tables 11.2a and 11.2b compare the evolution of external linkages with that of internal corporate changes or restructuring (new subsidiaries, sale of subsidiaries, dismantling of operations, and reorganization of activities). Restructuring occurs jointly or as a response to external growth. Firms that grow by M&A and, to a lesser extent, agreements have to reorganize the scale and scope of their activities and may be prompted to modify their organizational structure. However, these organizational changes show a less regular trend than agreements and M&As over the same period, for reasons that include a less accurate diffusion of information in the press.

Figures 11.2a. and 11.2b also compare the evolution of external growth (M&As and agreements) with internal growth (new subsidiaries), which represents an important share of total internal corporate changes or restructuring discussed above. Both US and European firms have mostly

Table 11.2 *External linkages and corporate change, 1984–1992;*
a European firms

	1984–6	1987–9	1990–2	1984–92	(%)	CAGR[b]
Total external links, of which:	50	100	110	260	100.00	10.97
M&As	12	41	51	103	39.62	29.68
Agreements[a]	38	59	59	157	60.38	6.26
Corporate change, of which:	42	28	47	117	100.00	− 6.76
New subsidiaries	23	6	7	36	30.77	− 14.99
Sold subsidiaries	2	3	5	10	8.55	10.40
Disinvestments	7	10	13	30	25.64	− 8.29
Reorganizations	10	9	22	41	35.04	9.05

b *US firms*

	1984–6	1987–9	1990–2	1984–92	(%)	CAGR[b]
Total external links, of which:	73	88	217	378	100.00	34.00
M&As	47	61	45	153	40.48	13.00
Agreements[a]	26	27	172	225	59.52	43.00
Corporate change, of which:	34	56	67	157	100.00	− 1.00
New subsidiaries	15	14	30	59	37.58	− 2.00
Sold subsidiaries	2	3	6	11	7.01	0.00
Disinvestments	4	18	13	35	22.29	0.00
Reorganizations	13	21	18	52	33.12	8.88

Notes
[a] Agreements include JVs, minority stakes, licensing agreements and other agreements.
[b] CAGR = Percentage annual compound growth rate 1984–92. The CAGR of sales of subsidiaries by European firms and disinvestments by US firms refers to the period 1985–92. The growth rate of the reorganizations by US firms was calculated for the period 1985–91.

centered their growth on external linkages rather than internal growth. This is explained by the need to reach a minimum efficient scale fast. External linkages allow firms to increase the scale of their operations (particularly M&As) and to exploit the external economies of being part of a network of collaborative agreements.

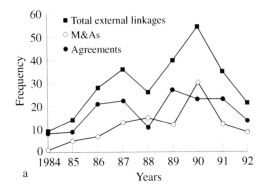

a

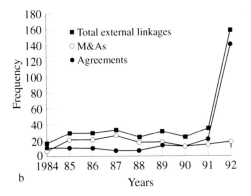

b

11.1 External linkages
a European firms.
b US firms.

Aims of external linkages

External linkages may be used to overcome two types of failure in the
market for knowledge: the lack of private incentives to undertake innovations and the lack of capabilities complementary to innovative skills (e.g.
commercialization capabilities).[5] Accordingly, external linkages can be
classified as *research oriented linkages*, which mainly focus on the first type
of market failure, and *market oriented* or *complementary resource-seeking
linkages*, aiming to cope with the second form of market imperfection.

Research oriented linkages, may involve rival firms (e.g. consortia for the
definition of common standards or joint R&D agreements) or firms

[5] In the economic literature, imperfections in the market for knowledge are associated with
the public-good nature of knowledge and with imperfect information (and its consequences,
such as adverse selection and moral hazard).

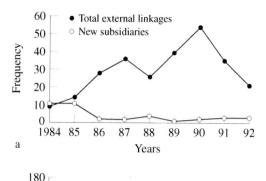

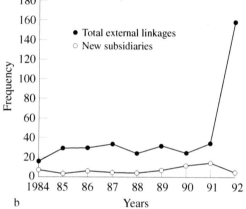

11.2 External and internal growth
a European firms.
b US firms

specialized in different stages of a technological "*filière*." They allow firms to share the risks and the costs associated with the production of multi-disciplinary, complex knowledge, thus increasing the private incentive to invest in R&D activities. Moreover, they allow the acquisition of new technological capabilities whose in-house development would require a longer time and higher costs.

Market oriented linkages are usually set up by firms that operate in different stages of a technological "*filière*" (e.g. operating systems' suppliers and turn-key systems' developers) or in different regional markets. They may provide access to complementary capabilities (e.g. distribution capabilities) that cannot be acquired in the market (because of complex interdependencies between these capabilities and technological or production

Table 11.3 *Total external linkages and corporate change by objective, 1984–1992*

	Research[a]	(%)	Market[b]	(%)	Financial	(%)	Total	(%)
European firms								
Total external links[c]	62	24	186	73	8	3	256	100
Corporate changes[d]	17	14	73	61	29	25	119	100
US firms								
Total external links[c]	128	34	246	65	2	1	376	100
Corporate changes[d]	16	10	114	73	25	17	155	100

Notes:
[a] Research includes links with a R&D content.
[b] Market includes all links without any R&D content. Joint production agreements are included
[c] Total links include M&As, JVs, minority stakes, licensing agreements, and other agreements. Eight links cannot be classified.
[d] Corporate changes includes new subsidiaries, sold subsidiaries, disinvestments, and reorganizations. One operation cannot be classified.

capabilities) and cannot be accumulated in-house for various reasons, including the time required for their accumulation.[6] These linkages may help to reduce a specific form of market failure – that is, a socially insufficient production of assets complementary to R&D capabilities. This has important implications for innovators because the commercial success of an innovation depends on the supply of specialized and co-specialized inputs (Teece, 1986; Geroski, 1992). The access to complementary assets may take the form of M&As, minority participations, JVs and other agreements, reflecting the importance of different factors (including economies of scale and scope, the degree of complex interdependencies among complementary knowledge and capabilities and appropriability conditions).

Table 11.3 shows the main purposes of agreements and internal re-organizations. The operations have been grouped in accordance with the classification discussed earlier: operations that involve R&D activities (Research), operations that do not involve any R&D activity (Market), and purely financial operations (Financial).[7] All these operations may involve competitors or firms located in different stages of this "technological *filière*."

---

[6] The economic literature has provided other explanations for the adoption of alternative organization of economic activities which draw on transaction costs (Williamson, 1975).
[7] Market operations may include commercial and production activities. Research operations may include production and commercial activities.

Over 70 percent of external operations signed by the European firms were *market oriented*, against about 24 percent of *research oriented* operations involving R&D activities. The sample firms have signed market oriented linkages to gain access to specialized commercial assets or service expertise, and new markets. The cross-marketing deal between Sema Group and Finsiel signed in 1992 is a case in point. Active licensing agreements were also classified as market oriented operations because they aim to find new markets for the licensor's technology. Examples of research oriented linkages are the joint development of a videotext software package for IBM mainframes by Cap Gemini and IBM in 1984 and the acquisition of an 80 percent stake in Technologies Machine Art, a robot manufacturer, by Cap Gemini in 1987.

The share of *research oriented* operations is higher for US firms as compared with European firms (34 percent). This difference is probably due to the large number of US firms specialized in packaged software which show a comparatively high involvement in R&D activities. An insignificant share of total operations have a pure financial content (3 percent and 1 percent for the European and the US firms, respectively).

Overall, the different number of market and research operations was expected. A firm may aim to set up many external linkages with different partners to achieve economies of scale and scope in the extensive use of its knowledge and capabilities. By contrast, the number of potential research partners is limited by the distribution of scientific and technological capabilities across firms. Moreover, a firm that looks for a research partner may want to focus on a few firms endowed with the best scientific or technical capabilities available on the market.

These data indicate that through external linkages software firms aim to gain access to both general scientific or technological knowledge and to more context-specific knowledge (linked to particular markets, users, and applications). The software firms use different types of external links (from M&A to technological and cooperative agreements) along with internal investments (e.g. new subsidiaries). Different forms of coordination are adopted according to the purposes and competencies of the firms involved in the knowledge exchange and pooling. For example, Novell, a US company specialized in LAN operating systems (NetWare) in 1989 acquired another US firm with competencies in networking software, Excelan. Novell's NetWare gateway to IBM's SAA network architecture is based on Excelan expertise (*Datamation*, June 15 1994, 76). The acquisition in this case is justified by the relatedness of the two firms' core businesses. A second example is that of Cap Gemini, a large French firm specialized in computer services which in 1990 jointly developed with Nynex International, a telecommunication-services firm, a network-control system for France Telecom. The complementary capability of these firms and the fact that telecommunication services were outside Cap Gemini's main business may explain the choice of an agreement as an alternative to M&A. By contrast, Cap Gemini has resorted to M&As and minority stakes to gain access to the resources of software firms such as Volmac, Programmator, Hoskyns, and Sema Group, whose activities fall within Cap Gemini's core business.

The evidence of a large share of external operations aiming at the reorganization of commercial networks and the creation of new market opportunities indicates that the use of the firm's stock of knowledge and competencies on a larger scale represents a major objective of inter-firm agreements. In a context of high economic complexity and uncertainty firms are forced to interact with other agents, which are potential sources of tacit knowledge and specific information. In the computer software industry there is a large number of firms between software producers and the customers – e.g. distributors, commercial agents, retailers, value-added retailers, etc. Although some of these firms will probably disappear with the evolution of the industry, many will survive because, on the whole, they have knowledge of a variety of specific phases, applications and users' needs that no single software producer can economically control.

A similar share of the operations classified as internal restructuring has a Market content for the European and US firms (61 percent and 73 percent of total internal restructuring operations, respectively), confirming the importance of commercialization activities in this industry and the linkages between internal growth and internal restructuring. Unlike external operations, a large share of internal restructuring operations shows a financial dimension, particularly for the European firms (25 percent of total operations against 17 percent of the US firms) (see table 11.3). This category of internal restructuring includes equity issues to finance firms' expansion, management acquisitions of share capital, etc. – for instance, in 1984 Cap Gemini announced that 37.5 percent of its stake would be acquired by the company management. Notice that, besides the management and other company stockholders, operations with a financial object often involve external institutions. In 1986 Cap Gemini issued shares and convertible bonds to finance its growth and in 1987 it was acquired for 8 percent of its stake by Financière Suez.

Trajectories of growth in software firms

Table 11.4 shows external operations (separated into M&As and agreements) classified into three categories: operations in the firm's main business, operations in related business sectors (computer hardware,

Table 11.4 *External links by distance from the firms' main business, 1984–1992*

	Links in the main business sector	(%)	Links in related business sectors	(%)	Links in unrelated sectors	(%)	Total links[a]	(%)
European firms								
Total external links, of which:	190	76	55	22	5	2	250	100
M&As	85	87	12	12	1	1	98	100
Agreements[b]	105	69	43	28	3	3	152	100
US firms								
Total external links, of which:	285	78	72	20	7	2	364	100
M&As	128	83	25	16	1	1	154	100
Agreements[b]	157	75	47	22	6	3	210	100

Notes:

[a] 24 external links cannot be classified.

[b] Agreements include JVs, minority stakes, licensing agreements and other agreements.

telecommunications equipment and services, or electronic components), and operations in unrelated business sectors. The latter also include general corporate consulting (for instance, in 1990 Cap Gemini acquired a 67.5 percent holding in Gamma International, a French management consulting firm).

European firms in the sample signed over 76 percent of total external linkages in the area of their main business (SIC code 7370–7379). Only 2 percent of total external linkages were made in unrelated business sectors. The remaining linkages focused on related sectors (about 20 percent of total linkages). A similar pattern is shown for the US firms.

A large share of agreements in the area of the firms' main business also emerges when one looks at the number of agreements with an R&D content. About 77 percent of the Research linkages (both M&As and agreements) were signed in the main business by the European firms, against about 20 percent of Research links in related business sectors, and only 3 percent in unrelated business sectors. Moreover, there are no significant differences between Research and Market links with respect to the area of business. The US and European firms, again, show a similar pattern of diversification through external linkages.

Some differences emerge between M&As and agreements with respect to this issue. Agreements represent a privileged channel for diversifying into related business sectors compared with M&As, particularly for the European firms (28 percent of their total agreements were drawn up in sectors related to the firms' main business against 12 percent of M&As). This may be explained by the fact that agreements are a more flexible form of investment as compared with M&As in that they generate fewer "sunk" costs. Therefore, they may be utilized to monitor related business areas or new market niches and as an option. However, the majority of agreements are also in the firm's core business and in related sectors (only 3 percent are in unrelated sectors).

Finally, our empirical analysis indicates that external and internal growth do not differ significantly with respect to the direction of diversification.

So far, we have described the diversification of external linkages during the period 1984–92. The next step of our analysis is centered on the relationship between this pattern of diversification and diversification before 1984. Table 11.5 compares the diversification of 1983 subsidiaries with that of external growth during 1984–92. The diversification is measured with the specialization rate (SR) and the Herfindahl Index (H). The first is the share of the firm's largest sector, while the latter is the sum of the squares of the shares of the variable. In this case, the Herfindahl Index was calculated on three classes corresponding to the main business, related sectors, and unrelated sectors. The Herfindahl then varies between 0.33 (maximum diversification – equal shares) to 1 (maximum specialization – share of the highest sector equal to 1). This analysis was also performed by using another measure of diversification – entropy, $\Sigma s_i; \ln(s_i)$ (where s_i are shares of the variable in each class). These produce very similar results.

All firms, except for Cap Gemini, Programmator, Logica, and Pansophic, have increased or maintained stable their degree of diversification during 1984–92 compared with 1983. This is shown by the comparison of the Herfindahl Index and the specialization rate for total 1984–92 external growth operations with the corresponding indexes for 1983 subsidiaries.

This comparison, however, confirms that the majority of external operations have centered on software activities, thus reinforcing the starting specialization. The average SR index is above 80 percent and its minimum value is 53 percent for the US firms (Computer Services) and 55 percent for their European counterparts (SD–Scicon). As expected, agreements are more diversified than M&As for reasons discussed above. But, again, over 70 percent of total agreements focused on computer software and services.

It is interesting to note the different degree of specialization of US firms compared with European firms in 1983. All US software firms, except for one (Pansophic), were perfectly specialized in 1983. By contrast, European firms were more diversified (the average H83 is 0.86 compared with 0.98 for US firms). This difference may depend on two factors. First, the large size of the US market which has favored the achievement of economies of scale and specialization by local firms. Second, the large number of US firms which entered the market as start-ups early in the 1980s. Firms such as Lotus Development, founded by people spun off from Visicalc in 1981, Autodesk (founded in 1982), and Sterling Software (1983) grew during the 1980s by exploiting the high technological and market opportunities arising from software and related activities (including computers). The presence of network externalities has represented an important reinforcing mechanism which has given rise to increasing returns and the emergence of market leaders which have built their fortune on few software products (packages). For instance, Microsoft in 1994 held over one-third of the world market for personal computers' applications (*Business Week*, January 9 1995, 46).

In Europe, many software firms have spun off from electronics and non-electronics firms, often maintaining close links with their parent companies. For example, Finsiel was affiliated to Istituto Bancario S. Paolo and IRI in 1983, Scicon Computers was taken over by Systems Designers (SD) from British Petroleum in 1988, and Istel was a British Leyland's subsidiary (BL Systems) in 1983. These firms did not have a market large enough to allow a degree of specialization and growth comparable to that of their US

Table 11.5 *1983 diversification and 1984–1992 external growth (M&As)*

a European firms

Firm (1)	Hsub 1983[i] (2)	H 1984–92[i] (3)	SR 1983[i] (4)	SR 1984–92[i] (5)	HM&A 1984–92[i] (6)	HAgr 1984–92[i] (7)	SRM&A 1984–92[i] (8)	SRAgr 1984–92[i] (9)
CAP–Gemini–Sogeti	0.57	0.73	0.73	0.84	0.80	0.67	0.88	0.79
Finsiel	1.00	0.68	1.00	0.80	1.00	0.64	1.00	0.77
SD–Scicon[a]	0.68	0.50	0.80	0.55	0.56	0.50	0.67	0.50
Sligos[b]	1.00	0.72	1.00	0.83	0.88	0.56	0.93	0.67
Sema Group[c]	0.63	0.54	0.75	0.67	0.50	0.56	0.67	0.67
Concept[d]	1.00	1.00	1.00	1.00	1.00	1.00	1.00	1.00
Datev[d]	1.00	1.00	1.00	1.00	–	1.00	–	1.00
Hoskyns Group[h]	1.00	0.88	1.00	0.94	1.00	0.76	1.00	0.86
GSI	1.00	1.00	1.00	1.00	1.00	1.00	1.00	1.00
Programmator	0.56	1.00	0.67	1.00	1.00	–	1.00	–
Volmac	1.00	0.76	1.00	0.86	1.00	0.72	1.00	0.83
Logica[h]	0.52	0.73	0.60	0.84	0.72	0.73	0.83	0.84
Telesystèmes	0.56	0.56	0.67	0.67	0.50	0.58	0.50	0.70
Thorn–EMI Software[e]	1.00	1.00	1.00	1.00	1.00	–	1.00	–
SAP[d]	1.00	0.72	1.00	0.83	1.00	0.56	1.00	0.67
CGI[d]	1.00	1.00	1.00	1.00	1.00	1.00	1.00	1.00
Istel[f]	1.00	0.46	1.00	0.60	0.52	0.68	0.60	0.80
Software AG	1.00	0.60	1.00	0.73	1.00	0.68	1.00	0.80
AVG	0.86	0.77	0.90	0.84	0.80	0.65	0.84	0.72
SD	0.20	0.19	0.15	0.15	0.28	0.29	0.27	0.29

b US firms

Firm (1)	Hsub 1983[i] (2)	H 1984–92[i] (3)	SR 1983[i] (4)	SR 1984–92[i] (5)	HM&A 1984–92[i] (6)	HAgr 1984–92[i] (7)	SRM&A 1984–92[i] (8)	SRAgr 1984–92[i] (9)
Microsoft	1.00	0.53	1.00	0.67	0.59	0.53	0.71	0.67
Computer Associates	1.00	1.00	1.00	1.00	1.00	1.00	1.00	1.00
Oracle Corp.	1.00	0.70	1.00	0.82	1.00	0.68	1.00	0.80
Lotus Development	1.00	0.81	1.00	0.89	0.79	0.82	0.88	0.90
D&B Software Services	1.00	1.00	1.00	1.00	1.00	—	1.00	—
WordPerfect[d]	1.00	1.00	1.00	1.00	1.00	1.00	1.00	1.00
McDonnell Douglas[g]	1.00	0.44	1.00	0.54	0.46	1.00	0.58	1.00
Novell	1.00	0.72	1.00	0.83	0.88	0.68	0.93	0.80
Policy Management Sys.	1.00	0.56	1.00	0.67	0.50	1.00	0.50	1.00
American Management	1.00	1.00	1.00	1.00	—	1.00	—	1.00
ASK Computer Systems	1.00	0.50	1.00	0.50	0.56	1.00	0.67	1.00
SAS Institute	1.00	1.00	1.00	1.00	1.00	—	1.00	—
Autodesk[d]	1.00	0.71	1.00	0.83	0.78	0.63	0.88	0.75
Ashton–Tate	1.00	1.00	1.00	1.00	1.00	1.00	1.00	1.00
Pansophic Systems	0.50	1.00	0.50	1.00	1.00	1.00	1.00	1.00
Cadence Design Systems	1.00	0.54	1.00	0.64	0.72	0.50	0.83	0.50
Mentor Graphics	1.00	0.51	1.00	0.55	0.56	0.78	0.67	0.88
Computer Sciences	1.00	1.00	1.00	1.00	1.00	1.00	1.00	1.00
Sterling Software	1.00	0.72	1.00	0.83	0.78	0.63	0.88	0.75
Computer Services	1.00	0.50	1.00	0.53	0.52	0.50	0.60	0.50
AVG	0.98	0.76	0.98	0.82	0.76	0.74	0.81	0.78
SD	0.11	0.22	0.11	0.19	0.27	0.32	0.25	0.31

Table 11.5 (*cont.*)

Notes

[a] The number of 1983 subsidiaries was calculated by aggregating the subsidiaries of Systems Designers (SD) and Scicon Computer Services, which was taken over by SD in 1988 from British Petroleum.

[b] In 1983, Sligos was a Tymshare's subsidiary, a US computer-services firm, acquired by McDonnell Douglas in 1985.

[c] Sema Group was born in 1989 by the merger between the British UK CAP Group and the French Sema Metra.

[d] Predicasts' data available for 1990 or 1992.

[e] Thorn–EMI Software was created after 1983 by Thorn–EMI, which in 1983 had four subsidiaries in the computer sector.

[f] In 1983 Istel was a British Leyland subsidiary (BL Systems). It was acquired by AT&T in 1989.

[g] Formerly McDonnell Douglas' Data System division.

[h] Hoskyns was acquired by Cap–Gemini–Sogeti in 1990.

[i] H = Herfindahl Index was calculated for 1983 subsidiaries (Hsub1983), total external operations (Hsub1983), total external operations (H1984–1992), M&As (HM&A1984–1992) and Agreements (HAgr1984–1992). SR = specialization rate (percentage of the largest line of business) was calculated for 1983 subsidiaries and 1984–1992 external operations.

counterparts. Moreover, as mentioned before, most of them have positioned in different market niches of limited size by offering customized, ad hoc software and professional services for large customers. In some cases, their largest customer is still the parent company (e.g. the public administration for Finsiel) and most revenues arise from the regional or national market. The opportunities to enter the larger, global market for packaged software were limited by early entry and market pre-emption by US firms.

External growth during the period 1984–92 made European and US firms more similar than in 1983. On average, both European and US firms became more diversified. To take a closer look, however, few software firms, including those that grew fast through M&As and other external linkages, tried to diversify their activities in businesses unrelated to software activities. Few software firms entered the computer (hardware) business. For instance, Cap Gemini acquired IBAT, a process control and robotics manufacturer in 1986. In the same year, Microsoft acquired Citation, a CD-ROM manufacturer, and since then it has increased its efforts in the multimedia business. In 1992 Microsoft signed an agreement with Compaq Computer to joint develop computer audio functions and Novell signed an agreement with Stratus to joint develop fail-tolerant PC networks.

Another target of diversification for software firms was telecommunication services such as electronic mail. This is the case for the joint ventures between Computer Associates and MCI Communications in 1986 and with Radio Schweiz in 1989. In 1984 McDonnell Douglas announced a JV with Marubeni of Japan for the development of value-added network services, and in 1985 Scicon acquired 80 percent of Telecom International, a satellite communications company.

Discussion

During the 1980s and early 1990s software firms tried to increase the scale of their operations through external growth and internal restructuring. Scale is particularly important in the market for software packages, where market concentration is relatively high and the market leaders are all US firms (with the exception of SAP of Germany). In customized software and services, where European firms specialize, size is increasingly important as well. This explains the importance of market oriented linkages. External linkages enable firms to increase the size of their operations and to achieve economies of scale and scope. This is true in particular for firms which have made significant investments in structured development methodologies and have developed large libraries of documentation and programs that can be re-used for different customers. The fixed costs associated with these intangible assets are an important source of economies of scale and scope which can be exploited through either direct commercial channels or indirect channels, as in the case of minority participations or non-equity commercial agreements with other service providers located in a specific market.

Software firms have not diversified in unrelated business sectors, except for a few cases such as Microsoft's acquisition of a 26 percent share of the book publisher Dorling Kindersley in 1991. Similar to other forms of knowledge acquisition (e.g. innovative or imitative R&D), the absorption of new information through the establishment of external links is a costly activity that requires previous investments in evaluation and absorptive capabilities (Cohen and Levinthal, 1989). The costs of acquisition of knowledge are positively related to the distance between the firm's stock of knowledge and the new information. Besides the computational and organizational costs associated with the acquisition of new pieces of information, there are additional costs caused by the evaluation of the quality of information (which increase with the distance from the firm's stock of knowledge).[8] This is one explanation for the difficulties in diversifying shown by several firms from different sectors. In the history of the computer and software industry there are several examples of attempts at diversifying business activities. Philips is notable: after several attempts to remain in the computer industry (including numerous agreements) it has abandoned this sector to focus on its main business (which is still quite diversified). During the 1980s many firms in the IT sector also refocused their activities. Despite technological convergence among different branches of the IT sector, most attempts to diversify through alliances and M&As between firms specialized in telecommunications, computers, and electronic components, have failed (e.g. IBM's acquisition of Rolm). A major reason for these failures is linked to the high fixed costs in acquiring market- and user-specific knowledge, which give rise to increasing returns to scale. Rolm's limited market share hampered IBM's attempt to reach a minimum efficient scale in the market for private branch exchanges (PBXs) in the 1980s (Gambardella and Torrisi, 1998), for instance.

Some software firms have also refocused their activities after attempts at diversifying within the same software sector. In 1989 Pansophic, a US firm specialized in system software, tried to diversify into graphics applications, but failed. This failure may be linked to different reasons, including cost

---

[8] We do not take into account the costs of monitoring the behavior of the supplier of knowledge. These costs may induce firms to internalize the source of knowledge through M&As. But vertical integration does not necessarily reduce these costs because of asymmetric information and moral hazard. After all, there are few reasons to believe that "integration transforms a hostile supplier into a docile employee" (Grossman and Hart, 1986, 693).

and time for the acquisition of technological and market knowledge, and managerial bottlenecks. More recently, Cap Gemini, a computer service provider which grew through M&As during the 1980s, started a restructuring plan to sell activities outside its core business, including Cisi, a French computer services firm acquired a few years before (*Tribune–Côte–Desfosses*, March 10 1994, 12). SD–Scicon sold its US energy systems business to Combustion Engineering in 1988, its scientific control systems subsidiary to Cap Gemini in 1990, and its artificial intelligence activities to former employees (who founded a new firm, Integrated Solutions) with the purpose of focusing on manufacturing process control systems and financial communications services (*Computer Weekly*, 1990).

Finally, many software firms (e.g. Cap Gemini and Logica) have refocused their activities towards telecommunication services and multimedia. The business area resulting from the convergence between software and telecommunication services creates new windows of opportunities for new and established firms, including European services' providers. This explains the number of external linkages established by the sample firms in this field.

Conclusions

This chapter analyzes the process of growth and external linkages of large European software firms in comparison with their US counterparts. This is a quite young industry that has grown at a high annual rate compared with other IT segments, including computers. The positive externalities coming from technological convergence, the unbundling of software sales from that of hardware products, and the rising complexity of software applications have encouraged the outsourcing of software activities from user firms and vertical disintegration. They have also attracted many new firms into the software industry.

The conclusions emerging from the analysis of software firms' growth and restructuring in the period between 1984 and 1992 can be summarized as follows. First, analysis of collaborative agreements and other external growth operations provides some insights into the reasons why software firms set up these linkages. Many of these external links are a way to reach new markets and to exploit economies of scale and scope in the use of the firm's stock of knowledge (*market oriented* links). These operations provide software firms with the access to complementary capabilities that they do not possess (and maybe do not have incentives to develop) in-house. A smaller number of external growth operations aims to absorb or develop jointly new technological knowledge (*research-oriented* links). These linkages provide firms with private incentives to undertake innovative activity that they would not try alone.

Second, this study shows that software firms increased their diversification through external growth during the period under scrutiny. However, a closer analysis showed that most operations appeared to focus on technologically related activities (e.g. telecommunication services). Moreover, there are no significant differences among different forms of external growth with respect to the directions of diversification. Although collaborative agreements, particularly joint R&D agreements, are more diversified than M&As, they also focus on software and related businesses. This undermines the hypothesis that collaborative agreements, particularly joint research agreements and minority stakes, represent an important way to explore unfamiliar business sectors. The evidence provided in the chapter may be explained by the high growth rate of the software market, which offers significant investment opportunities compared with other sectors. There are decreasing returns to unrelated diversification owing to loss of managerial control, misallocation of internal resources, and organizational inertia that firms may experience even when they diversify in related businesses, as shown by some examples mentioned in this chapter. Future research on this topic should try to test more carefully the association between decreasing returns to diversification and the factors mentioned above.

Finally, at the beginning of the 1980s the differences between US and European firms were significant in terms of their production profile and diversification. European firms were more diversified in 1983; many of them belonged to an electronics or non-electronics group and focused on computer services. By contrast, US firms were very specialized. Most produced one or a few software packages and did not belong to any industrial group. The different degree of diversification between US and European firms declined as a consequence of 1984–92 developments. However, European and US software firms still show a different specialization – only one European firm (SAP of Germany) maintains an international position as a producer of software packages (Software AG, the second German software packages producer in 1990, has now refocused its activities towards services). The remaining firms have reinforced their activities in computer services and, more recently, have diversified in telecommunication services. This points out the difficulty in diversifying from software services to packaged software, which depends on the different commercial capabilities required in these two market segments. Another major barrier to entry into the market for packaged software arises from increasing returns linked to dynamic economies of scale and network externalities.

References

Cohen, W., and D. Levinthal (1989). "Innovation and Learning: The Two Faces of R&D," *Economic Journal,* 397(99), 569–96

Computer Weekly (1990) *Guide to Resources,* Sutton: Computer Weekly Publications

Gambardella, A. and S. Torrisi, (1998). "Does Technological Convergence Imply Convergence in Markets? Evidence from the Information Technology Industry," *Research Policy,* 27(5), 445–63

Geroski, P. A. (1992). "Vertical Relations between Firms and Industrial Policy," *The Economic Journal,* 102, 139–47

Gotlieb, C.C. (1985). *The Economics of Computers: Costs, Benefits, Policies and Strategies,* Englewood Cliffs, NJ: Prentice-Hall

Grossman, S. J. and O. H. Hart, (1986). "The Costs and Benefits of Ownership: A Theory of Vertical and Lateral Integration," *Journal of Political Economy,* 94(4), 691–719

IDC (1990). *European Software and Services. Review & Forecast,* Paris: International Data Corporation, European Research Centre

Jensen, M. and W. Meckling (1976). "Theory of the Firm: Managerial Behaviour, Agency Costs, and Capital Structure," *Journal of Financial Economics,* 3, 305–60

Malerba, F. and L. Orsenigo (1996). "Schumpeterian Patterns of Innovation are Technology-Specific," *Research Policy,* 25(3), 451–78

Malerba, F. and S. Torrisi (1996). "The Dynamics of Market Structure and Innovation in the Western European Software Industry," in D. Mowery (ed.), *The International Computer Software Industry: A Comparative Study of Industry Evolution and Structure,* New York: Oxford University Press, 165–96

Montgomery, C. A., and B. Wernerfelt (1988). "Diversification, Ricardian Rents, and Tobin's *q*," *Rand Journal of Economics,* 19(4), 623–32

Nelson, R.R. and S. Winter (1982). *An Evolutionary Theory of Economic Change,* Cambridge, Mass. and London: The Belknap Press of Harvard University Press

Patel, P. and K. Pavitt (1994). "The Continuing, Widespread (and Neglected) Importance of Improvements in Mechanical Technologies," *Research Policy,* 23, 533–45

Pavitt, K. (1991). "Key Characteristics of the Large Innovating Firm, *British Journal of Management,* 2(1), 533–45

Penrose, E. (1959). *The Theory of the Growth of the Firms,* Oxford: Basil Blackwell

Perry, M. K. (1989). "Vertical Integration: Determinants and Effects," in R. Schmalensee, and R. Willig (eds.), *Handbook of Industrial Organization,* Amsterdam: North-Holland, 183–255

Predicasts Company Thesaurus (1983). *Annual Edition,* Company Section, Cleveland Oh.: Predicasts Inc

Predicasts F&S Index (1984–92a). *United States, Annual Edition,* vol. 2, Cleveland, Oh.: Predicasts Inc

Predicasts F&S Index (1984–92b). *International, Annual Edition*, vol. 2., Cleveland Oh.: Predicasts Inc

Rosenberg, N. (1976). *Perspectives on Technology*, Cambridge: Cambridge University Press

Rotemberg, J.J. and G. Saloner (1994). "Benefits of Narrow Business Strategies," *American Economic Review*, 4(5), 1330–49

Rumelt, R.P. (1995). "Inertia and Transformation," in C.A. Montgomery (ed.), *Resource-Based and Evolutionary Theories of the Firm*, Dordrecht: Kluwer Academic, 1010–32

Steinmueller, W. E. (1996). "The US Software Industry: An Analysis and Interpretative History," in D. Mowery (ed.), *The International Computer Software Industry: A Comparative Study of Industry Evolution and Structure*, New York: Oxford University Press, 15–52

Stigler, G. (1951). "The Division of Labour is Limited by the Extent of the Market," *The Journal of Political Economy*, 59(3), 185–93

Teece, D. J. (1986). "Profiting from Technological Innovation: Implications for Integration, Collaboration, Licencing and Public Policy," *Research Policy*, 15(6), 285–305

Teece, D.J., R. Rumelt, G. Dosi, and S. Winter (1994). "Understanding Corporate Coherence: Theory and Evidence," *Journal of Economic Behavior and Organization*, 23, 285–305

Torrisi, S. (1998). *Industrial Organization and Innovation: An International Study of the Software Industry*, Cheltenham, UK and Northampton, Mass.: Edward Elgar

Williamson O. E. (1975). *Markets and Hierarchies: Analysis and Antitrust Implications*, New York: Free Press

Winter, S.G. (1993). "On Coase, Competence and the Corporation," in O.E. Williamson and S.G. Winter (eds.), *The Nature of the Firm*, New York: Oxford University Press, 179–95

12 European biotechnology: learning and catching-up

Margaret Sharp and Jacqueline Senker

Introduction

There have been fears that Europe may have been placed at a competitive disadvantage in biotechnology because of the late entry of its firms and the slow development of dedicated biotechnology firms in this new area of technology. In particular, there are fears that with capabilities developing fast elsewhere it may be unable to catch up. The purpose of this chapter is to compare the evolution and structure of the biotechnology sector in the United States and Europe, and consider the implications for European competitiveness in biotechnology.

Three themes emerge from this chapter. The first, that of the commercialization of biotechnology, is seemingly relatively straightforward. This new technology has emerged from rapid advances during the last half-century in the life sciences, particularly in the area of molecular biology and molecular genetics. These have revolutionized traditional routes to new drug discovery, new plant species, and a host of related activities, and are now opening the way to new gene-related therapies. The leading edge of the new technology established itself in the United States, fueled by that country's massive expenditure to support basic research in the life sciences which, in combination with a ready venture capital market and an entrepreneurial culture, led to a rapid process of commercialization by small, new, dedicated biotechnology firms (DBFs).

The initial lack of a small-firm sector in Europe meant that the commercialization of biotechnology was until recently dominated by the existing, predominately large, chemical and pharmaceutical companies, and the story of how these companies have accessed and assimilated the new technology constitutes the second theme of this chapter. Large European-based multinationals in chemicals and pharmaceuticals, in

This study was undertaken as part of the STEEP (Science, Technology, Energy, and Environment Policy) Research Program funded by the ESRC at the Science Policy Research Unit.

269

pursuit of the necessary knowledge and skills in biotechnology, have through arrangements of one sort or another widely penetrated the American knowledge base. We explore the effects of these US linkages on European skills and capabilities in biotechnology. Small dynamic biotechnology companies were slow to emerge in Europe but recent surveys have found that there are now increasing numbers of European DBFs. The reasons for their late development and the factors and changes which have helped them to emerge are the third theme of the chapter. We conclude by considering the emerging structure of the European biotechnology industry and its capability to compete with the United States.

The emergence of biotechnology

Biotechnology, by its broadest definition, is "the application of biological organisms, systems, and processes to manufacturing or service industries" (ACARD, 1980). In this sense, biotechnology has been around since the New Stone Age when humankind first learnt the art of cross-breeding plants and animals and of using yeast to leaven bread and ferment alcohol. For many centuries broad empiricism sufficed as technology, but by the beginning of the twentieth century this was replaced by a more systematic attempt to screen and categorize the role and variety of micro-organisms existing in the natural environment and to exploit those that had useful application – penicillin being a prime example. This was the so-called "second generation of biotechnology."

The new or "third-generation" biotechnology dates from the early 1970s when two breakthroughs in molecular biology – the discovery of a mechanism by which part of a foreign gene could be inserted into another and change its characteristics (recombinant DNA) and techniques for fusing and multiplying cells (hybridomas) – heralded the coming of genetic engineering. Using the methods of recombinant DNA the genes of micro-organisms such as yeast could be reprogrammed to produce useful proteins. The applications of these radical new techniques were rapidly appreciated. By the early 1980s a number of proteins of recognized therapeutic value such as insulin, human growth hormone and Factor VIII (for the treatment of haemophilia) had been cloned into a variety of micro-organisms and scale production was under way. These developments led in turn to the emergence of a whole new generation of protein drugs based on naturally occurring proteins in the body's immune system. Many of these drugs are currently being launched on world markets, with further "generations" of new products in the pipeline. Current developments in gene therapy, and other new drugs which are being developed as a result of recent breakthroughs in sequencing and mapping the human genome, open the way to a wholesale revolution in medical technology.

Applications for biotechnology outside the pharmaceutical industry also rapidly became apparent. In agriculture, genetic engineering had application to both animal husbandry and plants. In animals it led to the development of sheep capable of expressing valuable therapeutic proteins in their milk and pigs with "human" organs which can be used for transplants. But such "mutant" species have raised ethical questions (is it right to use animals in this way?). Even the breeding of special mice prone to cancer to expedite research in this area (the Harvard mouse) has caused problems. In plants, it led to the rapid development of hybrid plant species incorporating such desirable characteristics as resistance to frost or drought, fungi, pests – even resistance to particular types of herbicide. But there has also been concern that such products could lead to dangerous mutant species of plants invading the countryside and authorities have moved slowly in allowing field trials. As a result, few new products have yet been launched in this area.

More than any other technology, except perhaps nuclear power, the development of biotechnology has been led by academic scientific research (OTA, 1984, 1988). As a consequence, the industrial exploitation of biotechnology has been characterized first, by the prominent role played by universities and other scientific institutions and, secondly, by the emergence of many and varied forms of linkage between these scientific institutions and industry. This means there are three important "players" in the biotechnology innovation process: the universities and other major scientific institutions who are the main repositories of scientific knowledge; small and medium-sized firms (SMEs), dedicated to exploiting this knowledge (DBFs); and the large chemical and pharmaceutical companies who regard this new technology as a major source of product and process innovation but also as a potential threat to their existing way of life.

Among these players, universities and research institutes have benefitted from high levels of public funding for the life sciences, reflecting the high priority accorded by them to health care. In particular, the fight against cancer (and, more recently, AIDS) has attracted funds from both public and private sources. As a result, as table 12.1 shows, in all countries approximately one-third of the public basic research budget has been devoted to the life sciences, while in the United States the proportion rises to almost one-half. Indeed in both proportionate and absolute terms, expenditure on the life sciences in the United States dwarfs that of any other country. This helps to explain why the United States has captured the leading edge of research: there is just much more research being undertaken in the United States than anywhere else in the world.

Table 12.1 *Breakdown of national expenditures on academic and related research, by main field, 1987, $ million and percent*

	Expenditure[a]						
	UK	FRG	France	Neth.	USA	Japan	Average[b]
Engineering	436	505	359	112	1,966	809	
	15.6	12.5	11.2	11.7	13.2	21.6	14.3
Physical	565	1,015	955	208	2,325	543	
sciences	20.2	25.1	29.7	21.7	15.6	14.5	21.2
Environmental	188	183	172	27	859	136	
sciences	6.7	4.5	5.3	2.8	5.8	3.7	4.8
Maths and	209	156	175	34	596	88	
computing	7.5	3.9	5.4	3.5	4.0	2.3	4.4
Life sciences	864	1,483	1,116	313	7,285	1,261	
	30.9	36.7	34.7	32.7	48.9	33.7	36.3
Social sciences	187	210	146	99	754	145	
(and psychology)	6.7	5.2	4.6	10.4	5.1	3.9	6.0
Professional and	161	203	67	82	490	369	
vocational	5.7	5.0	2.1	8.5	3.3	9.9	5.8
Arts and	184	251	218	83	411	358	
humanities	6.6	6.2	6.8	8.6	2.8	9.6	6.8
Multi-disciplinary	6	32	3	1	217	28	
	0.2	0.8	0.1	0.1	1.5	0.8	0.6
Total	2,798	4,037	3,212	958	14,904	3,736	
	100	100	100	100	100	100	100

Notes:
[a] Expenditure data are based on OECD "purchasing power parities" for 1987, calculated in early 1989.
[b] This represents an unweighted average for the six countries (i.e. national figures have not been weighted to take into account the differing sizes of countries).
Source: Irvine, Martin, and Isard (1990), 219.

The commercialization of biotechnology

The first commercial exploitation of biotechnology occurred in the United States, and owes much to the prescience of Robert Swanson, a US venture capitalist, who appreciated the commercial potential of genetic engineering and in the early 1970s saw the opportunity for founding a specialist biotechnology company on the same lines as the specialist electronics firms

then "swarming" in Silicon Valley. Swanson compiled a list of top professors in the field and approached each with a partnership proposal. A
successful approach to Herbert Boyer, co-inventor of recombinant DNA
(rDNA), the gene-splicing process, led to the launch of Genentech in 1976.
The successful outcome of the company's initial research project, using
genetic-engineering techniques to produce the human growth hormone,
somatostatin, from bacteria, demonstrated the commercial potential of
rDNA techniques (Hall, 1988).

With the founding of Genentech, the biotechnology industry was born
in the United States. In the initial phase of commercialization neither large
corporations nor banks showed much interest in investing in the new and
untested technology and early start-up funds were provided by so-called
"business angels" – often locally based millionaires who are looking for
promising new opportunities – and venture capitalists – financiers who
provide capital to companies in return for a share in the equity and a seat
on the board of directors. Until recently, venture capital was an American
phenomenon. Karl Compton, president of the Massachusetts Institute of
Technology (MIT), prompted the establishment of the first venture capital
fund, the American Research and Development Corporation, shortly after
the end of the Second World War. Its aim was to supply risk capital to new
companies based on scientific research and it inspired the formation of
similar technically oriented venture-capital firms in other regions and
countries. With the emergence of many small electronics and software firms
in Silicon Valley and around Harvard and MIT, they came into their own.
By 1979 there were 250 US venture-capital firms, many of which had been
stimulated by American Research and Development's example (Etzkowitz,
1993).

Unlike the electronics industry, where most start-ups involved skilled
corporate engineers spinning off from large firms to form their own companies, biotechnology was academically based. The genetic engineering
skills needed to commercialize biotechnology were scarce and mainly
restricted to those who had been doing research in universities and research
institutes. Entrepreneurs who were eager to exploit the promise offered by
biotechnology had to solicit professors to become involved in the foundation of new genetic-engineering companies, although by 1980 scientists
were beginning to catch on and it was not unusual for them to approach
venture capitalists with business plans. Venture capitalists lured other professors to work for the start-up companies as directors, consultants, or to
sit on scientific advisory boards. Typically, these DBFs were launched with
private funding, and then raised initial capital investments of anything
between $1 and $10 million from venture capital firms. By 1991 there were
approximately 1,000 DBFs in the United States, with company formation

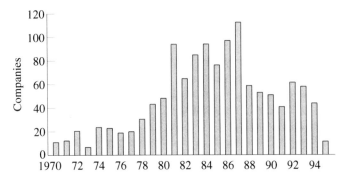

12.1 The biotechnology industry, by year of company foundation
Source: Ernst & Young (1995).

reaching its peak in 1987 (see Figure 12.1). As firms died, so others were born and the total population of DBFs in the United States has remained remarkably stable since the mid–1980s (OTA, 1991, chapter 4). The areas of primary focus of these firms are human health care, followed by agriculture, plant biotechnology and chemicals (Dibner, 1991).

The explosion of small firms in the United States cannot be disassociated from its *entrepreneurial climate*. The concept of "climate" in this context "includes the whole system of values in a society: attitudes towards science, towards economic and social change, towards private enterprise, and towards risk" (Piatier, 1984). US culture, which has been described as putting a high value on entrepreneurship (Rothwell and Zegveld, 1982), has influenced the way university faculties regard their relationship with industry. There is a long tradition in the United States of faculty consulting for industry and in some technology-related universities, such as MIT and Stanford, consulting is positively encouraged. Professors are traditionally allowed to spend up to 52 days per year consulting (Kenney, 1986). Goodeve (1967) notes that MIT "encourages its staff to spend up to one day a week in term time and much of their holidays (i.e. about a third of their total time) on industrial work, either as consultants or as outside directors." Education for entrepreneurship for both students and the wider community is also a recognized course offered by many institutions of higher education (McMullan, 1986). In biotechnology, by contrast with electrical engineering and computer science, professors have generally not resigned their faculty appointments, perhaps because they perceive that this is the best way to remain at the leading edge of biotechnology research (Kenney, 1986). Thus the new DBFs retain strong links with academic science.

Table 12.2 *R&D spending, by selected US DBFs, 1993 and 1995*

	$ million		As % of Sales	
	1993	1995	1993	1995
Amgen	255.3	451.7	18	23
Biogen	79.3	87.5	53	65
Centocor	66.1	66.2	83	83
Chiron	140.0	343.8	44	34
Genentech	299.4	345.9	46	40
Genetics Institute	102.1	122.4	95	71
Gensia	54.3	38.8	163	32
Genzyme	48.3	83.0	17	22
Immunex[a]	49.7	83.5	52	53
Medimmune	14.9	26.4	89	96
Scios Nova	39.5	27.9	73	57
Xoma	26.9	22.1	640	1,841

Note:
[a] 1993 figure for June 2–December 31, after merger with oncology business of Lederle Laboratories.
Sources: 1993 data, *Chemical and Engineering News* (1994); 1995 data, *Nature Biotechnology* (August 1996).

These small firms essentially created and maintained the US lead in biotechnology. It is significant, for example, that all 33 new biopharmaceuticals which had been approved for market by April 1995 had emerged from either DBF or university research and none from the traditional source of new drugs, the research labs of the large pharmaceutical firms (Ernst & Young, 1995). Table 12.2 gives an indication of the high levels of R&D spending of some of these firms in the 1990s. Faced with long lead times and costly clinical testing, DBFs entered into research contracts, with the large companies, selling their capabilities and knowledge to any who would buy them. Many such contracts were for as little as $1million or $2million, a small amount for the large companies but vital for the finances and credibility of the small ones.

The DBFs performed two very useful functions in this contract research role. First, they acted as intermediaries between the large companies and the academic base. With their close academic links they were able quickly to put together the cross-disciplinary teams required to exploit biotechnology: in contrast, the big firms, with their traditional contacts in chemistry not biology, found it difficult to find the right people (Kenney, 1986). Secondly, they enabled the large companies to hedge their bets and avoid long-term and expensive employment commitments at a time when it was still uncertain where biotechnology was going. (The strategies adopted by large chemical–pharmaceutical companies for biotechnology are discussed in more detail on pp. 277–86.) For their part, few DBFs saw themselves as long-term research contractors. Their long-term objective was in most cases to become a fully integrated pharmaceutical company, the hope being to take one or two "blockbuster" drugs through the various phases of testing into products yielding multi-million dollar profits.[1] Few companies have actually achieved this to date. Genentech, the largest and in many ways the most successful, managed to launch its tissue plasminogen activator (tPA) in 1989 after 10 years of development, but over-extended itself in the process and was therefore in no position to fight the effective takeover bid from Hoffmann LaRoche the following year.[2] Although the company retains its formal independence, in practice it now acts as a Roche subsidiary. Centocor and Cetus, companies strong in the late 1980s, fell at the last hurdle, when products failed the crucial final phase of testing.[3] By the mid–1990s a new generation of leading players has emerged. Amgen, for example, has succeeded in launching first its erythropietin (Epogen) and then its colony-stimulating factor, Neupogen, and now has sales approaching $3 billion per annum. Centocor is re-emerging as a strong player and Chiron, although now 60 percent owned by Ciba–Geigy (since 1996 Novartis) also has a strong product portfolio. There are also an increasing number of specialist genomics companies, such as Craig Venter's Human Genome Sciences, now playing a vital role in research. Indeed, it looks as if Amgen will be something of an exception as an integrated firm while, at the same time, many large firms "unbundle" some part of the R&D process to specialists.

The difficulty of achieving fully-fledged status as a pharmaceutical company, however, does not deter the DBFs. Indeed, what is impressive is the successive generations of DBFs which have sought to scale these heights. As the work of Mark Dibner (1991) and Ernst & Young (1995, 1996a) shows so well, although the total population of DBFs in the United States had stabilized at approximately 1,000 by 1990, births and deaths mean that there is much movement within that population, with new com-

---

[1] This is well illustrated in Werth (1994), which describes the frantic early years of the Vertex company in Boston.

[2] One of the problems Genentech faced was that in order to recoup its heavy R&D spend it priced its tPA at the top end of the price spectrum. This led to Medicare and many insurance companies in the United States refusing to pay for its use and insisting on cheaper alternatives, especially after a damning report which suggested it was no more efficacious than these alternatives. As a result sales were lower than anticipated, share prices fell and help had to be sought. See "An Appetite for Technology: Hoffmann LaRoche", *Bio/Technology* (August 1992).   [3] For instance, Centocor's septic-shock antibodies.

panies emerging to fill the gaps left by those who go out of business and/or get swallowed up by larger companies.

Many, including one of the present authors (Sharp, 1985a; Orsenigo, 1989), predicted that once the major companies began to make big investments in biotechnology and establish in-house competence, the small companies would disappear, either as a result of takeover by one of the big companies or through attrition. Regulations for pharmaceuticals and in relation to biotechnology itself has meant long and expensive trials and tests before products could be launched on the market; patent uncertainties and the possibility of major litigation to defend patents gave substantial advantage to well established companies. As biotechnology matured, it was argued, the small company would be squeezed out by the big.

Contrary to these predictions, the small biotechnology firm has survived and flourished. What fuels this continued dynamism? The most important factor is that the science base itself continues to move forward. The techniques of DNA, so scarce in the mid–1970s, are now part of the undergraduate curriculum. Meanwhile, new technologies such as polymerase chain reaction (PCR), gene sequencing, bio-informatics, and combinatorial chemistry have taken over at the leading edge, providing continuing opportunities for the formation of new specialist firms. The DBFs play an important part in pushing the technology forward and, with their privileged links into the science base, perform a vital intermediary function in helping diffuse new technologies among the industrial community. Indeed, their aspirations to become leading players fuels the competition among them, helping to propel the leading edge of the technology. Nevertheless, the DBFs remain capital-hungry, if for no other reason than that it takes 10–12 years and $250 million to launch a new drug, and they lack the distribution facilities, marketing knowledge, and capabilities necessary to bring these new products to market. The mutual dependence of the large and small firms in this sector therefore persists.

Large-firm strategy in the assimilation of biotechnology

Biotechnology, with its impact on drug discovery and new plant species, has to date had most impact on the chemical industry. The modern chemical industry is a large, heterogeneous industry whose boundaries, at their broadest, have been set by technology – the understanding and manipulation of molecules. It comprises, at one extreme, the low value-added, bulk chemicals and, at the other, speciality products such as dyes and paints, food additives and photographic supplies, and the production of highly sophisticated chemicals used as ingredients for pharmaceuticals, requiring many manufacturing steps and selling for thousands of dollars a gram.

Table 12.3 *The world's largest chemical-pharmaceutical companies, ranked by sales, 1985 and 1995*

	1985		1995	
Rank	Company	Sales[a] ($ billion)	Company	Sales[a] ($ billion)
1	BASF[b]	18.15	Hoechst[b]	36.40
2	Bayer[b]	17.79	BASF[b]	34.47
3	Hoechst[b]	16.55	Bayer[b]	31.10
4	ICI[b]	15.50	Dow[c]	20.20
5	Du Pont[c]	15.04	Johnson & Johnson[c]	18.84
6	Dow Chemical[c]	11.54	Du Pont[ac]	18.43
7	Shell[b]	9.18	Ciba-Geigy[b]	17.50
8	Union Carbide[c]	9.00	Rhône-Poulenc[b]	16.87
9	Ciba–Geigy[b]	8.85	Merck[c]	16.68
10	DSM[b]	8.76	ICI[bd]	16.21
11	Montedison[b]	8.49	Bristol Myers[c]	13.76
12	Rhône-Poulenc[b]	7.48	Akzo[b]	13.38
13	Monsanto[c]	6.75	Am Home Products[c]	13.37
14	Exxon[c]	6.67	Sandoz[b]	12.89
15	Akzo[b]	6.54	Norsk Hydro[b]	12.58

Notes:
[a] Chemical sales only (including pharmaceuticals).
[b] European-based.
[c] US-based.
[d] Figures exclude Zeneca's sales (demerged from ICI in 1993).
Source: 1985 data, *Bio-Technology* (July 1993), 801; 1995 data, *Chemical and Engineering News* (June 1996).

The industry is marked by a strong innovative tradition in which the in-house R&D department has provided the dynamic force, acting in effect as a nucleus which, via its external links into the research base, has proved a constant source of regeneration and renewal. This innovative tradition helps to explain both the presence and the longevity of the large conglomerate chemical company ("conglomerate" in the sense of spanning many sectors *within* the industry). Complete mastery of core technology, synthetic organic chemistry, has led to innovation across all fields. Table 12.3 lists the leading firms in the industry. Two factors are worth noting from this table. First the dominance of European names. Secondly, that many of these companies – for example, Hoechst and Bayer – have dominated the industry since the early part of this century. It is also interesting to note that the new entrants to the "big league" are companies such as Sandoz, Roche, and Merck, whose strength lies in pharmaceuticals and fine chemicals. Those who have lost position during the 1980s are companies whose fortunes were based on processing bulk chemicals and especially petrochemicals.

These changes reflect the collapse of profitability in bulk petrochemicals and their downstream derivatives (plastics, fibers, fertilizers) that came with the two oil crises and recessions of the 1970s and early 1980s. The 1980s also witnessed the entry of three important new sets of players into the industry – companies from the Gulf States, the newly industrializing countries (NICs) of South East Asia, and the transition economics of Eastern Europe. Under severe competitive pressure, the industry moved in two directions. First, there was major restructuring and rationalization, achieved through a mixture of closure, merger, and acquisition, which led to a substantial "reshuffling" of assets amongst firms and an increasing concentration of activities. The low value-added upstream bulk-chemical activities in particular have become more concentrated, often in the hands of the oil and gas company entrants, while the older chemical companies have tended to concentrate on the higher value-added, research-intensive activities.

Among such activities, the pharmaceuticals and agro-chemicals sectors offered obvious attractions. Both markets are highly oligopolistic, with intense competition within each market segment. R&D provided the crux of this competition as companies vied with each other to introduce new products, but R&D also underpinned firms' ability to move rapidly into a competitor's market and meet health and safety regulations. In this sense, such competition was a major barrier to entry and an excuse to maintain high profitability. Since the 1960s, when health and safety regulations were first introduced, R&D as a proportion of turnover has steadily increased: in pharmaceuticals, by 1992, R&D averaged 16 percent of net output, with it taking, typically, 12 years to bring a new drug to market at a cost of up to \$240million.[4] New companies did not enter easily.

By the mid–1980s, however, the rising costs of R&D and the increasing tightness of public sector budgets, led to a double squeeze on the profits of the major companies. In their search for new activities which might bring

---

[4] Only one in every 10,000 new chemical entities (NCE) screened for therapeutic properties makes it to the market. This \$240 million is the *average* cost of each new NCE which makes it to the market, including failures, and using present-value accounting to allow for the time profile of costs incurred over the 10-year period of R&D, clinical trials, etc. (DiMasi *et al.*, 1991).

higher profits and/or lower costs, biotechnology offered obvious attractions. The problem was the lack of internal competence – the companies, as noted above, were founded on synthetic chemistry, not biology. A 1983 report noted that

By and large, the big companies are counting on ... affiliations to tide them over until their own research staff gain sufficient knowledge and experience to perform advanced research in-house. (McGraw-Hill's *Biotechnology Newswatch*, 1983)

While some companies such as Dow Chemicals and DuPont developed in-house programs to spearhead their efforts in biotechnology, many firms entered into collaboration with DBFs (Sapienza, 1989) or university centers (Webster, 1994) to build up their capability in the new technology. By 1988 a survey of 53 major US corporations by the Office of Technology Assessment (OTA) found that

major corporations are building up their in-house R&D capabilities while simultaneously complementing their research with outside sources of innovation. (OTA, 1988)

In contrast to their US counterparts, few of the large European chemical–pharmaceutical companies played much part in the first decade of "the new biotechnology." Most companies were uncertain what to make of the new technology and especially of the hype surrounding its development. Some had experience of fermentation technology through the production of biological pharmaceuticals such as penicillin, or through the use of enzymes. The latter, however, tended to be the preserve of specialist companies such as Gist Brocades or Novo rather than the large firms. A number of the larger companies had experimented with single-cell protein, including Shell, BP, Hoechst, and ICI, but the experience had tended to reinforce their skepticism (Sharp, 1985a).

This combination of uncertainty, skepticism, and inexperience led to what might be called a "minimalist strategy" of participation in biotechnology on the part of many of these European firms. While avoiding large investments, most companies built up teams of researchers large enough to keep abreast of the science and to monitor developments and competitors. Thus Bayer, ICI, and Ciba–Geigy all established small research teams in their corporate R&D laboratories with a fairly free rein to explore ideas as they wished (Sharp and Galimberti, 1993). Other companies – for example, BASF – left even these moves until later, having only a minor interest in pharmaceuticals and being very uncertain whether biotechnology would have any relevance to their main interests in areas such as plastics and fibers (Sharp, 1985a).

There were two important consequences of this strategy of "watching and waiting" (Sharp, 1985b). First, it conceded leadership in the development of the new technology to the small companies which were closely linked into the academic base. In this phase of development relatively few of the major European chemical firms formed partnerships with US DBFs. Hoechst, in placing a $67million, 10-year contract in 1981 with the Massachusetts General Hospital (MGH), bought itself directly into the US academic base, and even made arrangements for its researchers to be trained there, a move implicitly acknowledging the limitations of its indigenous science base in Germany. Other companies – among them Glaxo, Wellcome, and Bayer – chose not to try to buy themselves into the new technology, but instead to expand their own research, setting up laboratories which were able to link directly into the US research base.[5]

The second result of the "watching and waiting" strategy was to create a policy void. The hype surrounding the DBFs in the United States led to demands for government action in Europe, but governments were uncertain what to do, and received no guidance from their corporate partners. Provided they were not expected to make major commitments, most companies were willing to explore options opened up by government funding. Governments, for their part, generally resorted to supporting the science base and promoting technology transfer. Such programs often involved little commitment on the part of companies, helped to keep them abreast of wider developments – and, more to the point, helped train a cadre of scientists to work in cross-disciplinary teams. Technology-transfer schemes promoted linkage between companies and academic science, giving the companies knowledge of developments in the science base and access to leading academics who were well linked into international scientific networks. As they built up in-house teams, such linkage became more, rather than less, important to the large companies.

By the mid–1980s the period of watching and waiting was over. Most of the large companies recognized that, whatever their original reservations, biotechnology had established itself as an important *enabling* technology (i.e. a route to new techniques) and would be essential for future product innovation. Investments therefore needed to be made. Two developments in particular influenced these decisions. First was the emergence of new techniques such as polymerase chain reaction, protein engineering, and antibody engineering, which gave credence to ideas of rational drug design and targeted-delivery systems. Just as in electronics the emergence of the microchip in the 1970s led firms to envisage successive generations of computer

---

[5] Burroughs Wellcome established a research laboratory in Research Triangle Park, North Carolina, in the late 1970s and used this as a launch pad for its links with the US academic base. Glaxo followed suit in 1983, establishing new research laboratories in 1986 at Research Triangle Park. Bayer expanded its operations on the site of the Miles Laboratories at West Haven, Conn., having taken over Miles in 1979 (Sharp, 1985a).

technology, so these new developments opened up the vision of successive generations of the new biotechnology. Secondly, developments in plant biotechnology – in particular, the successful application of rDNA techniques to plant science and the "engineering" of new transgenic plant species – held out a vision of a whole new world in agriculture which would radically affect traditional markets for fertilizers, herbicides, and pesticides (Sharp, Thomas, and Martin, 1993).

The strategies chosen varied from company to company. All were concerned to build up in-house competencies. Some chose to do this internally, using existing and new linkages into academic science; others bought in competencies through the acquisition of new biotechnology firms or through merger with American counterparts; yet others chose to retain external linkages with American and/or European DBFs (see pp. 286–92, for detailed discussion of this phenomenon). All involved investments of $100million or more a year, building up internal teams of up to 700 researchers.[6] Initially many of these researchers were grouped together in special Biotechnology Divisions but, as time went by, these were disbanded and the biologists and biotechnologists within them dispersed among project-based multi-disciplinary teams.[7] The investments in new plant and capacity brought regulatory issues to the forefront. Most companies were prepared to accept the strict containment principles laid down by OECD guidelines of best (laboratory) practice (OECD, 1987) but problems encountered by Hoechst in trying to bring their genetically engineered insulin plant on-stream in Frankfurt in 1987 and the discussion of a five-year moratorium on genetic research in West Germany raised fears about the future.[8]

Given the need to build up in-house competencies, companies put pressure on governments to improve the indigenous science base and its links to industry. These concerns reflected the difficulties some European companies faced in recruiting staff for new biotechnology laboratories. Sanofi, for example, when it opened its Labège laboratory in Toulouse, recruited half its staff from overseas (Sharp, 1985a) and even Ciba–Geigy had difficulty recruiting for its Basel laboratory (Galimberti, 1993).

Governments, for their part, were anxious, insofar as funding was

---

[6] This was the number of researchers reckoned by Bayer to be engaged in biotechnology at the peak of its activities (see Sharp and Galimberti, 1993).

[7] The timing of these moves and the way in which they were handled, varied from company to company. Ciba–Geigy, for example, made such moves fairly early; by contrast, the Italian firm Carlo Erba–Farmitalia left the moves until much later and remarked on the difficulty of penetrating the "chemical" traditions of the pharmacologists until this had happened (see Galimberti, 1993).

[8] For a full discussion of the regulatory problems encountered in West Germany, see Shackley (1993).

increased, to see it linked to technology-transfer schemes which would ensure that companies used indigenous academic research, and that the research itself was "relevant" to industrial needs. In Britain, France, and Germany various schemes were introduced aimed at improving university–industry linkages. For the first time, too, came an attempt to identify strategic sectors within biotechnology. The British Protein Engineering Club – a collaborative industry–academic scheme – was mirrored by an attempt to get similar programs off the ground in France, Germany, and the Netherlands.

The European Commission also played its part. Early EC programs, the Biomolecular Engineering Program (BEP), 1982–6 and the Biotechnology Action Program (BAP), 1985–9, funded mainly academic research, bringing together researchers from different EC countries. BRIDGE (Biotechnology Research for Innovation, Development, and Growth in Europe), introduced in 1990, aimed to broaden the program to include greater industrial participation.

The third (and final) phase of the development has seen biotechnology products beginning to appear on the market, and a growing interdependence between large and small companies. Given the increasing emphasis on bringing products to market, the issues of regulation and intellectual property rights have become more pressing and, from the company point of view, take precedence over all other issues of public policy. Within Europe, the focus of policy on these issues has shifted to EU level, but differences of view between Commission, Council and Parliament have held up implementation of proposed directives.[9] The European Parliament finally approved the Life Patents Directive in May 1998, after excluding the procedures for human cloning and the patenting of human embryos. The Directive, which EU countries must incorporate into national legislation within two years, will make life easier for industry (Abbott, 1998).

The steady trickle of new biopharmaceuticals on to the market in the 1990s is anticipated to grow year by year. Jurgen Drews, head of R&D at Hoffmann LaRoche, commented in 1993:

A conservative estimate would expect 30–40 of the recombinant proteins now under development to become successfully marketed products over the next 5–6 years. This means that an average of 5–8 novel proteins should become available each year

---

[9] The differences of view broadly reflect the differences between the industrial lobby, which was influential in shaping both Commission and Council views, and consumer–Green worries about the longer-term implications of developments in biotechnology. Under the Maastricht Treaty procedures, attempts have been made to reconcile these differences. The European Parliament rejected a Directive on patenting in 1995, and left companies dependent on a variable patchwork of regulations implemented by member states. Progress is also being made on Directives for regulating genetically modified organisms (Ward, 1996a).

... If we assume an average sales volume for the forthcoming recombinant proteins equal to the average revenues generated by today's recombinant drugs, the portfolio of recombinant proteins now in clinical trials should amount to $10–20 billion in today's currency. (Drews, 1993, p. S17)

Looking beyond the 10-year horizon, Drews foresaw the arrival first of the cytokine-based drugs which will treat various kinds of cancer, many based on novel combinations of proteins and other chemical entities. Diseases such as Parkinson's and Alzheimer's and neural disorders are high on the list of targets. The most far-reaching of current developments, however, come from another source – from work involved with understanding the human genome (and, concomitantly, unravelling genes' physiological function and roles in disease processes). Current initiatives in genome mapping are helping to identify many new potential drugs and to illuminate routes to their development.[10] Gene therapy itself – direct intervention to alter the genetic make-up of cells or to block particular pathways – will have far-reaching effects on both pharmaceutical and health care industries.

The implications of these developments are interesting. Although they show a maturing of biotechnology, they also show that it remains an area of active – indeed, dynamic – development by both large and small firms in the industry. DBFs continue to exist because they have established synergistic relationships with the larger companies. Increasingly, as table 12.4 shows, it is these firms who are the source of new product ideas, but the small companies still depend on the larger firms not only to market these products but to carry them through the expensive development stages (which means taking them through Phase II and III trials).[11] The large firms also remain a key source of finance. The two sectors of the industry remain therefore mutually dependent upon each other. Hence, while the DBF sector is as active as ever, the larger firms are also increasing their commitments.

It is worth putting these developments into perspective. In 1995 the total R&D spend of the 216 leading biotechnology firms amounted to $4.04 billion – an average of $18.7 million per company – with sales at $8.2 billion ($38 million per company). By contrast, the figures for the 15 leading pharmaceutical companies show R&D at $13 billion (an average of $866

[10] Jurgen Drews has recently updated his earlier overview: A careful analysis of the Human Genome Project's potential suggests that 3000–10000 interesting new molecules – "drug targets" in pharmaceutical vernacular – may emerge from it over the next six years. (Jurgen Drews, "Genomic sciences and the medicine of tomorrow," *Nature Biotechnology*, November 1996, 1516–17).

[11] Phase II clinical trials are the first administration to patients suffering from the disease for which the drug is intended. Phase III is the expansion of therapeutic trials, once efficacy and relative safety have been established.

Table 12.4 *Top 10 biotechnology drugs on the market, 1993 and 2000*

Product	Developer	Marketer	1993 net sales ($ million)	Projected sales 2000 ($ million)
Neupogen	Amgen	Amgen	719	1,593
Epogen	Amgen	Amgen	587	1,200
Intron A	Biogen	Schering–Plough	572	1,000
Humulin	Genentech	Eli Lilly	560	1,300
Procrit	Amgen	Ortho Biotech	500	1,100
Engerix–B	Genentech	SmithKline Beecham	480	na
RecombiNAK HB	Chiron	Merck	245	na
Activase	Genentech	Genentech	236	450
Protropin	Genentech	Genentech	217	500
Roferon–A	Genentech	Hoffmann LaRoche	172	800
Total sales of top 10			$4,288	>8,000
Total industry sales			$7,700	

Sources: Med Ad News, quoted in Ernst & Young (1994); 2000 projections, *Scrip* Magazine (November 1995).

million) with sales at $79 billion (average $5.26 billion per company). Even if each pharmaceutical company spent only 10 percent of its R&D on biotechnology (almost certainly an under-estimate), its spending would amount to five times the DBF average.[12]

While large-firm investment has been growing, it has also become increasingly targeted. The last few years has seen a marked shift away from the broad learning strategies of the mid–1980s towards a more focused approach. Ciba–Geigy (now part of Novartis), for example, cut back on its portfolio of interests in biopharmaceuticals in 1989 in order to concentrate more narrowly on the development of a few products with market potential. For Bayer, targeting involved pulling out of biotechnology research in agro-chemicals and concentrating on pharmaceuticals. Hoffmann LaRoche has likewise pulled out of agro-biotechnology to concentrate its interests in the pharmaceuticals area. Rhône Poulenc, a relatively late entrant into mainstream biotechnology, has made up for lost time by an aggressive policy of acquisition and alliance. Like Ciba–Geigy and ICI, it has maintained interests in both

[12] "Public companies spend over $4 billion on R&D," *Bio/Technology* (August 14 1996), 934–5.

the pharmaceutical and agricultural aspects of biotechnology and has bought itself into the seed industry. German and Swiss firms suffered more than their British and French counterparts from uncertainties over regulation. The influence of the Greens in Germany, although less strident in the 1990s, has left an inheritance of delays and uncertainties which caused these companies to shift some of their biotechnology activities to already well established subsidiaries in the United States where the regulatory framework was clearer. This has been particularly so for plant biotechnology where experimentation perforce involves environmental release, albeit carefully controlled and monitored. (For more detail see Galimberti, 1993, especially the chapters on Bayer and Ciba–Geigy.)

For most of the large companies, however, the most notable feature of the 1990s was increased activity to access the US science base. This development is explored in the next section.

US activities of European multinationals

Many of the leading multinational firms (MNEs), including both British-, French-, and German-based companies, have accessed US knowledge and capabilities by a variety of methods including setting up (or extending existing) offshore laboratories, and negotiating contracts with both US academic laboratories and/or DBFs. These developments, which peaked in the late 1980s – early 1990s, gave rise to fears that, while European-owned multi-nationals might, by this process, be retaining their own competitive edge in biotechnology, they would not be transferring the skills, capabilities, and knowledge back to their home laboratories. As a result, European capabilities in biotechnology would fall behind. Recent research, however, throws doubt on this interpretation of events. On the contrary, it finds European MNEs using overseas laboratories and linkages with the US DBFs as a means of strengthening their European-based R&D activities. This section examines the evidence on both sides.

Corporate alliances

The outstanding feature of the early 1990s was the very large number of corporate alliances which European multinationals established with US DBFs. Table 12.5 summarizes the data. By 1994, Ciba–Geigy, one of the first companies to break with tradition in the early 1980s and contract out key research on biotechnology, had 29 known alliances, but was closely followed by Hoffmann LaRoche with 27, and Hoechst with 24. By contrast, the British companies ICI and Zeneca (demerged in 1993) between them had only two alliances. Other companies not included in table 12.5 also had

Table 12.5 *Alliances and JVs between US DBFs and leading European multinationals in the chemical–pharmaceutical industry, 1990–1994*

Company concluded (1)	Total no. of alliances (2)	No. 1990–4 (3)
Ciba–Geigy	29	17
Hoffmann LaRoche	27	10
Hoechst	24	10
Rhône Poulenc	19	12
Sandoz	18	14
Bayer	12	7
Akzo	11	6
BASF	4	0
ICI–Zeneca	2	1

Source: Sharp (forthcoming).

significant numbers of alliances: Glaxo, the British pharmaceutical company, boasts 17 agreements and SmithKline Beecham a total of 15 (*Bioscan*, February 1994).

Column (2) in table 12.5 – the number of agreements concluded between 1990 and 1994 – shows an increasing number of alliances between these two sets of players in the last five years – a time when, as indicated in the previous section, these companies have themselves been investing heavily in biotechnology. The data upon which table 12.5 is based indicates that there has been a shift over the course of the last 10 years from R&D agreements, which dominated in the early years, towards marketing and licensing agreements. In other words, whereas 10 years ago alliances supplemented large companies' internal research, today they fulfill a more important role – namely, as a key supplier of potential new products.

While table 12.5 illustrates how deeply some European companies are networked into the US biotechnology system, it gives little perspective on the relative position of European firms *vis-à-vis* those from other parts of the world. Table 12.6 summarizes data from *Bioscan* (1994) on the nationality of alliance partners for a sample of 72 leading DBFs in the United States. It shows that European firms are considerably more active than Japanese firms in linking up with US DBFs. However, the majority of alliances are forged between US companies. Similar conclusions derive from two other studies of the geographical spread of DBF alliances, shown in tables 12.7 and 12.8.

Both tables suggest that approximately 25 percent of alliances are

Table 12.6 *Alliances concluded by 72 of America's leading DBFs, to end-1993*

	No.	(%)
Number of DBFs on sample	72	
Total number of alliances	718	100
Number of alliances with foreign firms	259	36
Number with European firms	141	20
Number with Japanese firms	90	12.5

Source: Sharp (1995).

Table 12.7 *US-DBFs involved in biotechnology alliances, 1982–1991*

	No.	(%)
Total no. of alliances noted	2,079	
of which detailed data on	1,303	100
of which involving a Japanese partner	183	14
of which involving a European partner	346	27
of which UK	76	6
Swiss	71	5.5
German	45	3.5
French	36	3.0
Italian	36	3.0
Swedish	27	2.0
Dutch	9	1.0

Source: Dibner and Bulluck (1992).

Table 12.8 *Biotechnology alliances, 1992–1994 (June–June)*

	%	
Geography of deal partner	1992–3	1993–4
N. America	63	65
Europe	24	24
Japan	11	8
Other	2	3

Source: Ernst & Young (1994), table 13.

concluded with European firms compared to a 10–12 percent share with the Japanese, and an over 60 percent share with North America (including Canada).

Mergers, acquisitions, and overseas laboratories

Many European MNEs have overseas laboratories in the United States which have been acquired as a result of mergers and acquisitions (M&As). Bayer, for example, acquired two medium-sized US pharmaceutical firms, Miles and Cutter, in the late 1970s and their laboratories in West Haven, Conn. and California have formed the basis of Bayer's research presence in the United States. Ciba–Geigy's animal health laboratory in the United States was acquired from Bristol Myers Squibb in 1990 in the "reshuffling" of assets that took place after that firm's merger. Ciba–Geigy's plant-breeding laboratories in North Carolina, on the other hand, and its pharmaceutical laboratories in New Jersey derive from earlier decisions to develop these facilities in America. Both are located close to university campuses. Research Triangle Park in North Carolina has proved a popular location for European multinationals: Glaxo, Wellcome, Ciba–Geigy and Roche all have research laboratories in the area. Rhône Poulenc is a company which has pursued an aggressive policy of growth by acquisition; together with its subsidiary Institut Mérieux, it bought Connaught Biosciences, Canada's largest biotechnology firm, in 1989, to form the world's largest producer of vaccines. In 1990, it bought Rorer, a fairly substantial US pharmaceutical company, to form Rhône Poulenc Rorer (RPR), and all the company's pharmaceuticals research in the United States is now undertaken in the Rorer facilities. The Rorer laboratories also spearheaded the company's 1994 "network collaboration" – RPR–Gencell – which coordinates and integrates research by French academics and 14 US DBFs in the genome-sequencing area. Rhône Poulenc has also been actively acquiring seed companies.

Academic links

A study which analyzed European and Japanese company research laboratories in the United States (Dibner, Stock, and Greis, 1992) located 76 sites where the companies concerned were engaged in biotechnology R&D, of which 60 belonged to European parent firms and only 16 to Japanese parents. Table 12.9 highlights not only the large number of US laboratories run by European multinationals, but the extensive linkages which these laboratories have with US universities. It shows that on average European-owned sites are much more strongly linked into the American university

Table 12.9 *Linkages between US-based facilities of European and Japanese companies involved in biotechnology research*

	European-owned sites	Japanese-owned sites
No. of sites	60	16
Linkages with		
Universities (av.)	6.04	2.42
Biotechnology firms (av.)	0.93	0.17
Other corporations (av.)	1.00	0.58
Total collaborations (av.)	7.42	3.17

Note:
av. = average.
Source: Dibner, Stock, and Greis (1992).

system than the Japanese, reinforcing the impression that European companies in this sector are embedded in the US system, and more deeply rooted there than their Japanese counterparts.

An exception to this general picture was ICI–Zeneca which, although it has substantial laboratories at Wilmington, Penn., had few linkages with DBFs. Other United Kingdom firms such as Glaxo and SmithKline Beecham have also been slow until recently to develop US linkages. Equally, all three companies are deeply networked into the United Kingdom science base, playing an active part in 1980s initiatives to promote university–industry links in biotechnology and establishing and supporting laboratories at leading British universities.

How do MNEs use overseas laboratories and links to DBFs?

Despite some British companies seemingly finding that links with the United Kingdom science base are a sufficient resource to acquire the necessary knowledge and skills in biotechnology, the balance of the evidence cited above suggests that large European-based multinationals have widely penetrated the American knowledge base. The irony of the situation is that such linkages, forged between these European multinationals and the American science base, actively help to promote the competitiveness of these companies. It is not a question of European-based companies losing out, they have no difficulty holding their own among their global competitors. But it is unclear whether these companies are transferring skills and capabilities, as well as profits, back to their home base. If no state-of-the-art work in biotechnology is being undertaken in European laboratories, then there is an obvious danger that the European skill base in the area will fall behind, with knock-on effects for Europe's long-run ability to support a modern biotechnology industry.

It was important therefore to find out precisely how Europe's MNEs were using these links. To explore this issue, case studies of 10 leading multinationals in Germany, France, and the United Kingdom were undertaken. The case studies were based on desk research and semi-structured interviews with senior managers responsible for biotechnology research at European and US laboratories. The interviews covered five broad issues: the relative numbers of biotechnology researchers in Europe and the United States; differences in the nature of biotechnology R&D between Europe and the United States; methods for acquiring and transferring biotechnology capabilities in and between home and overseas laboratories; the factors influencing the location of company biotechnology research in the United States; and the effect of overseas research on European biotechnology capabilities (Senker, Joly, and Reinhart, 1998).

The study found four main reasons why European multinationals were locating research in the United States: the size of the market; the opportunity to gain tax concessions on US research activities; the need to comply with FDA regulations; and the ability to tap into US science. Of these, the first three were just as compelling as the last – indeed most companies stressed the need to satisfy the FDA inspection requirements, especially for biopharmaceuticals. They emphasized that they were constantly increasing in-house competencies through external collaborations with university researchers, both those local to their US laboratories, and those local to European laboratories. Strategic alliances between European laboratories and US-based DBFs were handled most frequently from the European end. Collaborations with local universities in Europe were used to search for new ideas, techniques, and new people, and for specific research contracts. By contrast, alliances with US DBFs – which frequently absorbed the major share of the MNEs' external research budget – were strategic, in the sense that they were used to enable firms to gain critical expertise and to move quickly into new areas of research. The main direction of knowledge flow from these strategic alliances was from the United States to Europe. Finally, the research revealed that the European MNEs employed roughly twice as many biotechnology researchers in laboratories in Europe as in the United States. Therefore, in spite of appearances to the contrary, it would seem that biotechnology R&D is not leaving Europe for the United States, and thus that European research capabilities are as strong as ever.

The study also highlighted issues that need to be addressed if Europe is to keep up with the United States. The strongest criticism was of the lack of critical mass in Europe with the fragmentation of the science base between the various European countries, a factor exacerbated by the chauvinism of the public sector research systems, which support national rather than other European companies. Companies, for their part, appear to have little knowledge of academic expertise outside their own country, while the sheer transparency of the US system means it is easy to find expertise there. In some areas of research there are perceived gaps in expertise in Europe: microbial physiology, virology, bio-informatics, gene therapy, genomics and combinatorial chemistry were all mentioned as areas where the United States was ahead. The research found, however, that companies' strategic alliances with US DBFs were helping to increase their biotechnology capabilities in these areas of weakness (Senker, Joly, and Reinhard, 1998).

European DBFs

If Europe's MNEs are stronger than originally perceived, what about Europe's small firms? From the 1980s onwards there was concern that US-style DBFs were not emerging in Europe to play a similar key role in the commercialization of biotechnology. A variety of factors were thought to explain their absence – lack of venture capital, an under-developed science base, lack of knowledge of the new technology and its commercial potential by existing firms, and the negative attitude of European academics towards industry. Many European countries developed broadly similar policies to rectify the deficiencies. The science base was strengthened by redirecting public research funds into academic biotechnology research, links were created between that science base and industry and the formation of small firms was promoted (Sharp, 1985a; Walsh, Niosi, and Mustar, 1995).

In Germany, for example, the relative neglect of molecular biology and molecular genetics meant there was a lack of well qualified young scientists in the early 1980s. In 1985 the government set up a program to help Germany catch up. The "Applied Biology and Biotechnology" program of 1986–9 financed academic research and provided grants for SMEs to purchase biotechnology know-how and services from research laboratories. It also met the cost of academic research in collaborative research projects between small firms and academics. The program was judged to be a success and, from 1990, was continued and extended with the "Biotechnology 2000" program (BMFT, 1989, 1993).

Similarly, recognition of France's rather weak position in biotechnology led, in 1982, to the introduction of a Mobilization Plan to strengthen the R&D infrastructure and encourage French companies to acquire genetic-engineering technologies and know-how (Sharp, 1985a; Sharp and Holmes,

1989). Subsequent evaluation revealed that a major achievement of the program was the construction of new links between industry, universities, and the public sector research laboratories (Hodgson, 1994). France also has a small but increasing number of small biotechnology firms whose growth has been stimulated by changes in venture capital availability and activities of government agencies such as the National Association for the Application of Research (ANVAR). Since 1983, ANVAR has provided funds to support the commercialization of public sector research by providing seed capital for start-up firms and awarding them grants or interest-free loans for innovative projects (Ramani, 1995; Walsh, Niosi and Mustar, 1995).

British government support for biotechnology was stimulated by the Spinks Report, published in 1980, which highlighted the importance of the technology and Britain's comparative scientific advantage in this field. The most targeted policy developments were in the academic sector, with the establishment in the early 1980s of the Biotechnology Directorate and its program aimed at promoting strategic university research and forging links between that research and industry. At about the same time, the Department of Trade and Industry (DTI) set up its Biotechnology Unit with the purpose of raising industrial awareness of opportunities in biotechnology and encouraging more R&D in industry. The Biotechnology Directorate and the Biotechnology Unit developed close links, including shared funding of several collaborative programs (Senker and Sharp, 1988).

Another outcome of the Spinks Report was the establishment of a DBF, named Celltech, backed by both the government and the City. Celltech was given first option rights to commercialize the results of research from the Medical Research Council[13] including monoclonal antibodies, and this gave the company a lead over competitors (Dodgson, 1991). Growth of DBFs in the United Kingdom was, however, slow. Unlike their US counterparts, few of those setting up such companies came from an academic background; over 64 percent of founders came from industry (Oakey *et al.*, 1990).

The slow emergence of European DBFs was also due to the lack of an entrepreneurial spirit among academic scientists. Government initiatives to support collaborative research between academic and industrial researchers did much to erode academics' anti-industrial values, and some universities have established companies to market their services or set up specialized research centers. Others, with the support of local government and/or EU funds, have joined together to establish technology transfer centers to commercialize the technology from their institutes (Monck *et al*,

---

[13] The Medical Research Council is a Government organization which funds medical research and postgraduate training in its own research institutes and in universities.

1988). At the same time, a decline in government funding for university research and rising insecurity of employment have made establishing or working in a small company an attractive option for some academic scientists.

The growing respectability of entrepreneurship for academics has been paralleled by easier access to investment capital. Early government initiatives to remedy the lack of British venture capital included the Business Enterprise Scheme (BES) which unfortunately was exploited as a tax loophole and failed to attract real venture-capital funds. The establishment of the United Kingdom Unlisted Securities (USM) and Over-the-Counter (OTC) Markets in the early 1980s helped to increase financing opportunities for new-technology companies, and by the late 1980s quite a number of new companies had emerged. Early investors, however, lacked an exit route for realizing their investments; both the OTC and USM required private placements. In 1993, after two British DBFs successfully floated on the US National Association of Securities Dealers Automated Quotation (NASDAQ), the London Stock Exchange relaxed its rules, allowing developing biotechnology companies to raise funds from this source. France has set up the Nouveau Marché and EASDAQ, a European version of NASDAQ, was set up in 1996. The result was to transform the position for DBFs. By the early 1990s, the United Kingdom, the Netherlands, and France all had developing venture-capital markets (Manigart, 1994). A study in the late 1980s, however, highlighted the differences between British venture-capital organizations, which adopted a "hands-off" approach to the firms they funded, offering investment under highly regulated terms and conditions, and their counterparts in the United States who offered expertise and guidance (Oakey *et al*, 1990). In other words, the successful founding of DBFs requires more than just money; too frequently, this lack of understanding of what venture capital was really about led to insurmountable hurdles for embryo biotechnology companies who could not offer quick profits.

A further beneficial effect on European DBFs flowed from a wave of mergers and downsizing among European multinationals during the early 1990s.[14] In the 1980s, the foundation of Celltech benefited from a "breakaway" from the Searle Laboratories at High Wycombe (Dodgson, 1991), while the foundation of British Biotechnology was prompted by the closure of those laboratories by Monsanto after its takeover of Searle (British Biotechnology Group, 1992). With "rationalization" taking place in the aftermath of merger it will become easier for European DBFs to recruit

---

[14] For example, the 1994 merger of Hoechst's and Schering's agro-chemicals interests as the joint venture AgrEvo, the 1995 Glaxo–Wellcome merger and the 1996 Novartis merger of Ciba and Sandoz.

Table 12.10 *EU vs. US biotech sectors*

Factor	Europe	USA
No. of companies	584	1,308
Turnover (K ECU)	1,158	9,663
R&D expenditure (K ECU)	605	5,859
No. of employees	17,200	108,000

Source: Extracted from Ernst & Young (1996a), table 3.

executives with product development experience, and some former pharmaceutical industry employees are setting up their own companies (Ernst & Young, 1996a).

In the 1990s, Europe has begun to see the emergence of significant numbers of DBFs. The situation varies considerably from country to country. The United Kingdom leads the field and there are increasing numbers of firms in Germany, France, Belgium, and the Netherlands, but almost none in Italy (Acharya, Arundel, and Orsenigo, 1998). Latest estimates suggest that there are approximately 584 DBFs in Europe: 150 in the United Kingdom, 85 in France, 80 in Germany, and 50 in Sweden, with lower numbers in other European companies. Table 12.10 shows that the considerable turnover, R&D expenditure and employment creation of these companies are still dwarfed by their US counterparts (Ernst & Young, 1996a).[15]

The position in Germany is especially interesting since this is widely quoted as a country where DBFs have found it difficult to gain a foothold. Research by Momma (Momma, 1996) has revealed a growing number of firms clustered in regions (e.g. around Munich, Berlin and Heidelberg) where there is a strong academic base. Many of these have been founded in the last six years and finance remains the greatest single hurdle for them to overcome, the German stock exchange remaining closed to such foundations; this situation may be eased by the establishment of EASDAQ in 1996 (Ward, 1996b). Momma identified 110 companies which were equivalent to US definitions of DBFs (i.e., operated in the new biotechnology using techniques based on genetic manipulations). Of these, a smaller proportion were found in the fields of biopharmaceuticals and diagnostics than in the United States or the United Kingdom, and more in areas which reflect Germany's core strength – equipment and the environment (Momma,

---

[15] This compares with 1,308 DBFs in the United States (Ernst & Young, 1996a).

1996). Germany also has the largest cluster of gene-therapy firms in Europe and a fast-developing combinatorial chemistry DBF (Ernst & Young, 1996a).

Comparison between the most widely used technologies of French and US DBFs showed that cell culture, hybridoma, protein engineering, and genetic engineering are common to DBFs in both countries. US firms, however, were well ahead in technologies close to the technological frontier – liposome, gene therapy, antisense and transgenics. As a result, they maintained a considerable capability gap over their French counterparts (Saviotti et al., 1998).

Various studies indicate that the United Kingdom not only has the greatest number, but also some of the most developed DBFs in Europe. Acharya, Arundel, and Orsenigo (1996) found a small group of United Kingdom firms which are close to the US model, aiming to become fully integrated pharmaceutical companies or at least to remain independent operators. Although some of these – for example, Celltech, British Biotechnology, and Cantab – are now well established, many were not founded until the early 1990s and are still at a relatively early stage of development. The greater maturity of British DBFs over their other European counterparts is also signaled by their strong involvement in strategic alliances or joint ventures (JVs) with large firms. Such links are rare amongst French or German DBFs (Estades and Ramani, 1996; Momma, 1996).

Collaborative links with large firms play a very important role in the development and growth of DBFs. A series of case studies of United Kingdom DBFs' strategic alliances (mainly with large US firms) found that in each case the DBFs, in return for finance, provided new product ideas. It was not, however, a one-way exchange of ideas and skills. The larger companies brought knowledge and capabilities about handling the later phases of development and coping with the regulatory authorities. They also brought marketing skills and know-how, and opened access to markets which would otherwise have been closed. Collaborations between partners frequently commenced with the DBF acting merely as a contractor to a large company, but the mutual respect and learning between the partners developed with time, and this frequently led to further rounds of collaboration involving closer partnership.

These case studies emphasized the fact that the DBFs gained more than finance from their participation in these collaborations. Nevertheless, this remained the crucial factor in the alliances. Collaborations with large well established firms gave the DBFs the credibility which was important both for raising bank finance and for developing further collaborations with other companies. Credibility gained from collaborations was also a key element in successful flotation on the Stock Market. Initial collaborations were also important as part of the learning process about how to set up further collaborations. And it was through collaboration that the DBFs learned how to conduct Phase II and Phase III clinical trials. Much of the learning was informal; the DBFs built up their knowledge and competencies through carrying out contract research and through the many day-to-day interactions with their partner's research team (Sharp, Senker, and Galimberti, 1995).

The fact that large US multinationals consider it worthwhile entering collaborations with European DBFs indicates that the latter possess specific knowledge not available in the United States. For instance, 1995 saw the setting up of a joint venture between a United Kingdom DBF and Pfizer to establish a British combinatorial chemistry firm (Ernst & Young, 1996b). Generally, however, the European multinationals have spurned local partners. Hence the recent growth in partnerships between European multinationals and European DBFs, especially in the United Kingdom,[16] may indicate that Europe's small biotechnology firms are beginning to catch up with their transatlantic brothers. These deals were, however, very much smaller in value than the deals concluded between European multinationals and US DBFs (Ernst & Young, 1996b).

Conclusions

The United States had a major advantage over Europe in the first decade of the emergence of biotechnology. Its massive expenditures on basic research on the life sciences and its entrepreneurial culture provided a fertile breeding ground for the new phenomenon of the small biotechnology firm "spinning-off" from university research. US chemical–pharmaceutical multinationals were also quicker than their European counterparts to form affiliations with these small firms, in order to absorb new knowledge and techniques. So was born the dedicated biotechnology firm – the DBF – and it is this which, above all, has pushed forward the frontiers of knowledge and opened up new opportunities for exploitation.

By contrast, the DBF was almost wholly absent from the European scene at that time. Some of these differences have lessened over time. European programs to build up a science base for the life sciences in universities and research institutes and to link that research with industry have paid off. These policies were an important mechanism for organizational learning by Europe's large chemical–pharmaceutical companies. They learned about

---

[16] In 1995, US partnerships accounted for 46 percent of alliances by UK DBFs, compared with 27 percent for inter-European alliances (Ernst & Young, 1996b).

developments in science, about who were the experts (and who was worth recruiting) and about collaboration. It was, however, a very necessary early phase of learning, and it was followed by a subsequent phase in which alliances with the US DBFs were added to the "package," supplementing the knowledge base and strengthening the product portfolio. The research reported in this chapter has shown decisively that the knowledge flows have been clearly from the United States to Europe and that, far from reducing Europe's capabilities and skills, they are adding to them.

After this slow and hesitant courtship, therefore, Europe's chem-ical–pharmaceutical companies now have the in-house capabilities to match global competition. The prognosis for Europe's DBFs, and their capability to match the performance of their counterparts in the United States is less clear-cut. Despite signs of recent growth, they still trail behind. Britain has the largest number of DBFs, some of which are beginning to resemble some of their more sophisticated US equivalents, but DBFs in other European countries are still in their infancy. Four factors, however, suggest they may see rapid development. First, the number of alliances with US and European multinationals is expanding fast and expected to produce substantial learning in the European DBFs. Secondly, the success of the British DBFs could have powerful demonstration effects on the wider European population. Thirdly, improved availability of European invest-ment capital is making it easier for firms to develop. Fourthly, the recruit-ment of experienced managers available as a result of pharmaceutical industry mergers and downsizing is likely to help DBFs achieve greater market success. The similarities which now appear to be emerging suggest that, as biotechnology matures, the industrial structure in the United States and Europe will converge.

If strategic alliances have proved an important route to learning, are they likely to prove only a short-term phenomenon? This seems unlikely. First, the underlying science base is still moving so fast that the need to retain ways of tapping into that base remain crucial to the success of the industry. In line with Gibbons et al.'s (1994) predictions, much of this "new produc-tion of knowledge" is coming from DBFs as well as the academic sector. Alliances will remain an important mechanism for knowledge (and tech-nology) transfer. Secondly, as a result of biotechnology – and particularly the exponential growth in possible drug targets as a result of the Human Genome Project – R&D has become a much more complex phenomenon. As Jurgen Drews says in his latest survey of the industry,

No single company has the in-house capability to accomplish all these facets of drug discovery alone. It will be necessary for the pharmaceutical company wishing to develop drugs rapidly from the Human Genome Project to form alliances with many partners – in both biotechnology and academia – to carry out the process as efficiently and effectively as possible.[17]

In other words, far from the small firm gradually dying away, it would seem that biotechnology has brought a permanent revolution to the industry in the way it handles research and that collaboration is here to stay. If this is the case, it is not too late for the European DBF to catch up.

Support for this view is provided by Acharya, Arundel, and Orsenigo (1996) who point out that views about whether European DBFs can catch up may depend on a proper interpretation of the role of US DBFs. They suggest that the assumption that DBFs are intermediaries which bridge fundamental and applied research is incorrect. Biotechnology innovations are not based on a linear process of technology transfer, from public sector institutions to DBFs and finally to multinationals. Rather,

[in] biotechnology, innovative activities do not appear to be easily separable into vertical stages, going from science to production and marketing. If anything, the division of labor (and therefore cooperation) is generated by the complexity of, and the rapid progress in, the knowledge base. (Acharya, Arundel, and Orsenigo 1996.)

Tendencies towards vertical integration between multinationals and DBFs, as well as the evolution of alliances, thus suggests that DBFs are increasingly performing an exploratory role. The main problem in the development of biotechnology, for both large and small companies, is to integrate different pieces of knowledge from a variety of sources. Far from writing off European capabilities, we should recognize developments for what they are – important building blocks in the learning process. Biotechnology is by no means a mature sector. The race has only just started, and it is too early to judge the outcome.

References

Abbot, A. (1998). "Europe's Life Patent Moratorium May Go . . .," *Nature*, 393(6682) (May 21), 200

ACARD (1980). *Report of the Joint Working Party of the Advisory Council on Applied Research and Development (ACARD), the Advisory Board of the Research Councils (ABRC) and the Royal Society*, London: HMSO (also known as the Spinks Report)

Acharya, R., A. Arundel, and L. Orsenigo (1996). "The Evolving Structure of the European Biotechnology Industry and its Future Competitiveness," a report for the European Commission, Maastricht: MERIT

Bioscan (1994). *Bioscan: The Worldwide Biotech Industry Reporting Service*, Phoenix, Ariz.: Oryx Press (February)

[17] Drews (1993), 1518.

British Biotechnology Group plc (1992). *International Offer of Shares*, 14

Der Bundesminister für Forschung und Technologie (BMT) (1989). *Programmreport Biotechnologie*, Bonn: BMFT

(1993). *Bundesbericht Forschung 1993*. Bonn: BMFT

Chemical and Engineering News (1994) (April 4), 16

Dibner, M. (1991). "Tracking Trends in US Biotechnology," *Bio-Technology*, 9 (December), 1334–7

Dibner, M. and J.A. Bulluck (1992). "US–European Strategic Alliances in Biotechnology," *Biotechnology Forum Europe*, 9, October, 628–35

Dibner, M., G. Stock, and N. Greis (1992). "Away from Home: US Sites of European and Japanese Biotech R&D," *Bio-Technology*, 10 (December), 1535–8

DiMasi, J.A., R.W. Hansen, H.G. Grabowski, and L. Lasajna (1991). "The Cost of Innovation in the Pharmaceutical Industry: New Drug R&D Cost Estimates," *Journal of Health Economics* (June)

Dodgson, M. (1991). *The Management of Technological Learning: Lessons from a Biotechnology Company*, Berlin: Walter de Gruyter

Drews, J. (1993). "Into the 21st Century. Biotechnology and the Pharmaceutical Industry in the next 10 years," *Bio-Technology*, 11, March

Ernst & Young (1994). *Reform, Restructure and Renewal*, 9th Annual Report on the Biotechnology Industry, Palo Alto: Ernst & Young LLP

(1995). *Biotech 96. Pursuing Sustainability*, 10th Industry Annual Report, Palo Alto: Ernst & Young LLP

(1996a). *European Biotech 96. Volatility and Value*, 3rd Annual Report on the European Biotechnology Industry, London: Ernst & Young International

(1996b). *UK Biotech 96. A Supplement to European Biotech 96. Volatility and Value*, London: Ernst & Young International

Estades, J. and S. Ramani (1996). "Technological Competence and the Influence of Decisive Networks: A Comparative Analysis of SMFs in the Biotechnology Sectors in France and Britain," paper presented at the final conference of COST A3 action on Management and New Technology (Madrid) (June 12–14)

Etzkowitz, H (1993). "Enterprises from Science: The Origins of Science-Based Regional Economic Development," *Minerva*, 31(3), 326–60

Galimberti, I (1993). "Large Firms in Biotechnology: Case Studies on Learning Radically New Technologies," DPhil thesis, Science Policy Reseach Unit, University of Sussex

Gibbons, M., C. Limoges, H. Nowotny, S. Schwartman, P. Scott, and M. Trow (1994). *The New Production of Knowledge*, London: Sage Publication

Glaser, V. and J. Hodgson (1996). "Public Companies Spend over $4 billion on R&D," *Nature Biotechnology*, 14(8) 934–35

Goodeve, Sir C. (1967). "A 'Route 128' for Britain?," *New Scientist* (9 February), 346–8

Hall, S. (1988). *Invisible Frontiers. The Race to Synthesize a Human Gene*, London: Sidgwick & Jackson

Hodgson, J. (1994). "The end of French biotechnology R&D?," *Bio-Technology Europroduct Focus*, (Spring), 5

Irvine, J., B.R. Martin, and P. Isard (1990). *Investing in the Future: An International Comparison of Government Funding of Academic and Related Research,* Aldershot: Edward Elgar

Kenney, M. (1986). *Biotechnology: The University-Industry Complex,* New Haven: Yale University Press

Manigart, S (1994). "The Founding Rate of Venture Capital Firms in Three European Countries (1970–1990)," *Journal of Business Venturing,* 9(6), 525–41

McGraw-Hill's *Biotechnology Newswatch* (1983). *Biobusiness World Data Base,* draft report by a US Government Interagency Working Group on Competitive and Transfer Aspects of Biotechnology, Amsterdam: Elsevier

McMullan, E. (1986). "The Economics of Entrepreneurship Education," in W. Brown and R. Rothwell (eds.), *Entrepreneurship and Technology: World Experiences and Policies,* Harlow: Longman, 101–12

Momma, S. (1996). "New Biotechnology Firms in Germany," MSc dissertation, Science Policy Research Unit, University of Sussex (August)

Monck, C., P. Quintas, R. Port, D. Storey, and P. Wynarczyk (1988). *Science Parks and the Growth of High Technology Firms,* London: Croom Helm

Oakey, R., W. Faulkner, S. Cooper, and V. Walsh (1990). *New Firms in the Biotechnology Industry: Their Contribution to Innovation and Growth,* London: Pinter

OECD (1987). *Recombinant DNA Safety Considerations: For Industrial, Agricultural and Environmental Applications of Organisms Derived by Recombinant DNA Techniques,* Paris: OECD

Office of Technology Assessment (OTA) (1984). *Commercial Biotechnology,* Washington,DC: OTA–US Government Printing Office

 (1988). *New Developments in Biotechnology: US Investment in Biotechnology,* Washington, DC: OTA–US Government Printing Office

 (1991). *Biotechnology in a Global Economy,* Washington, DC: Office of Technology Assessment, Congress of the United States

Orsenigo, L. (1989). *The Emergence of Biotechnology,* London: Pinter

Piatier, A. (1984). *Barriers to Innovation,* London: Frances Pinter

Ramani, S (1995). "The French Evolution of Biotechnology," *Bio-Technology,* 13(8), 757–9

Research Fortnight (1996). "Another Chance for Bio-patenting?," October: 16

Rothwell, R., and W. Zegveld (1982). *Innovation and the Small and Medium Sized Firm,* London: Frances Pinter

Sapienza, A. (1989). "R&D Collaboration as a Global Competitive Tactic – Biotechnology and the Ethical Pharmaceutical Industry," *R&D Management,* 19(4), 285–95

Saviotti, P., P.-B. Joly, J. Estades, S. Ramani and M.-A. De Looze (1998). "The creation of European dedicated biotechnology firms," chapter 5 in J. Senker (ed.), *Biotechnology and Competitive Advantage,* Cheltenham: Edward Elgar

Senker, J., P.-B. Joly, and M. Reinhard (1998). "Biotechnology and Europe's Chemical–Pharmaceutical Multinationals," chapter 7 in J. Senker (ed.), *Biotechnology and Competitive Advantage,* Cheltenham: Edward Elgar

Senker, J. and M. Sharp (1988). "The Biotechnology Directorate of the SERC: Report and Evaluation of its Achievements," Science Policy Research Unit, University of Sussex, mimeo

Shackley, S. (1993). "The Regulation of Biotechnology in Europe," DPhil thesis, submitted to University of Sussex

Sharp, M. (1985a). "The New Biotechnology: European Governments in Search of a Strategy," *Sussex European Paper*, 15, available from Science Policy Research Unit, University of Sussex

(1985b). "Biotechnology: Watching and Waiting," chapter 6 in M. Sharp, (ed.), *Europe and the New Technologies,* London: Pinter

(forthcoming). "The Science of Nations: European Multinationals and American Biotechnology," *International Journal of Technology Management*

Sharp, M and Galimberti, I (1993). "Coherence and Diversity: Europe's Chemical Giants and the Assimilation of Biotechnology," case study undertaken for the EC FAST Project: *Coherence and Diversity in Europe's Industrial System,* Science Policy Research Unit, University of Sussex, mimeo

Sharp, M. and P. Holmes (1989). *Strategies for New Technologies: Six Case Studies from Britain and France*, Oxford: Phillip Allan

Sharp, M., J. Senker and I. Galimberti (1995). "Co-operative Alliances and Internal Competencies: Some Case Studies in Biotechnology," Science Policy Research Unit, University of Sussex, mimeo

Sharp, M., S. Thomas, and P. Martin (1993). "Technology Transfers and Innovation Policy: Chemicals and Biotechnology," *STEEP Discussion Paper* 6, Science Policy Research Unit, University of Sussex

Walsh, V., J. Niosi, and P. Mustar (1993). "Small Firm Formation in Biotechnology: a Comparison of France, Britain and Canada," *Technovation,* 15(5), 303–27

Ward, M (1996a). "Another Push to Revise Eurobiotech Directives," *Bio-Technology* 14 (February)

(1996b). "EASDAQ Opens, with Some Unease," *Nature Biotechnology*, 14(9), 1075–76

Webster, A. (1994). "University–Corporate Ties and the Construction of Research Agendas," *Sociology*, 28(1), 123–42

Werth, B. (1994). *The Billion Dollar Molecule*, New York: Knopf

13 The research network and the new economics of science: from metaphors to organizational behaviors

Paul David, Dominique Foray, and W. Edward Steinmueller

Introduction and overview

Effective policies for the promotion of competitiveness and long-term economic growth through innovation in any society must rest upon a clear picture of the ways in which it generates, distributes, and exploits scientific and technological knowledge. Understanding the social norms and economic incentives that govern the behavior of researchers and institutions within this system is essential for evaluating and improving public funding policies and institutional arrangements.

To say that scientific research is an important factor in modern industrial development and long-run economic growth is to state the obvious. Today it is widely recognized and acknowledged that there are complex and dynamic interdependencies linking the progress of basic research with the advance of technology.[1] Indeed, there are numerous indications of a tightening of the inter-connections between research carried on under the institutionalized norms of "open science" associated with university and public research institution-based science on the one hand, and the mission oriented, commercially directed performance of R&D pursued in corporate laboratories on the other. Narin and Olivastro (1992) have documented a significant upward trend in the citations of scientific publications in US patents during the 1980s, and have found that the median age of scientific papers thus cited declined appreciably over the course of that decade. These developments have become a subject interest among economists – as well as among science administrators, university leaders, and business managers.

Although economists continue to strive for a deeper understanding of the insides of the "black box" of technology, it has been apparent for many

---

[1] See David (1992) for a reasonably representative review, and extensive references to literature that goes beyond the now-discarded simple linear-sequence model of the connections between scientific discovery, invention, innovation, and diffusion.

years that far more is understood about resource allocation in the world of proprietary technologies and company-financed R&D than is systematically known about such matters in the world of academic science, and of publicly funded R&D more generally. In view of the foregoing perceptions of the tightening links between technological innovation and academic science and engineering research activities, the comparative lack of attention paid to the incentive structures and institutional constraints affecting the organization and performance of research activities conducted in the latter sphere is both surprising and unfortunate.[2] Within the past decade, however, the situation has begun to change.

Studies of network collaboration involving public institutions (such as some of the contributions to part II of this volume) are part of a larger program of research that is being undertaken to correct the gross imbalance in the distribution of economists' attentions between the Republic of Science and the Realm of Technology. Some among the participants in the broader research enterprise have taken to styling what they do as "the new economics of science."[3] Simply expanding our knowledge about the economics of the pursuit of scientific and engineering knowledge carried on with public sector support is the proximate goal of those endeavors. Yet, it is to be hoped that the findings will lay more solid theoretical and empirical foundations for the formulation and implementation of public policies; of special concern in this regard are questions pertaining to policies affecting the relationships and the balance between technological applications-oriented R&D, on the one hand, and the array of research activities presently subsumed under the rubric "basic science," on the other. In order to provide a broader context for appraising this work, in the next section we set out a brief overview of the conceptual framework, and a number of the pertinent hypotheses that have guided empirical explorations in the "new economics of science."

Sociologists of science, working during the 1960s and 1970s in the tradi-

---

[2] On the need to redress this comparative neglect through research on the microeconomics of resource allocation within publicly supported science, see Dasgupta and David (1987, 1988), David (1994c), and the surveys by Diamond (1996) and Stephan (1996). While not opening the "black box" of the microeconomics of scientific research, Nathan Rosenberg (1982, Chapter 7) has led the modern vanguard calling upon economists to recognize that the state of scientific knowledge should not be treated as exogenous to the economy's development – because the scientific enterprise is being shaped in many ways by technological concerns. This general argument for the "endogeneity" of science had been articulated in Merton's (1938/1970) classic "externalist" interpretation of the scientific revolution of the seventeenth century. But the latter has not gone uncontroverted by historians of science, whereas Rosenberg makes the persuasive point that in the twentieth century the pursuit of scientific knowledge has increasingly been driven by technological aspirations and capabilities.

[3] See Dasgupta and David's (1994) call: "Towards a New Economics of Science" – and web site: <http://www.nd.edu:80/~econsci>, for echoes from the NSF-sponsored conference organized by Philip E. Mirowski and Esther-Mirjam Sent (at the University of Notre Dame) (March 1997).

tion of Robert K. Merton (1973) and his students, have been concerned especially with analyzing institutionalized features of the characteristic reward systems of "academic" science communities; they were occupied in studying the functioning of scientific academies, the role of archival publications and peer review as mechanisms for establishing collegiate reputations, and the influence of these upon the career patterns of scientists.[4] At the same time, contributors to both that stream and the more recent branches of the sociological literature, as well as historians of science who have come under its influence, fully recognize the important part in the functioning of scientific communities that is played by informal patterns of interpersonal communications and social interactions among individual researchers. The relational concept of a "network" has for a long time been central in research on the formation and functioning of "invisible colleges" among the practitioners of science. The network has figured with increasing prominence in efforts to describe and understand the evolving cognitive structures of scientific knowledge. It is employed both metaphorically in historical accounts and analytically in attempts to infer the structures of informal communication, influence and research collaboration from the bibliometric evidence of citation patterns in scientific (and related) publications. D. J. de Solla Price pioneered use of the network concept, both metaphorically and a technique of statistical analysis, and was also responsible for re-introducing and extending the meaning of the seventeenth-century term "invisible college." The latter was coined originally by Robert Boyle in referring to the small group of natural philosophers whose intellectual transactions with one another anticipated the formation of the Royal Society in the early 1660s.[5]

More recently, methodological advances in the bibliometric analysis of collaboration patterns[6] continue to refine the statistical approach initiated by Price (1965), and to probe more deeply into the foundational concept of "collaboration" in scientific publication (see, for example, Katz and Martin, 1995). The concept of "networks" has been considerably extended and elaborated by the particular conceptual and quantitative approach to science and technology studies – the so-called "translation school" –

---

[4] See, for example, Ben-David (1991), Cole and Cole (1967), Cole and Cole (1973); Cole (1978); Crane (1972); Hagstrom (1965); Gaston (1978); Whitley (1984); Zuckerman and Merton (1971); Ziman (1968).

[5] See Price (1963, 1965, 1986, 83ff.). It is interesting to note that around the same time, if not even earlier, the network metaphor was being employed in much the same epistemological context by Kuhn (1962: 7), when he wrote of "the network of theory through which [a scientific community] deals with the world." Numerous works dealing with the existence of informal networks of correspondence and cooperation among the mathematicians, mechanical philosophers, and the followers of Baconian science in the seventeenth century and after, are discussed in David (1995b). Crane (1972) carried the "invisible college" concept forward into studies of academic science communities.

[6] See Hicks and Katz (1995), Katz and Hicks (1994, 1995).

associated with the work of Michel Callon and his colleagues at the Ecole des Mines in Paris.[7]

Studies in the new economics of science, quite naturally, have also begun to concern themselves with both theoretical and empirical analyses of "research networks."[8] This line of inquiry is confluent with the recent direction of attention among economists generally to the implications of social communication behaviors and other non-market transactions among rational agents. We comment below (pp. 314ff.) on this aspect of the growing popularity of applications of "the network metaphor" in economics and other fields of social science research, because it serves to suggest broader areas of application, where the conceptual approaches and techniques developed by recent quantitative studies of collaborative arrangements involving networks of public sector research units and institutions may prove particularly germane.

It should be appreciated that the systematic investigation of European public research networks undertaken by Alfonso Gambardella, Walter Garcia-Fontes and Aldo Geuna, part of which appears in chapters 14 and 15 in the present volume, constitutes a novel and significant departure within the new economics of science program (novelty thus compounded).[9] This work has widened the scope of empirical investigations of "network" phenomena in science, by shifting attention upwards from the behaviors of individual researcher and cooperative research teams, and systematically analyzing concurrent and intertemporal collaborative relationships among larger organizational entities and institutions.[10] The focus of the discussion

---

[7] Callon (1989, 1991, 1992), Callon *et al.* (1992). One device developed in these works is to employ statistical clustering and network-analysis techniques to graphically display the codified knowledge products (scientific publications and patents) upon which bibliometric studies focus exclusively, as being "embedded" in webs of association with individual researchers, entrepreneurs, financial and other agents, as well as material artifacts (see Pestre, 1997). On recent studies that examine the existence and significance of historical precursors of the modern intertwining of interpersonal scientific networks and commercially oriented "networks of innovation".

[8] In addition to the contemporary empirical works noticed below, attention may be drawn to the analytical and historical treatment of networks among research scientists and engineers by Antonelli (1994), Dasgupta and David (1994), David (1995b, 1997b), David and Flemming (1996).

[9] See Gambardella and Garcia-Fontes (1996a, 1996b); Garcia-Fontes and Geuna (chapter 14 in this volume); Geuna (1996); Geuna (chapter 15 in this volume).

[10] This shift parallels recent efforts (for example, by Arora, David, and Gambardella, 1998) to study systematically the determinants of the productivity of research *units*, thereby going beyond the preoccupations of both the literature in quantitative sociology that had focused on the productivity of individual researchers, and related econometric studies by economists of life-cycle publication rates among academic scientists (surveyed by Stephan, 1996). In the older sociological literature, the work of Andrews (1979) and Stankiewicz (1980) represented important exceptions to the general neglect of the performance of research groups and institutions in favor of individual researchers, as the chosen units of analysis.

and econometric analysis in these studies centers upon "research networks" that were formally organized within the context of the publicly funded cooperative R&D programs of the European Economic Community and the European Union. This shifts attention further upwards, from the research group to the level of the institutional participants involved in formal collaborative arrangements that span a range of public and private non-profit entities conducting scientific and engineering research – university departments and research centers, independent institutes, and national and regional laboratories, as well as R&D units situated within business corporations. In effect, they are pioneering a field of investigation for science studies that is in some regards parallel to (but, in other regards, intersects immediately with) the inter-firm agreements and R&D collaborations involving business corporations which have recently become subjects of intense study among industrial organization economists.

The connections that may be drawn between investigations of the economics of publicly supported research networks and those devoted to inter-firm R&D collaborations, such as are presented in chapters 9–11 in this volume, are immediately transparent and so require little further notice here. We shall therefore direct most of our substantive discussion (pp. 314–317) to the need for theoretical and empirical studies of the dynamics of network participation and performance at levels of analysis above that of the individual researchers can expand the agenda of policy issues addressed by the "new economics of science."

Our concluding section emphasizes the particular importance for science and technology policy discussions of explicitly considering the organization norms and behavioral styles characteristic of individuals and teams situated in the institutions (and firms) that participate in collaborative networks. The incentive structures under which they operate, and the nature of the contractual and institutional constraints that are imposed upon the participants, affect the kinds of networks that will or will not be formally or informally constructed. They thus powerfully shape activities and expected performance attributes. Invoking the metaphor of "a network" tends to foster the notion that "a network is a network," – a distinct species of organization whose characteristics are more alike than they are differentiated. That simplification, of course, has shown itself to be very fruitful in stimulating new and important directions for studies of the organization of scientific and technological research. Yet, one must remain wary of the problems that such simplified, homogenized images may create when the network metaphor is employed to suggest that it is just the connections and not the node to which we need to attend; that each and every "connect-able" network would *ipso facto* become endowed with the potential to exhibit the desirable flexibilities, the range of cognitive and

integrative capabilities, the extent and heterogeneity of mobilized member-
ships, all of which are often taken to be the salient and beneficial features
of this organizational "species" – considered *tout ensemble*. We insist, therefore, that as the discussion proceeds further along the path toward R&D
policy-making – whether in the sphere of private industry or in the public
sector – it is essential to avoid the pitfalls that are created whenever meta-
phoric rhetoric is allowed to substitute for explicit and systematic economic
analysis.

The "new economics of science" – the conceptual approach and leading hypotheses

The general conceptual orientation that has been associated with the label
"new economics of science" (NES) emerges from the fusion of insights
drawn primarily from two areas of the social sciences.[11] One set comprises
propositions from the modern economics of information, and industrial
organization analyses of the behavior of agents in games of incomplete
information; the other is the functionalist perspective and empirical findings drawn from the Mertonian tradition of studies of the sociology of scientific institutions.[12]

The aspects of the approach derived from modern industrial organization economics touching upon network behavior will be spelled out more
fully in the following section, but throughout much of the work in the new
economics of science genre, the problems of asymmetric information,
agency and reputation formation are seen as central, and they are compounded by other problems peculiar to the production and distribution of
knowledge – a commodity that has some of the attributes of a pure public
good.[13] Further, the methodological touchstone for this application of eco-

---

[11] In addition to contributions to the present volume, works closely associated with the label
include: Arora (1994), Arora, David and Gambardella (1995, 1998); Arora and
Gambardella (1994, 1997); Cowan and Foray (1996); Dasgupta and David (1987, 1994);
David (1992, 1994a, 1995a, 1995b, 1995c, 1996, 1997, 1998); David and Flemming (1995),
David and Foray (1995, 1996), David, Geuna, and Steinmueller (1995), David and Maude-
Griffin (1995); David, Mowery and Steinmueller (1992); Gambardella (1995); Gambardella
and Garcia-Fontes (1996a). But, see also Trajtenberg, Henderson and Jaffee (1992); Jaffe,
Trajtenberg, and Henderson (1993); and Henderson, Jaffee, and Trajtenberg (1995).

[12] See Dasgupta and David (1994)for further discussion; also David (1997a), for an effort to
formally bridge the work of Merton (1973) by integrating the function of norms governing
communication behavior and entry into invisible colleges with some perspectives from the
"sociology of scientific knowledge," concerning the cognitive content of science and the
epistemological functions of research communities.

[13] The classic pair of pure public goods properties exhibited by knowledge and information
are infinite expansibility or "non-rival" usage, and high costs of assuring exclusive possession. It is important to insist on a sharp distinction drawn between the assertion that such
properties exist, and other, derivative propositions as to whether or not, and in which cir-

nomic analysis has been to insist that explicit notice be taken of the distinctive institutional settings which distinguish public from private sector research activities; and to further differentiate between government procurement and direct research management arrangements, on the one hand, and the devolved state patronage arrangements now typical of university-based science, on the other.

For example, in the latter case the scientific reward system assigns payoffs to researchers and research organizations, according to "priority" in the knowledge production process; being first is all that really matters. This differs markedly from the commercial world where innovators are often displaced by imitators.[14] The formation of networks for the production of knowledge that will be carried on under subscription to the norms of "open science" thus reflects a rather different set of incentives than those driving many commercial joint ventures (JVs), and structuring contractual forms in principal–agent relations.[15]

One implication of this difference is that the cumulative self-reinforcing advantage processes operating in the case of successful university research networks may be what is actually responsible for their observed stability, in contrast to the comparatively high rates of turnover that seem to typify the world of inter-firm R&D collaborations. "Success" in the case of firms is governed by many other considerations than the outcome of their joint research activities, including competitive strategies in other domains that may undermine the perpetuation of those cooperative agreements. In much of the industrial organization literature devoted to explaining such

cumstances, it is feasible and socially desirable to leave the fruits of "science as a process" (i.e. knowledge products) in the public domain rather than allowing their commercial exploitation to be protected as a property right. See David (1994a). This distinction, familiar to economists and intellectual property lawyers, is sometimes obscured, with many resulting confusions. Such have appeared, for example, in Callon (1994).

[14] The difference arises from the implicit role of the priority system as a mechanism for monitoring and enforcing assignment of rights to "moral possession" of intellectual property, and the reputational reward mechanisms based on such claims. This system does not protect the rights of the discoverer to the subsequent use of the discovery, as does the commercial patent system. On the contrary, "public disclosure" is a condition for receiving credit and the world's patent systems generally exclude such scientific discoveries from protection (i.e. facts of nature are not patentable). Instead, the "ownership rights" conferred by the priority system are rights of moral possession which delineate conditions under which credit may be legitimately claimed by individuals and groups for discoveries and inventions, without reference to their intellectual property ownership status. Claims made within this system are not adjudicated formally and are reinforced only by the credits assigned through citation in journals and texts. See Dasgupta and David (1994), and David and Foray (1995) for further discussion and references.

[15] There is some overlap between the incentive systems in the case of "patent races," in which it is also true that there are disproportionate rewards for being first. For a number of reasons, patent races do not seem to dominate the conduct of industrial research, although they are important in a few sectors such as pharmaceuticals.

persistence as can be found in patterns of inter-firm R&D collaboration, the salient explanatory factor is the hypothesized existence of superior "efficiency in contracting."[16] But, quite possibly this phrase should be understood to refer to the greater ease in some cases of finding coalition partners whose long-term commercial strategies are both aligned with, and dominated by, the complementarities achieved through cooperative R&D.

In the latter contrast one can see the influence of perspectives drawn from institutional and organizational sociology and the sociology of scientific knowledge. The many studies undertaken following those approaches have highlighted the role of networks of scientists and technologists in constructing the research agenda, as well as shaping public opinion about scientific and technological issues.[17] Individuals and institutions within the research community are motivated, as are any other work organizations, to create a more comfortable and congenial material and social environment. Through their recurring interactions emerge structures of "social norms" that directly or indirectly serve to stabilize the community and the larger social formations upon which it is dependent.[18] A relevant example of a "social norm" in the present context is the regulation of information exchanges among individual researchers, which is an important issue for the health of institutional groups. Too little information flow increases the risk of duplication and the pursuit of futile lines of investigation, whereas too much information increases the risk that rival research organizations will use the information to win the priority race.

At the level of society as a whole, researchers are seen to have strong incentives to form not only epistemic communities, but communities of professional interest in order to more effectively make claims on societal resources. The social dimensions of the research system thus have a political content that is important to recognize and elucidate for purposes of policy analysis, but which the new economics of science has not yet made headway in examining. One must begin here with simple questions and build towards being able to tackle more intricate issues: are differences in scientific opinion aligned with particular competing networks? Do protracted research disputes take the form of collisions between networks of researchers competing for scarce external resources, or are these sustained because they have other, internal (e.g. "loyalty-inducing") functions? How

---

[16] See, for example, Hladik (1985); Mowery (1988). For dynamic theories of stability in inter-firm agreements, see chapter 10 by Bureth, Wolff, and Zanfei and chapters 9 and 11 in this volume.

[17] On the latter especially, see MacKenzie and Wajcman (1985) for representative contributions.

[18] As is noticed below (pp. 316–17), there are some evident parallels between this sociological formulation and the "coordination equilibrium" approach to the analysis of social norms in the economics literature. See also, in the same vein, the discussion in David (1994b).

does the pre-alignment of networks with respect to particular approaches and research techniques affect the resolution of scientific disputes, and the award of "priority" credits? How, in turn, may public agencies' decisions regarding funding shape the size, structure, and methodological alignment of those networks? Are there ways in which policy-makers can solicit expert scientific opinion (including judgments about directions for funding of future research programs) that will minimize the incentives thereby created for rent-seeking by expert members of experts' networks? Mapping the structure of scientific and technological networks can provide important fundamental data for understanding these processes and, eventually, being in a position better to manage and utilize the competencies represented by "networked" research systems.

The synthesis of these approaches has yielded the following set of basic precepts, working hypotheses, and policy propositions that are distinctive of the positive and normative contributions to the new economics of science (NES). By contrast the older literature on the economics of science has been largely preoccupied with the theoretical implications of incomplete private appropriation of the economic benefits of basic research. It thus focused on the calculation of private and social rates of return on public R&D expenditures, the economic returns from investment of human capital in the form of formal scientific education, the typical life-cycle productivity profiles of academic scientists, and the dynamics of the markets for Ph.D. scientists and engineers (see Dasgupta and David, 1994; Diamond, 1996; Stephan, 1996).

First, for NES it is crucial to study the elaborately articulated set of science institutions that have grown up in the West, and which define *reward structures* to which professional scientists respond. These structures are distinguishable from, and can be distorted by, the material rewards available to scientists and engineers engaged in proprietary, market oriented research. Yet they can coexist with, and inter-connect in some highly productive ways with the networks of innovation and commercial exploitation – even to the extent of engaging some individuals as active participants in both research and the world of business affairs (see David, Mowery, and Steinmueller, 1992).

Second, it is observed that an important feature differentiating the academic and non-military public research from the conduct of R&D in the business sector, and in "classified" military research, is that the *rapid and complete disclosure of new scientific findings* is called for by: (1) the idealized norms of the open science community; (2) the prevailing collegiate reputational reward systems which are based on validated claims to priority in discovery and inventions; (3) the avowed goal of academic research to achieve rapid growth in the stocks of "reliable knowledge" – that is to say, to maximize the expansion of the accessible knowledge base, rather than the flow of economic rents from existing "knowledge assets."

Third, in addition to research findings that readily are rendered in explicit, codified forms, and therefore more easily disseminated through archival publications and other impersonal broadcast media, *tacit knowledge* plays an important role in the practice of science, as well as in technological pursuits. One must observe that because the transfer of research findings is rendered more complicated, and more costly, when it requires arranging also for the interpersonal communication of tacit knowledge (by direct demonstration, training, and the like), such activities can constitute a significant cost element in conducting science even under "open", cooperative arrangements.[19] Indeed, as such knowledge transfers among members of academic research networks take on some characteristics of "reciprocated altruism" – involving either bilateral exchanges in kind (barter), or the construction of more complicated multilateral patterns in the movement of personnel among laboratories. The transactions costs entailed thereby may well exceed even those imposed by the process of negotiating commercial contracts for "training and related services" in order to effect transfers of tacit knowledge that complements the (codified) patent information whose use is licensed among business firms.[20]

Fourth, it is acknowledged that an *internal tension* arises in the practical conduct of academic science as a consequence of the competition for priority in discovery, and the intertemporal implications of the latter in the competition among researcher and research programs for future funding. At the margin the effects of those pressures are not unlike the competition among business firms to secure profits from possession of new knowledge gained through R&D, in that they are likely to encourage secretive forms of rivalrous behavior, rather than fully cooperative "team pooling" of information. This may occur even among research groups that are engaged with one another in ostensibly common collaborative programs.

Fifth, the foregoing propositions suggest a number of general, systemic policy orientations that would be conducive to *sustaining* a rapid pace of science-based technological innovation:

(1) A well functioning set of scientific institutions and organizational policies is one that manages to keep within bounds the tension between

---

[19] See Cowan and Foray (1996), David (1998), David and Foray (1995).

[20] The work of Arora (1991, 1995) points out that many of the inherent difficulties of contracting in tacit knowledge can be overcome by bundling the necessary services with the licensing of patent rights. But, it will be observed that within the academic research community the introduction of such mechanisms would fundamentally transform the nature and functioning of the reward system and the norms of "cooperation."

cooperation in problem-solving and competition among individuals and research units for "priority of discovery." One way in which this is accomplished is by facilitating the spontaneous formation of more extensive and internally diversified, and hence more "collectively competent" (private) knowledge-pooling networks among cooperating researchers. The latter are likely to emerge spontaneously, and operate rather like voluntary "clubs" (whose rules and behavioral norms usually are inexplicit but nonetheless understood) when the participants have been trained and socialized within scientific research communities that share common intellectual and institutional traditions.

(2) An effective institutional infrastructure for science and technological research is one that manages to maintain a proper balance between the requirements of openness and autonomy of investigation (as required for the rapid growth of the stock of knowledge) on the one hand, and the need for delays and restrictions upon the full disclosure of all new information (which facilitate the appropriation of economic returns that are needed to sustain investment expanding the knowledge base), on the other. Movements away from initial conditions of institutional and organizational policies that have favored either of the polar extremes (complete openness, or unrestricted proprietary control) can be expected to elicit an acceleration of the rate of industrially applicable scientific findings.

(3) Direct transfers of knowledge between open science communities and the proprietary R&D organizations of the private business sector are especially problematic to institutionalize. The coexistence of two reward systems within any single organization makes the behaviors of the participants difficult to anticipate, and tends to undermine the formation of coherent cultural norms that promote cooperation among team members. Specially designed institutions – having a research mission distinctive from that of either traditional academic science or profit oriented R&D labs – may therefore be more effective in maintianing such knowledge transfers.

Underlying the patterns of organizational participation in scientific ventures, however, are the myriad linkages among individual researchers, research teams, and the web of professional associations and business connections. Many of these collaborative relationships are at once less formal and more persistent than the contractual coalitional arrangements that may be observed at the institutional level. Corresponding personal network connections exist in the world of private industry, of course, even though there they have generally been ignored, or suppressed by the conventions of analysis in industrial organization economics. The standard modes of analysis treat the participating individuals as "purchased inputs;" a black-box conceptualization of "the firm" is invoked uniformly in analyzing the behavior of organizational entities varying in size and internal complexity, from an owner-operated clothing boutique or a small legal partnership to a multi-plant automobile manufacturing company or a transnational banking and financial corporation. One of the challenges for the new economics of science, then, is to successfully integrate the theoretical and empirical study of research network formations at the micro-level of the individual, the meso-level of the research group, and the macro-institutional level of the university and business corporation.

In other words, in this field as in others, it is the "network," in its variegated forms, that is emerging as a critical conceptual construct and a promising unit for empirical study. Why that should be the case at this moment in time is itself a question that may repay brief further consideration.

The "network" metaphor, and its wonderful career

The "network" appears well on its way to becoming the transcendent symbol and dominant metaphor of the coming "information century." Nowadays it seems that wherever we look, networks can be seen. Some are physical structures that have been on the scene for a very long time – such as electrical and power networks, telephone networks, national highway systems, rail networks (and, in some places, still functioning remnants of the age of canal networks). There also are the newer additions to the set of less tangible network organizations – such as the national postal systems, airline networks, private express mail courier systems, news agency networks (e.g. Reuters), and the broadcast networks, which use the electromagnetic spectrum to transmit signals for land-based and earth-orbiting stations. Still other "networks," increasingly, are perceived as relational patterns of interaction – such as wholesale and retail trade distribution networks, inter-company procurement networks involving contractors and sub-contractors – all of which may be supported by a variety of physical transport layers for messages, people, and tangible artifacts.

The shift taking place in everyday language both mirrors and contributes to the formation of these perceptions. Not so long ago it was almost automatic in the West to allude to machinery as the ideal of the orderly interoperation of the many constituent parts of an intricate social system (such as an economy), or to invoke the smooth meshing of gears as the metaphor of choice when describing the coordination of action in human affairs (in references to a "well-oiled political machine," for example). Now, by contrast, we have more and more regular recourse to a new, contextually flexible terminology to signify the objects and relational entities of the world around us. When describing some intricate technological, economic, social, or political arrangement, we are inclined in place of "clockwork" to say "network," possibly with not much more self-awareness and critical effort than was expended when employing the previous metaphor.

Economists have not been backward in invoking the image of the network as a new mode of achieving order in human affairs, a form of social arrangement that eludes placement within the conventional dichotomy between resource allocation methods that work via the price system and those that depend upon commands. Networks are seen in the recent literature as standing somewhere between markets and hierarchies, and somehow able to produce coherence without contract or command. Workers on the theoretical frontiers of economics, thus, have come to embrace – perhaps too often without explicit recognition – many of the essential ideas about the roles of informal social networks that are commonplace among sociologists, and have long been familiar in the sociology of science.[21] Unfortunately, application of the fashionable term of the moment itself offers little to indicate the particular characteristics, properties, or implications of the economic phenomena (structures and processes) with which it is now being associated. According to the *Oxford English Dictionary on Historical Principles* "Network", simply refers to something that has been wrought in a form resembling a net – and, "a net" is a thing rather difficult to describe or explain to someone who has not already seen one.[22]

The recent linguistic shift, of course, is part of a larger and more profound cultural and intellectual transformation. It seems all but self-evident that popular thought and expression has been encouraged in its use of network metaphors by the startlingly rapid and convergent advances in computer and telecommunications technologies, which have been transforming information industries and the users of their services. Whether in conscious or unconscious signification of the now trendier conceptualization of systems of production and social organization,

---

[21] See, for example, Granovetter (1973, 1978); Granovetter and Soong (1986); for interpersonal networks and the sociology of science, see Luhmann (1984, 1990), Ziman (1984, chapters 4 and 5).

[22] It may be questioned whether the physical analogies evoked by this usage are apposite, inasmuch as nets are utilized to entrap things or screen them out (as in the cases of fish, and insects). The nodes and links play completely passive roles in those physical "nets," whereas the modern usage envisages a complex set of (non-exclusionary) links and interactions among the connected nodes of the "net"-work. Indeed, rather than being conceptualized as a pre-designed and passive instrument, the network increasingly is being viewed as an active agent developing its own objectives and competencies.

economics too has taken up the study of networks – and not only in connection with the fashionable issues of telecommunication and computer network externalities, and questions concerning compatibility standardization.[23] Social networks also are now treated formally in modeling many contexts involving strategic interdependence, where they are represented as conveying information and forging mutual trust through repeated transactions, even when the connections among the players are highly localized and can be presumed to be effected without sophisticated technological support.

Although the economic and social importance of such informal structures has long been recognized in practical affairs, networks appear recently to have acquired new significance as a distinctive organizational form in business. Particularly noteworthy in this connection has been the lively interest among industrial organization economists in understanding the filiation of individual agents, and of firms that have, through cooperative agreements of diverse forms, created networks for purposes of innovation. Imai and Baba (1989), for example, emphasize the role of "transborder networks" of corporate participation in the development of new system products; whereas Teubal, Yinnon, and Zuscovitch (1991) draw the analogy explicitly between the function of a telephone switchboard ("a PBX") and that of the intermediary firms or agents that initially overcome the problem of coordinating independent suppliers of multi-component systems, or facilitate producer–user interactions in the development and marketing of a new technology.

Several lines of inquiry in game theory have converged recently upon local network structures as the terrain for analyzing the equilibrium properties of games characterized by strategic complementaries and interactive learning among the players. Each player is assumed to interact directly with some sub-set of the entire ensemble of players, i.e. those constituting the player's immediate "neighborhood." Interest in this literature has focused upon the strategic problem which arises when (as it is supposed) players cannot adapt their behaviors to deal with each of those neighbors individually but, instead, must select a strategy that is uniform with regard to all their neighbors.[24] The conditions under which the dynamics of local interaction games of this kind will give rise to equilibria characterized by correlated beliefs or behaviors have been studied, both in deterministic decision frameworks, and in dynamic stochastic models that make use of results from Markov random field theory to show how local network externalities

---

[23] See, for example, the general compatibility standards literature surveyed by David and Greenstein (1990) and David (1995a); see Steinmueller (1995) specifically on data communication standards.

[24] See, for example, Blume (1993); Ellison (1993); Bala and Goyal (1995); Morris (1996).

can lead to *de facto* standardization of technologies and the spontaneous formation of conventions.[25]

So, perhaps it really has been the transformation of the artifactual environment by the breathtaking advance of information technology (IT) which has succeeded, where ample opportunities for direct observation of human society hitherto generally proved unavailing, in persuading economists that there was something to the sociologists' perspecive after all. Reared as they were for so long a time on a solid diet of theorizing about the choices made by atomistic individualists, economists have begun at last to acknowledge the importance of human agents being "embedded" in inter-personal and inter-organizational networks. Technological progress can indeed have many unexpected cultural repercussions!

Network competition and cooperation in the European science system: a future research agenda

Scientific and technological research involves the formation of epistemic communities motivated by common disciplinary, topical, or methodological interests. In recent years, however, changes in the missions and in the process of scientific research appear to have altered the relative weight of these motivations. Traditionally, research networks were strongly bound to disciplines where internally developed agendas strongly influenced the direction of search for new knowledge and the evaluation of research results. More recently, research at the interstices and boundaries among disciplines, which we will refer to as "transdisciplinary" research,[26] have proven enormously fruitful for producing conventionally defined scientific outputs and in contributing to the development of commercially useful knowledge. While this change is generally appreciated, policy-makers and social scientists have only recently begun to grapple with the origins and implications of this change.[27]

The growing significance of transdisciplinary research implies that many of the scientific indicators of inputs and outputs presently used are

---

[25] See David (1988, 1993a, 1993b); Kirman (1993); David and Foray (1994a, 1994b); Dalle (1995); David, Foray and Dalle (1998); Ellison and Fudenberg (1995); Morris (1996).

[26] See Knorr-Cetina (1982) for a related approach.

[27] Various reasons have been suggested as origins for the increases in transdisciplinary research: (1) the particular effectiveness of non-traditional technical disciplines in transferring research results and accepting research questions from the experiences of industry (Blume, 1990); (2) the growing significance of computer modeling and simulation in combining disciplinary approaches (Arora and Gambardella, 1994); (3) the convergence of relevant "application knowledge" into a common knowledge infrastructure in areas such as microelectronics (Steinmueller, 1996); (4) the role of some of the new missions that science is being asked to address, such as environmental questions, in motivating research that spans disciplinary boundaries (Metcalfe *et al.*, 1992; Rothwell and Dodgson, 1990).

measuring a mixture of activities: some may reasonably be identified with traditional disciplinary research, while others are associated with transdisciplinary activities. The best means of sorting out this measurement problem will be to examine the pattern of network formation and operation over time, in order to identify the emergence of transdisciplinary research activities and to restructure existing indicators to reflect the new mixture of disciplinary and transdisciplinary research. Quantitative techniques for identifying the reconfiguration of networks are available in the use of cluster analysis and related methods.[28]

Once input and output measures are devised more accurately to reflect the division of activities between disciplinary and transdisciplinary research, a number of important policy-related questions may be addressed. Is the entire European science and technology system developing recognizable specializations in transdisciplinary research? How are these specializations distributed across member state and regional boundaries? What sorts of universities and other institutions are most likely to be sites for substantial levels of transdisciplinary research? What is the interaction between funding sources in the development of such research activities? Answering many of these questions will require a deeper understanding of the formation and operation of networks.

The economics of network formation and development

A deeper understanding of network formation and operation requires examining the underlying incentive structures governing individual and institutional participation in them.[29] The industrial organization literature on the "networked firm,"[30] as well as earlier literature on joint ventures (JVs) and the determinants of industrial contracting behavior, offers several approaches that are worth adapting to the problem of scientific networks.

[28] The methods for analyzing these networks, and associating their characteristics with other social and economic variables in ways that are analytically robust and lead to statistical methods for hypothesis testing has advanced substantially over the past 30 years. These methods are based on work in graph theory (Alba, 1973); cluster analysis (Everitt, 1993); and the econometric methods involving discrete and qualitative variables (Amemiya, 1985; Maddala, 1983; Manski and McFadden, 1981). Examples of the application of these methods in the analysis of the formation and functioning of networks include Antonelli (1994), David and Foray (1994b).

[29] Microeconomic modeling of the behavior of individual researchers with regard to participation, and cooperation in informal networks – such as has been undertaken by Dasgupta and David (1994), and by David (1995c, 1998) – remains in a rather primitive state; it does not address the internal distributional issues and the phenomenon of internetwork competition that are tackled in the study by Garcia-Fontes and Geuna (see chapter 4 in this volume).

[30] The "networked firm" has been considered by many authors including Imai and Baba (1991); Foray (1991); Fransman (1990).

Within the networked firm approach, a key concept is the identification and focus on key "core competencies" that influence decisions about the division of labor between the firm and its suppliers.[31] In scientific networks formed along disciplinary lines, individual reputation standings are established on the basis of contributions to archival publications, professional recognition in appointments of positions in academies, governmental panels, invited presentations at conferences, awards of prizes, and so forth. The processes of institutional or organizational reputation formation are intertwined with those of the individuals associated with their direction, but applications "results" and other dimensions reflecting group performance also enter. Besides, there may be significant lags in the adjustment of organizational reputation to reality, especially in institutional settings where the turnover of personnel is rapid. Problems of the latter sort are especially severe in the less formal network organizations that form for purposes of applied, transdisciplinary research.

Nevertheless, the move from a strong disciplinary orientation to a topical and methodological motivation has made it possible to redefine the role of researchers and research institutions. It is now increasingly possible for some of these participants in the research process to receive professional recognition and research funding for developing specializations that are complementary to the conduct of research in a number of disciplinary areas. The development of high-power synchrotron equipment, for example, has initiated important research in materials science and biology. A "core competence" in the practical applications of synchrotron radiation[32] can thus provide a viable basis for the organization of research facilities and the employment of researchers. The formation of networks employing these "core competencies" may, perhaps, be identified using bibliometric methods, as well as through direct peer evaluations of known types of competencies.[33]

The JV literature (see Hladik, 1985) calls attention to another feature of the network-formation process, the problem of aligning the distribution of inputs with the distribution of returns. In industry, JVs are established as a means for the founding firms to clearly establish the value of contributions

---

[31] See, for example, Richardson (1972); Teece (1987 and 1992) for further development.

[32] Synchroton radiation was first observed by the early developers of cyclotrons as an interesting and potentially hazardous byproduct of their apparatus. Depending on the nature and operation of the accelerator, synchrotron radiation can be generated over a wide range of electromagnetic frequencies at high and controllable intensities. Many of the applications in recent years have involved the ultra-short frequencies commonly known as X-rays.

[33] From a policy viewpoint, one may ask how the development of identifiable core competencies have been influenced by funding patterns and rules about institutional collaboration, the location and concentration of such competencies within the European Union, and the prospects for targeted development of such competencies in other locations within the European Union.

and the entitlements to return. The scientific and technological research system contains a large number of collective activities at both the national and transnational levels that could usefully be characterized as JVs because of pre-agreement about contributions of effort and entitlement to credit from research outputs. A scientific "JV" may be distinguished from an informal network not only through the prior existence of agreements about contribution and credit, but also through the degree of contractual specification or institutionalization of the relationship among researchers, the expected duration of the activity (in time or in relation to funding objectives), and the nature of the venture's funding arrangements (whether it seeks continuing funding from multiple sources or is a "one-program" creature).

The history of industrial JVs indicates that this pattern of organization is risky, with high rates of infant mortality, large numbers of ventures that ultimately prove unsatisfactory to the partners and that are divested, and a few that are very successful. A key factor in the success of such ventures is the time it takes for them to generate returns that are of recognizable value to the founders. Employing the correspondence between industrial and scientific and technical JVs, and using research methods including bibliometric analysis to identify outputs, one may ask whether similar patterns of risk are observable in the latter and, if so, what the distinguishing factors (including the lag between formation and outputs) are in those that do prove successful. Policy implications of this line of research include methods for "benchmarking" the performance of collective scientific activities that have a JV structure, determining the influence of funding patterns and rules on their formation, and addressing the prospects of targeted efforts to create such JVs.

The industrial structure literatures dealing with regulation theory and "mechanism design" have highlighted the role of principal–agent relationships in the division of labor among companies.[34] In the science and technology system there are several types of principal–agent relationships. The most obvious of these is the relationship between the funding agency and

---

[34] This literature (see Levinthal, 1988; Shavell, 1979, for an introduction), draws attention to the possible divergence of interest between the principal who contracts with the agent to perform a service. The principal's interest may be characterized as receiving the highest level of service for the least cost. The agent wishes to maximize returns in providing the service, which can be achieved by maximizing the spread between their costs of performance and the consideration paid by the principal. Conflicts arise when one or the other party gains at the expense of the other – e.g. the agent maximizes the spread by reducing the quality of the service without reducing the fee expected from the principal. This problem may be partially addressed by careful design of the rules underlying the contract; however, such rules may be expensive to craft and enforce. "Repeat play" is another possible means to reduce the opportunistic behavior of agents: the conditionality of future contracts on past performance will narrow the divergence of principal and agent interests.

the recipient, but there are also important principal–agent relationships at other levels of the system. Researchers are employed within institutions that are often directly responsible for accounting for research performance to the funding source. Similarly, within scientific networks, prior agreements among participants about the distribution of credit for outputs may create principal–agent-type problems in the incentives facing particular members of the network.[35] There are a number of methods for illuminating these issues using bibliometric data and data on participations of institutions in research contracts.

The most straightforward of the implications of the principal–agent relationship to test is the influence of "repeat play" on the stability of established networks. The empirical studies by Garcia-Fontes and Geuna (1998), and by Geuna (chapter 15 in this volume) are a contribution to this approach, in showing how one may measure and test statistically the persistence of particular networks within the European science and technology system. In addition, it is possible to compare the identities of funding applicants with the credits assigned to research outputs, the mechanisms by which research institutions deal with the problems of researcher non-performance or departure, and the rules governing the transfer of research projects or funding within networks after funding. Each of these research areas offers opportunities for policy-relevant research addressing the trade-offs between network stability and policy actions: are the terms and conditions of national and regional funding programs, and their interactions, on balance supportive or disruptive of the stability of networks?

The economic welfare implications of network stability, however, are not unambiguous. A stable network may reflect efficiency in agreements, "contracting efficiency" in the division of labor. But, this efficiency gain may be offset by a loss of research variety if the stability of the network relies upon a particular division of labor among participants. Moreover, the stability of networks may be reinforced by other mechanisms than contracting efficiency, conferring further ambiguity as to whether stability is socially desirable. The subject of the next focus area, the Matthew effect, illustrates this problem in greater depth.

The Matthew effect and mechanisms of cumulative advantage

An alternative approach to the issue of network formation and stability is suggested by considering generalizations of the so-called "Matthew effect" in science. This was first noted by Merton (1968), who used the term to

---

[35] While prior agreement on the assignment of credit produces principal-agent-type problems, attempts to reach *ex post* agreements on attribution of credit among research team members have a long history of producing controversy.

highlight and account for the fact that distributions of scientific recognition and marks of achievement are extremely left-skewed.[36] Distributions of scientific publications (and citations) exhibit the same phenomena of concentration and persisting stratification. Approximately half of the papers published in a given field are contributed by 10 percent of the scientists, and the top 20 percent of researchers account for 65–75 percent of the published "output" in that field. The Matthew effect – or, more generally, the operation of self-reinforcing, "cumulative-advantage" processes in the allocation of research resources – has been proposed to explain the progressively increasing concentration of scientific publication that is observed over the life of scientific cohorts in specific fields.

A central tenet of the cumulative-advantage hypothesis is that scientific recognition is rewarded with greater access to research resources, which in turn reinforces the initial recognition and provides still greater access to research resources. Researchers and research groups that have established higher reputational standings within their respective disciplines are further advantaged in competing for incremental resources.[37] This would contribute to tendencies to even greater polarization and stratification of research communities producing, on the one hand, a layer of scientific "elites" that are highly regarded, well equipped, and secure in pursuing long-term projects and, on the other, a larger mass of researchers who are indifferently regarded, modestly supported, and chained to shifting short-term objectives.

The Matthew effect raises many issues about the functioning of the resource-allocation system for scientific and technological research. Why should there be such great inequality in scientific productivity and recognition, fame, and other rewards to the prolific few? Are those prizes necessary incentives or simply a kind of economic rent that is being reaped by the exceptionally talented – or, perhaps, the exceptionally lucky? Does it really reflect a highly unequal distribution of underlying talents? Are we justified in supposing that the prevailing system of allocating recognition and material resources on the basis of performance-based reputations is identifying the most talented researchers? Although efforts have been made to

---

[36] Robert Merton's (1968) description of the self-reinforcing processes affecting collegiate reputation among scientists as the "Matthew effect" is a New Testament allusion (Matthew, 13:3 and 25:29): "For unto everyone that hath shall be given, and he shall have abundance; but from him that hath not shall be taken away even that which he hath." Merton's students (Cole and Cole, 1973; Zuckerman, 1977; Gaston, 1978) reformulated the Matthew effect in broader terms, proposing that self-reinforcing processes affect productivity as well as reputation, making the Matthew effect largely synonymous with the "cumulative-advantage" hypothesis which has been summarized by Allison, Long, and Krauze (1982).

[37] See, for example, David (1994c) for further discussion and references.

address these questions in regard to the performance of individual researchers who have remained in the academic science system, far less is known about scientists who have moved between the ivory tower and the corporate lab. Moreover, we are only just beginning to ask comparable questions about the distribution of competencies and performance indicators among multi-agent research units. It does appear that there are, indeed, pronounced differences among research units in their productivities gauged in terms of current rates of scientific publication and reputational standings based upon past publication activity (see for example, Arora, David, and Gambardella (1995, 1998). If these correspond to the variation of core competencies among them, then institutions and social norms in science might be said to be functioning well, in the sense that the highly productive units in the population have been selected and given the resources to realize their potential.

Nevertheless it is also possible that some of the disparities of this kind may be generated by failures of the attribution mechanisms upon which the science reward system, and the quantitative measures of productivity, rely. In the case of individual researchers, the "new economics of science" literature has highlighted some potentially serious problems with the existing attribution mechanisms that credit published "contributions" to the prolific elite. In fact these contributions depend upon the complementary efforts and abilities of the supporting cast – the myriad of trained scientific co-workers who perform as research associates, postdoctoral students, technical and administrative assistants, and as teachers responsible for preparing new cadres of researchers (see Dasgupta and David, 1994; and David and Maude-Griffin, 1995). These co-workers are not being evaluated on the basis of publications in scientific journals. This problem is not only one of social equity in recognizing the contribution of co-workers supporting the operation of research networks, it is also an important issue in evaluating the institutional structure of the scientific and technological system. The complementarities derived from the presence and contributions of colleagues – locally, regionally, nationally, and across national boundaries – is an important issue for the allocation of research funding. The relative contributions of such complements may be highly attenuated by geographical or institutional distance in some instances, while being much broader in others. Identifying the conditions where complementary relationships are highly localized, and where they span institutional, regional, and national boundaries is an essential step in describing the likely outcomes of funding patterns and rules governing inter-institutional collaborations.

The contributions of Garcia-Fontes and Geuna, and other work in the "new economics of science" genre,[38] call attention to the point that public funding agencies face an inherent long-run vs. short-run trade-off in allocating public funds for research. Were they to seek to maximize short-run research productivity, in a way that would deliver "successes" for which those responsible in the agency could justly claim political credit, they would be led towards concentrating resources on institutions and research units that already possessed demonstrable research capabilities, and hence offer the sponsoring agency a greater degree of certainty about obtaining some positive results. Such a strategy has the effect of reinforcing and amplifying the heterogeneity of initial capabilities, and tends to widen already existing "competence gaps" amongst research institutions. This may reduce long-run scientific research productivity because many institutions with satisfactory, or even greater, potential for research will be discouraged. Thus, national science policy objectives, and ECE policy guidelines for cooperative research programs (and, in the case of the European Union, the ways in which the latter interact with the behaviors of the national R&D funding agencies) will have an impact upon the formation of scientific research networks in Europe. For example, at the simplest level of analysis, if the European Union seeks to support long-run goals, networks will include both prominent and less prominent institutions. This is because the presence of the latter will be thought to increase the odds of obtaining the contract. Conversely, if the Union has short-run objectives, there will be a tendency towards smaller gaps in capabilities between members of any network, and a more marked stratification of the population of networks into high- and low-status groupings of scientific research institutions and business firms.[39]

The preceding remarks can draw for support upon the findings that a significant positive relationship exists between past funding levels and the probability of receiving additional research funding in the EU's BRITE-EURAM program. Moreover, in the most recent of the detailed studies of the experience of research units participating in an Italian (CNR) publicly funded biotechnology research program, undertaken by Arora, David, and

---

[38] Garcia-Fontes and Geuna (chapter 14 in this volume), Geuna (chapter 15 in this volume). See also David and Maude-Griffin (1995) and Arora, David, and Gambardella (1999), for works that examine the issue, and its potential quantitative importance by means of simulation modeling, and in the context of empirical investigation of public agency funding decisions, respectively. Arora and Gambardella (1997) extend the point, by a theoretical analysis showing that policies encouraging industry to fund academic science would be likely, for informational reasons, to have the effect of further amplifying the bias of public agencies to concentrate resources in the hands of researchers with "proven capabilities" to deliver quick and predictable results.

[39] For a sketch of a formal model of stratification in research network formation, see David (1995b), in which ideas on "convergence clubs" from Quah (1994) are put to use in a context that, arguably, is more appropriate than the one in which they originated.

Gambardella (1995, 1998), indications were found that the size of project budgets requested and granted was positively related to measures of the units' scientific reputational standing, which also positively affected the likelihood of their selection for funding under the program, and the probability of their funding. Perhaps most important, the estimated magnitudes of the parameters in that model imply that if cumulative advantage mechanisms were not operating, size-adjusted levels of funding among the research units would tend to even out over time.

What has been missing from all the empirical studies discussed here, however, is the ability of the econometrician to control for differences in the larger funding situation of the research groups that are under examination. This is the context shaped by the interactions of national and EU public funding, as well as some projects that have brought project support from industrial collaborations and contracts. A more comprehensive approach to data collection and analysis is therefore essential in future studies of this kind. It is no longer appropriate, if it ever was, to study the national and EU systems as two separate entities; they are becoming increasingly interrelated, and are exerting unintended as well as intended effects upon each other. Elucidating these is therefore an important future task for both modeling and empirical studies of the European science and technology system.

National and transnational funding of scientific research networks

This will call for a foundational understanding of the incentive structures and system relationships guiding the operation and evolution of public research programs and institutions that are funded at the national level. Starting from the current literature (such as Senker, 1991; Picard, 1990; Meyer-Kramer, 1992), it is necessary first to identify specific incentive mechanisms operating at the national level that interact with EU research funding and administrative rules. A particular direction of inquiry in such work is to determine how the funding patterns and rules of national systems contribute to the formation and stability of European research networks.[40] For example, do national funding systems that emphasize the assembly of domestic competencies cut against the participation of researchers in international research networks? Are there meaningful distinctions between the institutional incentives created by these national systems for the development of particular types of competencies?

---

[40] An exploratory effort to do this has been made by David, Geuna, and Steinmueller (1995), on the basis of limited access to unpublished EU Framework Programs statistics made available to the authors through the STOA office of the European Parliament, and other national data sources. Changes in EU data access policies would permit much more systematic investigation of the interactions between national and regional funding policies.

Answering either of these questions requires working backward from an identification of patterns of scientific and technological networks to the institutional differences across countries, taking into account the effect of cumulative advantage processes such as the "Matthew effect" in academic science. Traditional indicator data may reveal that a particular country has developed an important specialization in a particular area of research. This indication may be the result of several different mechanisms. It may reflect an early entry of particular national research institutes into that area, and the subsequent reinforcement of their leading position (and ability to attract a network of participating researchers) through the usual operation of positive feedback mechanisms involving learning and reputation-based access to national R&D resources. Alternatively, it might be the intended product of deliberate national efforts to assemble a special scientific and technological competence in the area in question – which could be identified and distinguished from the former process through careful examination of the history of network development. Then again, the comparative international salience of a nation's research institutions in a particular field could arise from the unintended interaction of national R&D funding programs that developed "core competencies" in those units, enabling them subsequently to exploit the opportunities created subsequently by applications oriented regional R&D programs. In short, identifying the mechanisms generating traditional indicators of differential research capability are far more important for assessing and formulating policy than are the indicators themselves.

In recent years, the funding of national science efforts has been put under increasing stress by the efforts to reduce total government expenditures throughout Europe, and by the growth in competing claims for public resources. Examining how these fiscal stresses have been translated through specific national funding systems is crucially important for understanding the future health and performance of European science and technology. Fiscal stresses have been translated into funding priorities and rules that are only partially related to the changing missions of the universities and its connection with the issues of network formation. How have these changes in funding priorities and rules influenced the formation and stability of research networks, as well as the incentives and trade-offs at individual and institutional levels? What useful lessons can be learned from the comparative experience of different national funding systems in responding to fiscal stress that could inform future policies if such stress continues or accelerates (as appears likely)? Given the importance of these questions, it seems remarkable how little systematic attention has been paid to them at the European level.

Bridging scientific networks

Direct transfers of knowledge between open science communities and the proprietary R&D organizations of business are especially problematic to institutionalize, however much they are called for by policy-makers. Mixing reward systems within a single organization makes the behaviors of the participants difficult to anticipate and undermines the formation of coherent cultural norms that promote cooperation among team members. Consequently, it is worth considering the possibility that specifically designed, "bridging institutions" – having a research mission distinctive from that of either traditional academic science or profit oriented R&D labs – may be more effective in effecting such knowledge transfers. Europe has led the world in the establishment of institutions that, among other missions, are meant to perform bridging functions between academic and private business research networks. Such organizations include the Fraunhofer Gesellschaft in Germany, the CNRS in France, and the CNR in Italy. More detailed evaluations are needed of the strengths and limitations of these organizations as "gateway nodes" linking distinctive networks, and it is especially important to examine the extent to which their success may depend upon the specific adaptations of the internal career incentives provided to participating researchers by firms and universities in their respective national settings. Such adaptations may contribute strongly to their success *in situ, while limiting the scope for replicating that success* by simply copying their internal organizational forms and procedure in other national contexts.[41]

The interaction between public and private R&D networks is particularly important for the issue of knowledge transfer. Studies of the relations between public and private research institutions[42] have indicated that one of the difficulties of this transfer process is that different research organizations may develop approaches and descriptive language for research problems that differ enough for transfer to be impeded. This is directly germane to the interactions between private and public research networks, because the participants in such networks generally are not "freelance" research consultants but, instead, at any given stage in their careers have more persistent forms of commitment to one or another on-going organizational entity. It therefore becomes interesting to ask: what patterns in the duration of participation in a particular line of research, by public and private

---

[41] See David and Foray (1995) on the general point about the historical, path-dependent character of national institutional infrastructures, and the limitations this imposes on the usefulness of a "mix-and-match" approach to improving national technological innovation performance by importing so-called "best-practice" features from various national "ecologies."   [42] See OECD (1984); Stankiewicz (1985, 1986).

networks, are associated with the formation of effective "bridges" between them? Can we detect patterns of mobility between public and private research networks that suggest opportunities for enhancing the transfer of knowledge? Are public policies that have increasingly emphasized university–industry collaboration changing the pattern of industry or university scientific publication or patenting activities? Can measures of research output be used to characterize the division of labor between public and private research networks? Is it true, for example, that joint participation of university and industry researchers in a network leads to an increase in publications by the former and patents by the latter relative to the baseline activities of university and industry research activities? To what extent are these networks developing similar, overlapping, and possibly duplicative, competencies (as may be revealed by close examination of patterns in their respective scientific publication and patenting activity in specific areas), rather than maintaining distinctive but complementary specializations?

Within Europe, the development of such bridging functions remains uneven and it is possible that there are significant opportunities to improve European cohesion by increasing our understanding of how the existing knowledge-transfer mechanisms work, including the degree to which they are abetted or hampered by labor market regulations and features of the intellectual-property-rights regime affecting trade secrecy. More concerted inquiries directed along these and the foregoing lines would yield useful insights into the design of appropriate policies for jointly augmenting and increasing the accessibility of the new additions to the distributed knowledge base in science and engineering that the growing multiplicity of networks can contribute.

Science policy and the limitations of metaphor

As is well known, the study of the economics of science and technology has freed itself from the grip of a heuristic device, the old "simple linear model." One formulation of this conceptual construct was the "pipeline" representation of the generation of technological innovations: an initiating process of knowledge creation was carried forward by the flow of information through a sequence of distinct (but linearly connected) institutional "containers" – pure science in university laboratories, applied science in departments of engineering and company research groups, technical development in the design and production engineering divisions of firms that would use or market the new processes and products, and so on. The descriptive deficiencies of this hydraulic fantasy were manifold. It held "science" in the exogenous part of the schema, seemingly isolated from market influences affecting the motivation for research and the provision of R&D resources; it ignored the role of technologies in shaping aims, methods, and the research productivity of both "basic" and "applied" research; and it particularly suppressed the systemic contributions of exploratory research by-products in the form of trained scientists and engineers, and novel research instruments.

Set against the background of all those distortions, the new metaphor of scientific and technological research as a multi-node, multi-channel network process offers an attractively flexible and potentially more accurate heuristic framework. In this new representation, institutional boundaries can be left fuzzy rather than being sharply drawn; feedback loops abound, and so everything can be seen to depend upon everything else, in at least two ways. This certainly provides a more suitable guide in quantitative assessments of the economic returns on research activities of various kinds: direct effects, indirect effects, and feedbacks can be taken into account, or the biases due to their omission can be readily identified in attempts to evaluate the long-run societal payoffs from basic research. Still other conceptual advantages are afforded, in the natural support that such pictures give to the analysis of issues raised by the phenomena of "network externalities," the tension between uniformity and diversity, the importance of complementary investments, the creation and strategic placement of knowledge-transfer channels, and many other policy-relevant topics. But that is not the end of the new metaphor's appeal: the network representation suggests opportunities for applying sophisticated mathematical methods of analysis (such as branching theory, and percolation theory), and of mobilizing the powerful statistical techniques for exploratory data analysis (such as statistical network and cluster analysis) to uncover some important properties that may be of critical importance for understanding the economic fundamental and practical realities of systems of knowledge production and distribution.[43]

There are however, potential problems of which we must be wary. These lie along the tempting but slippery slope between the use of "the network" as a heuristic relational representation (for purposes of studying the intellectual and organization of science and technology), and the acceptance of network metaphors as the guiding rationale for resource allocation and policy initiatives affecting the funding and organization of scientific research. There are two specific dangers that deserve at least brief notice in the present connection. One comes from idealizing networks as a single

[43] On the application of Markov random field and percolation models in the context of competitive diffusion of technology standards, see David and Foray (1994a, 1994b); the use of these frameworks for stochastic modeling of interpersonal communication networks in scientific research communities is explored in David (1998).

organizational form, the other from presenting that form as superior to other, more institutionalized modes of organizing the production of scientific and technological knowledge. We shall take these up in turn.

The first of the paths towards policy error follows from excessive abstraction, seeing "the network" as an idealized organizational form with certain generic capabilities, and so neglecting to perceive that networks are not one thing, but many things. In actuality, the dynamics of their development and the ways in which they channel and augment the capabilities of the participating agents will depend upon the particular rules, the common understandings, and the shared experiences and initial competencies of their membership. Industrial organization economists have made great progress in recent years in moving beyond the abstraction of "the firm," and even beyond the construct of "the representative firm". They now recognize the enormous heterogeneity in firms' "competencies," and appreciate the roles of "corporate cultures" and the historical idiosyncrasies of the processes through which the latter are formed. Network relationships, however, whether among firms, academic research groups, or sets of individual researchers, being bonds of a "weaker" and potentially more transient form, are inherently more difficult to study through "institutionalized" sources. Consequently, as fashionable as it has now become to speak of R&D networks and "networks of innovation" in generally approving terms, their evolution and performance have not yet been made the subject of extensive systematic studies in the way that the universities, and the business companies of different countries have been, and the empirical groundwork upon which to erect classification schemes still remains to be provided. "Network" cannot be read as labeling *an* organizational instrument for the conduct of research; rather, it might be suitable as the label for a large bag containing a highly variegated class of tools, each needing much more detailed descriptive tagging.

The point to be made here about the elaboration of such taxonomies is, simply, that their existence would serve forcibly to remind us that we ought not proceed on the casual assumption that "a network is a network". We should hardly expect that the same capabilities, or the same cost structures, will characterize all members of the *genus* "network." After all, the latter comprises, at one end of the spectrum, the inter-personal network relationships that form spontaneously and can persist with scant incremental administrative monitoring or control functions. These are exemplified by the shadowy circles of mechanical philosophers, instrument-makers, chemical alchemists, and "projectors" of evanescent commercial schemes whose existence has been discerned by historians of mid-seventeenth century science in England, and by today's small, loose cliques among academic scientists who periodically attend many of the same conferences and communicate via e-mail in the interim. The incentives for, and results from, formation of those sorts of networks are likely to differ markedly from those found toward the opposite, more structured end of the spectrum – i.e. among the various contractually specified agreements involving teams of university-based researchers and their respective laboratory facilities, or on-going joint research consortia among corporations, or formal R&D projects that engage research personnel from various public institutions and design and production engineers from several manufacturing firms for fixed durations.

Public policy programs aiming at encouraging the formation of "networks" need to have in mind which among the wide array of such formations, and what peculiar "network processes and outcomes" it is that are believed to be especially deserving of subsidization. Very specific purposes are likely to require specialized competencies and customized organizational structures – "horses for courses", as the English colloquialism puts it. But, from a very broad welfare-analytic perspective it seems clear enough that quite familiar general arguments in the economics of R&D should also apply: open network organizations, in which knowledge is not made proprietary and the core participants operate under incentive structures conducive to the rapid and complete disclosure of new knowledge, will be those whose organizational form tends to generate the maximum spillovers, *ceteris paribus*. Consequently, they should have prior claim for public support over other, "knowledge-value-appropriating" network structures.[44]

The second source of potential misuse of the network metaphor in policy discussions is the presentation of "the network" as a spontaneously emergent, and extremely plastic alternative organizational form that can, and in many situations should, supplant apparently more inflexible, formally structured, institutional entities in which scientific and technological research has previously been carried on. There is a fashionable argument today that Western societies are already embarked upon a transition to a new dominant mode of knowledge production – "Mode 2", as it has been dubbed in the work of Michael Gibbons *et al.* (1994) – the morphology of which is neatly conveyed by the network metaphor. This new mode of knowledge production is described as being organized in externally oriented integrative and interactive units, which are well suited to transdisciplinary inquiry, owing to the fluidity with which research groups can be assembled, reconfigured, and disbanded. It is thus favorably contrasted with the image of an antecedent regime ("Mode 1") based upon freestanding, quasi-auktarkic research entities: the corporate central research laboratories with their "not-invented-here" mindsets, discipline-bound academic departments, and specialized, single-purpose scientific institutes.

---

[44] This is the burden of one of the policy positions advanced by David, Mowery, and Steinmueller (1992), as well as by David and Foray (1995).

In the vision of some scholars, the future clearly lies with the "post-modern" research system, and the withering, or thorough reform of the latter, "old modern" system should be no cause for concern. Indeed, in the future scenarios painted by Michael Gibbons and his co-authors, efforts to preserve Mode 1 in the face of the imminent emergence of Mode 2 are depicted as definitely retrograde:

An alternative model [to "large university-based institutes with tenured faculty," or mission-oriented government laboratories, and "permanent research units with tenured research staff set up for specific monocultural research"] might involve the creation of lean "centers" employing few administrators with a budget to stimulate *networks of innovators,* in units attached to diverse institutions, agencies or firms. They would be periodically evaluated in terms of their effectiveness in process management. When their jobs were completed, or when decreasing returns became evident they would be disbanded ... any policy that tended to entrench institutions, or encourage autarkic attitudes, is anachronistic. (Gibbons *et al.,* 1994, 162. emphasis added)

How are we to interpret a proposal such as that? If it is read as calling for experimentation in *a new organizational paradigm for science-based innovation,* then one certainly has to agree with the critical point made by the historian of science, Dominique Pestre (1997), regarding the proclamation of "Mode 2" as the newly emerging, post-modern way of producing scientific and technological knowledge. There really is nothing new to the history of the modern West about the involvement of scientists in networks that could be described as heterogeneous, transdisciplinary, organizationally diverse, and built upon multiple criteria of quality control. Granted that the rhetoric associated with the rise of institutionalized science has emphasized its conduct in contexts of cultural excellence and distinction, and accepting that the announced academic research goal of pursuing knowledge as an end in itself presented science as qualitatively allied with humane studies, as mathematics was in the tradition of the Renaissance, the reality – as historians of science have been telling us for some time – was, as it continues to be, the engagement of researchers from that world in a variety of "contexts of application."[45]

---

[45] Pestre (1997, 165–6) notes that during the seventeenth and eighteenth centuries the networks of "Baconian," or "practical science" centered in London took different, and more immediately commercially oriented forms from those in France, where *les académiciens* were part of the state apparatus. In the latter context, the practitioners of "mixed mathematics" worked directly with military and civil royal engineers in mapping the royal kingdom, improving astronomically based techniques of maritime navigation, and the interchangeability of parts for military production; whereas Buffon, Réaumur, and others from the academy claimed to possess the scientific means to explain and partially codify common practices and knowledge of an artisanal nature, and on that basis suggested ways that the entire process of production could be rationalized (against the narrow interests of the guilds) for the benefit of the realm as a whole.

Yet, there is reason enough to suppose that the proponents of Mode 2 are historically sophisticated and aware of the antecedent existence of networks linking "contexts of application" with research activities and researchers on the frontiers of scientific knowledge. Correspondingly, one must infer that what they have in mind is truly a far more radical organizational transformation. Proposals such as the one quoted above, therefore, should be read as venturing beyond speculation about future trends to recommend the deliberate and continuing withdrawal of public support from the main elements of the institutional infrastructure undergirding the science base in most of the world's advanced industrial economies; and the redeployment of those resources through "networks," which would mobilize transdisciplinary research teams at transient "sites of application" in the public and private sectors.

Yet, in this vision of a "flexible" future, the invocation of the power of the network is one that is essentially magical. There is no analysis of how the new equilibrium would come to be stabilized, or what the resulting system would look like. That its organizational and behavioral features would be quite different from the initial conditions seems undeniable, for, the "networks of innovators" recruited by those tightly budgeted administrators operating from "lean centers" are not supposed to pay the overhead support costs of the facilities and staffs of university and corporate laboratories upon which their teams will need to draw – lest they contribute thereby to persisting institutional "entrenchments." Organizations of the favored (Mode 2) form can be assembled and, as has been evident, will function successfully in a symbiotic, parasitical manner so long as their (Mode 1) institutionalized hosts remain adequately nourished from other sources. But, the strategy of promoting the multiplication of lean and impermanent network organizations *at the expense* of those "hosts" is surely likely to have perverse consequences, and prove eventually to be infeasible.

Only a little analysis of the economics of organizational behavior is needed to see how insubstantial are the vague, chimerical conjurings up of "networks of innovators" as the solution to the serious challenge of maintaining creativity in science systems where the work of people with long and highly specialized training, who require increasingly complex and costly durable facilities, must be paid for as well as managed in a coordinated fashion. In the world according to Gibbons *et al.* (1994), would not the acceleration of already severe financial pressures push those responsible for the running of high fixed-cost organizations such as universities and large-scale research establishments, whether operated by business corporations or managed as public laboratories, soon to insist that "external" personnel attached to them in any way bring corresponding contributions to the overhead?[46] Similarly, pressure would mount to restrict the collaborative freedoms of those researchers who drew "inside" support – lest they participate in external network projects that competed with, or simply diverted their effort from, grants and contracts that would help pay for their own institutions' fixed costs.

Perhaps, then, the "networks of innovation" would tend to disconnect themselves from academic institutions, whose maintenance of libraries, discipline-based departments, and attendant administrative cadres geared to fulfilling their educational missions, have come to be widely regarded as hindering the growth of transdisciplinary inquiry within their immediate precincts, and as adding unnecessarily to the fixed costs of research. Would the separation of teaching from innovative problem-solving not be detrimental in the long run to the effectiveness with which both activities could be carried on? Would not the withdrawal of public patronage from academic research institutions and institutes that preserved and transmitted the ethos of "open science" not foster greater recourse to increasingly restrictive intellectual property mechanisms for appropriating some part of the economic value flowing from the work of those on their payrolls. Worse yet, would it not encourage secrecy and direct exploitation by university-owned "consulting firms"? Of course they would, for trends in these directions are already discernible around us.[47]

In short, the "networking" metaphor has been too casually appropriated on behalf of ill-conceived science and technology policies that would aim to raise the degree of *connectivity* within the system while jeopardizing the continued functionality of its *nodes*. Indeed, on closer analysis the features of the *equilibrium* structure that one can envisage for the brave new world of knowledge production dominated by "Mode 2" appears less and less to be those characterizing a dense network of recurring interactive relationships among differentiated and complementary institutional research contexts. Rather, it seems more closely akin to something resembling competitive "spot markets" for consultants' services, and a market for "cut-price research motels" where temporary lodgings can be found for the transdisciplinary teams assembled by administrator–contractors operating from those "lean centers." The accompanying structure of incentives facing the researchers, and the "know-who brokers" and "boffin-contractors" – who are to provide the necessary intermediating services of "temporary help agencies" in this flexible scientific labor market – is not likely to be such as would encourage commitment to extended programs of exploratory

---

[46] For an introductory discussion of manifestations of these issues at the global level, see David (1997b), David; Foray, and Steinmueller (1997).

[47] See, for example, David (1996) for some evidence on restrictions of US university-based researchers' freedom to disclose results in the context of university–industry collaborative research centers.

investigation. Nor, indeed, do we have any reason to suppose it will be conducive to significant intellectual risk-taking on the part of researchers, obliged as they would be to market their most proven forms of expertise in one evanescent "applications context" after another, without the measure of professional security that in a past era had been afforded by the "anachronism" of tenured faculty and staff appointments.

The now-fashionable metaphor of "a network" is not the same thing as a well worked out economic model from which one can legitimately move, by way of institutionally grounded empirical inquiries, towards a fundamental re-orientation of policies to affect the allocation of resources for science and technology. It is important to remember that an emblem is not a rationale, especially because we recognize the power that some emblems have had to precipitate unreasoned action.

The particular metaphor in question here, to be sure, may claim to have had an honorably benign, indeed, a most fruitful career, as a heuristic device with which to elucidate and further probe many issues concerning the production and distribution of knowledge. From the ingenious, painstaking, and illuminating economic studies reviewed here, and the agenda of future research on the formation and performance of these organizational entities, it should be evident that its career in such service is far from over. But, by the same token, it has been seen that the network metaphor is trustworthy as a point of departure, not as a substitute for careful economic policy analysis.

References

Alba, R. (1973). "A Graph–theoretic Definition of a Sociometric Clique," *Journal of Mathematical Sociology*, 1

Allison, P., S. Long, and T. Krauze, (1982). "Cumulative Advantage and Inequality in Science," *American Sociological Review*, 47(5), 615–25

Amemiya, T. (1985). *Advanced Econometrics*, Cambridge, Mass.: Harvard University Press

Andrews, F. M., (ed.) (1979). *Scientific Productivity: The Effectiveness of Research Groups in Six Countries*, New York: New York University Press

Antonelli, C. (1994). "Localized Knowledge, Percolation Processes and Information Network, *Working Paper*, Department of Economics, University of Torino

Arora, A. (1991). "The Transfer of Technological Know-how to Developing Countries: Technology Licensing, Tacit Knowledge, and the Acquisition of Technological Capability," unpublished Ph.D. dissertation, Stanford University

(1995) "Licensing Tacit Knowledge: Intellectual Property Rights and the Market for Know-How," *Economics of Innovation and New Technology*, 4(1), 41–59

Arora, A., P.A. David, and A. Gambardella, (1995). "Increasing Returns to

Knowledge Capital in Scientific Research," Paper Presented to NBER Summer Workshop on Industrial Organization, Cambridge Mass

(1998). "Reputation and Competence in Publicly Funded Science: Estimating the Effects on Research Group Productivity," *Les Annales d'Economie et de Statistiques*, Numero 49/50

Arora, A., and A. Gambardella (1994). "The Changing Technology of Technological Change: General and Abstract Knowledge and the Division of Innovative Labour," *Research Policy* 23, 523–32

(1997). "Public Policy Towards Science: Picking Stars or Spreading the Wealth?," *Revue d'économie industrielle,* 79

Bala, V. S. and S. Goyal (1995). "Learning from Neighbors," *Econometric Institute Report*, 9549, Erasmus University, Rotterdam (September)

Ben-David, J. (1991). *Scientific Growth: Essays on the Social Organization and Ethos of Science*, ed. with an introduction by G. Freudenthal, Berkeley, Cal.: University of California Press

Blume, L.E. (1993). "The Statistical Mechanics of Strategic Interaction," *Games and Economic Behavior*, 4, 378–424

Blume, S. (1990). "Transfer Sciences: Their Conceptualization, Functions and Assessment," conference paper, "Consequences of the Technology Economy Programme for the Development of Indicators," (Paris) (July 2–5)

Bureth, A., S. Wolff, and A. Zanfei, (1998). "Cooperative Learning and the Evolution of Inter-firm Agreements in the European Electronics Industry," chapter 10 in this volume

Callon, M. (1989). *La science et ses réseaux: Genèse et circulation des faits scientifiques*, Paris: La Découverte

(1991). "Techno-economic Networks and Irreversibility," in John Law (ed.), *A Sociology of Monsters: Essays on Power, Technology and Domination*, London: Routledge & Kegan Paul

(1992). "The Dynamics of Techno-economic Networks," in R. Coombs, P. Saviotti and V. Walsh, (eds.), *Technological Change and Company Strategies*, London: Academic Press, 72–102

(1994). "Is Science a Public Good?," *Science, Technology and Human Values*, 19(4), 395–424

Callon, M., P. Laredo, V. Rabeharisoa, T. Gonard, and T. Leray (1992). "The Management and Evaluation of Technological Programs and Dynamics of Techno-Economic Networks: The Case of AFME," *Research Policy*, 21, 215–36

Cole, J. and Cole, S. (1973). *Social Stratification in Science*, Chicago: Chicago University Press

Cole, S. (1978). "Scientific Reward Systems: A Comparative Analysis," in R. A. Jones (ed.), *Research in Sociology of Knowledge, Sciences and Art*, Greenwich, Conn.: JAI Press, 167–90

Cole, S. and Cole J. (1967). "Scientific Output and Recognition," *American Sociological Review*, 32, 377–90

Cowan, R. and D. Foray (1996). "The Economics of Codification and the Diffusion of Knowledge," unpublished working paper, IMRI, University of Paris-

Dauphine (March)

Crane, D. (1972). *Invisible Colleges*, Chicago: University of Chicago Press

Dalle, J.-M. (1995). "Dynamiques d'adoption, coordination et diversité: la diffusion des standards technologiques," *Revue Economique*

Dasgupta, P. and P.A. David, (1987). "Information Disclosure and the Economics of Science and Technology," in G. Feiwel (ed.), *Arrow and the Ascent of Modern Economic Theory*, New York: New York University Press, 519–42

   (1988). "Priority, Secrecy, Patents and the Economic Organization of Science and Technology," *CEPR publication*, 127, Stanford University (March)

   (1994). "Towards a New Economics of Science," *Research Policy* 23: 487–521

David, P.A. (1988). "Path-dependence: Putting the Past into the Future of Economics," *Institute for Mathematical Studies in the Social Sciences Technical Report*, 533, Stanford University (November)

   (1992). "Knowledge, Property and the Systems Dynamics of Technological Change," in L. Summers, and S. Shah, (eds.), *Proceedings of the World Bank Annual Conference on Development Economics 1992*, (Washington DC) (published March 1993)

   (1993a). "Historical Economics in the Long Run: Some Implications of Path Dependence," in G.D. Snooks (ed.), *Historical Analysis in Economics*, London: Routledge

   (1993b). "Path Dependence and Predictability in Dynamic Systems with Local Network Externalities: A Paradigm for Historical Economics," in D. Foray and C. Freeman (eds.), *Technology and the Wealth of Nations*, London: Pinter

   (1994a). "Intellectual Property Institutions and the Panda's Thumb: Patents, Copyrights, and Trade Secrets in Economic Theory and History," chapter 2 in M. B. Wallerstein, M. E. Mogee, and R. A. Schoen (eds.), *Global Dimensions of Intellectual Property Rights in Science and Technology*, Washington, DC: National Academy Press

   (1994b). "Les standards des technologies de l'information, les normes de communication et l'Etat: un problème de biens publics," in A. Orléan (ed.), *Analyse économique des conventions*, Paris: Presses Universitaires de France

   (1994c). "Positive Feedbacks and Research Productivity in Science: Reopening Another Black Box," in O. Granstrand, (ed.), *Economics of Technology*, Amsterdam and London: North-Holland

   (1995a). "Standardization Policies for Network Technologies: The Flux between Freedom and Order Revisited," chapter 3 in R. Hawkins, R. Mansell and J. Skea (eds.), *Standards, Innovation and Competitiveness: The Politics and Economics of Standards in Natural and Technical Environments*, Aldershot, Edward Elgar

   (1995b). "Reputation and Agency in the Historical Emergence of the Institutions of 'Open Science'," paper presented to the National Academy of Sciences Colloquium on the "Economics of Science and Technology," (Beckman Center, Irvine University College, (October 20–21)

   (1995c). "Stratification in Research Network Formation — A Sketch-model of the World without the EU: Discussant's Comments," presented to the conference on "New Research Findings: The Economics of Scientific and

Technological Research in Europe," (University of Urbino), (February 24–25), unpublished

(1996). "Science Reorganized? Post-modern Visions of Research and the Curse of Success," in *Measuring R&D Impact – Proceedings of the Second International Symposium on Research Funding*, Ottawa: NSERC of Canada

(1997). "Resource Allocation and the Global Science Infrastructure: International Cooperation and the Economics of Access to Large-scale Research Facilities," paper presented to the "International Workshop on the Global Science System in Transition," IIASA (Laxenburg), (May 23–25)

(1998). "Communication Norms and the Collective Cognitive Performance of 'Invisible Colleges'," in G. B. Navaretti *et al.*, *Creation and Transfer of Knowledge: Institutions and Incentives*, New York: Physica-Verlag

David, P. A. and T. Flemming (1996, 1995). "Communications, Creativity and Research Network Dynamics: An Elementary Economic Model of Scientific Communities," paper presented to the International "Conference on Creation and Transfer of Knowledge," (Castelgandolfo) (September 1995); revised for presentation to the All Souls College Seminar on the Economics of Information Diffusion (Oxford) (May 1996)

David, P.A., and Foray, D. (1994a). "Dynamics of Competitive Technology Diffusion through Local Network Structures: The Case of EDI Document Standards," in L. Leydesdorff and P. van den Besselaar, (eds.), *Evolutionary Economics and Chaos Theory: New Developments in Technology Studies*, London: Pinter

(1994b). "Percolation Structures, Markov Random Fields and the Economics of EDI Standards Diffusion," in G. Pogorel, (ed.), *Global Telecommunications Strategies and Technological Changes*, Amsterdam: North-Holland

(1995). "Accessing and Expanding the Knowledge-base in Science and Technology," *STI Review – Science, Technology and Industry*, 16, Paris: OECD

(1996). "Information Distribution and the Growth of Economically Valuable Knowledge: A Rationale for Technological Infrastructure Policies," in M. Teubal *et al.* (eds.), *Technological Infrastructure Policy: An International Perspective*, Dordrecht and London: Kluwer Academic

David, P. A., D. Foray, and J.-M. Dalle (1998). "Marshallian Externalities and the Emergence and Spatial Stability of Technological Enclaves," vol. 6, 2–3

David, P. A., D. Foray, and W. E. Steinmueller (1997). "The Global Science System in Transition: Framing the Workshop Issues," paper presented to the "International Workshop on the Global Science System in Transition," IIASA, (Laxenburg) (May 23–25)

David, P.A., A. Geuna, and W. E. Steinmueller (1995). "Additionality as a Principle of European R&D Funding," report for the STOA Program of the European Parliament, MERIT Research Memorandum 2/95/012, Maastricht: Rijksuniversiteit Limburg

David, P.A. and S. Greenstein (1990). "The Economics of Compatibility Standards: An Introduction to Recent Research," *Economics of Innovation and New Technology*, 1 (1–2), 3–42

David, P. A. and R.C. Maude-Griffin (1995). "Contingency, Competition and Cumulative Advantage in Basic Science: A Stochastic Simulation Model of

Public Resource Allocation and Research Productivity," *HTIP Working Paper*, Center for Economic Policy Research, Stanford University (May 1994) (revised and expanded June 1995)

David, P. A., D. Mowery, and W. E. Steinmueller (1992). "Analyzing the Payoffs from Basic Research," *Economics of Innovation and New Technology* 2(4)

Diamond, A. M., Jr. (1996). "The Economics of Science," *Knowledge and Policy* (Special Issue), 9 (2–3), 6–49

Ellison, G. (1993). "Learning, Local Interaction, and Coordination," *Econometrica*, 61, 1047–71

Ellison, G. and D. Fudenberg (1995). "Word-of-mouth Communication and Social Learning," *Quarterly Journal of Economics*, 110(1), 93–126

Everitt, B. (1993). *Cluster Analysis*, London: Heinemann Educational

Foray, D. (1991). "The Secrets of Industry are in the Air: Industrial Cooperation and the Organizational Dynamics of the Innovative Firm," *Research Policy*, 20(5), 393–405

Fransman, M. (1990). *The Market and Beyond: Cooperation and Competition in IT in the Japanese System*, Cambridge: Cambridge University Press

Gambardella, A. (1995). *Science and innovation*, Cambridge: Cambridge University Press

Gambardella, A. and W. Garcia-Fontes (1996a). "Regional Linkages through European Research Funding," *Economics of Innovation and New Technology*, 4, 123–38

(1996b). "European Research Funding and Regional Technological Capabilities: Network Composition Analysis," (revised version of paper presented to the conference "New Research Findings: the Economics of Scientific and Technological Research in Europe," (University of Urbino) (February 24–25, 1995); *Economics Working Paper*, 97, Universitat Pompeu Fabra, Barcelona, (March, 1996)

Garcia-Fontes, W. and A. Geuna (1998). "The Dynamics of Research Networks in Europe," chapter 4 in this volume

Gaston, J. (1978). *The Reward System in British and American Science*, New York: Wiley

Geuna, A. (1996). "The Participation of Higher Education Institutions in Community Framework Programs," *Science and Public Policy*, 23(5), 287–96

(1998). "Patterns of University Research in Europe", chapter 15 in this volume

Gibbons, M., C. Limoges, H. Nowotny, S. Schwartzman, P. Scott, and M. Trow (1994), *The New Production of Knowledge. The Dynamics of Science and Research in Contemporary Societies*, London: Sage

Granovetter, M. (1973). "The Strength of Weak Ties," *American Journal of Sociology*, 78, 1360–80

(1978). "Threshold Models of Collective Behavior," *American Journal of Sociology*, 83, 1420–43

Granovetter, M. and R. Soong (1986). "Threshold Models of Interpersonal Effects in Consumer Demand," *Journal of Economic Behavior and Organization*, 7(1), 83–100

Hagstrom, W. O. (1965). *The Scientific Community*, New York: Basic Books

Henderson, R., A. Jaffe and M. Trajtenberg (1995). "Universities as a Source of

Commercial Technology: A Detailed Analysis of University Patenting 1965–1988," *National Bureau of Economic Research Working Paper*, 5068, (March)

Hicks, D. and S. Katz, (1995). "A Profile of British Science: An Overview of Comprehensive, Time Series, Bibliometric Data," *SPRU Working Paper*, University of Sussex

Hladik, K.J. (1985). *International Joint Ventures*, Lexington, Mass.: Lexington Books

Imai, K. and Y. Baba (1989). "Systemic Innovation and Cross-border Networks," paper presented to the International Seminar on the Contributions of Science and Technology to Economic Growth," (June), Paris: OECD Division of Science, Technology, and Industry

(1991). "Systemic Innovation and Cross-border Networks, Transcending Markets and Hierarchies to Create a new Techno-economic System," in OECD (ed.), *Technology and Productivity: The Challenges for Economic Policy*, Paris: OECD

Jaffe, A., M. Trajtenberg, and R. Henderson (1993). "Geographic Localization of Knowledge Spillovers as Evidenced by Patent Citations," *Quarterly Journal of Economics*, 63, 577–98

Katz, S. and D. Hicks, D. (1994). "The Classification of Interdisciplinary Journals: A New Approach," paper presented at Fifth International Conference on "Scientometrics and Informatics," (River Forest, Ill.)

(1995). "Questions of Collaboration," *Nature*, 375 (11 May); 99

Katz, S. and B.H. Martin, (1995). "What is a Research Collaboration?," *Research Policy*, 24

Kirman, A.(1993). "Ants, Rationality and Recruitment," *Quarterly Journal of Economics*,108 ,137–56

Knorr-Cetina, K.D. (1982). "Scientific Communities or Transepidemic Arenas of Research? A Critique of Quasi-economic Models of Science," *Social Studies of Science*, 12, 101–30

Kuhn, T. S. (1962). *The Structure of Scientific Revolutions*, Chicago: University of Chicago Press

Levinthal, D. (1988). "A Survey of Agency Models of Organizations," *Journal of Economic Behavior and Organization*, 9

Luhmann, N. (1984). *Soziale systeme. Grundriss einer allgemeinen Theorie*, Frankfurt-am-Marn: Suhrkamp

(1990), *Die Wissenschaft der Gesellschaft*, Frankfurt-am-Marn: Suhrkamp

MacKenzie, D. and J. Wajcman, (eds.) (1985). *The Social Shaping of Technology*, Buckingham: Open University Press

Maddala, G.S. (1983). *Limited-dependent and Qualitative Variables in Econometrics*, Cambridge: Cambridge University Press

Manski, C.F. and D. McFadden (eds.) (1981). *Structural Analysis of Discrete Data with Econometric Application*, Cambridge, Mass.: MIT Press

Merton, R. K. (1938/1970). *Science, Technology & Society in Seventeenth Century England*, New York: Harold Fertig, first published as vol. IV, part 2 of *Osiris: Studies on the History and Philosophy of Science, and on the History of Learning and Culture* (1938)

(1968). "The Matthew Effect in Science," *Science* 159, 56–63

(1973). in N.W. Storer (ed.), *The Sociology of Science: Theoretical and Empirical Investigations*, Chicago: University of Chicago Press

Metcalfe, J.S., L. Georghiou, P. Cunningham, and H.M. Cameron (1992). *Evaluation of the Impact of European Community Research Programmes upon the Competitiveness of European Industry – Concepts and Approaches*, Monitor/Spear, EUR 14.198 EN

Meyer-Kramer, F. (1992). "The German R&D-System in Transition," *Research Policy*, 21(5), 423–34

Morris, S. (1996). "Strategic Behavior with General Local Interaction," Department of Economics Working Paper, University of Pennsylvania (March)

Mowery, D. (1988). *International Collaborative Joint-ventures in US Manufacturing*, Cambridge Mass.: Ballinger

Narin, F. and D. Olivastro, (1992). "Status Report – Linkage between Technology and Science," *Research Policy*, 21(3), 237–49

OECD (1984). *Industry and University: New Forms of Co-operation and Communication*, Paris: OECD

Pestre, D. (1997). "La production des savoirs entre académies et marché: une relecture historique de livre 'The New Production of Knowledge' édité par M. Gibbons," *Revue d'Economie Industrielle*, 79, 163–74

Picard, J.F. (1990). *La république des savants: la recheche française et le CNRS*, Paris: Flammarion

Price, D.J. de Solla (1963). *Little Science, Big Science*, New York: Columbia University Press

(1965). "Networks of Scientific Papers," *Science*, 149, 510–15

(1986), *Little Science, Big Science and Beyond*, New York: Columbia University Press

Quah, D. (1994). "Ideas Determining Convergence Clubs," *Department of Economics Working Paper*, London School of Economics (September)

Richardson, G. B. (1972) "The Organization of Industry," *Economic Journal*, 82, 383–96

Rosenberg, N. (1982). *Inside the Black Box: Technology and Economics*, New York: Cambridge University Press

Rothwell, R. and M. Dodgson (1990). "Technology Policy in Europe," in J. de La Mothe, and L.M. Ducharme, *Science, Technology and Free Trade*, London: Pinter

Senker, J. (1991). "Evaluating the Funding of Strategic Science: Some Lessons from British Experience," *Research Policy*, 20, 29–43

Shavell, S. (1979). "Risk Sharing and Incentives in the Principal and Agent Relationship," *Bell Journal of Economics*, 10

Stankiewicz, R. (1980). *Leadership & the Performance of Research Groups*, Research Policy Institute, University of Lund, Sweden

(1985). "A New Role for University in Technological Innovation," in G. Sweeney (ed.), *Innovation Policies: An International Perspective*, London: Pinter

(1986). *Academics and Entrepreneurs: Developing University–industry Relations*, London: Frances Pinter

Steinmueller, W. E. (1995). "The Political Economy of Data Communication Standards," chapter 16 in R. Hawkins, R. Mansell, and J. Skea, (eds.), *Standards, Innovation and Competitiveness: The Politics and Economics of Standards in Natural and Technical Environments*, Aldershot: Edward Elgar

(1996). "Technological Infrastructure in Information Industries," in M. Teubal *et al.*, (eds.), *Technological Infrastructure Policy: An International Perspective*, Dordrecht and London: Kluwer Academic, 117–140

Stephan, P. (1996). "The Economics of Science," *Journal of Economic Literature*, 34(3), 199–235

Teece, D. J. (1987). "Profiting from Technological Innovation: Implications for Integration, Collaboration, Licensing, and Public Policy," in D.J. Teece, (ed.), *The Competitive Challenge*, Cambridge, Mass.: Ballinger

(1992). "Competition, Cooperation and Innovation – Organizational Arrangements for Regimes of Rapid Technological Progress," *Journal of Economic Behavior and Organization*, 18, 1–25

Teubal, M., T. Yinnon and E. Zuscovitch (1991). "Networks and Market Creation," *Research Policy*, 20, 381ff

Trajtenberg, M., R. Henderson, and A. B. Jaffe, (1992). "Ivory Tower versus Corporate Lab: An Empirical Study of Basic Research and Appropriability," *National Bureau of Economic Research Working Paper*, 4146 (August)

Whitley, R. (1984). *The Intellectual and Social Organization of the Sciences*, Oxford: Clarendon Press

Ziman, J. (1968). *Public Knowledge: An Essay Concerning the Social Dimension of Science*. Cambridge: Cambridge University Press

(1984). *An Introduction to Science Studies: The Philosophical and Social Aspects of Science and Technology,* Cambridge: Cambridge University Press

Zuckerman, H. (1977). *The Scientific Elite: Nobel Laureates in the United States*, New York: Free Press

Zuckerman, H. and R. K. Merton (1973). "Institutionalization and Patterns of Evaluation in Science," in N.W. Storer, (ed.), R. K. *Merton, The Sociology of Science: Theoretical and Empirical Investigations*, Chicago: University of Chicago Press

14 The dynamics of research networks in Europe

Walter Garcia-Fontes and Aldo Geuna

Introduction

The European Commission has been pursuing an active policy of funding research since its inception. The Commission R&D projects aim to be of a strategic nature – i.e. they are aimed at changing the objectives and methods of research, rather than simply augmenting the search for new knowledge. On the one hand, the Commission has the objective of improving the competitiviness of European industry by the invention and development of new processes and products, and on the other it wants to trigger projects that would not be initiated without this funding. Another goal is to promote links between academic and industrial research. These objectives have to be set against the goal of European cohesion, trying to expand research capabilities to institutions in under-developed regions.

This wide and diverse set of objectives is not always internally consistent. Attempts to foster pre-competitive research while trying to be market oriented produce clashes of interest, as is often the case for industry oriented R&D research programs. In some of these programs the funding effort is supposed to contribute to the process of European cohesion, but at the same time the projects must be selected on technical and scientific merit alone. Another typical conflict arises from the fact that picking a mix of institutions with different research capabilities contributes to the diffusion of new techniques and results and therefore improves the research

We would like to express our thanks for the comments received from participants at the conferences "New Research Findings: The Economics of Scientific and Technological Research in Europe", (University of Urbino), and EARIE, 1995 (Juan Les Pins), and useful discussions with Paul David, Alfonso Gambardella, and Edward Steinmueller. We are grateful for the data supplied by the services of the European Commission, as well as the financial support of the European Union Human Capital and Mobility Program (Contract no. ERBCHRXT920002 and no. ERB4050PL930320). Walter Garcia-Fontes acknowledges the financial support of grant DGICYT PB95–0980.

capabilities of the European scientific community taken as a whole, while funding the most reputed institutions allows the programs to achieve high research yields only in the short run.

These conflicts can be studied by means of a simple framework. The funding agency, in this case the Commission, demands scientific results and supplies funds for research, while the research units demand funds and supply results. We do not have information about scientific results, but we have very detailed information on the funding effort by the Commission and about the participation of research units in the BRITE-EURAM program.

In this chapter we study the effects of the funding effort by the Commission on the supply and the demand of funds, and on the participation of research units in the networks formed. We study the contracts signed under the BRITE-EURAM program for the Second and Third Framework. Particular attention is given to the core of the network – that is, main contractors or originators of networks that span different networks and different years, accounting for a substantial proportion of the total participation in networks. We use a model of coalition formation and spillins within the coalition (see Olson and Zeckhauser, 1966, or Sandler and Murdoch, 1990) to formulate an empirical model and analyze the effects of Commission funding on the networks, by assessing how the role of the core and the evolution of the networks have changed throughout the two Frameworks.

The interaction among research institutions in networks funded by the European Union has been studied by Gambardella and Garcia-Fontes (1996). They showed that complementary factors in research capabilities matter in the formation of networks, since research coalitions are formed by linking together the most technologically advanced institutions. This suggests that the Commission funding policy for research tends to favor short-run goals versus long-run cohesion. An important limitation of this analysis is that it is static and cross-sectional. The current chapter, instead, uses a panel of networks to study both cross-sectional and dynamic characteristics of the research networks.

The chapter is organized as follows: we present a theoretical model of network interaction, and then describe the main features of the BRITE-EURAM program. This allows us to identify some dynamic features of the contracts signed. The theoretical model is implemented empirically, and tested. Finally, we present our conclusions.

A model of research coalitions

We start by proposing a model of network interaction, based on similar models that have been proposed in the literature for the production of joint public goods.[1]

We consider the networks as coalitions of researchers which engage in research activities that provide both private knowledge output, which is institution-specific, and public knowledge output, which is network-specific.

Let q^i be the private knowledge and k^i the public knowledge produced by member i of a network, and l^i the general research activities provided by the ith component of the network. The joint production relationships for q^i and k^i are given by:

$$q^i = f_i(l^i) \tag{14.1}$$

and

$$k^i = g_i(l^i) \tag{14.2}$$

where both $f_i(\cdot)$ and $g_i(\cdot)$ are assumed to be twice continuously differentiable and concave.

Consider the total public knowledge produced within the network, K. Since K is a pure public good within the network, each partner receives the knowledge that he/she produces, k^i, and the common knowledge spilled in from the rest of the network, $\tilde{K}^i = \Sigma_{j \neq i} k^j$. Hence, each partner receives:

$$K = \tilde{K}^i + k^i.$$

If the network has n members, the knowledge that spills in to participant i derives from the aggregate activities $\tilde{L}^i$ of the $n-1$ partners according to the following relationship:

$$\tilde{K}^i = s(\tilde{L}^i); \ s' > 0, \ s'' < 0. \tag{14.3}$$

We model the choice of network activity by the utility function of a representative member of the network (network members do not need to be identical):

$$u^i = u^i(x^i, q^i, \tilde{K}^i + k^i); \tag{14.4}$$

where x^i represents the numeraire, or the choice of other goods (income effects are assumed to be negligible).

Substituting (14.1), (14.2) and (14.3) into (14.4), we obtain:

[1] For a survey of this kind of model see Sandler (1992, chapters 4 and 5). The version that we present here closely follows Sandler and Murdoch (1990).

$$u^i = u^i(x^i; f_i(l^i); g_i(l^i) + s(\tilde{L}^i)) = v^i(x_i, l^i | \tilde{L}^i):$$

There are two ways of obtaining demand functions from this model: (1) the Nash–Cournot equilibrium concept implies that each agent chooses the level of activity which maximizes her utility subject to an income budget constraint and to the prevailing contributions of public knowledge from the rest of the network, $\tilde{L}^i = \Sigma_{j \neq i} l^j$, and (2) the Lindahl equilibrium concept, which assumes that network members communicate and exchange information concerning the level of the public knowledge that they are going to share in the network, but meet the costs by individualized cost shares (the shares must sum to 1, so that costs are covered).

Since $l^i = Li - \tilde{L}^i$, the maximization problem for the ith agent in the case of Nash-Cournot equilibrium can be written as:

$$\max_{xi,Li} \{v^i(x^i; L^i | \tilde{L}^i) l^i + p \tilde{L}^i = p_x x^i + pL^i\}$$

where p_x and p are the prices of x and L^i respectively, and $l^i + p\tilde{L}^i$ is income. Notice that the maximization problem is now written in terms of the network-wide research activities demanded by institution i.

The solution to this maximization problem is the demand function for total network research activity by institution i:

$$L^i_N = L^i_N(I^i + p\tilde{L}^i, p_y, p, \tilde{L}^i) \tag{14.5}$$

where the subscript N stands for Nash–Cournot. The network demand for research activity depends on prices, income, and the level of research spillins. In equilibrium, all members of the network will demand the equilibrium level of total network research activity – that is, $L^e = L^i_N$ for all i.

For a research coalition, we can also take into account the fact that the search for scientific results can be considered a race against other research teams, and therefore the research expenditure of other similar networks can be considered as a "threat," T, for any given coalition of researchers. If we condition all the analysis to this threat, we have to include this new variable in the demand function:

$$L^i_N = L^i_N(I^i + p\tilde{L}^i, p_y, p, \tilde{L}^i, T). \tag{14.6}$$

In the case of the Lindahl equilibrium concept, each partner in the network is assumed to have preferences represented by the following utility function:

$$u^i = u^i(x^i, q^i, K) \tag{14.7}$$

where again

$$K = \tilde{K}^i + k^i \tag{14.8}$$

and the joint production relationships are

$$q^i = f_i(L) \tag{14.9}$$

and

$$K = g(L) \tag{14.10}$$

In this case, the total level of the collective research activity, L, produces both the private and public knowledge experienced by each partner of the network. The Lindahl equilibrium concept implies a cooperative game, and therefore the partners choose the equilibrium level of joint research. Each partner contributes a private effort to the relationship and is assigned a share in the aggregate cost of the project, θ^i.

Substituting (14.8), (14.9) and (14.10) into (14.7) and taking into account the budget constraint:

$$p_x x^i + \theta^i pL = I^i$$

allows us to formulate the maximization problem for the ith partner as follows:

$$\max_{xi,L}\{ U^i(x^i,L) | p_x x^i + \theta^i pL = I^i\}$$

The solution to this problem gives the following demand functions:

$$L^i_H = L^i_H(I^i,p_y, \theta^i p, T) \tag{14.11}$$

where H stands for Lindahl.

We will base our estimating equations on (14.6) for the Nash–Cournot case and (14.11) for the Lindahl case.

We will use this model to investigate the demand functions for the Commission's contribution of different types of participants at different moments in time. It is necessary first to identify and describe the relevant types of participants, and how participation has evolved over the Second and Third Framework of the BRITE-EURAM program.

The BRITE–EURAM shared-cost projects

The following analysis focuses on the Research and Technological Development (RTD) contracts signed in the period 1989–93 in the BRITE-EURAM I and BRITE-EURAM II (henceforth BE program).[2] In the appendix we provide a detailed description of the creation and character-istics of the BE program. BE represents a particularly suitable program for

---

[2] The contracts signed under RAW and AERONAUTICS are not included.

our purpose. First, its technological focus represents a heterogeneous set of participants (Commission, 1992, 41, 1993a, 10). Second, its orientation involves not only applied and development work, but also more basic research with industrial applicability. Third, if we consider both the number of participations and the funding level for shared cost actions, BE is the second most important program throughout this period.[3]

We obtained the original data set from DG XII (Director-General, Science, Research and Development) of the EC. The contracts signed were, respectively, 352, with 1,783 participations,[4] in the Second Framework (SF) and 703, with 2,056 participations, in the Third Framework (TF). For each contract we were provided with the following information: title of the project, duration of the contract, cost and Commission contribution,[5] participants' names and locations, and participants' position in the network (main contractor, secondary contractor, sub-contractor, etc.). However, we did not succeed in obtaining information on the organizations: type of institution (large enterprise, small–medium enterprise, university, research organization, etc.) and its dimensions. As we were interested in the research network, we decided to focus our analysis only on shared-cost collaborative research projects. We therefore excluded from our database the following types of contracts: feasibility award, first-step CRAFT, concerted action, other "like-grant" action, and time amendments. Instead, we considered the institutions involved in contribution amendments as normal contractors taking part in the network. The database constructed in this way thus takes into account about 90 percent of the contracts (of those involving shared-cost actions) signed during the Second Framework Program, and 80 percent of those signed during the Third Framework Program.[6]

As shown in table 14.1 and 14.2 we have a population of 3,440 participations sub-divided into 673 contracts, with 350 contracts in the SF and 323 in the TF. The type of cost – MAR or ECO – identifies the participants that receive up to 100 percent of the additional cost (MAR, limited to higher education institutions, HEIs), and the other participant type (ECO), to

---

[3] For an analysis of the technologies generated under the BRITE-EURAM program, as well as its economic effects and the impact on European industry, see Commission (1993b, 1996, 1997).

[4] In this part of the chapter "participation" means a contractor of any category, including also institutions involved in time/contribution amendments. In the descriptive analysis, on the other hand, participations come only from contractors involved in shared-cost actions.

[5] The Commission reimburses up to 50 percent of the project costs to companies or institutes that operate a project-costing system. Universities, higher-education establishments and similar non-commercial bodies receive up to 100 percent of the additional costs.

[6] The Third Framework lasted up to the end of 1994, thus 80 percent represents an estimate of the contracts signed up to March 1, 1994.

Table 14.1 *Participation in the Second and Third Frameworks, breakdown by type of cost*

Cost type	Second Framework (%)	Third Framework (%)	Total (%)
ECO	1,302 (73.2)	1,221 (73.5)	2,523 (73.3)
MAR	476 (26.8)	441 (26.5)	916 (26.7)
Total	1,778	1,662	3,440

Source: Elaboration of Commission data

Table 14.2 *Main contractors' participations, in the Second and Third Frameworks, breakdown by type of cost*

Cost type	Second Framework (%)	Third Framework (%)	Total (%)
ECO	278 (79.4)	263 (81.4)	541 (80.4)
MAR	72 (20.6)	60 (18.6)	132 (19.6)
Total	350	323	673

Source: Elaboration of Commission data.

whom the Commission reimburses up to 50 percent of the project costs (ECO).

When we look at the total population, we can see that HEIs account for approximately one quarter of participations. They play quite a relevant role both in the SF and the TF. But, when we look at main contractor figures not only is their relevance less evident, but also their share declines from the SF to the TF. Therefore, if we assume that projects directed by a HEI are more focused on pre-competitive research, we can highlight a strong and increasing market orientation for the program. To reinforce this observation, in table 14.3 we show the data concerning the Commission contribution. While in the SF the share of Commission contribution to HEIs and the shares of their participations are about the same, in the TF they are different owing to a drop in the Commission contribution of about 4 percent.[7] In the TF, HEIs have therefore not only played a less important role in establishing the research effort, with a subordinate position as the main

---

[7] Comparing these figures with those of the total framework (see, for example, Commission, 1994b) we note that the BE programs are characterized by a lower level of HEI participation, and a higher level of HEI funding. Therefore, compared to the aggregate figure, HEIs in the BE program are strong players even if in relative terms they are less important.

Table 14.3 *Commission contribution in Second and Third Frameworks, breakdown by type of cost (million ECU)*

Cost type	Second Framework (%)	Third Framework (%)	Total (%)
ECO	275 (73)	293 (77)	568 (74)
MAR	101 (27)	88 (23)	189 (26)
Total	377	380	757

Source: Elaboration of Commission data.

contractor, but they have also received fewer funds from the Commission, thus further weakening their impact.

To understand the differences between BE I and BE II we develop a more detailed analysis of the Commission contribution. We subdivide the variable Commission contribution into six categories: (1) 0–25,000 ECU; (2) 25,000–100,000 ECU; (3) 100,000–200,000 ECU; (4) 200,000–300,000 ECU; (5) 300,000–500,000 ECU and (6) > 500,000 ECU. We classify the contracts (in this case one for each participation) in relation to these classes. In figure 14.1 we show the allocation of Commission total contribution. Each bar represents the number of contracts present in that class. The distribution is very similar in the two frameworks. The TF, as expected, has slightly lower values than the SF. Only in the first and in the last category does it have a higher number of contracts. In particular, the increase of the first class is mainly due to an increase in the number of HEI contracts.

As figure 14.2 illustrates, going from the SF to the TF a larger number of HEIs have participated in a contract with a contribution under 25,000 ECU. While the first category is more than double, the fifth has lost about 30 percent of participations.

On the other hand, (see figure 14.3), enterprises and research centers have reduced their participation in low budget contracts (class 2 has lost a significant number of contracts) and they have increased their presence in the top class.

The increase in the total number of participations with a contract in the sixth category is caused only by this last dynamic feature. We can therefore, again reconfirm and definitely support the previous observation that HEIs' role has become less important in BE programs.

As we highlighted previously, the share of participations and the quota of Commission contributions have about the same value in the SF and slightly different in the TF.

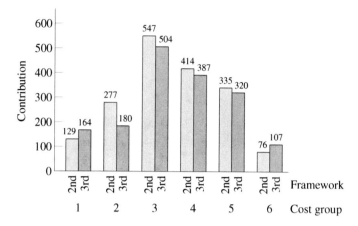

14.1 Commission, total contribution

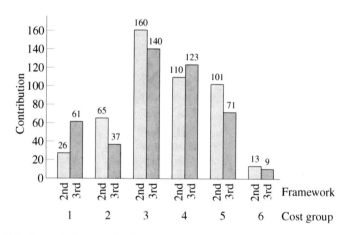

14.2 Commission, "MAR" contribution

Network formation and the hard core

Up to now, we have regarded participants as anonymous institutions without soul and we have ignored the network dimension completely. In this section we try to remedy this shortcoming.

In table 14.4 we show the participation distribution according to the position in the network (100 = main contractor, 200 = second contractor, etc). We can highlight two changes in the networks from the SF to the TF.

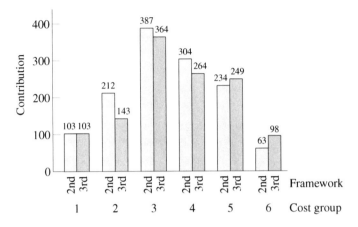

14.3 Commission, "ECO" contribution

First, there has been an important increase in the number of sub-contractors,[8] networks have become more branched in small components. The number of network linkages with different priority levels has therefore increased. Networks are usually characterized by the relationship among contractors at the international level on the one hand, and that between contractors and subcontractors at the local level, which existed prior to the RTD projects, on the other. The increase in sub-contractors implies an increased probability of having networks composed by parts of already pre-existing ones. Networks of the TF are therefore becoming less novel.

Second, up to the third contractor there are no big differences between the two Frameworks. The share of participants identified as "fourth contractor" has fallen strongly in the TF, so in the last Framework the networks are composed by a smaller number of contractors. Typically in the TF there are three contractors and a certain number of sub-contractors; in general, the TF's networks are thus characterized by a lower number of contractors and a larger number of sub-contractors.

When we take into account the average network size, the distinction between contractors and sub-contractors becomes less important. In table 14.5 we show the network distribution by size (number of partners) in the two Frameworks. While the mean number of partners is about five for both Frameworks, in the TF slightly less than 50 percent of the projects are carried out by networks with four or fewer participants. This is due to the fact that an extremely high number of networks (91) have only three par-

---

[8] Each contractor is entitled to sub-contract part of his research to other institutions that become his specific sub-contractors.

Table 14.4 *Distribution of participation type, Second and Third Frameworks*

Participation type	Second Framework	(%)	Third Framework	(%)	Total	(%)
100	350	19.7	323	19.4	673	19.5
200	337	19.9	312	18.8	649	18.9
300	305	17. 1	296	17.8	601	17.5
400	258	15.5	196	11.8	454	13.2
500	178	10.0	135	8.1	313	9.1
Other contractors	130	7.3	142	8.5	272	7.9
Sub-contractors	220	12.4	258	15.6	478	813.9
Total	1778	100	1662	100	3440	100

Source: Elaboration of Commission data.

Table 14.5 *Networks, Second and Third Frameworks, by number of partners*

No. of partners[a]	Second Framework	(%)	Third Framework	(%)	Total	(%)
1	7	2.0	3	0.9	10	1.5
2	22	6.3	7	2.2	29	4.3
3	44	12.6	91	28.2	135	20.1
4	58	16.6	52	16.1	110	16.3
5	94	26.9	54	16.7	148	22.0
6	61	17.4	42	13	103	15.3
> 6	64	18.3	74	22.9	138	20.5
Total	350	100	323	100	673	100

Note:
[a] The number of partners is given by the sum of coordinators, contractors, sub-contractors, and contribution amendment contractors.
Source: Elaboration of Commission data.

ticipants. On the other hand, in the SF the networks with five participants are the ones with the highest share. So, going from the Second to the Third Framework we can highlight a shrinking network size, with a polarization of projects within the three-participant network structure.

In general, without taking into account the participants' position in the network, the Fourth Framework Program is characterized by smaller networks. When we look also at the type of participants, the networks of the TF are not only smaller but are also characterized by a larger amount of

Table 14.6 *Concentration in participation, Second and Third Frameworks*

	Second Frame-work	(%)	Third Frame-work	(%)	Total	(%)
Single participation (A)	711 (40%)	71.2	780 (47%)	75.3	1,184 (34.4%)	69.6
Repeated participation (B)	287	28.8	256	24.7	516	30.4
Total no. of institutions $(C) = (A) + (B)$	998	100	1,036	100	1,700	100
Expanded participations (D)	1,067 (60%)		882 (53%)		2,256 (65.6%)	
Total participations $(E) = (A) + (D)$	1,778 (100%)		1,662 (100%)		3,440 (100%)	

Source: Elaboration of Commission data.

sub-contractors than by an increasing number of probably pre-existing one-to-one relations. It seems therefore that this kind of evolution can hinder the process of diffusion of the new technologies (and of related knowledge bases and capabilities) which lie at the heart of European science and technology policy. On the other hand the shrinking of networks dimension may also be due to organizational inefficiencies related to the management of large networks. So it can be considered as a necessary cost – i.e. fewer institutions involved means less diffusion of new knowledge – to obtain the generation of new technologies – i.e. fewer partners means easier management and a greater likelihood of successful research.

To study the effectiveness of the Commission diffusion policy we decided to analyze concentration in participation. We assigned a name (A, B, C, etc.) to the various participating institutions and identified them in the different projects in both Frameworks. The result is shown in table 14.6. An institution can be involved in RTD projects only once (single participation), or more than once (repeated participation). For the latter type of organization, it is then possible to calculate how many times, including the first, it has taken part in a project (expanded participation). The analysis of these variables enables us to compare the two Frameworks and to draw some conclusions on the real impact of Commission funding in terms of diffusion policy:

• The average number of participations for the institutions with repeated participation (D/B) is decreasing, from 3.72 participations in the SF to

3.45 in the TF. In other words, the institutions with only one participation obtained in the TF a higher share of contracts (from 40 percent to 47 percent).

- When we consider the two Frameworks together we can highlight a higher value for the average number of participations (4.37). This is due to the presence of institutions that are in both the SF and the TF.
- There are 334 institutions present at least once in both Frameworks. This group of institutions is characterized by an average number of participations of 5.41. Moreover, these 334 institutions, after the first participation, are involved another 1,474 times in a project. Considering that in the two Frameworks together there are 1,740 participations that are repetitions, it follows that the 334 institutions are responsible for 85 percent of the repetitions (1,474 is approximately 85 percent of 1,740). They represent only 19.6 percent of the population, but they account for 1,808 contracts – that is to say 52.6 percent of the total contracts signed during the two Frameworks.
- The 516 institutions with repeated participation in the two Frameworks together can be divided in two groups. The first is formed by the 334 institutions with a mean participation of 5.41 and the second by the 182 institutions with an average number of participations of 1.46 (266/182, where 266 = 1740–1474). Finally, the 1,700 institutions present in both frameworks can be characterized as follows:
  - the "singles," formed by 1,184 institutions that got only one contract
  - the "networkers," formed by 182 institutions that got more than one contract, but in only one Framework
  - the "hard core," comprising 334 institutions that got more than one contract in both Frameworks.

From the descriptive analysis in this section we can already draw some interesting policy implications. We stated in the introduction that a dynamic framework could help us better understand the trade-off between short-run and long-run goals. What we find in this section is that this trade-off can be improved. The EC has made an effort to enlarge the population of institutions involved in RTD projects. In the TF there is indeed a larger variety of participants (sub-contractors). There are also more institutions that participate in only one network (singles). The increase in the number of single participants can be interpreted as a positive indicator of the impact of the Commission diffusion policy. In other words, even though funding focuses on a few reputed institutions, these may involve less reputed institutions to a greater extent. It is therefore important to stress the role of the set of institutions that we defined as the "hard core" of the networks. These represent 13 percent of the institutions participating, but get 52 percent of the contracts, implying that more than half of the Commission funds are directed to the same group of institutions. Assuming that these are outstanding organizations, and ruling out every kind of bureaucratic inertia and all types of possible industrial lobbying, this implies that the distribution of funds is heavily shaped by the merit criterion, and thus strongly influenced by cumulative and self-reinforcement mechanisms.[9] But since the hard core is networking with a greater set of institutions, from the point of view of the Commission funding policy, in principle one could keep funding the hard core over time and this could have an indirect positive effect over long-run cohesion goals.

It seems that participants included in the hard core, networkers and singles, may display significantly different behavior within the networks. We will try to provide evidence on this differential behavior by estimating the theoretical model presented above. This will also allow us to provide evidence on the relation of the hard core to the rest of participants in the research networks.

Estimation of the demand for funding

In this section we estimate the demand functions derived above. We assume a log-linear relation for the demand functions. As the dependent variable we use total Commission contribution to the network, which we associate with its total research activity.

As explanatory variables we use the total income that each participant has, which is given by the total cost committed to the project. Income from other sources for each partner of a network is not available, and therefore we have to adopt the assumption that preferences are strongly separable and that the budget constraint depends only on the total budget assigned to the project. We do not have information about knowledge prices, but assuming that prices of the rest of goods and knowledge prices move together, and taking into account the 0-degree homogeneity of the demand functions, we can formulate the demand functions only in terms of income and spillins or cost shares, by deflating all variables by a common price deflator. As a deflator we use a real effective exchange rate index against the ECU, since all values are given in this currency unit. As the threat variable, T, we use the average Commission contribution for networks of the same size in the same framework.

---

[9] Institutions that are successful in getting funds for their research have a higher probability of producing exploitable research, which improves their probability of joining other projects in the future (see David, 1994, Dasgupta and David, 1994). Geuna (1996) finds empirical evidence in favor of this cumulative effect in the selection process of European research grants.

Equation (14.6) for the Nash–Cournot case is then formulated as:

$$\log CONTRIBUTION_t^j = \beta_{i0} + \beta_{i1}\log INCOME_{it}^j + \qquad (14.12)$$

$$\beta_{i2}\log SPILL_{it}^j + \beta_{i3}\log THREAT_t^j + \epsilon_{it}^N$$

where $CONTRIBUTION_t^j$ is the total contribution of the Community to network j at framework t, $SPILL_{it}^j$ is the total contribution to network j *minus* the contribution for institution i at Framework t, $THREAT_t^j$ is the average Commission contribution to networks of equal size to network j at framework t, and $INCOME_{it}^j$ is total income approximated by the total cost of the project for institutions i in network j at Framework t *plus* $SPILL_{it}^j$. We add a random perturbation term ϵ_{it}^N.

Equation (14.11) for the case of Lindahl equilibrium is formulated as:

$$\log CONTRIBUTION_t^j = \delta_{i0} + \delta_{i1}\log COST_{it}^j + \qquad (14.13)$$

$$\delta_{i2}\log SHARE_{it}^j + \log THREAT_t^j + \epsilon_{it}^{II}$$

where $COST_{it}^j$ is the total cost of the project for institution i in network j at framework t, $SHARE_{it}^j$ is the individual cost share (contribution received by the institution over total contribution received by network j), and ϵ_{it}^L is a random perturbation term.

In (14.12) the variables $INCOME$ and $SPILL$ are simultaneously determined in the theoretical model with the Commission contribution, and are therefore correlated with the error term. Similarly in (14.13) the variable $SHARE$ is correlated with the error term. Consistent estimates can be obtained by applying an instrumental–variable estimation procedure, such as two-stage least squares.

It is standard in the literature on coalitions to assume that total individual income is strictly exogenous and used as an instrument (for instance, Sandler and Murdoch, 1990, use GNP as an instrument on a defense spending equation). In our case, we lack information on the total individual income of each institution, and assuming strong separability we take it that the total cost of the project represents the total income that each institution allocates to it. We therefore propose to use the following instruments: total cost of the project ($COST$) for the institution, the size of the network ($SIZE$), the threat variable ($THREAT$), and a constant. While the $THREAT$ variable can be safely assumed to be exogenous, some discussion is needed with respect to the exogeneity of the $COST$ and $SIZE$ variables. $COST$ represents the total cost of the project – that is, the total amount of income allocated by the institution to this particular project. While the dependent variable, $CONTRIBUTION$, is the total grant received by the *network*, and it is therefore agreed within the network, $COST$ is determined individually by each institution according to its total budget, and depends on the institution size and research record, which are given in our sample. It is not therefore unreasonable to assume that it is exogenous in this relationship. On the other hand, the size of the network (*SIZE*) is restricted by the criteria of the Commission and the type of project in hand.

We show the results in table 14.7. Column (1) presents the pooled regression over both frameworks and types, while the other columns list separate regressions for both Frameworks and types of participants. The pooled model is rejected in favor of the separated regressions for both specifications. We show first the results for the Nash and Lindahl model, and afterwards conduct a test to discriminate between these two.

For the Nash–Cournot equilibrium models, the estimated elasticities are positive and significant in all cases. This provides support for the joint-product model. Both activities, public common knowledge and private appropriation of knowledge, have elasticities which are less than unity, showing that these are normal goods. The estimated elasticities show an increase in spillin effects from the Second to the Third Framework. The spillin effects seem also less important for the core and the networkers, which is consistent with their role as network spanners. Single participants, on the other hand, receive the highest proportion of spillins within the networks.

In the case of the Lindahl specification, the negative coefficient of the *SHARE* variable is consistent with the Slutzky equation for a Lindahl equilibrium. There is also a significant increase in the absolute value of this coefficient from the Second to the Third Framework for the core and the networkers, and a decrease for the singles. This is consistent with the results obtained for the Nash equilibrium.

The results obtained for the variables *SPILL* and *SHARE* in both specifications are consistent with the descriptive analysis. We find greater spillins from the core to the other participants, especially the singles, and an increase of spillin effects from the SF to the TF. This evidence reinforces the observation that the trade-off between short- and long-run goals can be improved through funding the hard core. In a dynamic setting, Commission policy can improve the short-run vs. the long-run trade off, by financing the hard core and letting this type of institution "invite" other less reputed institutions. The importance of spillins can also be interpreted as a flow of public knowledge produced by the hard core to other participants. This is especially important in the context of non-cooperative behavior (Nash), since the level of public knowledge cannot be decided cooperatively and the hard core is able to produce knowledge more efficiently.

It is interesting to distinguish between these two models, to provide evidence on the degree of cooperative behavior within the networks. We

Table 14.7 Nash–Cournot and Lindahl coalition models, Second and Third Frameworks, dependent variable: total Commission contribution

	Pooled[a] regression	Second Framework			Third Framework		
		Hard core	Networkers	Singles	Hard core	Networkers	Singles
Nash equilibrium[b]							
Intercept[b]	0.003[c]	0.77	1.23[c]	0.56[c]	0.76	0.50[c]	−0.07[c]
	(0.12)	(0.30)	(0.71)	(0.30)	(0.20)	(0.39)	(0.37)
INCOME	0.59	0.61	0.54	0.58	0.59	0.59	0.59
	(0.01)	(0.02)	(0.04)	(0.01)	(0.02)	(0.02)	(0.01)
SPILL	0.23	0.17	0.14	0.28	0.28	0.41	0.32
	(0.02)	(0.04)	(0.18)	(0.03)	(0.04)	(0.06)	(0.06)
THREAT	0.17	0.16	0.23	0.10	0.08	−0.04[c]	0.09[c]
	(0.02)	(0.04)	(0.16)	(0.05)	(0.04)	(0.09)	(0.07)
Lindahl equilibrium							
Intercept	−0.15[c]	1.06[c]	2.14[c]	1.07[c]	1.11	−0.35[c]	−1.34
	(0.22)	(0.67)	(1.35)	(0.81)	(0.40)	(0.76)	(0.59)
COST	0.45	0.45	0.31	0.55	1.45	0.53	0.44
	(0.02)	(0.03)	(0.10)	(0.06)	(0.04)	(0.12)	(0.07)
SHARE	−0.41	−0.40	−0.27	−0.52	−0.44	−0.59	−0.40
	(0.03)	(0.05)	(0.13)	(0.08)	(0.05)	(0.16)	(0.10)
THREAT	0.54	0.46	0.53	0.34	0.45	0.46	0.63
	(0.03)	(0.06)	(0.16)	(0.11)	(0.06)	(0.17)	(0.12)

Notes:
[a] All data for both Frameworks and type of participants pooled.
[b] Standard errors in brackets. All coefficients are significant at a 5 % level unless otherwise noted.
[c] Not significantly different from zero at 5 % level.

Table 14.8 J-*test for distinguishing between Nash and Lindahl behavior*

	Hypothesis 1			Hypothesis 2		
	α_L	t-ratio	Conclusion	α_N	t-ratio	Conclusion
Second Framework						
Hard core	−0.49	−2.3	Reject	1.60	53.0	Reject
Networkers	−0.95	−1.7	Fail to reject	1.77	18.1	Reject
Singles	−0.69	−3.3	Reject	1.39	27.4	Reject
Third Framework						
Hard core	−0.05	−0.3	Fail to reject	1.15	38.6	Reject
Networkers	0.42	0.6	Fail to reject	0.94	10.6	Reject
Singles	0.04	0.2	Fail to reject	1.23	39.1	Reject

conduct a non-nested J-test.[10] The methodology consists of two new regressions, which are constructed as follows: first a regression is run on the Lindahl model, and then the predicted values of this regression are added as a new explanatory variable to the Nash model. If the estimated coefficient for this new variable, which we call α_L, turns out to be significantly different from 0, then the Lindahl model is supported (Hypothesis 1). If it is not significantly different from 0, then there is evidence against the Lindahl model. The second regression consists of this procedure reversed – that is, a regression is run with the original Lindahl model *plus* the predicted values of the Nash model, obtaining a new coefficient α_N (Hypothesis 2). We conduct this test for the six models – that is, for the two Frameworks and the three types of participants. The results are shown in table 14.8. Our data seem to support non-cooperative behavior in the interaction of networkers, especially in the Third Framework. For that framework the Nash model cannot be rejected, while the Lindahl model is rejected in all instances.

The fact that our data supports competitive vs. cooperative behavior has important policy implications. The Lindahl equilibrium is socially efficient because externalities are internalized, while the Nash equilibrium implies an under-provision of the public good (public knowledge), since each researcher does not take into account that her own research activity implies a positive externality within the research coalition taken as a whole. Since we reject the Lindahl specification in favor of the competitive specification, we find evidence that there is room for improving the "social" product of

---

[10] See MacKinnon, White, and Davidson (1983) on the methodology of this test.

the networks by favoring more cooperative behavior. Relating this last result to our previous results, while we find that the hard core can act in ways that improve the trade-off between short-run vs. long-run objective of Commission funding, at the same time there is still room for increasing the efficiency of the funding effort by encouraging more cooperation within the networks.

Moreover, the absence of evidence in favor of cooperative behavior means that it is important to clearly define who receives Commission money. Since there is no joint determination of the level of public knowledge that should be produced, funds should go to the participants who are able to produce private and public knowledge more efficiently. This may therefore provide some justification for the concentration of funds on the hard core, which would in turn be able to produce more public knowledge that could spillin to the rest of participants.

Concluding remarks

In this chapter we have investigated the dynamics of network formation within the BRITE-EURAM program. This is a program implemented by the European Union to foster industry–university R&D research with the objective of improving the competitiveness of European industry.

We unveiled some dynamic features for the role of the core of the networks, main contractors, and the behavior of followers. We found that a small group of institutions account for most of the participations within the networks, but that going from the Second to the Third Framework of projects, the presence of sub-contractors and single participants increases. The most reputed institutions are receiving most of the funding, but at the same time an increasing number of participants are receiving spillins from the core.

This interpretation is reinforced by a testable model of coalition formation and spillins of public knowledge within the coalitions. We model networks as coalitions formed with the objective of jointly producing private knowledge and common knowledge which is public within the networks. In this kind of model, we find that institutions that account for most participations receive smaller spillins than institutions that participate many times but only in one Framework or institutions that participate only once. Spillins also seem to increase from the Second to the Third Framework.

We think that the empirical evidence found in the panel of BRITE–EURAM contracts has important implications for the funding policy of the Commission. The inherent trade-off between short-run productivity of research and long-run cohesion of technological capabilities within the European Union is being improved in practice, thanks to the fact that the hard core involves more partners over time. But we also found that there is empirical evidence in favor of a competitive behavior on the networks, and owing to the public good nature of knowledge this may imply an under-provision in the joint production of public knowledge within the research networks. This implied loss in the "social" product of the networks may be reduced by encouraging greater cooperation among the participants of cost-shared contracts financed by the Commission. This suggests that the Commission should not only look at the selection process and formation of research networks, but also at the implementation of networks, taking special care to encourage cooperation among participants. Cooperation could be favored by improving the channels of communication and encouraging information exchange among participating research institutions. Over time, attention should be given to the refinancing of existing networks, as presumably a longer relationship would improve the mutual knowledge of the participants and promote cooperative behavior.

Appendix *The BRITE-EURAM family of research programs*

The first BRITE-EURAM program was built on the experience and the achievements emerging from the separate BRITE (Basic Research in Industrial Technologies for Europe) and EURAM (European Research on Advanced Materials) programs. In particular, under BRITE (1985–8) 215 shared-cost research projects were developed. The Commission allocated 180 million ECU (MECU) to that program. The most relevant aim of the program was to develop the applications of new technologies and new materials in traditional industrial sectors. During the same time span under the EURAM (1986–9) program the Commission approved 91 projects, for about 30 MECU. The program had as its main goal to stimulate the development of research in new materials (Commission, 1992, 65).

The BRITE-EURAM I (1989–92) program (henceforth BE I) is the aggregation and extension of these two programs. It was approved by the Council of Ministers in March 1989. It was budgeted under the Second Framework Program for about 500 MECU. The main aim of this four-year program was to improve the competitiveness of European manufacturing industry in the world market. The following strategic objectives were also indicated: (1) to foster trans-frontier collaboration in strategic industrial research; (2) to support the transfer of technology across Community frontiers and between sectors, particularly those with many small and medium-sized enterprises (SMEs); (3) to underpin the process of European cohesion (Commission, 1993a, 9–16). Even if the program was devoted to pre-competitive research it was characterized, more than the previous two, by market oriented activity. The Program covered five R&D areas:

(1) Advanced materials technology,
(2) Design methodology and assurance,
(3) Application of manufacturing technologies,
(4) Technologies for manufacturing processes,
(5) Aeronautics.

To assist SMEs, the program included not only shared-cost research contracts, but also concerted actions and feasibility awards.[11] Emphasis on SMEs and market orientation of research distinguished the BE I program from the previous two.

In September 1991, within the Third Framework Program, the Industrial and Material Technology program (BRITE-EURAM II) was approved for the period 1991–4 by the Council of Ministers. The operating budget of the program was approximately 670 MECU. This program arose from the merging of the two programs BE I and Raw Materials and Recycling (1990–2).[12] Following the previous program, the basis of BRITE-EURAM II (henceforth BE II) was the revitalization of European manufacturing industry. Its main aims were: (1) to increase the competitiveness of European industry in the face of strong international challenges, particularly in strategic sectors of advanced technology; (2) to strengthen European economic and social cohesion consistent with the pursuit of scientific and technical excellence; (3) to increase implementation of advanced technologies by SMEs; (4) to increase involvement of manufacturing SMEs in European RTD, thereby developing links with other enterprises (Commission, 1992, 7–11).

The program was characterized by a focus on advanced technology, the relevance given to the process of European economic and social cohesion and by the particular support for the SMEs' participation.[13] The program included three main technical areas – i.e. areas of research:

[11] "Concerted Actions" are projects to support the coordination of broad-based, pan-European collaborative research activities in promising new technologies with the benefit of real added-value as a result of cross-border collaboration. The EC supports the coordination costs, but not the research cost. "Feasibility Awards" are a special type of contract, available to SMEs, that covers up to 75 percent of the costs of research undertaken within nine months (subject to a maximum of 30,000 ECU) to establish the feasibility of a concept, process or material for a collaborative BRITE-EURAM project.

[12] During the two-years life of the RAW program, 69 shared-cost research projects for about 23 MECU were carried out.

[13] The Cooperative Research Action for Technology (CRAFT) is designed to provide enterprises, especially SMEs not having their own research facilities, with the possibility to contract outside research institutes to carry out research on their behalf (Commission, 1992, 13).

(1) Materials and raw materials:
    (1A) Raw materials and recycling
    (1B) New and improved materials and their processing
(2) Design and manufacturing
    (2A) Design
    (2B) Manufacturing and engineering
(3) Aeronautics.

Industrial enterprises, universities, research centers and other institutions have taken part in the program through five different support schemes. (1) shared-cost collaborative research projects – in particular, about 90 percent of the available Community research budget was ascribed to the two subcategories Industrial research (80 percent) and Focused fundamental research (10 percent); (2) Concerted actions already implemented in BE I; (3) Accompanying measures, particularly important among which were the Feasibility awards; (4) Cooperative research actions for technology; and (5) Targeted research actions, which imply that for specific subjects of common interest (e.g. environmentally friendly technologies and flexible and clean manufacturing) industrial research projects may be grouped together and be subject to special coordination to ensure synergy between the separate projects. What is interesting is the continuity between the two BRITE-EURAM programs. Indeed, BE II can be seen as a further step in the process of definition of a European program. As a result of the Maastricht Treaty and the feedback from the previous program, BE II turned out to be a program with a clearer strategic orientation and an improved and enlarged variety of support schemes.

The new research and technological development program in the field of industrial and materials technologies, BRITE-EURAM III (1994–8) (henceforth BE III) was approved by the Council of Ministers in July 1994. The operating budget of the program is about 1,700 MECU. The concern with the competitive position of European manufacturing industry is still at the heart of the program – in particular, competitiveness is seen as the most effective means of maintaining and even increasing employment. As a result of the economic recession (1990–3) and increased concern about pollution levels, the program aims to stimulate industry's capacity to "develop technology for human-centered production system taking account of human factors and based on clean technologies" (Commission, 1994a, 7). Three specific objectives are identified. They are:

[(1)] in the short term, priority should be assigned to research for the adaptation of existing technologies, or for the development of new technologies ... particularly in sectors where the level of technology is lower; SMEs in these sectors account for a large proportion of European industry; [(2)] in the medium term, research will focus on industries which are already developing innovative technologies and strategies allowing better use of human resources while endeavoring to reduce the adverse environmental impact of production; [(3)] in the long term, research will focus on new technologies for the production and the design of products which allow new industries or markets to be created in a context of sustainable growth. (Commission, 1994a, 8).

The program will include three main technical areas – i.e. areas of research – which are:
(1) Production technologies for future industries
(2) Technologies for product innovation
(3) Technologies for means of transport.

While the first two, with a different name and different sub-classes, are similar to the first two areas of BE II, the third has been broadened to include not only aeronautics but also other technologies for transportation. The program will be implemented through the same schemes of support used in BE II. The only new tool is the Pre-normative research project linked to the fulfillment of the general goal of the Fourth Framework Program of supporting the other Community policies through pre-normative research. Finally, the observation we made for the evolution of BE II in comparison with BE I, can also be made for the new program vs. the previous one. What we want to underline here is the existence of an *evolution process* which can be linked to the change of external economic and non-economic factors. However, the various modifications do not affect the group of consolidated features of the "BRITE-EURAM family."

References

Commission of the European Communities (1992). "A Universe of Possibilities: Industrial and Material Technologies. Information package, Brussels
    (1993a). "Evaluation of the BRITE/EURAM program (1988 1992) – (areas 1 to 4), Report EUR 15070, Brussels
    (1993b). "Economics Evaluation of the Effects of the BRITE/EURAM programs on European industry," Report EUR 15171, EN, Brussels
    (1994a). "Proposal for a Council Decision Adopting a Specific Research and Technological Development Program in the Field of Industrial and Materials Technologies, Brussels
    (1994b). "The European report on science and technology indicators 1994," Report EUR 15897 EN, Brussels
    (1996). "Evaluation of the Economic Effects of the Programmes EURAM, BRITE and BRITE-EURAM I," Report EUR 16877, EN, Brussels
    (1997). "Evaluation and Analysis of the Technological Transfer Generated by the Programmes EURAM, BRITE and BRITE-EURAM I," Report EUR 16878, EN, Brussels
Dasgupta, P. and P. A. David (1994). "Towards a New Economics of Science," *Research Policy*, 23, 487–521

David, P. A. (1994). "Positive Feedbacks and Research Productivity in Science: Reopening Another Black Box," in O. Granstraad, (ed.), *Economics of Technology*, Amsterdam: Elsevier Science Publisher

Gambardella, A. and W. Garcia-Fontes (1996). "Regional Linkages through European Research Funding," *Economics of Innovation and New Technology*, 4, 123–38

Geuna, A. (1996). "The Participation of Higher Education Institutions in Community Framework Programmes," *Science and Public Policy*, 23, 287–296, see chapter 15 in this volume

MacKinnon, J., H. White, and R. Davidson (1983). "Test for Model Specification in the Presence of Alternative Hypotheses: Some Further Results," *Journal of Econometrics*, 21, 53–70

Olson, M. and R. Zeckhauser (1966). "An Economic Theory of Alliances," *Review of Economics and Statistics*, 18, 266–79

Sandler, T. (1992). *Collective Action: Theory and Applications*, Ann Arbor: University of Michigan Press

Sandler, T. and J. Murdoch (1990). "Nash–Cournot or Lindahl Behavior?: An Empirical Test for the NATO Allies," *Quarterly Journal of Economics*, 105, 875–94

15 Patterns of university research in Europe

Aldo Geuna

Introduction

From the early 1980s onwards a transition took place from the post Second World War rationale for scientific funding to what can be referred to as the "competitive approach" to university research behavior and funding. Governments exerted increasing pressures on universities to focus their research on national economic priorities, and the funding of science has shifted from a period of continuous expansion to one of constant or shrinking budgets.[1] Policies aimed at concentration and selectivity of research funds – and, more generally, at a higher level of accountability and cost reduction – have been implemented. The new rationale for resource allocation to a university is based on an *ex post* evaluation of university performance via market forces or simulated market actions. Consumers, such as students, government, and other organizations, buy the services supplied by universities, giving in this way a direct evaluation of their output.

In Europe, the United Kingdom system based on *ex post* institutional accountability for performance quality is a clear example of the new market-steering approach. Although direct competition is not permitted, government can simulate market actions by adjusting its demand of university services in relation to absolute or relative institutional performance (Massy, 1996). Other European countries, such as the Netherlands, have started to implement similar approaches to university funding.[2] National policies aimed at concentration and selectivity of research funds may be

The comments and suggestions of Cristiano Antonelli, Anthony Arundel, Paul David, Alfonso Gambardella, Paola Garrone, Stephane Malo, Ed Steinmueller, and Katy Wakelin are gratefully acknowledged, as well as the financial support of the European Union Human Capital and Mobility Program, Contract no. ERB4050PL930320. This chapter draws heavily upon Geuna (1996, 1998).
[1] See Ziman (1994) for the analysis of science in a "steady state."
[2] For a description of the changes in the Dutch higher-education system, see Maassen, Goedegebuur, and Westerheijden (1993); van Vught (1997). Van Vught suggests that the new government strategy towards higher education in the Netherlands is the outcome of both government planning and market coordination.

further reinforced by EU research actions. The four Framework Programs of the Commission of the European Communities for the support of R&D cooperative projects have been characterized by a highly competitive approach to research funding (see also chapter 14 in this volume). Higher-Education Institutions (HEIs), almost exclusively universities, have increasingly taken part in these R&D cooperative projects. In the Fourth Framework Program they became the largest single type of institution both in terms of the number of times they participated in an EU-funded R&D cooperative project and in terms of the funds received.

The increasing participation of HEIs in each successive Framework Program may influence the structure of university research funding in both direct and indirect ways.[3] The EU contribution is small relative to the total budget of a university; nonetheless, it is relevant when compared to similar sources of funds. As an example, consider the situation in the United Kingdom. A comparison of funding for each university from Community sources vs. research grants and contracts of Research Councils in 1992–3 shows that, on average EU funds are 21 percent of Research Councils' funds. However, for about 10 percent of the institutions EU funding represents more than 50 percent of Research Councils' funds.

The purpose of this chapter is to study university participation in EU-funded R&D cooperative projects. Specifically, the analysis focuses on the determinants of university participation. It will be highlighted how, among other factors, the characteristics and behavior of the universities, the behavior of the funding agency, and the unintended consequences of the selection mechanisms for allocating funds are relevant for the understanding of university participation.

The unit of analysis can vary from the most disaggregated level of the research group to the entire institution. For the present study, we develop a cross-country analysis at the university level.[4] To generate an unbiased analysis, the availability of information on the reference population – i.e. participants and non-participants – is extremely important. In our case, it is possible to consider the totality of recognized universities in the EU countries as the total population, without over-imposing any selection bias. For each of these institutions, on top of institutional information, we gathered the number of times they took part in a R&D cooperative project in the First, Second, and Third Framework Programs. On the basis of this original data set, we formulated an empirical model to test for the relevance of different factors on both the probability of joining an EU-funded R&D project and the actual number of times a university participated.

[3] See David, Geuna, and Steinmueller (1995) for the analysis of the unintended effects of EU university research funding on the UK university system.
[4] For the reasons for this choice see p. 376.

This study has to be understood in the framework of an analysis of resource-allocation criteria.[5] Together with chapters 13 and 14 in this volume, it represents one of the outputs of a larger research program for understanding the institutional mechanisms and resource-allocation criteria characterizing publicly financed research.

The chapter is organized as follows. We discuss the increasing participation of HEIs in cooperative R&D projects of the Community Framework Programs, then present the unit of analysis, describe the data set and introduce some of the factors that influence university participation in EU-funded R&D projects. The econometric model and the interpretation of the results are then set out and finally, some policy implications and conclusive remarks are offered.

HEI participation in community programs

Efforts of the European Union to establish a targeted program for improving industrial competitiveness through the mechanism of funded research began officially with the First Framework Program (1984–7). The Framework was set up with the goal of strengthening strategic areas of European competitiveness. The mechanisms selected for the Framework included: (1) funding the R&D effort of private firms, research institutes, and higher-education institutes[6] in strategic areas; and (2) attempting to allocate funding to stimulate the formation of research networks spanning organizational and national boundaries. With the Second Framework Program (1987–91), the Community decided to use it as "the basis and instrument of European research and technology policy ... thus providing a clear structure for long-term overall objectives."[7] A comprehensive political strategy on technology, enjoying equal status with other key Community policy areas, was set out. The Third Framework Program (1990–4) was characterized by the regrouping of activities around three strategic areas with 15 separate programs and by the reinforcement of the aim of convergence among the member states of the Union. Nonetheless, as is clearly stressed in Commission (1992, 11) "where projects are evenly matched in qualitative terms, preference will be given to projects involving participants from technologically less well developed regions" the Community shows a lexicographic structure of preferences, with convergence subordinated to quality. The Fourth Framework Program (1994–8)

---

[5] See, among others, Arora, David, and Gambardella (1998); Dasgupta and David (1994); David (1994); Geuna (1997).
[6] The Community reimburses up to 50 percent of actual project costs to companies or research institutes, and to universities and other higher-education establishments it reimburses 100 percent of additional costs.   [7] See Commission (1992).

Table 15.1 *The Framework Programs*

Program	Duration	EU contribution
First Framework	1984–7	3,750 MECU
Second Framework	1987–91	5,396 MECU
Third Framework	1990–4	6,600 MECU
Fourth Framework	1994–8	13,100 MECU[a]
Fifth Framework	1998–2002	14,000 MECU[b]

Notes:
[a] Includes activities that were not encompassed in the other three Frameworks. The original amount of 12,300 MECU was increased after the enlargement of the Union.
[b] The Commission proposed a budget of 16,300 MECU in April 1997. On February 12 1998, the Council of Ministers approved a reduction of 2.3 MECU.
Sources: Commission (1994, 1997).

pursues the guidelines of the previous one, putting more emphasis on consistency between national and Community policy. The Program is structured in 13 "vertical" programs and three "horizontal" actions. Two new areas of research – transport and socio-economic research – have been added. In April 1997 the Commission put forward a proposal for a Fifth Framework Program (1998–2002). The new Program is characterized by a "problem-solving" approach with a focus on generic technologies. The aims of the Program have also been broadened, giving higher importance to the socio-economic impact of research.

In the course of implementing the succession of Frameworks, EU research and technological development policy has expanded in budgetary scope, as illustrated in table 15.1, and has developed a few key goals. In particular, the total budget of the Fifth Framework is about four times that of the First Framework Program in nominal value. However, the budget of the Fifth Framework is slightly inferior to that of the previous one in real terms.

The institutions that participate in the Framework Program are classified by the Commission[8] in one of the following five categories: Big Companies (BIG); Small and Medium Enterprises (SMEs); Public or Private Research Centres (RECs); Higher Education Institutions (HEIs); Others. Table 15.2 shows the distribution of the five types of institutions in terms of (a) number of times they participated in an R&D cooperative project and (b) funding for shared cost action for the Second and Third Framework Program.

[8] The participant in a project is required to classify her institution in one of these categories.

Table 15.2 *Distribution of participation and funding, by organizational type: Second, Third, and Fourth Frameworks*

	Second Framework program Part.[a]	Third Framework program Part.	Fourth Framework program Part.[b]	Second Framework program Funds	Third Framework program Funds	Fourth Framework program Funds[b]
BIG	21.9	21.3	19.3	41.1	34.2	26.8
SMEs	18.1	14.5	17.3	18.7	16.4	16.1
RECs	29.5	29.8	25.1	20.8	23.5	23.9
HEIs	29.2	31.5	29.3	18.9	22.5	27.4
Others	1.2	2.9	9.1	0.6	3.4	5.9

Notes:
[a] Part. = participation.
[b] The figures refer to the period January 1, 1994–December 31, 1996.
Source: Elaboration of Commission data (1994, 1997).

Three main observations emerge from the analysis of table 15.2. First, Big Companies suffered an important decrease between the Second and Fourth Framework, both in their participation level and in their funding. Part of the 14.3 percentage-point cut in Big Companies' funding was redistributed to public or private research centers and, especially, to higher-education institutions and other organizations, with the result that the funding of HEIs approached 28 percent in the Fourth Framework Program, up from 19 percent during the Second. Second, the share of HEIs has increased, accounting for somewhat less than one-third of the total participation in projects. Universities, almost the totality of HEIs,[9] became in the Fourth Framework Program the largest single type of institution, both in terms of the number of times they participated in an EU-funded R&D cooperative project and in terms of funds received. Third, in all three periods "research institutions" have a higher share of participation than their share of funds. This means that funds are more thinly spread, on average, across participating units in the research centers and higher-education community than among participating businesses. For HEIs, the difference in share of participation and funding shrank in an important way between the Second and Fourth Framework Program.

[9] Among the 427 HEIs participating in Community Framework Programs 97 are post-secondary education institutions (PSIs) that are not recognized as universities. However, each of these PSIs has participated in few projects, accounting for only 4.3 percent of the total number of times HEIs participated in EU-funded R&D cooperative projects (Geuna, 1996).

Table 15.3 *Collaborative links involving HEIs and RECs, Second and Third Frameworks*

Organization type	Second Framework		Third Framework[a]	
	HEIs (%)	RECs (%)	HEIs (%)	RECs (%)
HEIs	25.6	36.0	29.8	42.4
RECs	36.7	28.6	40.6	28.5
BIG	19.6	18.5	14.8	14.1
SMEs	16.6	15.4	12.1	11.8
Others	1.5	1.5	2.7	3.1
Total	100	100	100	100

Notes:
[a] The figure for the Third Framework Program refers to some 85% of the contracts.
Source: David, Geuna, and Steinmueller (1995).

HEIs play an important role in the EU's research and technological development policy. On the one hand, they supply basic knowledge needed by business enterprises and, on the other, they benefit from gaining access to complementary expertise and instrumentation in Big Companies' R&D laboratories. Moreover, for HEIs, participation in a Framework project means not only access to EU funding, but also the opportunity to interact with industry and other research organizations in the formation of new, high-quality research networks. This is especially important for countries with lower scientific and technological resources because it enables them to overcome the constraints imposed by the small size of their research community.

Table 15.3 describes the evolution of collaborative links[10] by organization type for HEIs and RECs. In moving from the Second to the Third Framework Programs, the number of HEIs' links with other HEIs and with research centers increased; nonetheless, 29 percent of their links are still with industrial partners. The number of links is affected by the increasing numbers of HEIs and RECs participating in the Framework, but despite this increase, university–industry collaborations remain important in the Third Framework.

When one considers the total number of collaborative links between the same and different types of participants (see table 15.4), it is possible to

[10] "Collaborative links" are connections established between each of the participants in a research and technological development contract. For the calculation of the number of collaborative links a participant may be the coordinator, a contractor, or an associate contractor (Commission, 1994).

Table 15.4 *Total collaborative links, Second and Third Frameworks*

	BIG		SMEs		RECs		HEIs		Others		Total	
	Second FP	Third FP[a]	Second FP	Third FP[a]	Second FP	Third FP[a]	Second FP	Third FP[a]	Second FP	Third FP[a]	Second FP	Third FP[a]
BIG	6,609	3,703	4,753	3,954	3,770	3,569	3,898	3,914	81	558	19,111	15,698
SMEs	4,753	3,954	2,643	2,227	3,135	2,986	3,305	3,194	73	630	13,909	12,991
RECs	3,770	3,569	3,135	2,986	5,813	7,204	7,320	10,706	305	789	20,343	25,254
HEIs	3,898	3,914	3,305	3,194	7,320	10,760	5,091	7,876	307	700	19,921	26,390
Others	81	558	73	630	305	789	307	700	25	311	791	2,988

Note:
[a] The figure for the Third Framework Program refers to some 85% of the contracts.
Source: Elaboration of Commission data.

identify three relevant groups. First, the *industrial* group – i.e. collaborative links BIG–BIG, SMEs–SMEs and BIG–SMEs – with about 30 percent and 19 percent of the links in the Second and Third Frameworks, respectively. Second, the *research* group – i.e. collaborative links HEIs–HEIs, RECs–RECs and HEIs–RECs – which have not only the largest but also an increasing share of links about 39 percent and 50 percent, respectively. Third, the *hybrid* group – i.e. collaborative links across the institutions of the two previous groups – with about 30 percent and 27 percent, respectively. The cooperation between "research institutions" and industry, characteristic of the hybrid group, although decreasing, is nonetheless a significant part of the picture.

Finally, EU contractual funding across different programs managed by DG XII (Directorate-General, Science, Research and Development) of the Commission is analyzed. On the one hand, when one considers the share distribution for each program by type of participant, it is possible to identify a group of programs in which HEIs have about 50 percent of the funds. They are Step/Epoch, Bridge, and Science and Technology for Development,[11] in the Second Framework, and Environment, Marine Science and Technology, Biotechnology and Life Sciences; and Technologies For Developing Countries, in the Third Framework.[12] On the other hand, when the share distribution for each type of participant by program is considered the previous group of university oriented programs loses importance. The two industrially oriented programs – Esprit and BRITE-EURAM – and their continuation under the Third Framework Program, are always the most important sources of HEIs' funding.[13]

In the Fourth Framework Program HEIs became the largest single type of institution, in terms both of the number of times they participated in an EU-funded R&D cooperative project and of funds received. They have developed collaborative links especially with other research institutions, but also taking part in a significant number of projects with industrial partners. Finally, although they are the dominant player in a few Framework Programs particularly oriented towards HEIs, they also participate in a respectable number of projects in the industrially oriented programs.

Four main observations can be drawn from this analysis. First, if the financial trend of the first part of the Fourth Framework Program is sustained throughout to its end, the distribution of funds by type of partici-

---

[11] Because of their specific character the programs under the heading Improvements to European Scientific and Technological Cooperation, Medical and Health; BCR; and Fusion are not included in the analysis.

[12] Because of their specific character the programs under the heading Human Capital and Mobility and Fusion are not included in the analysis.

[13] Only Environment, among the programs of the previous group, receives in absolute terms a relevant share of funds (16 percent).

pant will tend to become more homogeneous across the groups. Second, the increasing share of HEIs, within a Framework Program characterized by a growing budget, implies growing impact over time of EU funds on the higher-education finance system. In particular, in a period of budget cuts, restructuring and internationalization of the European higher-education system, the availability of a new competitive source of funds can have extremely important consequences.[14] Third, the growing budget of the Framework Program represents a vital opportunity for institutions in countries with few resources to overcome the constraints imposed by the small size of their national research community. Fourth, in the course of the four Framework Programs HEIs have developed varied ways to draw upon EU funds. They have joined cooperative projects that range from grants to university consortia for basic research to university–industry cooperation in market oriented research.

With these issues in mind, it becomes crucial to understand why some universities and other PSIs are taking part with different frequency in cooperative projects within the EU Framework Program. After the presentation of the unit of study and the description of the data set, we shall focus our analysis on the understanding of the determinants of university participation in EU-funded R&D cooperative projects. We shall then estimate an econometric model for university participation.

University participation in EU-funded R&D cooperative projects

In Europe there is no standardization on the definition of PSIs and Universities; in different countries, these terms carry varying connotations. However, in all the EU countries, the institutions granted University status have gone through a national selection process that can be considered more stringent then the one for the granting of PSI status. This category can therefore be considered more homogeneous. Moreover, most PSIs are teaching oriented institutions only marginally involved in research; those that are involved in research are generally more oriented towards a regional or national type of networking, and only when their scientific research quality is high will they try to access the EU funding system. For this reason, whereas all universities can be considered candidates for EU research funds, only a minority of PSIs would qualify. The totality of recognized universities in the EU countries is therefore considered the reference population here.

The ideal unit of analysis to understand university participation in EU-

---

[14] The impact and unintended effects of EU funding on the allocation of national public and private research funding going to higher-education institutions – i.e. university departments – in the United Kingdom are discussed in David, Geuna, and Steinmueller (1995).

funded R&D projects would be the research group or research center that applied for EU funds; this information is currently not available at the cross-country level. Although less informative, the analysis of university participation in EU-funded R&D cooperative projects at the aggregate level of the university can offer useful insights. Clearly, this unit of analysis has a size bias: large universities tend to have more research groups and consequently tend to participate more in EU projects. Nonetheless, controlling for size, other factors such as scientific research productivity, geographical localization, and scientific orientation are useful to explain participation in EU projects. Besides, the analysis at the institutional level has independent justifications. First, although the literature on R&D cooperation emphazises the centrality of the research group, particularly in this special case of international cooperation, the identity of the institution – i.e. Cambridge University vs. De Montfort University – plays an important role. In particular, because the funding agency – i.e. the Commission – is not perfectly informed, the institutional reputation or "the name" of the institution becomes a substitute for missing information on specific researchers or research groups. Second, to develop an international cooperation with a well known university means also to originate positive image externalities for the institution involved. The literature recognizes one of the main incentives for cooperation in the augmented image and prestige due to the link;[15] then, again, the institution itself comes to the fore. Third, taking the university as the unit of analysis enables us to have information on the total population – i.e. both the universities that have joined EU-funded R&D projects and the ones that have not taken part in them – and consequently the analysis at the university level will not have any selection bias. Fourth, from a methodological point of view, macro-analysis at the institution level enables us to draw the background picture of this particular area of R&D cooperation. In future research, micro-analysis at the research-group level will be carried out on the basis of the results of current work.

By 1992, there were 379 active universities in the EU.[16] We have classified an institution in the category "University" following the official national classification. In addition to the national classification systems, two other main sources of information have been used: (1) the *International Handbook of Universities* (International Association of Universities, 1991, 1993), and (2) the *World of Learning* (1995). When discrepancies between the sources were found, an institution has been classified in the category "University" if the institution was entitled to grant a doctoral (PhD) degree. In a few cases, mainly in Spain and Portugal, the most recent uni-

---

[15] See for example Malerba, Morawetz, and Paquaig (1991).
[16] Austria, Finland, Luxembourg, and Sweden are not included.

versities were not taken into account. When clearly distinguishable, Art, Physical Education, and Education schools were excluded.[17] The three institutions, Universitaire Centrum Antwerpen, Universitaire Faculteiten Sint-Ignatius te Antwerpen, and Universitaire Instelling Antwerpen, have been subsumed under the University of Antwerp. Finally, to calculate the number of United Kingdom universities the information from the *Universities' Statistical Record* was used. The resulting value of 71 is caused by the fact that the University of London is sub-divided into 22 colleges; both the University of Cambridge and the University of Oxford are included as single institutions (the different colleges forming them have not been considered); the three institutions, Manchester Business School, Manchester University, and UMIST, have been subsumed in the University of Manchester.[18]

The data regarding the participation of universities in EU-funded R&D cooperative projects have been provided by DG XII of the Commission. They refer to shared-cost actions funded by DG XII under the First, Second, and Third Framework Program.[19] However, the data for the First Framework Program are not complete because the database of DG XII was created only after the end of the program, and then only part of the data concerning the Program was stored in it. The information for the Third Framework Program is also only up to March 15 1994.

For each university, the geographical information and the number of contract partner links were made available, the latter representing the number of times a HEI has been involved in an EU-funded R&D cooperative project. No time or program information was released. Constructed in this way, the database comprises 330 universities, representing 86 percent of the total population of universities in the EU countries considered.

The 379 institutions forming the total population of European universities can be sub-divided into participants and non-participants. The following variables have been used to study both groups:

PART: The number of times a university has been involved in an EU-funded R&D cooperative project

NRES: The number of researchers, including the total of

[17] In most of the countries these schools are not included in the "University" category; in the few cases in which they have university status, they were not counted.

[18] In the case of both the University of Antwerp and the University of Manchester, the different institutions have been subsumed owing to the impossibility of identifying a more detailed institutional association of the scholars in publication counts.

[19] In both the Second and the Third Framework the research concerned with information and communications technologies was under the supervision of DG XIII, and is therefore not included in the data set. Some other small programs directed by DG VI, DG XIII and DG XIV are not included either. About 55 percent – 60 percent of the funds were administered by DG XII.

	full-time academic staff *plus*, when present, 50 percent of part-time academic staff in 1992; it is used as a proxy for the size of the university
PUBS:	The number of papers published within a certain institution in 1993; an all-author count, in which the paper is credited to each of the participating authors, has been applied,[20] the data source is the Science Citation Index, CD-ROM version 1993[21]
RATIO:	The ratio between the number of publications and the number of researchers (*PUBS/NRES*); it is used as a partial proxy for the scientific research productivity of the university
FIELDS:	The scientific fields in which the institution grants a doctoral degree; these are converted into a categorical variable to classify the institutions in relation to their disciplinary composition
NEWOLD:	The founding year of the institution; this has been turned into a categorical variable to classify the institutions in relation to their historical age.

Table 15.5 presents the descriptive statistics for the four continuous variables. 326 universities (four cases have been excluded owing to missing data) have participated from a minimum of one time to a maximum of 420 times in a cooperative project. They have participated on average in 56 projects. The high kurtosis (5.536) and the positive skewness (2.130), together with the high standard deviations (66) and large difference between min and max, indicate concentration in the values. Moreover, as the first three quartiles have respectively, the values 10, 32, and 78, one can describe the population of universities participating in EU-funded R&D projects as

---

[20] For an analysis of the problems connected with the data collection, see Commission (1994, 8–40). Special mention must be made of the peculiar role played by hospitals. Their weight in the presence count is not just over-estimated because of the effect of co-authorship, it is also often unclear whether they are linked to the university or not. Hence in some cases the publication is counted as "University" and in other cases as "Hospital". This varies among the European countries because of the widespread institutional variety. For an analysis of the shortcomings inherent in the use of publications count as an indicator of university research output see, among others, Johnes (1992); Martin and Irvine (1983); Moet, Burger, Frankfort, and Van Raan (1985).

[21] For humanities and social sciences there exists the specific Social Science SCI which, however, has not been utilized owing to the much lower propensity to publish of researchers in humanities and social sciences. These data are thus biased to the detriment of institutions with humanities or social science departments. However, under the first three Framework Programs only a minor part of the budget was indirectly committed to socio-economic studies, so that this is not considered a serious weakness for purposes of the present analysis.

Table 15.5 *Descriptive statistics for the main variables*

	Mean			Std. Dev.			Min			Max		
	TP[a,d]	P[b,e]	NP[c,f]	TP[d]	P[e]	NP[f]	TP[d]	P[e]	NP[f]	TP[d]	P[e]	NP[f]
EUPART	49	56	0	65	66	0	0	1	0	420	420	0
NRES	887	922	631	946	896	1232	15	36	15	7330	7000	7330
PUBS	415	461	84	519	530	258	5[g]	5[g]	5[g]	3185	3185	1397
RATIO	0.568	0.636	0.078	0.971	1.016	0.142	0.005	0.005	0.005	12.34	12.34	0.598

Notes:
[a] Total population; eight cases have been excluded owing to missing data.
[b] Participants.
[c] Non-participants.
[d] 371 valid cases.
[e] 326 valid cases.
[f] 45 valid cases.
[g] Estimate value.

composed of a large number of institutions with little participation and a small group of institutions involved in a large number of cooperative agreements. Similar observations can be made when the other three variables are analyzed. Finally, when the descriptive statistics for the total population are compared to those of participants and non-participants, small positive differences for each of the four variables are present in the participants' distribution, while important negative differences characterize the non-participants' distribution. Thus, participation or non-participation in cooperative R&D projects financed by the EU appears to be non-independent from the size and the scientific research productivity of the institution.

To control for other effects than size – scientific research productivity and country fixed effects – we have gathered information on the disciplinary composition, and on its age – i.e. period of establishment.

The widespread institutional variety of the European university system has always constrained the value of international comparisons. The Rheinish–Westphalian Technical University in Aachen, Germany, has few things in common with the Eindhoven Technical University in Eindhoven, the Netherlands, for example.[22] The former has faculties such as philosophy and education, while the latter is an engineering school. Nonetheless, starting from the fact that the requirements for the doctoral degree are approximately standardized among the EU countries, we have classified the institutions according to the scientific fields in which they grant the PhD degree. In particular, taking into account the OECD classification for scientific fields – Agriculture, Medicine, Natural Sciences, Engineering, Social Sciences, and Humanities – we have created 28 categories:

- Six for the universities defined as *mono-disciplined*, which grant the doctoral degree in only one scientific field; each of the six classes contains observations.
- 15 for the universities defined as *bi-disciplined*, which grant the doctoral degree in two scientific fields; only nine of them include some institutions.
- Seven for the universities defined as *multi-disciplined*; in this group are included all the institutions that award a doctoral degree in three or more scientific fields. To better classify these universities we have controlled for the presence of Engineering, Medicine, and Natural Sciences. We have then sub-divided the group into seven categories, all of which contain observations.

For each institution, we have identified the founding year. In relation to this, we have classified the universities in one of the following four classes: (1) new post-war university (144 institutions) – all the institutions estab-

---

[22] The two cities are only 120 km from each other.

lished after 1945; (2) modern university (32 institutions) – including the institutions created between 1900 and 1945; (3) nineteenth-century universities (77 institutions) – as the name indicates, those founded between 1800 and 1900; and (4) old university (126 institutions) – embracing all the universities founded before 1800.

The number of times an institution participated in EU-funded R&D cooperative projects is a share of the number of its applications. Among other factors, the characteristics of the university – scientific research productivity, reputation, and disciplinary composition – influence the share of accepted applications. In turn, the total number of applications of a university is the sum of the applications of the single centers. It thus depends on the number of the centers – i.e. the size of the institution – and on the characteristics of the centers and of the university itself. In the following section, we shall develop an econometric model that analyzes the importance of a few institutional characteristics on university participation. In particular, we focus our analysis on the relevance of size and scientific research productivity.

An econometric test of the determinants of university participation

The aim of the regression analysis developed here is to test the relevance of size, scientific research productivity, and other fixed factors for university participation in EU-funded R&D cooperative projects.

As the number of times a university participated in cooperative projects (PART) takes values between 0 and 420, the OLS regression is not a suitable estimation procedure. Two different approaches can be used. One is a Tobit model with the number of times a university participated in projects as a censored dependent variable. The other is a two-equation model, where the first specification is a Probit model with a binary dependent variable which takes the value 1 when the university has participation, and 0 when it does not, and the second is a Truncated regression model for the non-limit observations – i.e. for a level of participation greater than zero. The two alternative approaches can be tested against each other.[23] The double specification can be tested as the unrestricted model against the restricted Tobit model.

The advantage of the two-equation model rests on the ability to separate the analysis of the participation in a project from the analysis of multi-participation. In this way, it is possible to separate the analysis of the probability of joining an EU-funded R&D project from the study of the level of participation in projects. The former informs us about the relevance of the

---

[23] See Cragg (1971) for the original specification of the two-equation model.

factors considered on the selection, while the latter provides information about the level of participation.

In the Tobit model (15.1), we regress the dependent variable *PART* on the independent variables number of researchers (*NRES*), and ratio between number of publications and number of researchers (*RATIO*). The first independent variable measures the size of the university, while the second is used as a proxy for its scientific research productivity. We assume a log-linear relation. Dummy variables (*DCOUNTRY*) for national fixed-effects and control dummy variables (*DSCIFIELD*) for scientific fields[24] are included. In the Probit model (15. 2) the dependent variable *Y* is the probability of being involved in a project, which takes the value 1 when the university has participation, and 0 when it does not. The same set of independent variables is used.[25] In the Truncated regression model (15.3) only the universities that have participated in at least one EU-funded R&D cooperative project are considered. The dependent variable *P* is the number of times a university participated in projects and is recorded only when it is greater than 0. The independent variables are the ones used in the previous two equations. As in the Tobit model, we assume a log-linear relation. The (15.1), (15.2) and (15.3) are then formulated as:

$$\ln (1 + PART) = \alpha + \beta_1 \ln NRES + \beta_2 \ln RATIO +$$
$$\Sigma_{i=1..n}\, \beta_i\, DCOUNTRY_i + + \Sigma_{j=1..m}\, \beta_j\, DSCIFIELD_j + \varepsilon_1 \qquad (15.1)$$

where n = number of countries = 10 and m = scientific fields categories = 8.

$$Y = \delta + \gamma_1 \ln NRES + \gamma_2 \ln RATIO + \Sigma_i$$
$$=_{1..n}\, \gamma_i\, DCOUNTRY_i + + \Sigma_j$$
$$=_{1..m}\, \gamma_j\, DSCIFIELD_j + \varepsilon_2 \qquad (15.2)$$

where $Y = 1$ if $PART > 0$ and $Y = 0$ if $PART = 0$; n = number of countries = 9 and m = scientific fields categories = 7.

$$\ln (1 + P) = \chi + \mu_1 \ln NRES + \mu_2 \ln RATIO +$$
$$\Sigma_i =_{1..n}\, \mu_i\, DCOUNTRY_i + + \Sigma_j$$
$$=_{1..m}\, \mu_j\, DSCIFIELD_j + \varepsilon_3 \qquad (15.3)$$

where P is observed only when $PART > 0$; n = number of countries = 10 and m = scientific fields categories = 8.

Taking (15.1) as the restricted model and (15.2) and (15.3) together as the unrestricted model, we have used a likelihood-ratio test (LLR) to decide the best specification. As LLR is equal to 136.66, using a Chi-squared test with

[24] The nine dummies for scientific fields orientation are the result of a recategorization of the original classification into 22 classes given by the variable *FIELDS*.

[25] The dummy variables for the Netherlands, Denmark, and Natural and medicine universities are not included in 15.2 because the related universities always have probability 1.

Table 15.6 *Estimation results*

VAR	Tobit[c]	Probit[ac]	Truncated[bc]
LLR	−495.46	−77.18	−349.95
Constant	−1.312 (0.01)	5.333 (0.88)	−1.552 (0.00)
ln NRES	0.847 (0.00)	0.197 (0.19)	0.888 (0.00)
ln RATIO	0.560 (0.00)	0.321 (0.00)	0.498 (0.00)
DCOUNTRY			
Belgium	0.769 (0.00)	−3.961 (0.94)	0.853 (0.00)
Denmark	0.78E−1 (0.84)	–	−0.112 (0.70)
France	−0.522 (0.00)	−3.958 (0.94)	−0.646 (0.00)
Germany	−0.809 (0.00)	−4.604 (0.94)	−0.707 (0.00)
Greece	0.706 (0.01)	−2.777 (0.96)	0.293 (0.20)
Italy	−0.457 (0.02)	−3.654 (0.95)	−0.595 (0.00)
Ireland	0.950 (0.01)	−4.280 (0.94)	1.139 (0.00)
The Netherlands	−0.18E−1 (0.95)	–	−0.283 (0.25)
Portugal	0.312 (0.29)	−3.997 (0.94)	0.346 (0.17)
Spain	−0.852 (0.00)	−4.465 (0.94)	−0.860 (0.00)
United Kingdom	–	−4.036 (0.94)	–
DSCIFIELD			
Eng and Agr	0.804 (0.00)	−3.653 (0.95)	0.930 (0.00)
Soc and Hum	−0.844 (0.00)	−5.067 (0.93)	0.100 (0.68)
Nat and Med	−0.318 (0.24)	–	−0.313 (0.13)
Mix–scientific	0.46E−1 (0.85)	−3.677 (0.95)	0.90E−1 (0.64)
Mix–technical	0.952 (0.00)	−3.329 (0.95)	0.924 (0.00)
Multi–Soc and Hum	−0.124 (0.58)	−4.240 (0.94)	0.87E−1 (0.61)
Multi–Scientific	−0.192 (0.26)	−3.896 (0.94)	−0.137 (0.29)
Multi–Technical	0.305 (0.101)	−3.798 (0.94)	0.331 (0.01)
Multi-disciplinary	–	−3.602 (0.95)	–

Notes:
[a] Non-linear Probit; dependent variable: Binary; no. obs. 371.
[b] Non-linear Truncated regression; dependent variable: Positive participation; no. obs. 326.
[c] Coefficient significance between brackets; marginal effects have the same significance of coefficients.

21 degrees of freedom, the Tobit model was rejected at 99 percent probability.

The results of our estimation are shown in table 15.6. In the Probit equation,[26] the scientific research productivity of the institution has a positive

[26] The Probit model correctly predicts 90 percent of the outcomes.

and significant effect on the probability of taking part in an EU-funded R&D cooperative project, while the size of the university is not significant. None of the dummy variables for country and scientific-field fixed-effect have a significant value. These results highlight the fact that the probability of taking part in a cooperative R&D project financed by the Commission depends primarily on the scientific research productivity of the university. This is consistent with the results of Arora, David, and Gambardella (1998) which showed that, in the case of publicly funded R&D projects, the scientific reputation of the research group – and, in particular, its weighted number of past publications – is the main factor influencing the probability of being selected. Moreover, these results seem to confirm that the Commission acted consistently with its stated policy objectives of awarding research funds primarily on grounds of scientific and technological excellence.

Important differences in the influence and significance of the explanatory variables are present in the result of the Truncated regression model. Both size and scientific research productivity have positive and significant coefficients. Consistent with our expectations, the size effect – i.e. large universities tend to have more research groups and consequently tend to participate more in EU-funded R&D projects – has an important positive impact on the level of participation. Nonetheless, given the size, institutions with higher scientific research productivity are involved in more projects. Thus, while the probability of being granted funds depends primarily on the scientific research productivity of the university, the participation in R&D projects is affected by the size of the institution and, given its size, by its scientific research productivity.

Major country fixed-effects[27] are present in the Truncated regression model. They can be sub-divided into three sub-groups. First, the dummy variables for France, Germany, Italy, and Spain have negative significant values. Given the size and scientific research performance, universities in these countries had a lower participation rate. Among the many possible explanations, the negative sign of these dummies could be related to the administrative and bureaucratic structure of their national university system. In predominantly publicly financed systems, the novelty of a competitive financing process has constrained the propensity to participate in EU-funded R&D projects. Although their university systems have a high quality, they are extremely bureaucratic and are not used to external cooperation and competitive fund-raising. Moreover, particularly in the case of France and Italy, a large portion of research is realized in public research organizations – CNRS (France), Max Planck Society (Germany), CNR

---

[27] The reference country is United Kingdom.

(Italy), CSIC (Spain) and other public research centers – and hence the research intensity of the university system tends to be lower than in other countries.

Second, the dummy variable for Ireland has positive and significant values. Other factors being equal, this indicates that Irish universities had an advantage in the level of participation. This advantage can be interpreted as the result of the policy objectives of the Commission. As we highlighted on p. 369, since the First Framework Program, technological and economic convergence among the member states of the EU has been a major policy aim. From the Third Framework Program onwards in particular, a clear technological cohesion policy has been developed. Projects involving partners from less favored[28] regions tend to be preferred to projects of the same quality but without members from less developed regions. Some results show that the cohesion policy probably also has a positive influence on the participation of Greek universities, while the statistical evidence does not support the same conclusion for those in Portugal.

Third, the dummy variable for Belgium has a positive and significant value. This indicates that, given the size and scientific research productivity, Belgian institutions succeeded in having a higher participation rate. A possible explanation is connected with the fact that the diffusion of information about how, where, and when to apply for EU funds has taken a relatively long period of time. Belgian universities, exploiting localization and information advantages, entered the system early and, consequently, developed a "first-entry advantage" that enabled the creation of "barriers to entry" to the disadvantage of later comers.[29]

The dummy variable for scientific field has been used to control for the bias inherent in the way we collected the number of publications and for the different propensities in publishing. In the chosen specification, the technology oriented institutions have positive and significant values.[30] The high value of their coefficients, on top of the control aspect, may also indicate the existence of an advantage for technology oriented universities. However, with the data available, no conclusive observations can be made.

Fixed effects to account for the age of the university have also been

---

[28] In the Council Regulation 93/2081/EEC, Greece, Ireland, and Portugal are still included as an entire country in the less favored regions.

[29] For the discussion of the creation of barriers to entry in the context of selection of publicly funded R&D projects, see Geuna (1996). For evidence on the phenomenon in the UK context, see Pike and Charles (1995).

[30] We have also estimated other more detailed specifications. The coefficients of the institutions focused on medicine were sometimes significant and negative, indicating the presence of a over-estimation of the scientific research productivity of these institutions (see n. 20 for the discussion of reasons). Also because of the small number of institutions with this characteristic, the test for the restricted against the unrestricted specification did not allow us to reject the null hypothesis. Thus, we chose the nine dummies specification.

included. We used four dummies for the founding year as proxies for the reputation effect – the older the university, the higher the reputation. Even if some evidence of a positive coefficient for the modern universities were found, the test for the restricted against the unrestricted specification rejected the latter.

The results of the estimations of the two-equation model presented above point to the existence of important differences in the significance of the factors when they are used to explain the probability of joining an EU-funded R&D project or to explain the actual number of times a university participated in projects. Given other factors, such as differences among countries and scientific fields, the scientific research productivity of the university influences both the probability and the level of participation, while the size is significant only when used to explain the latter.

Among other reasons, the different frequency in participation seems to be affected by the characteristics and behavior of the universities themselves, the behavior of the funding agency, and the unintended consequences of the selection mechanisms. A possible interpretation of the results of the estimations points to the existence of a set of factors that seems to have a significant influence on the frequency of participation. First, as the large universities tend to have more research groups – and, consequently, tend to have a high level of participation in EU-funded R&D cooperative projects – the size distribution of the total population of European universities may influence the skewness of the distribution of participation. Second, the existence of important differences in scientific research productivity and the presence of cumulative and self-reinforcement mechanisms could explain why only a small number of universities has a high participation rate. Third, the differences in the national systems of higher education may have created different incentives for participating in EU-funded R&D projects. Fourth, the priorities of EU R&D policy, especially as concerns cohesion policy and technology orientation, may influence the frequency of the distribution of participation. Finally, the localization and information advantage enjoyed by some institutions may as we saw above have enabled the creation of barriers to entry, permitting them a larger level of participation.

Conclusions

A growing share of the income of universities in EU countries is generated through research grants and contracts from both national agencies and the Union. This increased reliance upon contractual funding is the result of the process of re-examination and modification of the rationale for resource allocation to universities. To raise the short-term efficiency of higher-education institutions, governments make increasing use of competitive mechanisms for resource allocation, developing a market-steering approach to university research funding. EU funding of university research via the Framework Programs accounts for an important share of the research income granted by means of competitive mechanisms. In this context, the understanding of university participation in EU-funded R&D cooperative projects becomes an issue of crucial relevance.

This chapter has examined the determinants of university participation in EU-funded R&D cooperative projects. We studied an original data set describing the totality of European universities in terms of institutional characteristics and number of times the university participated in R&D cooperative projects of the three Commission Framework Programs. An econometric model has been developed to test for the relevance of different factors on both the probability of joining an EU-funded R&D cooperative project and the actual level of participation in projects.

Some evidence has been found to support the idea that scientific research productivity influences both the probability of joining an EU-funded R&D project and the number of times an institution has participated in projects, while research size has a positive influence only on the latter. Given the size and scientific research productivity of the university, other factors are important to explain the different frequency in participation. Among others, three seem to be consonant with the results of the estimations. First, the bureaucratization and lack of practice in competitive fund-raising of the university system may have a negative influence on the propensity to take part in EU-funded R&D cooperative projects. Second, the existence of techno-economic convergence aims for the Framework Programs tends to privilege the participation of institutions localized in less favored regions. Third, due to the unintended consequences of selection mechanisms, early entrants in the system tend to have advantages in repeated participation.

Our estimations suggest that scientific excellence is important in the decision process of the Commission, but we also found some evidence of the influence of cohesion policy. The importance given to scientific research productivity, through the effect of cumulative and self-reinforcement mechanisms, creates a repeated selection of a minority of high-research-intensive institutions. This tends to maximize short-term research outcomes. Nonetheless, longer-term goals are pursued when, following the guidelines of cohesion policy, universities in less favored regions have a priority advantage in participation.[31] In this way, especially in the case of university research, positive knowledge spillovers may increase those regions' research capabilities.

---

[31] For the development of this problematique in the case of the BRITE-EURAM program, see Gambardella and Garcia-Fontes (1996); see also chapter 14 in this volume.

Finally, if the consequences of selection based on the "quality principle" are reinforced by what we have called the first-entry advantage, another short-term vs. long-term trade-off should be considered. The characteristic of repeated selection may tend to reinforce the dominant research strategies (scientific paradigms and research programs), limiting research variety. The lack of incentives for path-breaking (and consequently more risky) research decreases the probability of scientific innovation,[32] potentially reducing the new knowledge base from which new technological innovations can emerge. On the other hand, the standardization of scientific knowledge enables increased communication and, as a result, a rise in the value of current science.

From a policy perspective, a better understanding of these two trade-offs, and of their interactions, is needed. Further analysis is also needed to evaluate the implications for the university funding structure of an increasing reliance on EU funding. In particular, improved indicators of scientific research activity – such as publication by scientific fields, publications weighted by their impact factor, and more detailed information on the universities participating in EU-funded R&D cooperative projects (for example, at the department level) – should be used.

References

Arora, A., P.A. David, and A. Gambardella (1998). Reputation and Competence in Publicly Funded Science: "Estimating the Effects on Research Group Productivity," *Les Annales d'Economie et de Statistiques*, 49/50, 163–98

Commission of the European Communities (1992). *EC Research Funding. A guide for Applicants*, Brussels

(1994). *The European Report on Science and Technology Indicators 1994*, Report EUR 15897 EN, Brussels

(1997). *Fifth Framework Programme for Research and Technical Development (1998–2002). Commission Working Paper on the Specific Programmes: Starting Points for Discussion*, COM (97) 553 Final, Brussels

Cragg, J. (1971). "Some Statistical models for Limited Dependent Variables with Application to the Demand for Durable Goods," *Econometrica*, 39, 829–44

Dasgupta, P. and P.A. David (1994). "Toward a New Economics of Science," *Research Policy*, 23, 487–521

David, P.A. (1994). "Positive Feedbacks and Research Productivity in Science: Reopening Another Black Box," in O. Granstraad (ed.), *Economics and Technology*, Amsterdam and London: North-Holland

David, P.A., A. Geuna, and W.E. Steinmueller (1995). "Additionality as a Principle of European R&D Funding," report for the STOA Program of the European

---

[32] For the discussion of scientific paradigms and research programs, see, respectively, Kuhn (1970) and Lakatos (1970).

Parliament, MERIT Research Memorandum, 2/95–012

Gambardella, A. and W. Garcia-Fontes (1996), "Research Linkages through European Research Funding," *Economics of Innovation and New Technology*, 4, 123–138

Geuna, A. (1996). "The Participation of Higher Education Institutions in Community Framework Programs," *Science and Public Policy*, 23(5), 278–96

(1997). "Allocation of Funds and Research Output: The Case of UK Universities," *Revue d'Economie Industrielle*, 79, 143–62

(1998). "Determinants of University Participation in EU-funded R&D Co-operative Projects," *Research Policy*, 26, 677–87

International Association of Universities (1991, 1993). *International Handbook of Universities*, London: Stockton Press

Johnes, G. (1992). "Performance Indicators in Higher Education: A Survey of Recent Work," *Oxford Review of Economic Policy*, 8, 19–34

Kuhn, T.S. (1970). *The Structure of Scientific Revolutions*, 2nd edn., Chicago: University of Chicago Press

Lakatos, I. (1970). "Falsification and the Methodology of Scientific Research Programmes," in I. Lakatos and A. Musgrave (eds.), *Criticism and the Growth of Knowledge*, Cambridge: Cambridge University Press

Maassen, A.M., C.J. Goedegebuure, and D.F. Westerheijden (1993). "Social and Political Conditions for Changing Higher Education Structures in the Netherlands," in C. Geller (ed.), *Higher Education in Europe*, London: Jessica Kingsley Publishers

Malerba, F., A. Maraeretz, and G. Pasqui (1991). "The Nascent Globalization of Universities and Public and Quasi-public Research Organizations," FAST Research in the Framework of the MONITOR Programme, Brussels

Martin, B.R. and J. Irvine (1983), "Assessing Basic Research: Some Partial Indicators of Scientific Progress in Radio-astronomy," *Research Policy*, 12, 61–90

Massy, W.F. (ed.) (1996). *Resource Allocation in Higher Education*, Ann Arbor: University of Michigan Press

Moet, H.F., W.J.M. Burger, J.G. Frankfort, and A.F.J. Van Raan (1985). "The Use of Bibliometric Data for the Measurement of University Research Data," *Research Policy*, 34, 131–149

Pike, A. and D. Charles (1995), "The Impact of International Collaboration on UK University–industry Links," *Industry and Higher Education*, 9, 264–76

Universities' Statistical Record (various years). *University Statistics, 3: Finance*, Cheltenham: Universities Statistical Record

Vught, F.A. van (1997). "Combining Planning and Market: An Analysis of the Government Strategy towards Higher Education in The Netherlands," *Higher Education Policy*, 10, 211–24

World of Learning (1995). London: Europa Publications

Ziman, J. (1994). *Prometheus Bound. Science in a Dynamic Steady State*, Cambridge: Cambridge University Press

Index

Lightning Source UK Ltd.
Milton Keynes UK
15 February 2011

167565UK00004B/72/P

9 780521 065719